Lecture Notes in Economics and Mathematical Systems

For information about Vols. 1–128, please contact your bookseller or Springer-Verlag

Vol. 129: H.-J. Lüthi, Komplementaritäts- und Fixpunktalgorithmen in der mathematischen Programmierung. Spieltheorie und Ökonomie. VII, 145 Seiten. 1976.

Vol. 130: Multiple Criteria Decision Making, Jouy-en-Josas, France. Proceedings 1975. Edited by H. Thiriez and S. Zionts. VI, 409 pages. 1976.

Vol. 131: Mathematical Systems Theory. Proceedings 1975. Edited by G. Marchesini and S. K. Mitter. X, 408 pages. 1976.

Vol. 132: U. H. Funke, Mathematical Models in Marketing. A Collection of Abstracts. XX, 514 pages. 1976.

Vol. 133: Warsaw Fall Seminars in Mathematical Economics 1975. Edited by M. W. Loś, J. Loś, and A. Wieczorek. V. 159 pages. 1976.

Vol. 134: Computing Methods in Applied Sciences and Engineering. Proceedings 1975. VIII, 390 pages. 1976.

Vol. 135: H. Haga, A Disequilibrium – Equilibrium Model with Money and Bonds. A Keynesian – Walrasian Synthesis. VI, 119 pages. 1976.

Vol. 136: E. Kofler und G. Menges, Entscheidungen bei unvollständiger Information. XII, 357 Seiten. 1976.

Vol. 137: R. Wets, Grundlagen Konvexer Optimierung. VI, 146 Seiten. 1976.

Vol. 138: K. Okuguchi, Expectations and Stability in Oligopoly Models. VI, 103 pages. 1976.

Vol. 139: Production Theory and Its Applications. Proceedings. Edited by H. Albach and G. Bergendahl. VIII, 193 pages. 1977.

Vol. 140: W. Eichhorn and J. Voeller, Theory of the Price Index. Fisher's Test Approach and Generalizations. VII, 95 pages. 1976.

Vol. 141: Mathematical Economics and Game Theory. Essays in Honor of Oskar Morgenstern. Edited by R. Henn and O. Moeschlin. XIV, 703 pages. 1977.

Vol. 142: J. S. Lane, On Optimal Population Paths. V, 123 pages. 1977.

Vol. 143: B. Näslund, An Analysis of Economic Size Distributions. XV, 100 pages. 1977.

Vol. 144: Convex Analysis and Its Applications. Proceedings 1976. Edited by A. Auslender. VI, 219 pages. 1977.

Vol. 145: J. Rosenmüller, Extreme Games and Their Solutions. IV, 126 pages. 1977.

Vol. 146: In Search of Economic Indicators. Edited by W. H. Strigel. XVI, 198 pages. 1977.

Vol. 147: Resource Allocation and Division of Space. Proceedings. Edited by T. Fujii and R. Sato. VIII, 184 pages. 1977.

Vol. 148: C. E. Mandl, Simulationstechnik und Simulationsmodelle in den Sozial- und Wirtschaftswissenschaften. IX, 173 Seiten. 1977.

Vol. 149: Stationäre und schrumpfende Bevölkerungen: Demographisches Null- und Negativwachstum in Österreich. Herausgegeben von G. Feichtinger. VI, 262 Seiten. 1977.

Vol. 150: Bauer et al., Supercritical Wing Sections III. VI, 179 pages. 1977.

Vol. 151: C. A. Schneeweiß, Inventory-Production Theory. VI, 116 pages. 1977.

Vol. 152: Kirsch et al., Notwendige Optimalitätsbedingungen und ihre Anwendung. VI, 157 Seiten. 1978.

Vol. 153: Kombinatorische Entscheidungsprobleme: Methoden und Anwendungen. Herausgegeben von T. M. Liebling und M. Rössler. VIII, 206 Seiten. 1978.

Vol. 154: Problems and Instruments of Business Cycle Analysis. Proceedings 1977. Edited by W. H. Strigel. VI, 442 pages. 1978.

Vol. 155: Multiple Criteria Problem Solving. Proceedings 1977. Edited by S. Zionts. VIII, 567 pages. 1978.

Vol. 156: B. Näslund and B. Sellstedt, Neo-Ricardian Theory. With Applications to Some Current Economic Problems. VI, 165 pages. 1978.

Vol. 157: Optimization and Operations Research. Proceedings 1977. Edited by R. Henn, B. Korte, and W. Oettli. VI, 270 pages. 1978.

Vol. 158: L. J. Cherene, Set Valued Dynamical Systems and Economic Flow. VIII, 83 pages. 1978.

Vol. 159: Some Aspects of the Foundations of General Equilibrium Theory: The Posthumous Papers of Peter J. Kalman. Edited by J. Green. VI, 167 pages. 1978.

Vol. 160: Integer Programming and Related Areas. A Classified Bibliography. Edited by D. Hausmann. XIV, 314 pages. 1978.

Vol. 161: M. J. Beckmann, Rank in Organizations. VIII, 164 pages. 1978.

Vol. 162: Recent Developments in Variable Structure Systems, Economics and Biology. Proceedings 1977. Edited by R. R. Mohler and A. Ruberti. VI, 326 pages. 1978.

Vol. 163: G. Fandel, Optimale Entscheidungen in Organisationen. VI, 143 Seiten. 1979.

Vol. 164: C. L. Hwang and A. S. M. Masud, Multiple Objective Decision Making – Methods and Applications. A State-of-the-Art Survey. XII, 351 pages. 1979.

Vol. 165: A. Maravall, Identification in Dynamic Shock-Error Models. VIII, 158 pages. 1979.

Vol. 166: R. Cuninghame-Green, Minimax Algebra. XI, 258 pages. 1979.

Vol. 167: M. Faber, Introduction to Modern Austrian Capital Theory. X, 196 pages. 1979.

Vol. 168: Convex Analysis and Mathematical Economics. Proceedings 1978. Edited by J. Kriens. V, 136 pages. 1979.

Vol. 169: A. Rapoport et al., Coalition Formation by Sophisticated Players. VII, 170 pages. 1979.

Vol. 170: A. E. Roth, Axiomatic Models of Bargaining. V, 121 pages. 1979.

Vol. 171: G. F. Newell, Approximate Behavior of Tandem Queues. XI, 410 pages. 1979.

Vol. 172: K. Neumann and U. Steinhardt, GERT Networks and the Time-Oriented Evaluation of Projects. 268 pages. 1979.

Vol. 173: S. Erlander, Optimal Spatial Interaction and the Gravity Model. VII, 107 pages. 1980.

Vol. 174: Extremal Methods and Systems Analysis. Edited by A. V. Fiacco and K. O. Kortanek. XI, 545 pages. 1980.

Vol. 175: S. K. Srinivasan and R. Subramanian, Probabilistic Analysis of Redundant Systems. VII, 356 pages. 1980.

Vol. 176: R. Färe, Laws of Diminishing Returns. VIII, 97 pages. 1980.

Vol. 177: Multiple Criteria Decision Making-Theory and Application. Proceedings, 1979. Edited by G. Fandel and T. Gal. XVI, 570 pages. 1980.

Vol. 178: M. N. Bhattacharyya, Comparison of Box-Jenkins and Bonn Monetary Model Prediction Performance. VII, 146 pages. 1980.

Vol. 179: Recent Results in Stochastic Programming. Proceedings, 1979. Edited by P. Kall and A. Prékopa. IX, 237 pages. 1980.

Vol. 180: J. F. Brotchie, J. W. Dickey and R. Sharpe, TOPAZ – General Planning Technique and its Applications at the Regional, Urban, and Facility Planning Levels. VII, 356 pages. 1980.

Vol. 181: H. D. Sherali and C. M. Shetty, Optimization with Disjunctive Constraints. VIII, 156 pages. 1980.

Vol. 182: J. Wolters, Stochastic Dynamic Properties of Linear Econometric Models. VIII, 154 pages. 1980.

Vol. 183: K. Schittkowski, Nonlinear Programming Codes. VIII, 242 pages. 1980.

continuation on page 325

Lecture Notes
in Economics and
Mathematical Systems

Managing Editors: M. Beckmann and W. Krelle

284

Helmut Lütkepohl

Forecasting Aggregated Vector ARMA Processes

Springer-Verlag
Berlin Heidelberg New York London Paris Tokyo

Managing Editors

Prof. Dr. M. Beckmann
Brown University
Providence, RI 02912, USA

Prof. Dr. W. Krelle
Institut für Gesellschafts- und Wirtschaftswissenschaften
der Universität Bonn
Adenauerallee 24–42, D-5300 Bonn, FRG

Author

Prof. Dr. Helmut Lütkepohl
Universität Hamburg
Institut für Statistik und Ökonometrie
Von-Melle-Park 5, D-2000 Hamburg 13, FRG

ISBN-13: 978-3-540-17208-6 e-ISBN-13: 978-3-642-61584-9
DOI: 10.1007/978-3-642-61584-9

2142/3140-543210

To

Sabine

PREFACE

This study is concerned with forecasting time series variables and the impact of the level of aggregation on the efficiency of the forecasts. Since temporally and contemporaneously disaggregated data at various levels have become available for many countries, regions, and variables during the last decades the question which data and procedures to use for prediction has become increasingly important in recent years. This study aims at pointing out some of the problems involved and at providing some suggestions how to proceed in particular situations.

Many of the results have been circulated as working papers, some have been published as journal articles, and some have been presented at conferences and in seminars. I express my gratitude to all those who have commented on parts of this study. They are too numerous to be listed here and many of them are anonymous referees and are therefore unknown to me. Some early results related to the present study are contained in my monograph "Prognose aggregierter Zeitreihen" (Lütkepohl (1986a)) which was essentially completed in 1983. The present study contains major extensions of that research and also summarizes the earlier results to the extent they are of interest in the context of this study.

This monograph is based on research I have carried out while I have been employed by the University of Bielefeld (1979-81), the University of Osnabrück (1981-84), the University of California, San Diego (1984/85), and the University of Hamburg (since 1985). I gratefully acknowledge the technical support by these institutions and many useful discussions and comments by my colleagues at these institutions.

Sabine Dornbusch has performed the computations reported in this study. I take this opportunity to thank her for outstanding research assistance during the last few years. Last not least I am most grateful to Mrs. Marlene Hakelberg for typing the final manuscript with patience and skill.

November 1986 Helmut Lütkepohl

CONTENTS

CHAPTER 1. PROLOGUE

1.1 OBJECTIVE OF THE STUDY

In making choices between alternative courses of action, decision makers at all structural levels often need predictions of aggregated variables. For example, in the process of planning a government budget, forecasts of annual tax revenues may be required. If quarterly or monthly figures of previous revenues are available then a time series model may be constructed for the generation process of the quarterly or monthly data. This model can then be used to obtain predictions for the next quarters or months and these forecasts can be aggregated to obtain annual forecasts of the tax revenues. Alternatively, the available monthly or quarterly data may be aggregated to obtain an annual series of tax revenues. Based on this series a model may be constructed to generate annual forecasts.

As a second example consider the manager of a retail firm with several branches who wants to place an order of a certain product to stock in for the next week. To minimize the storage space and at the same time minimize the risk of running out of stock, he or she needs a precise forecast of the demand in all branches during the next week. In other words, the manager will be interested in a forecast of a variable that is aggregated over time (temporally), adding up the sales of all days during the week, and over units (contemporaneously), summing up the sales for the individual branches. One possibility is to obtain the desired forecast by constructing and estimating a univariate time series model for the total sales data of the past weeks and use this model for generating a forecast. Alternatively, rather than using contemporaneously and temporally aggregated weekly total sales figures, a multiple time series model could be constructed for the disaggregate daily sales data of all separate branches. Such a model can be used to produce daily sales forecasts for the individual branches. The obtained forecasts can then be aggregated to give a total sales forecast for the next week. There are some other predictors that are relevant in the present context. For instance, the total daily sales, aggregated over all branches, can be predicted using univariate time series methods. A weekly forecast is then obtained by summing up the daily predictions. Another possibility would be to use temporally aggregated weekly data for predicting the sales for each branch for the next week and then add the forecasts for the individual branches to obtain an overall prediction.

In order to have a basis for choosing among the different alternatives the forecaster needs to know which one of the predictors is most accurate. In other words, time series of what level of aggregation provide the most accurate forecasts for a temporally and/or contemporaneously aggregated variable? It is the purpose of this study to compare the predictors corresponding to the different levels of aggregation.

In order to forecast a time series, a model is usually constructed for the data generation process, the parameters of the model are then estimated form the available data and predictors are obtained with the estimated process. Recently it has become popular to choose the model for the data generation process from the autoregressive moving average (ARMA) or autoregressive integrated moving average (ARIMA) classes. Vector ARMA processes are now becoming increasingly more popular as models for systems of time series. Therefore, in this study the data generation processes are assumed to be multivariate, nondeterministic, discrete-time stochastic processes that are stationary or can be made stationary by differencing. These processes are slightly more general than vector ARMA processes. In practice, however, ARMA approximations to these processes are likely to be of major importance. The reader may always think of vector ARMA processes where vector stochastic processes are considered, although in theoretical derivations the restriction to the vector ARMA class is often not necessary.

In this study the mean squared forecasting error (forecast MSE) will be used as a measure of forecast accuracy. The forecast MSEs of various predictors will be compared under the following alternative assumptions: (1) The data generating processes are completely known; (2) some parameters of the data generating processes are unknown and have to be estimated; (3) the processes are of possibly infinite order autoregressive type and have unknown orders and parameters. Where estimation results are involved, asymptotic theory and small sample results will be presented.

Properties of temporally and contemporaneously aggregated processes have been discussed recently by many authors. However, temporal and contemporaneous aggregation are usually considered separately. Moreover, some authors treat the case of known processes only and others investigate the relevant estimation problems and not the prediction problem. Furthermore some authors only deal with special processes and specific predictors. Where estimated coefficients are treated the model is usually otherwise assumed known including, for instance, the ARMA orders. References for many of the more special results and previous discussions will be given in the following chapters.

Although the theoretical results of this study remain formally valid for aggregating any number of component series over any number of time periods, in practice they are likely to be of major importance where merely a small number of component series is aggregated over a few time periods. For a discussion of the aggregation of large numbers of variables the reader is referred to work of Granger (1984).

In the following chapters, only discrete-time systems are considered. Admittedly, the aggregation of continuous-time systems is also of substantial theoretical interest. In practice, however, economic data are only available for discrete time. Therefore the question whether forecast improvements can be obtained by using continuous-time data is of little practical importance. The reader is referred to studies by Sims (1971), Geweke (1978), and Bergstrom (1984) for discussions of aggregation problems in continuous time.

1.2 SURVEY OF THE STUDY

In Chapter 2 the processes used in the remainder of the study are introduced and some of their properties are stated. Parameter estimation is discussed and some methods for model specification are considered. The estimation problem is treated under two different scenarios. The first one assumes that the data generation process is of finite order ARMA type and the ARMA orders are known. Special emphasize is given to the estimation of finite order AR (autoregressive) processes that play an important role in later chapters. The second scenario permits the actual data generation process to have an infinite AR order. It is assumed that nonetheless only finite order AR processes are fitted to the data. Asymptotic properties for the estimators are then obtained under the presumption that the AR orders of the fitted processes go to infinity with the sample size. The two alternative asymptotic scenarios will be used throughout the study.

The third chapter discusses forecasting the vector stochastic processes considered in Chapter 2. It is argued that the forecast MSE is a useful criterion for comparing predictors and optimal predictors are derived for known processes. Since in practice these forecasts are often used with estimated rather than known coefficients, the estimation consequences for the forecast MSEs are considered. Approximations to the forecast MSEs are derived using both asymptotic estimation theories of Chapter 2. The results and notation of the second and third chapters are basic for the remainder of the study as they are used repeatedly in the following chapters.

Chapters 4 and 5 are concerned with forecasting contemporaneously aggregated processes. Three predictors for a contemporaneous aggregate are compared. The first predictor is based on a multivariate model for the disaggregate components, the second one uses only the aggregate process and the third predictor is based on univariate models for the disaggregate components. In Chapter 4 the data generation processes are assumed known and it is shown that the first predictor is optimal whereas it depends on the structure of the underlying disaggregate process and the form of aggregation which one of the last two predictors is to be preferred. Necessary and sufficient conditions for the equality of the three predictors are given and some interesting consequences of these conditions are noted. In particular, a characterization of Granger-causality is obtained. Moreover, some properties of contemporaneously aggregated vector ARMA processes are derived. In Chapter 5 the asymptotic results of Chapter 3 are used to investigate the consequences of using estimated rather than known processes. In that case the first predictor is not necessarily optimal. This result is not only obtained from asymptotic considerations but is also confirmed for small samples by means of a Monte Carlo experiment.

In Chapter 6 the analysis is extended by allowing for temporal aggregation in addition to contemporaneous aggregation. Six predictors of potential interest are considered assuming again that the data generation processes are known. The first predictor is based on a multivariate model for the fully (temporally and contemporaneously) disaggregated system. The other predictors of interest use variables of different aggregation levels. In other words, they are based on the temporally and/or contemporaneously aggregated variables. In addition predictors based on the univariate components of contemporaneously disaggregated systems are considered. A general framework is provided in which all six predictors can be analyzed and compared. It turns out that the first predictor, based on the fully disaggregate system, is optimal. This result, of course, is not surprising since this predictor uses the largest information set. A number of other relations between the predictors are derived and necessary and sufficient conditions for their equality are given. In addition, some useful properties of temporally and contemporaneously aggregated vector ARMA processes are obtained as a by-product.

Although it is useful to have a general framework for comparing various predictors, in practice specific forms of aggregation are often of interest which are more easily dealt with. Two special forms of temporal aggregation are therefore treated in detail in Chapters 7 and 8. The first deals with temporal aggregation of stock variables like, for instance, the population of a city. For such a variable the value for a particular key date may be used as the monthly (temporally aggregated) figure. Thereby the values for all other days of the month are ignored. Thus, temporal aggregation of stock variables may be regarded as a missing observations problem. On the other hand, for flow variables like income, the annual (temporally aggregated) value is obtained by adding the values of each month. This form of temporal aggregation is considered in Chapter 8. For both stock and flow variables forecasts of the aggregate are assumed to be desired. The predictors based on the full, disaggregate series are compared to the predictors based on the temporal aggregates. The comparisons are performed for known and estimated processes. For stock variables, under special circumstances, the predictor based on the aggregate may outperform the one based on the disaggregate process, whereas for flow variables such a result is not obtained so that using the temporally disaggregate data is always preferable.

In Chapter 9 joint temporal and contemporaneous aggregation is considered again. The impact of the estimation variability on the relative forecast efficiencies is investigated for the six predictors introduced in Chapter 6. The relative effect of temporal and contemporaneous aggregation is of particular interest. Considering the predictor based on the fully disaggregated system and the predictor which is based on the temporal and contemporaneous aggregate, it is shown that efficiency losses due to temporal aggregation may be off-set by the gains due to contemporaneous aggregation when estimated processed are used. Relations between the MSEs of the other predictors are also derived.

Finally, in Chapter 10 the major findings of this study are summarized and some remaining problems are noted. In some chapters empirical examples are given using economic time series. The data are given in the Appendix of the book. The study concludes with a bibliography.

CHAPTER 2. VECTOR STOCHASTIC PROCESSES

In this chapter some notation is introduced and assumptions are discussed that will be used in later parts of the book. As explained in Chapter 1 the main concern of this study will be with forecasting economic variables of interest. Assuming that T observations x_{kt}, t = 1, ...,T; k = 1,...,K; for each of the K time series variables $x_1,\ldots,x_K$ are available one possible approach is to construct a model for the generation process of the multiple time series $\underline{x}_t = (x_{1t},\ldots,x_{Kt})'$, t = 1,...T, and use that model for predicting future values of the variables $x_1,\ldots x_K$. The model for the data generating process is chosen from the class of stochastic processes. In the following sections specific stochastic processes are introduced that are often suitable for modelling economic data. In Section 2.1 nondeterministic stationary processes are considered, in Section 2.2 an extension to certain types of nonstationary processes is provided and in Section 2.3 the special class of vector ARMA (autoregressive moving average) processes is discussed.

Usually the model specified for the data generating process contains unknown parameters. Estimation of these parameters is considered in Section 2.4. Possibilities and criteria for specifying a model for the data generating process are discussed in Section 2.5. Once a model has been specified and estimated it can be used for forecasting. This is the topic of Chapter 3.

2.1 DISCRETE-TIME, STATIONARY VECTOR STOCHASTIC PROCESSES

2.1.1 General Assumptions

A collection of random variables $\underline{x}_t = (x_{1t},\ldots,x_{Kt})'$, $t = t_o, t_o+1,\ldots,$ is called a K-dimensional, discrete-time vector stochastic process. Only discrete-time processes where the time index t assumes only integer values will be considered in this study since for most economic variables only data for discrete time are available. The starting point t_o of the stochastic process may be $-\infty$ and if nothing is said about t_o it will be assumed that the process has indeed been started at $t_o = -\infty$.

For notational ease the process will often simply be denoted by $\underline{x}_t$. On the other hand, $\underline{x}_t$ also denotes the random vector associated with time t or it may represent a realization of this random vector. In other words, the values of the corresponding multiple time series will also be represented by the same symbol. Similar conventions will be used for other stochastic processes. In all cases the specific meaning of a particular symbol should be clear from the context.

As forecasting is the objective certain assumptions about the constancy of characteristics of the distribution of the $\underline{x}_t$ are commonly made. Since in most cases moments up to the second order are of main interest, the following set of assumptions is a popular one:

$$E(\underline{x}_t) = \underline{\mu} \quad \text{for all } t. \tag{2.1.1a}$$

$$E(\underline{x}_t - \underline{\mu})(\underline{x}_t - \underline{\mu})' = \Sigma_{\underline{x}} \quad \text{for all } t. \tag{2.1.1b}$$

$$E(\underline{x}_t - \underline{\mu})(\underline{x}_{t+h} - \underline{\mu})' = \Gamma_{\underline{x}}(h) \quad \text{for all } t \text{ and } h. \tag{2.1.1c}$$

Here $\underline{\mu} = (\mu_1,\ldots,\mu_K)'$ is a (Kx1) vector and $\Sigma_{\underline{x}}$ and $\Gamma_{\underline{x}}(h)$ are (KxK) matrices. The elements of all nonrandom vectors and matrices are assumed to be finite numbers unless otherwise specified. A stochastic process $\underline{x}_t$ that satisfies the conditions (2.1.1) will be called stationary in the following. The first condition states that all members $\underline{x}_t$ of the process have the same finite mean vector. The second condition states that all $\underline{x}_t$ have the same finite variance-covariance matrix. Finally, condition (2.1.1c) requires that the covariance between two random vectors $\underline{x}_t$ and $\underline{x}_s$ depends only on the distance t-s the two are apart in time.

A stochastic process satisfying conditions (2.1.1) is sometimes called covariance stationary or weakly stationary in the literature. In contrast a process is called strictly stationary if for each h the joint distribution of $\underline{x}_t,\underline{x}_{t+1},\ldots,\underline{x}_{t+h}$ is identical to the joint distribution of $\underline{x}_s,\underline{x}_{s+1},\ldots,\underline{x}_{s+h}$, that is, the distribution does not depend on the particular time point t. Obviously, a strictly stationary process satisfies conditions (2.1.1) and is therefore stationary if the first and second moments exist. If for all integers t and h the sequences $\underline{x}_t$, $\underline{x}_{t+1},\ldots,\underline{x}_{t+h}$ have a joint, multivariate normal distribution, the process will be called Gaussian. For such a process strict stationarity and stationarity are equivalent properties.

A stationary process $\underline{x}_t$ for which the mean is zero, $\underline{\mu} = \underline{0}$, and all the covariances $\Gamma_{\underline{x}}(h) = 0$ for $h \neq 0$ will be called a white noise process. Processes of this type will be of particular importance in the following. A white noise process $\underline{x}_t$ for which $\underline{x}_t$ is independent of $\underline{x}_s$ will be referred to as independent white noise. Such a process is strictly stationary if the $\underline{x}_t$ have the same distribution for all t. Sometimes a white noise process with $\underline{\mu} = \underline{0}$ will be called zero mean white noise to distinguish it from a process with zero intertemporal correlation and nonzero mean. If nothing is mentioned about the mean, a white noise process will always be assumed to have zero mean.

In the foregoing it is not assumed that the covariance matrix $\Sigma_{\underline{x}}$ is nonsingular. In other words, it is possible that exact linear relationships exist among the components of $\underline{x}_t$. Allowing for this possibility is convenient when economic variables are under investigation since there are exact linear relationships between many variables. For instance, the Gross Private Domestic Investment is the sum of Fixed Investment and the Change in Business Inventories. On the other hand, some of the results given in later parts of this study hold only when $\Sigma_{\underline{x}}$ is a nonsingular matrix. Therefore, if not otherwise specified, the members of all stochastic processes will be assumed to have nonsingular covariance matrices.

For much of the theoretical discussion in this study it is convenient to assume that the considered processes have mean zero. For a stationary process this assumption is obviously not critical since for each such process $\underline{x}_t$ with nonzero mean vector $\underline{\mu}$ a corresponding zero mean process $\underline{z}_t = \underline{x}_t - \underline{\mu}$ can be defined and analyzed. In much of what follows, $\underline{x}_t$ will therefore be assumed to have zero mean.

Also it will be assumed that the considered processes are nondeterministic, that is, there are no parts like trends or seasonal cycles that can be predicted without error if the entire past of the process is assumed known. A more precise definition of a nondeterministic process can be given using the terminology introduced in Chapter 3 where predictors and their mean squared errors are defined. In those terms a stationary process $\underline{x}_t$ is called nondeterministic if the mean squared error matrices of its optimal linear predictors approach the covariance matrix $\Sigma_{\underline{x}}$ as the forecast horizon goes to infinity. In other words, as the forecast horizon approaches infinity, the optimal predictor converges to the process mean vector and thus does not use information from the past of the process.

2.1.2 The Wold or Moving Average Representation

Suppose $\underline{x}_t = (x_{1t},\dots,x_{Kt})'$ is a K-dimensional, nondeterministic, stationary stochastic process with mean zero. Then, by Wold's Decomposition

<u>Theorem</u> (e.g., Hannan, 1970), it has a moving average (MA) representation

$$\underline{x}_t = \underline{u}_t + \Phi_1 \underline{u}_{t-1} + \ldots = \sum_{i=0}^{\infty} \Phi_i \underline{u}_{t-i} \quad , \quad \Phi_0 = I_K \quad , \tag{2.1.2}$$

where I_K denotes the (KxK) identity matrix, the Φ_i are (KxK) coefficient matrices,

$$\det\left(\sum_{i=0}^{\infty} \Phi_i z^i\right) \neq 0 \quad \text{for } |z| < 1 \quad , \quad z \in \mathbb{C}, \tag{2.1.3}$$

$\mathbb{C}$ representing the complex numbers, $|z|$ denotes the modulus of z, and $\underline{u}_t$ is K-dimensional white noise with covariance matrix $E(\underline{u}_t \underline{u}_t') = \Sigma_{\underline{u}}$. Condition (2.1.3) means that the MA operator has no roots inside the complex unit circle.

Here and in the following an infinite sum of random variables is defined as the limit in quadratic mean (mean square) of the finite partial sums. For instance, $\underline{x}_t$ in (2.1.2) is defined such that

$$E\left[(\underline{x}_t - \sum_{i=0}^{n} \Phi_i \underline{u}_{t-i})'(\underline{x}_t - \sum_{i=0}^{n} \Phi_i \underline{u}_{t-i})\right] \xrightarrow[n \to \infty]{} 0 . \tag{2.1.4}$$

Sometimes the <u>lag operator</u> notation will be useful in the following. The lag operator L is defined such that $L\underline{x}_t = \underline{x}_{t-1}$ or $L^i \underline{x}_t = \underline{x}_{t-i}$. Using this operator, (2.1.2) can be written alternatively as

$$\underline{x}_t = \left(\sum_{i=0}^{\infty} \Phi_i L^i\right) \underline{u}_t = \Phi(L) \underline{u}_t \quad , \tag{2.1.5}$$

where $\Phi(L) = \sum_{i=0}^{\infty} \Phi_i L^i$.

The MA representation of a stochastic process is often convenient to work with. This is especially true when forecasting is of interest, as will become apparent in Chapter 3. Also, the covariances $\Gamma_{\underline{x}}(h)$ can be easily evaluated using (2.1.2). For $h \geq 0$,

$$\begin{aligned}
\Gamma_{\underline{x}}(h) &= E(\underline{x}_t \underline{x}_{t+h}') = E\left[\left(\sum_{i=0}^{\infty} \Phi_i \underline{u}_{t-i}\right)\left(\sum_{j=0}^{\infty} \Phi_j \underline{u}_{t+h-j}\right)'\right] \\
&= E\left[\left(\sum_{i=0}^{\infty} \Phi_i \underline{u}_{t-i}\right)\left(\sum_{j=0}^{h-1} \Phi_j \underline{u}_{t+h-j} + \sum_{j=0}^{\infty} \Phi_{j+h} \underline{u}_{t-j}\right)'\right] \\
&= \sum_{i=0}^{\infty} \Phi_i \Sigma_{\underline{u}} \Phi_{i+h}' .
\end{aligned} \tag{2.1.6}$$

Furthermore, $\Gamma_{\underline{x}}(h) = \Gamma_{\underline{x}}(-h)'$ and hence the $\Gamma_{\underline{x}}(h)$ for $h < 0$ can be obtained from (2.1.6).

2.1.3 Autoregressive Representation

If $\det(\Phi(z))$ in (2.1.3) has no roots on the complex unit circle, that is, $\det(\Phi(z)) \neq 0$ for $|z| \leq 1$, then $\underline{x}_t$ is called <u>invertible</u> and has an autoregressive (AR) representation,

$$\underline{x}_t = \sum_{i=1}^{\infty} A_i \underline{x}_{t-i} + \underline{u}_t \tag{2.1.7}$$

or in lag operator notation,

$$(I_K - \sum_{i=1}^{\infty} A_i L^i)\underline{x}_t = A(L)\underline{x}_t = \underline{u}_t \quad , \tag{2.1.8}$$

where $A(L) = I_K - \sum_{i=1}^{\infty} A_i L^i$.

Since $A(L)$ is the inverse of $\Phi(L)$ it is possible to express the A_i in terms of the Φ_i.

$$\begin{aligned} I_K = A(L)\Phi(L) &= (I_K - A_1 L - A_2 L^2 - \ldots)(I_K + \Phi_1 L + \Phi_2 L^2 + \ldots) \\ &= I_K + (\Phi_1 - A_1)L + (\Phi_2 - A_2 - A_1\Phi_1)L^2 + \ldots \\ &\qquad \ldots + (\Phi_j - \sum_{i=1}^{j} A_i \Phi_{j-i})L^j + \ldots \end{aligned}$$

and consequently,

$$\begin{aligned} 0 &= \Phi_1 - A_1 \\ 0 &= \Phi_2 - A_2 - A_1\Phi_1 \\ &\vdots \\ 0 &= \Phi_j - \sum_{i=1}^{j} A_i \Phi_{j-i} \\ &\vdots \end{aligned}$$

which implies $A_1 = \Phi_1$ and

$$A_j = \Phi_j - \sum_{i=1}^{j-1} A_i \Phi_{j-i} \quad , \quad j = 2,3,\ldots \quad . \tag{2.1.9}$$

Alternatively, if the AR representation (2.1.7) or (2.1.8) is given and

$$\det(A(z)) \neq 0 \quad \text{for } |z| \leq 1, \tag{2.1.10}$$

then $\underline{x}_t$ is stationary and thus has an MA representation. The MA coefficient matrices can be computed recursively as follows:

$$\Phi_0 = I_K,$$

$$\Phi_j = \sum_{i=0}^{j-1} \Phi_i A_{j-i} \quad , \quad j = 1,2,\ldots \quad . \tag{2.1.11}$$

Sometimes another AR representation than the one in (2.1.7) is useful. There exists an upper triangular matrix P with unit diagonal such that $P\Sigma_u P'$ is diagonal. Left multiplying (2.1.7) by that matrix results in an AR representation

$$\underline{x}_t = \sum_{i=0}^{\infty} D_i \underline{x}_{t-i} + \underline{v}_t \quad , \tag{2.1.12}$$

where $D_0 = I - P$, $D_i = PA_i$, $i = 1,2,\ldots$, and $\underline{v}_t = P\underline{u}_t$ is white noise with diagonal covariance matrix $\Sigma_v = P\Sigma_u P'$. The usefulness of this type of representation will become apparent in Sections 2.4 and 2.5.

It is perhaps worth noting that in practice it is often assumed that a process $\underline{x}_t$ has a finite order MA representation,

$$\underline{x}_t = \sum_{i=0}^{q} \Phi_i \underline{u}_{t-i} \tag{2.1.13}$$

or a finite order AR representation

$$\underline{x}_t = \sum_{i=1}^{p} A_i \underline{x}_{t-i} + \underline{u}_t \quad . \tag{2.1.14}$$

In the former case $\underline{x}_t$ is briefly called an MA(q) process and in the latter case $\underline{x}_t$ is said to be an AR(p) process. If x_t is a stationary <u>univariate</u> (1-dimensional) finite order AR(p) process with $p > 0$, then it will always have an infinite MA representation. Similarly, if x_t is a finite order invertible MA(q), then it has an infinite order AR representation. A multivariate vector process $\underline{x}_t$ may have both, a finite order MA and a finite order AR representation. Consider, for instance, the bivariate AR(1) process

$$\underline{x}_t = A_1\underline{x}_{t-1} + \underline{u}_t \quad , \tag{2.1.15}$$

where

$$A_1 = \begin{bmatrix} 0 & \alpha \\ 0 & 0 \end{bmatrix} .$$

Using (2.1.11) it is easy to see that the MA representation of this process is also of order 1, $\underline{x}_t = \underline{u}_t + A_1\underline{u}_{t-1}$.

For a finite order AR(p) process as in (2.1.14) the coefficient matrices can be recovered using the Yule-Walker equations, if the autocovariances $\Gamma_{\underline{x}}(h)$, $h = 0,\ldots,p$, are given. Post multiplying (2.1.14) by $\underline{x}'_{t-h}$, $h > 0$, and taking expectations gives the Yule-Walker equation

$$\Gamma_{\underline{x}}(-h) = A_1\Gamma_{\underline{x}}(1-h) + A_2\Gamma_{\underline{x}}(2-h) + \ldots + A_p\Gamma_{\underline{x}}(p-h) \ . \tag{2.1.16}$$

For $h = 1,\ldots,p$, the system

$$[\Gamma_{\underline{x}}(-1),\Gamma_{\underline{x}}(-2),\ldots,\Gamma_{\underline{x}}(-p)] = [A_1,\ldots,A_p]\Gamma_p \tag{2.1.17}$$

results. Here

$$\Gamma_p = \begin{bmatrix} \Gamma_{\underline{x}}(0) & \Gamma_{\underline{x}}(-1) & \ldots & \Gamma_{\underline{x}}(1-p) \\ \Gamma_{\underline{x}}(1) & \Gamma_{\underline{x}}(0) & \ldots & \Gamma_{\underline{x}}(2-p) \\ \vdots & \vdots & \ddots & \vdots \\ \Gamma_{\underline{x}}(p-1) & \Gamma_{\underline{x}}(p-2) & \ldots & \Gamma_{\underline{x}}(0) \end{bmatrix} = \Gamma'_p \ . \tag{2.1.18}$$

Thus,

$$[A_1,\ldots,A_p] = [\Gamma_{\underline{x}}(-1),\ \Gamma_{\underline{x}}(-2),\ldots,\ \Gamma_{\underline{x}}(-p)]\Gamma_p^{-1} \ . \tag{2.1.19}$$

This relationship will be used in Section 2.4 to estimate the AR coefficient matrices.

2.1.4 Spectral Representation

In the previous subsections time domain representations of stationary stochastic processes have been considered. Alternatively the information contained in the second moments of a process can be summarized in the frequency domain. A detailed introduction to the underlying basic concepts will not be given here since they are mostly avoided in the remainder of the text. In some instances they will prove useful however, and therefore some frequency domain results are summarized here. Details can be found in the books by Priestley (1981), Hannan (1970), Fuller (1976) and others.

Suppose $\underline{x}_t$ is a K-dimensional stochastic process with autocovariances $\Gamma_{\underline{x}}(h)$, $h = 0, \pm 1, \pm 2, \ldots$. Then the (KxK) matrix function

$$\underline{f}_{\underline{x}}(\omega) = \frac{1}{2\pi} \sum_{h=-\infty}^{\infty} e^{-i\omega h}\Gamma_{\underline{x}}(h) \quad , \quad -\pi \leq \omega \leq \pi \quad , \qquad (2.1.20)$$

is called the <u>spectral density matrix</u> of $\underline{x}_t$, provided it exists. The diagonal elements of $\underline{f}_{\underline{x}}(\omega)$ are the <u>spectral densities</u> of the component series x_{kt} and the off-diagonal elements are the <u>cross-spectral densities</u>. If $\underline{x}_t$ is stationary it can be shown that

$$\Gamma_{\underline{x}}(h) = \int_{-\pi}^{\pi} e^{i\omega h}\, \underline{f}_{\underline{x}}(\omega)\, d\omega \quad . \qquad (2.1.21)$$

Thus, the second moment characteristics of $\underline{x}_t$ can be represented either in terms of the autocovariances $\Gamma_{\underline{x}}(h)$ or, equivalently, in terms of the spectral density matrix.

If $\underline{x}_t$ has the MA representation (2.1.2) or (2.1.5), its spectral density matrix is

$$\begin{aligned} \underline{f}_{\underline{x}}(\omega) &= \frac{1}{2\pi} \Big(\sum_{j=0}^{\infty} \Phi_j e^{ij\omega}\Big) \Sigma_{\underline{u}} \Big(\sum_{j=0}^{\infty} \Phi_j' e^{-ij\omega}\Big) \\ &= \frac{1}{2\pi}\, \Phi(e^{i\omega})\, \Sigma_{\underline{u}}\, \Phi(e^{-i\omega})' \quad . \qquad (2.1.22) \end{aligned}$$

Note that $|e^{i\omega}| = 1$ and consequently

$$\det(\underline{f}_{\underline{x}}(\omega)) = \frac{1}{(2\pi)^K} \det(\Phi(e^{i\omega}))\det(\Sigma_{\underline{u}})\det(\Phi(e^{-i\omega})') \neq 0 \quad , \quad -\pi \leq \omega \leq \pi \quad , \qquad (2.1.23)$$

if $\underline{x}_t$ is invertible. In this case $\underline{f}_{\underline{x}}(\omega)$ is Hermitian positive definite for all $\omega \in [-\pi, \pi]$. In turn, if (2.1.23) is satisfied, the MA representation of $\underline{x}_t$ is invertible.

2.2 NONSTATIONARY PROCESSES

From the discussion in Section 2.1 it follows that a stochastic process $\underline{x}_t$ is nonstationary if any of the conditions (2.1.1) is violated. There are many ways nonstationarities can arise. For instance, the considered process may have a time varying mean (trend) and /or variance-covariance structure. In economics, for example, trending variables are quite common. In this study only very special nonstationary processes are considered, namely those where the nonstationarity can be removed by differencing. For instance, trends or seasonal components can often be removed in this way (see Box and Jenkins (1976)). For nonstationary processes it is often reasonable to assume a finite starting point t_o.

First consider the simplest case of a univariate nonstationary process x_t which is stationary after differencing once, that is, $x_t^s = x_t - x_{t-1}$ is stationary. In other words,

$$x_t = x_t^s + x_{t-1} = x_t^s + x_{t-1}^s + \dots + x_{t-n}^s + x_{t-(n+1)} \quad .$$

Thus, the variance of x_t will not be finite if n is allowed to grow without bounds. However, if the process x_t initiates at time t_o, say with $x_{t_o}^s$, then

$$x_t = \sum_{i=0}^{t-t_o} x_{t_o+i}^s$$

can have a finite variance which may leave some readers more comfortable. This problem of specifying an initial value for the process will be of little practical importance in the context of this study. For convenience it will usually be assumed that the stationary process x_t^s is started at $-\infty$. This assumption permits to ignore the initial value problem altogether for stationary processes. The stationary process x_t^s may, for instance, have an infinite AR representation,

$$x_t^s = \sum_{i=1}^{\infty} \alpha_i^s x_{t-i}^s + u_t \quad . \tag{2.2.1}$$

This notation would be meaningless if x_t^s were not defined for $t < t_o \neq -\infty$.

For the nonstationary process x_t only a finite AR representation is allowed and even that is not free of problems. For instance, if

$$x_t = \sum_{i=1}^{p} \alpha_i x_{t-i} + u_t \tag{2.2.2}$$

or

$$\alpha(L)x_t = (1-\alpha_1 L - \ldots - \alpha_p L^p)x_t = u_t \quad ,$$

then this expression is clearly only defined for $t - p \geq t_o$ or $t \geq t_o + p$. Suppose now that x_t^s has the finite AR representation

$$\alpha^s(L)x_t^s = (1-\alpha_1^s L - \ldots - \alpha_{p-1}^s L^{p-1})x_t^s = u_t \quad .$$

Then

$$(1-L)x_t = x_t^s = \alpha^s(L)^{-1}u_t$$

and thus,

$$\alpha^s(L)(1-L)x_t = u_t \quad , \quad t = t_o+p,\ t_o+p+1,\ \ldots$$

so that

$$\alpha(L) = \alpha^s(L)(1-L) \quad .$$

The fact, that for $t = t_o, \ldots, t_o+p-1$ the representation (2.2.2) is not valid will not be a serious worry in this study since it will always be assumed that t_o is sufficiently far back in the past so that the initial time period is not reached in any practical computations. It is perhaps worth noting that for the nonstationary process x_t the AR operator $\alpha(L)$ has a unit root i.e. $\alpha(1) = 0$, so that condition (2.1.10) is not satisfied. Similar comments apply if the difference operator $(1-L)$ has to be applied more than once or if a seasonal difference operator of the form $(1-L^s)$, where s is the seasonal period, has to be applied to obtain stationarity.

If the difference operator is applied to an already stationary series $x_t = \phi(L)u_t$ then the difference $x_t^s = (1-L)x_t = (1-L)\phi(L)u_t$ is still stationary. The MA operator $(1-L)\phi(L)$ of x_t^s has a unit root, though, and therefore has no convergent AR representation.

The situation becomes somewhat more complicated if $\underline{x}_t$ is a multivariate process. First, the components x_{kt} of $\underline{x}_t$ may have to be differenced a different number of times to obtain stationarity. Even if the individual components are stationary after differencing and have invertible univariate MA representations this does not imply that the multivariate process consisting of the differenced series also has an invertible MA representation (see Lütkepohl (1982a)). For instance, if each x_{kt} is stationary after differencing once, that is, $x_{kt}^s = (1-L)x_{kt}$ is stationary and has an invertible MA representation for $k = 1,\dots,K$, this does not mean that $\underline{x}_t^s = (x_{1t}^s,\dots,x_{Kt}^s)'$, as a K-dimensional multivariate process, has an invertible MA representation. This problem is of considerable practical importance since it is not uncommon to fit pure AR processes to a set of time series data.

In this study it will often be assumed that after differencing appropriately a stationary process $\underline{x}_t^s$ is obtained that has an invertible MA representation. In that case the discussion for univariate processes applies directly for the multivariate case.

2.3 VECTOR AUTOREGRESSIVE MOVING AVERAGE PROCESSES

2.3.1 Stationary Processes

Given the limited length of economic time series it is desirable to find a representation of a stochastic process with only a small number of parameters that can be estimated from the available data. If the K-dimensional process $\underline{x}_t$ has an invertible MA representation as in (2.1.5), it is often possible to write $\Phi(z)$ as the product of two operators

$$\Theta(z)^{-1}M(z) \tag{2.3.1}$$

where

$$\Theta(z) = I_K - \Theta_1 z - \dots - \Theta_p z^p \tag{2.3.2}$$

is of order p and is assumed invertible, i.e., $\det[\Theta(z)] \neq 0$ for $|z| \leq 1$, and

$$M(z) = I_K + M_1 z + \dots + M_q z^q \tag{2.3.3}$$

is of order q and is also taken to be invertible. The A_i, $i = 1,\dots,p$, and M_j, $j = 1,\dots,q$, are (KxK) coefficient matrices. The process $\underline{x}_t$ can now be written as

$$\underline{x}_t = \Theta_1\underline{x}_{t-1} + \dots + \Theta_p\underline{x}_{t-p} + \underline{u}_t + M_1\underline{u}_{t-1} + \dots + M_q\underline{u}_{t-q} \tag{2.3.4}$$

and is said to have a vector ARMA(p,q) representation (vector autoregressive moving average representation of order (p,q)). Using the lag operator it can be written in shorthand notation as

$$\Theta(L)\underline{x}_t = M(L)\underline{u}_t \quad . \tag{2.3.5}$$

Without further restrictions the ARMA representation of a stochastic process $\underline{x}_t$ is not unique. This fact is immediately obvious from the example in (2.1.15) where $\underline{x}_t$ has an ARMA(1,0) and an ARMA(0,1) representation. Also, left-multiplying (2.3.4) by a nonsingular matrix P yields an equivalent representation with AR and MA operators of orders p and q respectively. Here two representations are called equivalent if they represent zero mean processes with identical covariance structures or equivalently, if they possess the same MA representation (2.1.2).

Many dynamic econometric models have representations that can be obtained by multiplying (2.3.4) by an appropriate P matrix if deterministic terms are neglected (see Judge et al. (1985, Chapter 16)). A case of some importance in this study is obtained by using a triangular P matrix with unit diagonal which is such that $P\Sigma_u P'$ is a diagonal matrix. This choice of a transformation matrix yields

$$\underline{x}_t = D_0\underline{x}_t + D_1\underline{x}_{t-1} + \ldots + D_p\underline{x}_{t-p} + \underline{v}_t + \Psi_1\underline{v}_{t-1} + \ldots + \Psi_q\underline{v}_{t-q} \quad , \tag{2.3.6}$$

where $D_0 = I_K - P$, $D_i = P\Theta_i$, $i = 1,\ldots,p$, $\Psi_j = PM_jP^{-1}$, $j = 1,\ldots,q$, and $\underline{v}_t = P\underline{u}_t$ has a diagonal covariance matrix $\Sigma_v = P\Sigma_u P'$. Note that now $\underline{x}_t$ also appears on the right-hand side of the AR part.

Even if the zero order AR and MA matrices are required to be identity matrices this does not suffice to make the ARMA representation of a process unique. Again this is demonstrated by the example in (2.1.15). Also, simply left-multiplying (2.3.5) by any operator

$$P(L) = I_K + P_1L + \ldots + P_rL^r$$

with $\det[P(L)] \neq 0$ for $|z| \leq 1$ results in another equivalent ARMA representation of $\underline{x}_t$,

$$P(L)\Theta(L)\underline{x}_t = P(L)M(L)\underline{u}_t \quad . \tag{2.3.7}$$

One representation of particular practical importance results if P(L) is the adjoint $\Theta(L)^* = \det[\Theta(L)]\Theta(L)^{-1}$ of $\Theta(L)$. A typical element of

$\Theta(L)^*$ is a cofactor of $\Theta(L)$, i.e., the determinant of a matrix operator obtained by deleting one row and one column of $\Theta(L)$ appropriately multiplied by 1 or -1. Hence, $\Theta(L)^*$ is a finite order operator and (2.3.7) becomes

$$\det[\Theta(L)]\underline{x}_t = \Theta(L)^*M(L)\underline{u}_t \quad . \tag{2.3.8}$$

The virtue of this representation is that the same univariate AR operator is attached to each component of $\underline{x}_t$. This representation has been used in some empirical studies (e.g., Zellner and Palm (1974), Wallis (1977), Chan and Wallis (1978)).

For estimation purposes it is necessary to impose restrictions that make the process representation unique, that is, that restrict the class of permissible process representations in such a way that there is a one-to-one relationship between the covariance structures and feasible process representations. Various sets of restrictions have been proposed for that purpose by Hannan (1969, 1970, 1976, 1979), Deistler & Hannan (1981) and others. The following are examples (see Judge et al. (1985, Chapter 16)):

Suppose that $\Theta(L)$ and $M(L)$ are as in (2.3.2) and (2.3.3) respectively, and have no common left divisors, that is, $\Theta(L) = \Psi(L)\overline{\Theta}(L)$ and $M(L) = \Psi(L)\overline{M}(L)$ implies that $\det[\Psi(L)]$ is constant. Then any of the following three sets of conditions leads to unique ARMA representations (2.3.5):

1. $\Theta(L)$ is upper triangular and the degree of $\theta_{ii}(L)$ is not smaller than the degree of $\theta_{ij}(L)$ for all $i,j = 1,\dots,K$. Here $\theta_{ij}(L)$ is the ij-th element of $\Theta(L)$.

2. $\Theta(L) = \theta(L)I_K$, where $\theta(L) = 1 - \theta_1 L - \dots - \theta_p L^p$ is a scalar operator of degree p with $\theta_p \neq 0$.

3. In each class of equivalent ARMA models choose those with minimal MA degree q. Among these choose one with minimal AR degree p. The obtained representation will be unique if $[\Theta_p \quad M_q]$ has full rank K.

Although it is not always possible to write the MA operator $\Phi(L)$ of a stationary process in the form $\Theta(L)^{-1}M(L)$, that is, not every stationary nondeterministic stochastic process has a finite order ARMA representation, it is not difficult to see that any such process can be well approximated by an ARMA process in the sense that the mean squared forecasting errors of the considered process and the approximating ARMA process do not differ much. Forecasting will be considered in the next chapter.

On the other hand, any stationary process with an ARMA representation has a unique, pure MA representation of the type (2.1.2) satisfying (2.1.3). The coefficient matrices Φ_i of this representation can be obtained using the fact that $\Phi(z) = \Theta(z)^{-1}M(z)$. Denoting $\Theta(z)^{-1}$ by $C(z) = \sum_{j=0}^{\infty} C_j z^j$ the C_j matrices can be obtained recursively as

$$C_0 = I_K \quad ,$$

$$C_j = \begin{cases} \sum_{i=0}^{j-1} C_i \Theta_{j-i} & \text{for } j = 1,\ldots,p \\ \sum_{i=j-p}^{j-1} C_i \Theta_{j-i} & \text{for } j > p \end{cases} \tag{2.3.9}$$

(see (2.1.11)). Then the coefficient matrices Φ_j of $\Phi(z) = \sum_{j=0}^{\infty} \Phi_j z^j$ can be computed as

$$\Phi_0 = I_K \ ,$$

$$\Phi_j = \begin{cases} \sum_{i=0}^{j} C_i M_{j-i} & \text{for } j = 1,\ldots,q \\ \sum_{i=0}^{q} C_{j-q+i} M_{q-i} & \text{for } j > q \quad . \end{cases} \tag{2.3.10}$$

Uniqueness of the MA representation implies that any ARMA representation of a process will yield the same Φ_j matrices. This MA representation not only makes it easy to obtain the autocovariance structure of the process $\underline{x}_t$ (see (2.1.6)) but is also helpful in determining the forecast mean squared error (MSE) matrices as will be shown in Chapter 3, Section 3.1.

On the other hand for estimation and model specification purposes a pure AR representation is sometimes advantageous. If the MA part of (2.3.5) is invertible, a pure AR representation

$$\underline{x}_t = [I_K - M(L)^{-1}\Theta(L)]\underline{x}_t + \underline{u}_t = \sum_{i=1}^{\infty} A_i \underline{x}_{t-i} + \underline{u}_t \tag{2.3.11}$$

exists and the A_i can be obtained by recursions similar to those in

(2.3.9) and (2.3.10).

From (2.1.22) it follows that the spectral density matrix of (2.3.5) is

$$\underline{f}_{\underline{x}}(\omega) = \frac{1}{2\pi}\Theta(e^{i\omega})^{-1}M(e^{i\omega})\Sigma_{\underline{u}}M(e^{-i\omega})'\Theta(e^{-i\omega})'^{-1}, \quad -\pi \le \omega \le \pi , \quad (2.3.12)$$

provided $\underline{x}_t$ is stationary. Again, this matrix function contains all the information on the second moments of the process.

2.3.2 Nonstationary Processes

A K-dimensional ARMA process $\underline{x}_t$ of the form (2.3.4) - (2.3.5) is nonstationary if the AR operator $\Theta(L)$ has roots in or on the unit circle, that is,

$$\det[\Theta(z)] = 0 \quad \text{for} \quad \text{some } |z| \le 1 \quad . \quad (2.3.13)$$

For such a process it is again useful to assume that it starts at some finite time t_o. The variables $\underline{x}_{t_o}, \underline{x}_{t_o+1}, \dots, \underline{x}_{t_o+p-1}$ can be specified in a suitable manner and the ARMA representation (2.3.4) is assumed to be only valid for $t \ge t_o+p$. The MA part $\underline{u}_t + M_1\underline{u}_{t-1} + \dots + M_q\underline{u}_{t-q}$ may be assumed to be started at time $-\infty$.

Obviously in this case the autocovariances cannot be computed in the manner described in (2.1.6) since this formular is based on a pure MA representation which does not exist for the nonstationary case. The autocovariances will now depend on the initial variables $\underline{x}_{t_o}, \dots, \underline{x}_{t_o+p-1}$ and will in general vary with t.

As mentioned earlier, for practical purposes it is often assumed that nonstationarities can be removed by differencing individual components of $\underline{x}_t$. In this study it will usually be assumed that $\det[\Theta(z)] \ne 0$ for all $|z| \le 1$, $z \ne 1$. In other words, the only roots in and on the complex unit circle are unit roots. This assumption guarantees that a stationary multivariate process can be obtained by differencing. Some results given in the following chapters will still hold if the process under consideration has no invertible MA representation. On the other hand, when results for processes with estimated coefficients are discussed, the existence of an invertible MA representation will usually be important. Also, for the examples based on real life data the differenced data will be assumed to be generated by stationary processes with invertible MA parts. Following Box and Jenkins (1976) an univariate process x_t that has an ARMA(p,q) representation with invertible MA part after differencing d times will be called ARIMA(p,d,q) process (autoregressive integrated moving average process of order (p,d,q)).

2.4 ESTIMATION

If a given multiple time series is generated by a stationary Gaussian vector ARMA process with known orders, maximum likelihood (ML) procedures can be used for estimation. The resulting estimators have desirable asymptotic properties. The general case of estimating vector ARMA processes will be sketched in Section 2.4.1. If the generating process of the data under investigation is a pure AR process with known finite order, ML estimation is asymptotically equivalent to multivariate least squares (LS) estimation. This case is of particular interest in subsequent chapters of this study and will therefore be treated in more detail in Section 2.4.2. If the process orders are unknown it is still possible to fit finite order AR processes to the data using a multivariate LS procedure. An asymptotic theory for this case is summarized in Section 2.4.4.

2.4.1 Maximum Likelihood Estimation of Stationary Gaussian Vector ARMA Processes of Known Order

Let $\underline{x}_t$ be a K-dimensional, stationary, invertible, Gaussian vector ARMA(p,q) process

$$\Theta(L)\underline{x}_t = M(L)\underline{u}_t \quad , \tag{2.4.1}$$

where $\Theta(L)$ and $M(L)$ are as in (2.3.2) and (2.3.3) respectively. Suppose that $\Theta(L)$ and $M(L)$ are such that the ARMA representation is unique. Given a sample of size T, the negative log likelihood function is

$$\begin{aligned} -\ln \ell &= \frac{TK}{2} \ln 2\pi + \frac{T}{2} \ln \det \Sigma_{\underline{u}} + \frac{1}{2} \sum_{t=1}^{T} \underline{u}_t' \Sigma_{\underline{u}}^{-1} \underline{u}_t \\ &= \frac{TK}{2} \ln 2\pi + \frac{T}{2} \ln \det \Sigma_{\underline{u}} \\ &\quad + \frac{1}{2} \sum_{t=1}^{T} [M(L)^{-1}\Theta(L)\underline{x}_t]' \Sigma_{\underline{u}}^{-1} [M(L)^{-1}\Theta(L)\underline{x}_t] \quad . \end{aligned} \tag{2.4.2}$$

Without affecting the asymptotic properties of the estimators it may be assumed that the unobserved $\underline{x}_t$ for $t \leq 0$ are zero. Alternatively the sum on the right-hand side of (2.4.2) may be replaced by

$$\sum_{t=p+1}^{T} [\Theta(L)\underline{x}_t - (M(L)-I)\underline{u}_t]' \Sigma_{\underline{u}}^{-1} [\Theta(L)\underline{x}_t - (M(L)-I)\underline{u}_t] \quad , \quad (2.4.3)$$

where the $\underline{u}_{p+1-q},\ldots,\underline{u}_p$ are assumed to be zero and the $\underline{u}_t$, $t > p$, are obtained as

$$\underline{u}_t = \underline{x}_t - \Theta_1\underline{x}_{t-1} - \ldots - \Theta_p\underline{x}_{t-p} - M_1\underline{u}_{t-1} - \ldots - M_q\underline{u}_{t-q} \quad .$$

In any case, minimizing $-\ln \ell$ will in general be a highly nonlinear optimization problem.

Denoting the vector of all parameters by $\underline{\theta}$ and the corresponding ML estimator by $\hat{\underline{\theta}}$ it can be shown that $\hat{\underline{\theta}}$ is consistent, i.e.,

$$\text{plim } \hat{\underline{\theta}} = \underline{\theta} \quad , \quad (2.4.4)$$

and $\sqrt{T}(\hat{\underline{\theta}}-\underline{\theta})$ has an asymptotic normal distribution, i.e.,

$$\sqrt{T}(\hat{\underline{\theta}} - \underline{\theta}) \xrightarrow{d} N(\underline{0},\Sigma_{\hat{\underline{\theta}}}) \quad , \quad (2.4.5)$$

where $\xrightarrow{d}$ denotes convergence in distribution, $\Sigma_{\hat{\underline{\theta}}}$ is the inverse of the information matrix,

$$\Sigma_{\hat{\underline{\theta}}} = T\left[-E\,\frac{\partial^2 \ln \ell}{\partial\underline{\theta}\partial\underline{\theta}'}\right]^{-1} \quad ,$$

and the derivatives are evaluated at the true parameter vector (e.g., Anderson (1980)).

If $\underline{x}_t$ has a nonzero mean vector $\underline{\mu}$ the sample mean may be subtracted from each component prior to estimating the parameters $\underline{\theta}$. Asymptotically this is equivalent to estimating $\underline{\mu}$ by the ML method jointly with the other parameters. To see this, let $\underline{\eta} = (\underline{\mu}',\underline{\theta}')'$ and the negative log likelihood is

$$-\ln \ell = \frac{TK}{2}\ln 2\pi + \frac{T}{2}\ln \det\Sigma_{\underline{u}}$$
$$+ \frac{1}{2}\sum_{t=1}^{T}(\underline{x}_t - \underline{\mu})'[M(L)^{-1}\Theta(L)]'\Sigma_{\underline{u}}^{-1}M(L)^{-1}\Theta(L)(\underline{x}_t - \underline{\mu}) \quad .$$

Differentiating with respect to $\underline{\mu}$ and $\underline{\mu}'$ gives

$$- \frac{\partial^2 \ln \ell}{\partial \underline{\mu} \partial \underline{\mu}'} = \sum_{t=1}^{T} [M(1)^{-1}\Theta(1)]' \Sigma_{\underline{u}}^{-1} M(1)^{-1}\Theta(1)$$

$$= T[M(1)^{-1}\Theta(1)]' \Sigma_{\underline{u}}^{-1} M(1)^{-1}\Theta(1)$$

(see Judge et al. (1985, p. 939)) and

$$E\left[\frac{\partial^2 \ln \ell}{\partial \underline{\mu} \partial \underline{\theta}'} \bigg|_{\underline{\eta}}\right] = 0$$

since $\partial^2 \ln \ell / \partial \underline{\mu} \partial \underline{\theta}'$ is linear in $(\underline{x}_t - \underline{\mu})$ which has zero expectation. It follows that

$$\Sigma_{\hat{\underline{\eta}}} = T\left[-E\frac{\partial^2 \ln \ell}{\partial \underline{\eta} \partial \underline{\eta}'}\right]^{-1}$$

$$= \begin{bmatrix} \Theta(1)^{-1}M(1)\Sigma_{\underline{u}}[\Theta(1)^{-1}M(1)]' & 0 \\ 0 & \Sigma_{\hat{\underline{\theta}}} \end{bmatrix} \tag{2.4.6}$$

where $\hat{\underline{\eta}}$ denotes the ML estimator of $\underline{\eta}$. From the asymptotic normal distribution of $\sqrt{T}(\hat{\underline{\eta}} - \underline{\eta})$ it thus follows that $\hat{\underline{\mu}}$ is asymptotically independent of $\hat{\underline{\theta}}$. Furthermore, the upper left hand block of (2.4.6) is precisely the asymptotic covariance matrix of $\sqrt{T}(\bar{\underline{x}} - \underline{\mu})$, where $\bar{\underline{x}}$ is the vector of sample means.

In general $\Sigma_{\hat{\underline{\theta}}}$ has a complicated form which will not be given here. However, a special case which is of particular importance in later parts of this study will be considered next. More details and generalizations of the foregoing results can be found in Dunsmuir & Hannan (1976), Deistler, Dunsmuir & Hannan (1978), Hannan (1979), Hannan, Dunsmuir & Deistler (1980), Hillmer & Tiao (1979) and other articles.

2.4.2 Estimation of Vector Autoregressive Processes of Known Order

If the data generating process is of finite order AR type, the estimation problem reduces to running linear regressions. The system

$$\underline{x}_t = A_1\underline{x}_{t-1} + \dots + A_p\underline{x}_{t-p} + \underline{u}_t \quad , \quad t = p+1,\dots,T, \tag{2.4.7}$$

can be written as

$$\begin{bmatrix} \underline{x}^{(1)} \\ \underline{x}^{(2)} \\ \vdots \\ \underline{x}^{(K)} \end{bmatrix} = \begin{bmatrix} X_p & 0 & \dots & 0 \\ 0 & X_p & \dots & 0 \\ \vdots & \vdots & \ddots & \vdots \\ 0 & 0 & \dots & X_p \end{bmatrix} \underline{\alpha} + \begin{bmatrix} \underline{u}^{(1)} \\ \underline{u}^{(2)} \\ \vdots \\ \underline{u}^{(K)} \end{bmatrix}, \qquad (2.4.8)$$

where

$$\underline{x}^{(k)} = \begin{bmatrix} x_{k,p+1} \\ x_{k,p+2} \\ \vdots \\ x_{k,T} \end{bmatrix}, \quad \underline{u}^{(k)} = \begin{bmatrix} u_{k,p+1} \\ u_{k,p+2} \\ \vdots \\ u_{k,T} \end{bmatrix},$$

$$X_p = \begin{bmatrix} \underline{x}'_p & \underline{x}'_{p-1} & \dots & \underline{x}'_1 \\ \underline{x}'_{p+1} & \underline{x}'_p & \dots & \underline{x}'_2 \\ \vdots & \vdots & & \vdots \\ \underline{x}'_{T-1} & \underline{x}'_{T-2} & \dots & \underline{x}'_{T-p} \end{bmatrix} = \begin{bmatrix} \underline{X}'_p \\ \underline{X}'_{p+1} \\ \vdots \\ \underline{X}'_{T-1} \end{bmatrix}, \quad ((T-p)xKp), \qquad (2.4.9)$$

with $\underline{X}'_t = (\underline{x}'_t\ \underline{x}'_{t-1}\ \dots\ \underline{x}'_{t-p+1})$, and, denoting the column stacking operator by vec,

$$\underline{\alpha} = \text{vec}\begin{bmatrix} A'_1 \\ \vdots \\ A'_p \end{bmatrix}$$

is a K^2p-vector. Note that in (2.4.7)/(2.4.8) the first p observations of each variable are treated as "presample values". The LS estimator of $\underline{\alpha}$ is known to be

$$\hat{\underline{\alpha}} = I_K \otimes (X'X)^{-1}X' \begin{bmatrix} \underline{x}^{(1)} \\ \vdots \\ \underline{x}^{(K)} \end{bmatrix}, \qquad (2.4.10)$$

where $\otimes$ denotes the Kronecker product (see Judge et al. (1982, Chapter 11)). For a stationary Gaussian AR(p) process this estimator is consistent, asymptotically efficient and normally distributed,

$$\sqrt{T}(\hat{\underline{\alpha}} - \underline{\alpha}) \xrightarrow{d} N(\underline{0}, \Sigma_{\hat{\underline{\alpha}}}) \quad , \tag{2.4.11}$$

where

$$\Sigma_{\hat{\underline{\alpha}}} = \Sigma_{\underline{u}} \otimes \Gamma_p^{-1} \tag{2.4.12}$$

and $\Gamma_p = \Gamma_p'$ is as defined in (2.1.18), that is,

$$\Gamma_p = E(\underline{X}_t \underline{X}_t') \tag{2.4.13}$$

with $\underline{X}_t$ as in (2.4.9). For consistency and asymptotic normality of $\hat{\underline{\alpha}}$ it is actually not necessary that $\underline{x}_t$ is Gaussian. It suffices to assume that $\underline{u}_t$ is independent white noise with bounded fourth moments (see Fuller (1976, Theorem 8.2.3)).

The covariance matrix in (2.4.11) follows since

$$\begin{aligned}
&\operatorname{plim} T^{-1}(I\otimes X_p')(\Sigma_{\underline{u}}^{-1}\otimes I)(I\otimes X_p) \\
&= \Sigma_{\underline{u}}^{-1} \otimes \operatorname{plim} T^{-1}(X_p'X_p) \\
&= \Sigma_{\underline{u}}^{-1} \otimes \operatorname{plim}\left[\frac{1}{T-p}\left[\underline{X}_p, \ldots, \underline{X}_{T-1}\right]\begin{bmatrix}\underline{X}_p' \\ \vdots \\ \underline{X}_{T-1}'\end{bmatrix}\right] \\
&= \Sigma_{\underline{u}}^{-1} \otimes \operatorname{plim} \frac{1}{T-p}\sum_{t=p}^{T-1} \underline{X}_t\underline{X}_t' \\
&= \Sigma_{\underline{u}}^{-1} \otimes E(\underline{X}_t\underline{X}_t')
\end{aligned} \tag{2.4.14}$$

is known to be the inverse of the asymptotic covariance matrix of $\sqrt{T}(\hat{\underline{\alpha}} - \underline{\alpha})$ (see also Judge et al. (1985, Section 5.4.2)).

Consistent estimators of the white noise covariance matrix $\Sigma_{\underline{u}}$ are

$$\begin{aligned}
\hat{\Sigma}_{\underline{u}} &= \frac{1}{T-p}\begin{bmatrix}\hat{\underline{u}}^{(1)\prime} \\ \hat{\underline{u}}^{(2)\prime} \\ \vdots \\ \hat{\underline{u}}^{(K)\prime}\end{bmatrix}[\hat{\underline{u}}^{(1)}, \ldots \hat{\underline{u}}^{(K)}] \\
&= \frac{1}{T-p}\begin{bmatrix}(\underline{x}^{(1)} - X_p\hat{\underline{\alpha}}_1)' \\ \vdots \\ (\underline{x}^{(K)} - X_p\hat{\underline{\alpha}}_K)'\end{bmatrix}\left[(\underline{x}^{(1)} - X_p\hat{\underline{\alpha}}_1), \ldots, (\underline{x}^{(K)} - X_p\hat{\underline{\alpha}}_K)\right] \quad ,
\end{aligned} \tag{2.4.15}$$

where $\underline{\hat{\alpha}}_k'$ is the LS estimator of the k-th row of the (KxKp) matrix $(A_1, \ldots, A_p)$. Alternatively, using a correction for degrees of freedom,

$$\tilde{\Sigma}_{\underline{u}} = \frac{T-p}{T-Kp-p}\hat{\Sigma}_{\underline{u}} \qquad (2.4.16)$$

also gives a consistent estimator for $\Sigma_{\underline{u}}$. In the remainder of this study both $\hat{\Sigma}_{\underline{u}}$ and $\tilde{\Sigma}_{\underline{u}}$ will sometimes be used.

It follows from (2.4.14) that consistent estimators of the asymptotic covariance matrix $\Sigma_{\underline{\hat{\alpha}}}$ in (2.4.12) are

$$\hat{\Sigma}_{\underline{\hat{\alpha}}} = \hat{\Sigma}_{\underline{u}} \otimes \hat{\Gamma}_p^{-1} \qquad (2.4.17)$$

and

$$\tilde{\Sigma}_{\underline{\hat{\alpha}}} = \tilde{\Sigma}_{\underline{u}} \otimes \hat{\Gamma}_p^{-1} \quad , \qquad (2.4.18)$$

where

$$\hat{\Gamma}_p = \frac{1}{T-p}\sum_{t=p}^{T-1} \underline{X}_t\underline{X}_t' \quad . \qquad (2.4.19)$$

Note that the AR coefficients may be collected alternatively as

$$\underline{a} = \mathrm{vec}(A_1, A_2, \ldots, A_p) \quad , \qquad (2.4.20)$$

where vec is again the column stacking operator. It is sometimes advantageous to work with the K^2p-vector $\underline{a}$ and, denoting the LS estimator by $\underline{\hat{a}}$, it is not difficult to see that its asymptotic covariance matrix is

$$\Sigma_{\underline{\hat{a}}} = \Gamma_p^{-1} \otimes \Sigma_{\underline{u}} \quad ,$$

that is,

$$\sqrt{T}(\underline{\hat{a}} - \underline{a}) \xrightarrow{d} N(\underline{0}, \Gamma_p^{-1} \otimes \Sigma_{\underline{u}}) \quad . \qquad (2.4.21)$$

Also, it is possible to write the LS estimator using the Yule-Walker equations (2.1.17). Estimating $[\Gamma_{\underline{x}}(-1), \Gamma_{\underline{x}}(-2), \ldots, \Gamma_{\underline{x}}(-p)]$ by

$$\frac{1}{T-p}\sum_{t=p}^{T-1} \underline{x}_{t+1}\underline{X}_t'$$

and using (2.4.19) gives an estimator

$$[\hat{A}_1,\ldots,\hat{A}_p] = \left[\sum_{t=p}^{T-1} \underline{x}_{t+1}\underline{x}_t'\right]\left[\sum_{t=p}^{T-1} \underline{x}_t\underline{x}_t'\right]^{-1} , \qquad (2.4.22)$$

where the individual elements are just the LS estimators, that is, they are identical to the corresponding elements of $\hat{\underline{\alpha}}$ and $\hat{\underline{a}}$. This is easily seen by considering the k-th row of (2.4.22) which is

$$\left[\sum_{t=p}^{T-1} x_{k,t+1}\underline{x}_t'\right]\left[\sum_{t=p}^{T-1} \underline{x}_t\underline{x}_t'\right]^{-1}$$

$$= \left[\left[x_{k,p+1}, \;\ldots\ldots, x_{k,T}\right]\begin{bmatrix}\underline{x}_p' \\ \vdots \\ \underline{x}_{T-1}'\end{bmatrix}\right](X_p'X_p)^{-1}$$

$$= (\underline{x}^{(k)\,'}X_p)(X_p'X_p)^{-1} = \hat{\underline{\alpha}}_k' \quad .$$

Note that the so-called Yule-Walker estimator is often defined in a slightly different way. Instead of estimating $\Gamma_{\underline{x}}(-i)$ by

$$\frac{1}{T-p}\sum_{t=p}^{T-1} \underline{x}_{t+1}\underline{x}_{t-i+1}'$$

the estimator

$$\frac{1}{T}\sum_{t=i}^{T-1} \underline{x}_{t+1}\underline{x}_{t-i+1}' \quad ,$$

using all the sample information, is applied. Although the resulting estimator for $\underline{\alpha}$ is asymptotically equivalent to the LS estimator, Tjøstheim & Paulsen (1983) and Paulsen & Tjøstheim (1985) found that in small samples the Yule-Walker estimator tends to have a stronger bias than the LS estimator. Therefore, in this study the latter estimator is used.

The asymptotic efficiency of the multivariate LS estimator (2.4.10) is due to the fact that the regressors are the same in each equation of the system (2.4.7). In such a case each equation may be estimated by LS without loss of asymptotic efficiency. In later chapters subset AR models where some of the parameters are constrained to zero, will also be of interest. In that case, estimating each equation in (2.4.7) separately may result in a loss of asymptotic efficiency. Since $\not{\Sigma}_{\underline{u}}$ may be nondiagonal, a generalized LS procedure may be more efficient if in different equations different parameters are zero.

In general, if linear restrictions for the parameters are available, they can be expressed in the form

$$R\underline{\alpha} = \underline{r} \tag{2.4.23}$$

where R is a $(J \times K^2p)$ matrix and $\underline{r}$ is a $(J\times 1)$ vector. The restricted multivariate generalized LS (GLS) estimator for $\underline{\alpha}$ is obtained by minimizing

$$[\underline{X} - (I \otimes X_p)\underline{\alpha}]'(\Sigma_{\underline{u}}^{-1} \otimes I)[\underline{X} - (I \otimes X_p)\underline{\alpha}] \tag{2.4.24}$$

subject to $R\underline{\alpha} = \underline{r}$. Here $\underline{X} = \left[\underline{x}^{(1)\prime} \ \dots \ \underline{x}^{(K)\prime}\right]'$. The resulting restricted GLS estimator for $\underline{\alpha}$ is

$$\underline{\alpha}^* = \hat{\underline{\alpha}} + CR'(RCR')^{-1}(\underline{r} - R\hat{\underline{\alpha}}) \quad , \tag{2.4.25}$$

where

$$C = [\Sigma_{\underline{u}}^{-1} \otimes X_p'X_p]^{-1} = \Sigma_{\underline{u}} \otimes (X_p'X_p)^{-1} \quad .$$

Since $\Sigma_{\underline{u}}$ is usually unknown it may be replaced by a consistent estimator obtained from multivariate LS residuals. For instance $\hat{\Sigma}_{\underline{u}}$ or $\tilde{\Sigma}_{\underline{u}}$ may be used in (2.4.25) (see Judge et al. (1982, Chapter 11)). Under general assumptions (e.g. if $\underline{x}_t$ is Gaussian) $\underline{\alpha}^*$ is consistent and

$$\sqrt{T}(\underline{\alpha}^* - \underline{\alpha}) \xrightarrow{d} N(\underline{0}, \Sigma_{\underline{\alpha}^*}) \quad , \tag{2.4.26}$$

where the asymptotic covariance matrix is such that $\Sigma_{\hat{\underline{\alpha}}} - \Sigma_{\underline{\alpha}^*}$ is positive semidefinite. In general the difference between the two covariance matrices is nonzero and thus, $\underline{\alpha}^*$ is asymptotically efficient relative to $\hat{\underline{\alpha}}$.

Rather than using GLS estimation of (2.4.7) the transformed process

$$\underline{x}_t = D_o\underline{x}_t + D_1\underline{x}_{t-1} + \dots + D_p\underline{x}_{t-p} + \underline{v}_t \quad , \tag{2.4.27}$$

where D_o is upper triangular with zero diagonal and $E(\underline{v}_t\underline{v}_t') = \Sigma_{\underline{v}}$ is diagonal (see (2.3.6)), may be estimated by applying LS to each individual equation separately. If observations $\underline{x}_t$, $t = 1,\dots,T$, are available the system can be written as

$$\underline{x}^{(k)} = X_p^k\underline{\delta}_k + \underline{v}^{(k)} \quad , \quad k = 1,\dots,K \quad , \tag{2.4.28}$$

where $\underline{x}^{(k)}$ is defined as in (2.4.8), X_p^k is a matrix similar to X_p in (2.4.9) with all columns deleted that correspond to zero coefficients and columns added that correspond to nonzero elements of D_o, $\underline{\delta}_k$ contains the nonzero elements of the k-th row of the system (2.4.27), and

$$\underline{v}^{(k)} = \begin{bmatrix} v_{k,p+1} \\ v_{k,p+2} \\ \vdots \\ v_{k,T} \end{bmatrix} .$$

Hence, in (2.4.28) all zero constraints are taken into consideration and will be automatically satisfied in the LS estimation procedure.

The LS estimator of $\underline{\delta}_k$ is

$$\hat{\underline{\delta}}_k = (X_p^{k\prime} X_p^k)^{-1} X_p^{k\prime} \underline{x}^{(k)} \quad . \tag{2.4.29}$$

If $\underline{x}_t$ is Gaussian this estimator is consistent and

$$\sqrt{T}(\hat{\underline{\delta}}_k - \underline{\delta}_k) \xrightarrow{d} N[\underline{0}, \sigma_{v_k}^2 \operatorname{plim} T(X_p^{k\prime} X_p^k)^{-1}] \quad , \tag{2.4.30}$$

where $\sigma_{v_k}^2$ is the variance of v_{kt}, the k-th component of $\underline{v}_t$. This variance can be estimated consistently by

$$\hat{\sigma}_{v_k}^2 = \frac{1}{T-p}(\underline{x}^{(k)} - X_p^k \hat{\underline{\delta}}_k)'(\underline{x}^{(k)} - X_p^k \hat{\underline{\delta}}_k) \tag{2.4.31}$$

or by

$$\tilde{\sigma}_{v_k}^2 = \frac{T-p}{T-p-K_k} \hat{\sigma}_{v_k}^2 \quad , \tag{2.4.32}$$

where K_k is the number of parameters in the k-th equation of (2.4.28), that is, K_k is the number of elements of $\underline{\delta}_k$. Thus, a consistent estimator of the asymptotic covariance matrix of $\hat{\underline{\delta}}_k$ is

$$\hat{\Sigma}_{\hat{\underline{\delta}}_k} = \hat{\sigma}_{v_k}^2 \left[X_p^{k\prime} X_p^k/(T-p)\right]^{-1} \quad . \tag{2.4.33}$$

Of course, here $\hat{\sigma}_{v_k}^2$ may be replaced by $\tilde{\sigma}_{v_k}^2$.

Denoting the set of all parameters by $\underline{\delta}$, i.e., $\underline{\delta} = (\underline{\delta}_1', \ldots, \underline{\delta}_K')'$, and the corresponding LS estimator by $\hat{\underline{\delta}}$, it follows that

$$\sqrt{T}(\hat{\underline{\delta}} - \underline{\delta}) \xrightarrow{d} N(\underline{0}, \not{Z}_{\hat{\underline{\delta}}}) \quad , \tag{2.4.34}$$

where

$$\not{Z}_{\hat{\underline{\delta}}} = \text{plim } T[\underline{X}'(\not{Z}_{\underline{v}}^{-1} \otimes I_K)\underline{X}]^{-1}$$

and

$$\underline{X} = \begin{bmatrix} X_p^1 & & 0 \\ & \ddots & \\ 0 & & X_p^K \end{bmatrix} .$$

Hence,

$$\not{Z}_{\hat{\underline{\delta}}} = \text{plim } T \begin{bmatrix} \sigma_{v_1}^2 (X_p^{1\prime} X_p^1)^{-1} & & 0 \\ & \ddots & \\ 0 & & \sigma_{v_K}^2 (X_p^{K\prime} X_p^K)^{-1} \end{bmatrix}$$

and a consistent estimator can be obtained using (2.4.33).

Since $A_i = P^{-1}D_i$, $i = 1,\dots,p$, (see (2.3.6)), the vector

$$\begin{aligned} \underline{\alpha} &= \text{vec}[A_1 \; \dots \; A_p]' \\ &= \text{vec}([D_1 \; \dots \; D_p]'P^{-1\prime}) \\ &= (P^{-1} \otimes I_{pK})\text{vec}[D_1 \; \dots \; D_p]' \\ &= (P^{-1} \otimes I_{pK})\underline{\delta} \quad , \end{aligned} \tag{2.4.35}$$

where a well-known result for the column stacking operator vec has been used (e.g., Judge et al. (1985, p. 949)). Using the consistent estimator $\hat{P} = I_K - \hat{D}_o$ of P, where $\hat{D}_o$ is the LS estimator of D_o, an estimator

$$\underline{\alpha}_R = (\hat{P}^{-1} \otimes I_{pK})\hat{\underline{\delta}} \tag{2.4.36}$$

is obtained for $\underline{\alpha}$. For this estimator

$$\sqrt{T}(\underline{\alpha}_R - \underline{\alpha}) \xrightarrow{d} N(\underline{0}, \not{Z}_{\underline{\alpha}_R}) \tag{2.4.37}$$

with

$$\Sigma_{\underline{\alpha}_R} = (P^{-1} \otimes I_{pK}) \Sigma_{\hat{\underline{\delta}}} (P^{-1'} \otimes I_{pK}) \tag{2.4.38}$$

(see Judge et al. (1985, p. 189)). In general $\underline{\alpha}_R$ is efficient relative to the multivariate LS estimator $\hat{\underline{\alpha}}$, that is, $\Sigma_{\hat{\underline{\alpha}}} - \Sigma_{\underline{\alpha}_R}$ is positive semi-definite, since zero constraints are observed in estimating $\underline{\delta}$. It must be emphasized, however, that $\hat{\underline{\delta}}$ is only an efficient estimator of $\underline{\delta}$ if the system is given in the form (2.4.28) and the only restrictions that are available for the parameters are zero constraints.

If zero constraints are known for the system (2.4.7), it may be more efficient to use the restricted GLS estimator (2.4.25) for $\underline{\alpha}$ and then use a linear transformation to obtain an estimator for $\underline{\delta}$. Thus, the choice of the estimation procedure should depend on the type of prior information available.

In practice the time series under consideration frequently do not have a zero mean. In that situation intercept terms may be added to (2.4.7) or (2.4.27). In other words, for example, the system

$$\underline{x}_t = \underline{\nu} + A_1\underline{x}_{t-1} + \dots + A_p\underline{x}_{t-p} + \underline{u}_t \tag{2.4.39}$$

may be estimated by multivariate LS. For practical purposes this is a convenient form. Alternatively the sample means

$$\bar{x}_k = \frac{1}{T}\sum_{t=1}^{T} x_{kt} \quad , \quad k = 1,\dots,K \; ,$$

may be subtracted from the original data and the model

$$(\underline{x}_t - \bar{\underline{x}}) = A_1(\underline{x}_{t-1} - \bar{\underline{x}}) + \dots + A_p(\underline{x}_{t-p} - \bar{\underline{x}}) + \underline{u}_t, \tag{2.4.40}$$

where $\bar{\underline{x}} = (\bar{x}_1,\dots,\bar{x}_K)'$, may then be estimated by LS in exactly the manner described earlier. This procedure is sometimes more convenient in discussing theoretical results. Under general conditions the LS estimators for the AR coefficient matrices A_i resulting from (2.4.40) have the same asymptotic distribution as those obtained from

$$(\underline{x}_t - \underline{\mu}) = A_1(\underline{x}_{t-1} - \underline{\mu}) + \dots + A_p(\underline{x}_{t-p} - \underline{\mu}) + \underline{u}_t, \tag{2.4.41}$$

where $\underline{\mu} = E(\underline{x}_t)$.

Also, under general conditions (e.g., if $\underline{x}_t$ is Gaussian) $\bar{\underline{x}}$ is a consistent and asymptotically normally distributed estimator for $\underline{\mu}$, that is,

$$\sqrt{T}(\bar{\underline{x}} - \underline{\mu}) \xrightarrow{d} N(\underline{0}, \Sigma_{\bar{\underline{x}}}), \tag{2.4.42}$$

where

$$\Sigma_{\bar{\underline{x}}} = (I_K - \sum_{i=1}^{p} A_i)^{-1} \Sigma_{\underline{u}} (I_K - \sum_{i=1}^{p} A_i)'^{-1} \tag{2.4.43}$$

(see (2.4.6), Fuller (1976, Chapter 6) and Hannan (1970, Chapter IV)). Furthermore, $\bar{\underline{x}}$ is asymptotically independent of the LS estimators $\hat{A}_1, \ldots, \hat{A}_p$. These properties will be useful later on.

The foregoing results hold if the parameter restrictions and process orders are known. In practice this information is rarely available. Therefore the case of processes with unknown order will be discussed next.

2.4.3 Multivariate Least Squares Estimation of AR Processes With Unknown Order

Suppose the time series under investigation are known to be generated by a finite order AR process $\underline{x}_t$ as in (2.4.7) and its order p is unknown. In this case the estimation theory of the previous section is still relevant if an upper limit for the order can be specified. If such an upper limit, say P, is available, an AR(P) process can simply be estimated by multivariate least squares. The resulting estimators will be asymptotically inefficient if $p < P$ since possible zero restrictions are not observed. To improve the asymptotic efficiency of the LS estimators, a model selection criterion may be used to estimate the AR order p. If a criterion is used which estimates the order consistently, that is, the resulting estimator converges in probability to p, then the asymptotic distribution of the parameter estimates is the same as in the case where the order p is known. Similar comments apply for ARMA processes. Criteria for consistent order estimation are available and will be discussed in Section 2.5.

In the following it will be assumed that $\underline{x}_t$ is generated by an AR process and no upper bound for its order is available. In fact, the generating process may have an infinite AR structure. For this case Lewis & Reinsel (1982) have developed an asymptotic distribution theory (see also Bhansali (1978)).

For the stationary process $\underline{x}_t$ given in (2.1.7),

$$\underline{x}_t = \sum_{j=1}^{\infty} A_j \underline{x}_{t-j} + \underline{u}_t, \tag{2.4.44}$$

the following conditions are assumed to hold:

(i) $\underline{u}_t = (u_{1t},\dots,u_{Kt})'$ is identically distributed independent white noise with

$$E|u_{it}u_{jt}u_{kt}u_{lt}| < \infty \quad , \quad 1 \le i,j,k,l \le K. \tag{2.4.45}$$

(ii) $$\sum_{j=1}^{\infty} \sqrt{tr(\Phi_j'\Phi_j)} < \infty \, , \tag{2.4.46}$$

where the Φ_j are the MA coefficient matrices of the representation (2.1.2).

(iii) The order $\tilde{p}(T)$ of the AR model fitted to the series $\underline{x}_t$ is a function of the length T of the time series such that

$$\tilde{p}(T) \to \infty \, , \; \frac{\tilde{p}(T)^3}{T} \to 0$$

$$\text{and } \sqrt{T}\Big[\sum_{j=\tilde{p}(T)+1}^{\infty} \sqrt{tr(A_j'A_j)}\Big] \to 0 \quad \text{as} \quad T \to \infty. \tag{2.4.47}$$

Condition (i) allows for very general white noise processes $\underline{u}_t$. In addition to being independent and identically distributed the $\underline{u}_t$ are required to have finite fourth moments. The condition is, for instance, satisfied for a Gaussian white noise process.

The second condition is also not very restrictive and holds, for example, if $\underline{x}_t$ has a finite order ARMA representation. Note that (2.4.46) can be written alternatively as

$$\sum_{j=1}^{\infty} \sqrt{tr(\Phi_j\Phi_j')} < \infty.$$

The third condition requires that AR processes of increasing order be fitted to the data as the sample size T increases. However, the AR order must increase much more slowly than the sample size. The requirement

$$\sqrt{T} \sum_{j=\tilde{p}(T)+1}^{\infty} \sqrt{tr(A_j'A_j)} \xrightarrow[T\to\infty]{} 0 \tag{2.4.48}$$

is always satisfied if $\underline{x}_t$ is actually a finite order AR process and $\tilde{p}(T) \to \infty$. For infinite order AR processes this condition may impose a lower bound on the speed by which $\tilde{p}(T)$ goes to infinity. For example, if x_t is a univariate MA(1) process

$$x_t = u_t - \phi u_{t-1},$$

where $0 < |\phi| < 1$ to ensure invertibility, then

$$x_t = - \sum_{j=1}^{\infty} \phi^j x_{t-j} + u_t$$

and (2.4.48) becomes

$$\sqrt{T} \sum_{j=\tilde{p}(T)+1}^{\infty} |\phi^j| = \sqrt{T}\left[\frac{1}{1-|\phi|} - \frac{1-|\phi|^{\tilde{p}(T)+1}}{1-|\phi|}\right]$$

$$= \sqrt{T}\frac{|\phi|^{\tilde{p}(T)+1}}{1-|\phi|} \xrightarrow[T\to\infty]{} 0$$

In this case $\tilde{p}(T) = T^{1/r}$ with $r > 3$ is a possible choice which also satisfies $\tilde{p}(T)^3/T \to 0$. Also $\tilde{p}(T) = \ln T$ may be chosen for some ϕ for which $\sqrt{T}|\phi|^{\ln T}$ goes to zero for $T\to\infty$. This can be seen by noting that

$$\ln(\sqrt{T}|\phi|^{\ln T}) = \frac{1}{2}\ln T + \ln T \ln|\phi| = \ln T(\frac{1}{2} + \ln|\phi|)$$

and $\frac{1}{2} + \ln|\phi| < 0$ for $|\phi| < 0.6$. On the other hand, if $\tilde{p}(T) = \ln\ln T$ the term $\sqrt{T}|\phi|^{\tilde{p}(T)}$ does not go to zero since $\tilde{p}(T)$ goes to infinity too slowly. In general, the condition (2.4.48) implies a lower bound for the speed by which $\tilde{p}(T)$ goes to infinity when $T\to\infty$, while $p(T)^3/T \to 0$ provides an upper bound.

In practice, for a particular sample size T, the order is likely to be chosen by some order selection criterion. Some such criteria are presented in Section 2.5.1.

It is assumed that $AR(\tilde{p}(T))$ processes are fitted to the data by multivariate LS as discussed in the previous section. To distinguish between the parameter estimates obtained by fitting AR processes of different orders the matrix containing the first p AR coefficient matrices will be denoted by A(p), i.e.,

$$A(p) = [A_1, A_2, \ldots, A_p] \tag{2.4.49}$$

and

$$\underline{a}(p) = \text{vec } A(p) \tag{2.4.50}$$

is the $(K^2p \times 1)$ vector obtained by stacking the columns of A(p). Fitting an AR(p) to the data the estimated i-th AR coefficient matrix will be denoted by $\tilde{A}_{i,p}$. Furthermore

$$\tilde{A}(p) = [\tilde{A}_{1,p} , \tilde{A}_{2,p} , \ldots , \tilde{A}_{p,p}] \qquad (2.4.51)$$

and

$$\underline{\tilde{a}}(p) = \text{vec}\ \tilde{A}(p). \qquad (2.4.52)$$

Using the assumptions (i) - (iii), Lewis & Reinsel (1982) prove the following result:

<u>THEOREM 2.1</u>

Let $\underline{x}_t$ be an AR process as specified in (2.4.44) and suppose the conditions (i) - (iii) ((2.4.45) - (2.4.47)) are satisfied. Further assume that $\underline{\ell}(p)$, p = 1,2,..., is a sequence of $(K^2p \times 1)$ vectors such that

$$0 < C_1 \leq \underline{\ell}(p)'\underline{\ell}(p) \leq C_2 < \infty \quad , \quad \text{for all } p = 1,2,\ldots \qquad (2.4.53)$$

then

$$\frac{\sqrt{T-\tilde{p}(T)}\ \underline{\ell}(\tilde{p}(T))'[\underline{\tilde{a}}(\tilde{p}(T)) - \underline{a}(\tilde{p}(T))]}{\sqrt{\underline{\ell}(\tilde{p}(T))'(\Gamma_{\tilde{p}}^{-1} \otimes \Sigma_{\underline{u}})\underline{\ell}(\tilde{p}(T))}} \xrightarrow[T\to\infty]{d} N(0,1) \qquad (2.4.54)$$

where Γ_p is as defined in (2.1.18).

The Theorem implies that for a fixed p

$$\sqrt{T-\tilde{p}}(\text{vec}\{[\tilde{A}_{1,\tilde{p}}, \tilde{A}_{2,\tilde{p}}, \ldots, \tilde{A}_{p,\tilde{p}}] - [A_1, A_2, \ldots, A_p]\}) \qquad (2.4.55)$$

has an asymptotic multivariate normal distribution with mean vector $\underline{0}$ and covariance matrix $V\otimes\Sigma_{\underline{u}}$, where V is the upper left-hand (Kp x Kp) block of the inverse of

$$\Gamma_\infty = \begin{bmatrix} \Gamma_{\underline{x}}(0) & \Gamma_{\underline{x}}(-1) & \Gamma_{\underline{x}}(-2) & \ldots \\ \Gamma_{\underline{x}}(1) & \Gamma_{\underline{x}}(0) & \Gamma_{\underline{x}}(-1) & \ldots \\ \vdots & & \ddots & \end{bmatrix} . \qquad (2.4.56)$$

If the original multiple time series has a nonzero mean vector the sample means may be subtracted initially from the components of the series. Alternatively, intercept terms may be included in the regressions.

2.4.4 Nonstationary Processes

The asymptotic theory for estimating nonstationary processes is complicated by the fact that the asymptotic distribution of least squares estimators is in general not normal. For univariate finite order AR and ARMA processes the asymptotic distribution of LS estimators has been considered e.g. by Fuller (1976), Fuller, Hasza & Goebel (1981), Hasza & Fuller (1979, 1982), Dickey & Fuller (1979), Rao (1978) and Said & Dickey (1984, 1985), Dickey, Bell & Miller (1986).

In this study it is assumed that the nonstationary processes are such that the nonstationarity can be removed by differencing and the number of times the difference operator has to be applied is also assumed known. Furthermore it is assumed that the differenced process has an AR representation. Under these conditions the parameter estimation does not pose any severe problems, as the theory for stationary processes can be used.

2.5 MODEL SPECIFICATION

2.5.1 AR Order Determination

Usually the order of the generation process of a particular data set will be unknown. In that case the asymptotic theory of Section 2.4.3 can be used to derive the properties of the estimators provided the necessary assumptions are justifiable. The problem then remains to choose the function $\tilde{p}(T)$. Of course, the theory is valid for an arbitrary choice as long as (2.4.47) is satisfied. In fact, for a given sample size T, any finite number may be chosen and then a rule can be specified so that (2.4.47) holds for T approaching infinity. Therefore, in practice, it is desirable to have a rule for choosing $\tilde{p}(T)$ in a finite sample situation.

Three criteria (rules) will be used in this study:

$$AIC(p) = \ln \det \hat{\Sigma}_p + \frac{2K^2p}{T-P} \qquad (2.5.1)$$

(Akaike (1973, 1974)),

$$HQ(p) = \ln \det\hat{\Sigma}_p + \frac{2K^2 p \ln\ln(T-P)}{T-P} \qquad (2.5.2)$$

(Hannan & Quinn (1979), Quinn (1980)), and

$$SC(p) = \ln \det\hat{\Sigma}_p + \frac{K^2 p \ln(T-P)}{T-P} \qquad (2.5.3)$$

(Schwarz (1978), Rissanen (1978)), where K is the number of component series of $\underline{x}_t$, T is the length of the time series, P is the maximum AR order to be considered for the given series and $\hat{\Sigma}_p$ is the estimate for Σ_u given in (2.4.15) that results when an AR(p) is fitted. The only difference here is that always (for each p) the first P observed $\underline{x}_t$ vectors, $\underline{x}_1,\ldots,\underline{x}_P$, are treated as presample vectors. That is, $\hat{\Sigma}_p$ is only based on T-P residual vectors and in (2.4.15) T-P is used for T-p. Using any of the three criteria, AR(p) models are fitted to the data for p = 0,1,...,P and the AR order $\tilde{p}$ is chosen so as to minimize the selected criterion. For example, $\tilde{p}(AIC)$ is chosen such that

$$AIC(\tilde{p}(AIC)) = \min \{AIC(p) \mid p = 0,1,\ldots,P\}. \qquad (2.5.4)$$

The three criteria are based on different principles. Intuitively they can be interpreted as consisting of a term that decreases with increasing AR order ($\ln \det\hat{\Sigma}_p$) and a term that penalizes increasing the AR order. A criterion reaches its minimum when both are balanced in an optimal way. The penalty terms are different for the different criteria. For instance, for AIC it is $2K^2p/(T-P)$.

For the sample sizes considered in this study, out of the three criteria, AIC will always choose the largest AR order, while SC is the most parsimonious criterion. More precisely,

$$\tilde{p}(AIC) \geq \tilde{p}(SC) \quad \text{for} \quad T-P \geq 8, \qquad (2.5.5)$$

$$\tilde{p}(AIC) \geq \tilde{p}(HQ) \quad \text{for} \quad T-P \geq 16, \qquad (2.5.6)$$

and

$$\tilde{p}(HQ) \geq \tilde{p}(SC) \qquad (2.5.7)$$

for all sample sizes (see Lütkepohl (1985a)). Furthermore, SC and HQ are consistent criteria in the sense that $\tilde{p}(SC)$ and $\tilde{p}(HQ)$ converge in probability, as $T\to\infty$, to the true AR order p provided $\underline{x}_t$ is indeed a finite order, stationary AR(p) and the maximum AR order P is chosen such that $P \geq p$. In fact, SC and, for $K > 1$, also HQ are strongly consistent so that $\tilde{p}(SC)$ and $\tilde{p}(HQ)$ converge even almost surely to the true order p. In contrast, AIC overestimates the true AR order asymptotically with positive probability if $P > p$ (see Paulsen (1984), Tsay (1984), Quinn (1980), Shibata (1976, 1980), de Gooijer et al. (1985)).

A number of other criteria for AR order selection has been proposed in the recent literature. Most of them are either similar to AIC, SC or HQ or have inferior small sample properties in the sense that they provide models with inferior forecasting ability (see Lütkepohl (1985a)).

As an example the three criteria have been applied to the bivariate series $\underline{x}_t = (x_{1t}, x_{2t})'$ with x_1 and x_2 being the seasonally adjusted, quarterly U.S. Fixed Investment and Change in Business Inventories, respectively. The data and data source are given in the Appendix to the book. For specification and estimation purposes data covering the period 1947 to 1968 have been used. Since the original variables appear to have a trend (see Figures 2.1 and 2.2), first differences have been used. Thus, the stationary series x_{1t} and x_{2t} originate in the second quarter of 1947 leaving 87 observations for each of the variables. Using an arbitrarily chosen maximum AR order of $P = 14$, the following estimates obtain:

$$\tilde{p}(\text{AIC}) = 4 \quad \text{and} \quad \tilde{p}(\text{SC}) = \tilde{p}(\text{HQ}) = 1. \tag{2.5.8}$$

Once an AR order $\tilde{p}$ has been determined it makes sense to use only $\tilde{p}$ presample values and reestimate the process. This will always be done in the remainder of this study, when real life data are analyzed. The resulting estimated process for $\tilde{p} = 4$ is

$$\begin{bmatrix} x_{1t} \\ x_{2t} \end{bmatrix} = \begin{bmatrix} 0.78 \\ (0.29) \\ -0.55 \\ (0.57) \end{bmatrix} + \begin{bmatrix} 0.49 & 0.17 \\ (0.12) & (0.06) \\ 0.42 & -0.27 \\ (0.23) & (0.11) \end{bmatrix} \begin{bmatrix} x_{1,t-1} \\ x_{2,t-1} \end{bmatrix} + \begin{bmatrix} -0.17 & -0.07 \\ (0.13) & (0.06) \\ 0.05 & -0.10 \\ (0.25 & (0.12) \end{bmatrix} \begin{bmatrix} x_{1,t-2} \\ x_{2,t-2} \end{bmatrix}$$

$$+ \begin{bmatrix} 0.05 & -0.05 \\ (0.13) & (0.06) \\ 0.15 & -0.01 \\ (0.25) & (0.12) \end{bmatrix} \begin{bmatrix} x_{1,t-3} \\ x_{2,t-3} \end{bmatrix} + \begin{bmatrix} -0.18 & -0.07 \\ (0.11) & (0.06) \\ 0.13 & -0.45 \\ (0.21) & (0.12) \end{bmatrix} \begin{bmatrix} x_{1,t-4} \\ x_{2,t-4} \end{bmatrix} + \begin{bmatrix} u_{1t} \\ u_{2t} \end{bmatrix},$$

$$\tilde{\Sigma}_{\underline{u}} = \begin{bmatrix} 5.06 & 2.15 \\ 2.15 & 19.3 \end{bmatrix}, \tag{2.5.9}$$

and for $\tilde{p} = 1$, the process

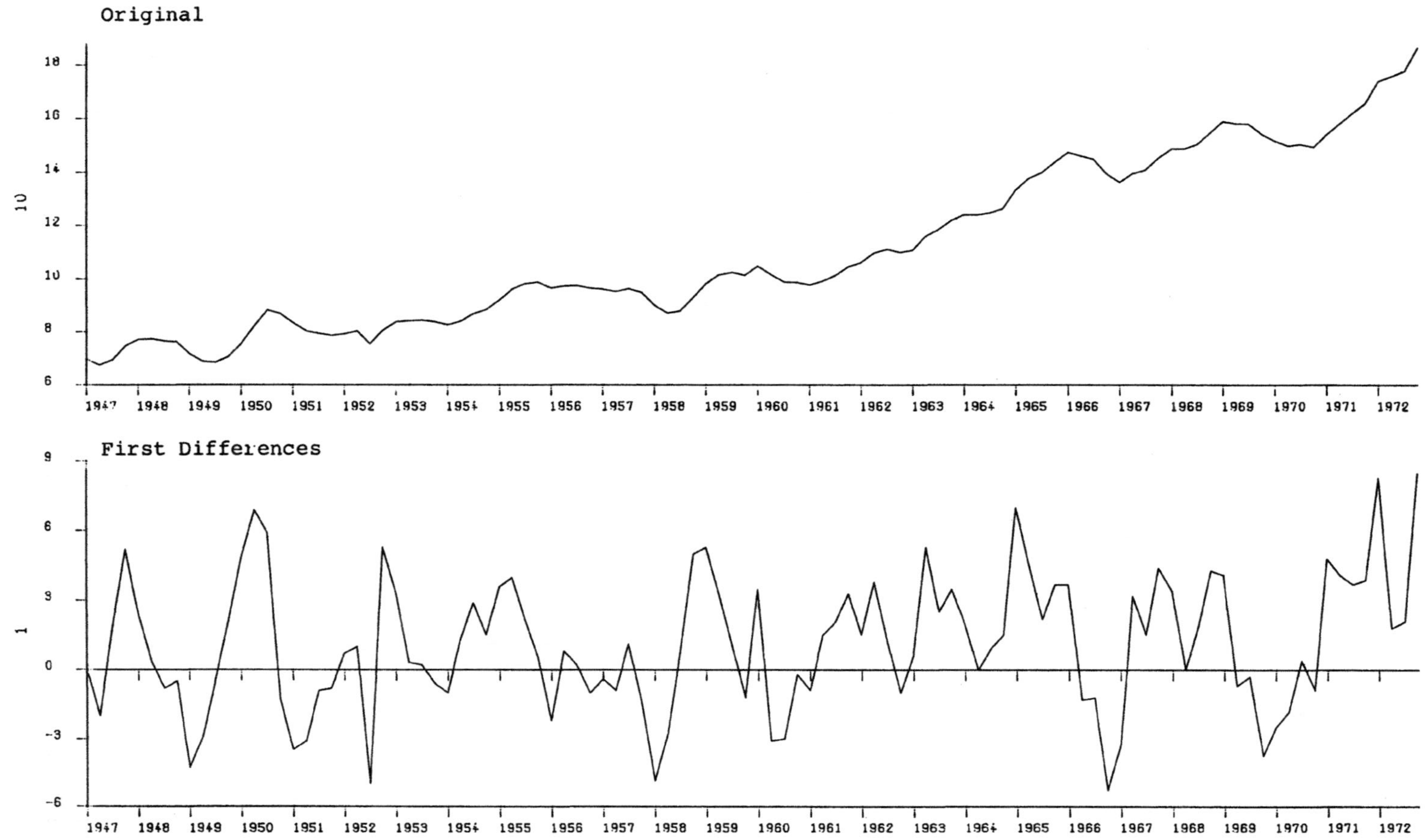

Figure 2.1. Quarterly, Seasonally Adjusted U.S. Fixed Investment

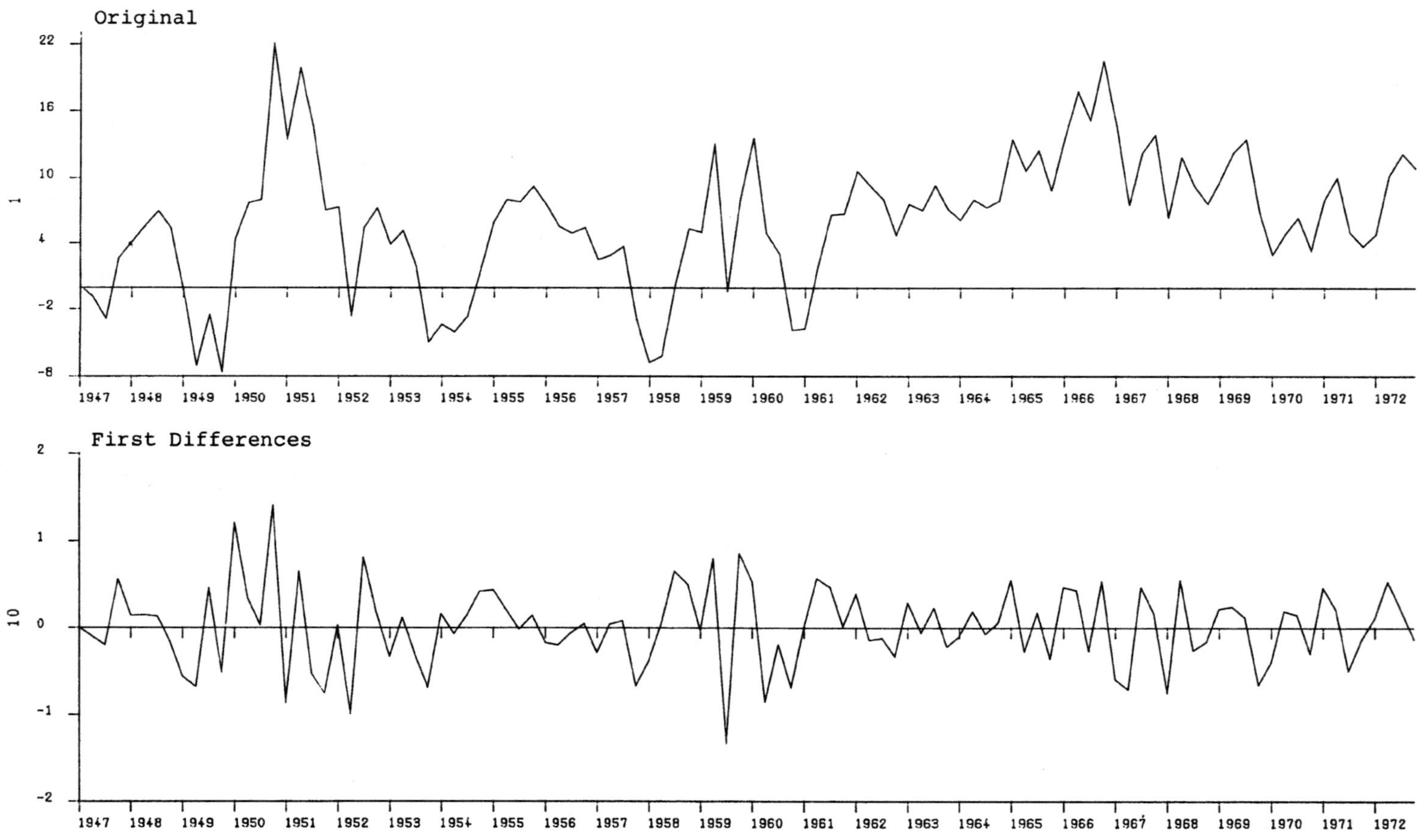

Figure 2.2. Quarterly, Seasonally Adjusted U.S. Change in Business Inventories

$$\begin{bmatrix} x_{1t} \\ \\ x_{2t} \end{bmatrix} = \begin{bmatrix} 0.62 \\ (0.27) \\ -0.32 \\ (0.53) \end{bmatrix} + \begin{bmatrix} 0.40 & 0.17 \\ (0.09) & (0.05) \\ 0.48 & -0.30 \\ (0.19) & (0.10) \end{bmatrix} \begin{bmatrix} x_{1,t-1} \\ \\ x_{2,t-1} \end{bmatrix} + \begin{bmatrix} u_{1t} \\ \\ u_{2t} \end{bmatrix},$$

$$\tilde{\Sigma}_{\underline{u}} = \begin{bmatrix} 5.64 & 2.58 \\ 2.58 & 21.8 \end{bmatrix} \qquad (2.5.10)$$

is obtained. Here the numbers in parentheses are estimated standard errors, that is, they are the square roots of the diagonal elements of $\tilde{\Sigma}_{\hat{\underline{\alpha}}}$ in (2.4.18). The intercept terms are kept in the models regardless of their significance. This will be done in all real life examples of this study.

Obviously, a number of parameter estimates in the AR(4) model (2.5.9) are smaller than their respective standard errors in absolute value. Thus, using the asymptotic distribution theory of Section 2.4.2, they are not significantly different from zero at any common significance level. Estimating too many parameters adversely affects the estimation efficiency and, as will be seen in the next chapter, also the forecasting efficiency. Therefore various suggestions have been made to limit the number of parameters involved. Possible strategies include fitting mixed vector ARMA models (Tiao & Box (1981)), index models (Sargent & Sims (1977), Reinsel (1983)) or subset AR models (Penm & Terrell (1982, 1984), Hsiao (1979)). In the latter case some of the coefficients of a full AR model are simply set at zero and in the following subsection one possible strategy to decide on the zero constraints will be considered. The method is a modification of Hsiao's (1979) procedure.

2.5.2 Subset Autoregressions

The general strategy for specifying a subset AR model is to search over a range of models and restrictions and choose the one that optimizes a prespecified criterion. It will be assumed that minimization of a criterion called CR is the objective. The criteria used in the empirical examples of later chapters will be described later on.

There are various possibilities to select a subset AR model. Ignoring the costs one would ideally search over all possible alternatives given some prespecified upper bound P for the model order. Such a strategy is often not practical as the costs may be extremely high even if the number of component series K and the maximal order P are only moderate. Also, degrees of freedom limitations may render a full search procedure impossible. For instance, if K = 5 and there are 15 years of quarterly data, that is, 60 observations are available for each variable, then, if P = 12, there will not be sufficiently many degrees of freedom for LS estimation. Since many macro economic variables change slowly over time multicollinearity problems may render the computation of estimates difficult even if 20 or 30 years of quarterly data are available. This problem is inherent in any specification strategy that requires the estimation of the full model at some stage of the search procedure.

Hsiao (1979) has suggested a method that is likely to avoid fitting the full model of maximal order. The procedure will be described here for the bivariate system

$$x_{1t} = \psi_1 + \delta_{11,1}x_{1,t-1} + \dots + \delta_{11,k}x_{1,t-k} + \\ + \delta_{12,0}x_{2t} + \dots + \delta_{12,n}x_{2,t-n} + v_{1t} \qquad (2.5.11a)$$

$$x_{2t} = \psi_2 + \delta_{21,1}x_{1,t-1} + \dots + \delta_{21,r}x_{1,t-r} + \\ + \delta_{22,1}x_{2,t-1} + \dots + \delta_{22,s}x_{2,t-s} + v_{2t} \qquad (2.5.11b)$$

Note that x_{2t}, the current value of the second variable, appears in the first equation. In other words, an AR representation of the form (2.4.27) is used. In the present context this representation has the advantage that the covariance matrix Σ_v of $\underline{v}_t = (v_{1t}, v_{2t})'$ is diagonal so that the two equations can be estimated efficiently by LS even though they will in general involve different sets of regressors. Note that the variables are allowed to enter with a different number of lags in different equations. Relaxing the assumption of having an equal number of lags for each variable in each equation may result in a substantial reduction of the number of parameters required. Since v_{1t} and v_{2t} are uncorrelated and the two equations may be treated separately, Hsiao's method will be discussed for the first equation in the following. The second equation can be treated analogously.

Hsiao proposes the following search scheme:

<u>Step 1:</u> Determine $\tilde{k}$ such that

$$CR(\tilde{k},-) = \min\{CR(k,-) \mid k = 0,1,\dots,P\}$$

where the dash indicates that the second variable is not

included in the model and thus a univariate model is fitted for the first variable. Note that for $k = 0$ the intercept is the only regressor in the equation.

Step 2: Choose $\hat{n}$ such that

$$CR(\tilde{k},\hat{n}) = \min \{CR(\tilde{k},n) \mid n = -,0,\dots,m\} .$$

Here $n = -$ means that the second variable is not included in the model. Due to omitted variables effects $\tilde{k}$ may not be the optimal lag length for the first variable and therefore a third step is carried out.

Step 3: Select $\hat{k}$ such that

$$CR(\hat{k},\hat{n}) = \min \{CR(k,\hat{n}) \mid k = 0,1,\dots,\tilde{k}\} .$$

The integers $\hat{k}$ and $\hat{n}$ are then used as estimates for the lag lengths in the first equation of (2.5.11). As mentioned earlier an analogous procedure can be used to determine the lag lengths in the second equation of (2.5.11). Note however, that the first variable x_{1t} does not enter with lag zero in the second equation.

The estimate $(\hat{k},\hat{n})$ is not necessarily the optimal pair that minimizes the criterion CR over all possible integer pairs. An example where the global minimum is not found by Hsiao's method is given in Judge et al. (1982, Chapter 26). The advantage of the procedure is that it usually avoids fitting a model with $k = n = P$ if P is large. It will now be described how a further reduction in the number of parameters can be obtained.

For simplicity the procedure is presented for a bivariate system such as (2.5.11). A generalization of the specification procedure will be obvious. Also, since the two equations may be treated separately, the method is described only for the first equation. The second equation can again be treated analogously.

Let $\underline{p} = (p_1,\dots,p_P)'$ be a vector with elements

$$p_i = \begin{cases} 1 & \text{if } \delta_{11,i} \neq 0 \\ 0 & \text{if } \delta_{11,i} = 0 \end{cases} \qquad i = 1,\dots,P, \qquad (2.5.12)$$

and $\underline{q} = (q_0,q_1,\dots,q_P)'$ is a vector with elements

$$q_i = \begin{cases} 1 & \text{if } \delta_{12,i} \neq 0 \\ 0 & \text{if } \delta_{12,i} = 0 \end{cases} \qquad i = 0,1,\ldots,P, \tag{2.5.13}$$

and P is the maximum lag length that is considered for the time series under consideration. CR($\underline{p}$,$\underline{q}$) denotes the value of the criterion to be minimized if the included and excluded parameters in the first equation are specified by $\underline{p}$ and $\underline{q}$. The coefficients to be retained in the first equation are determined in the following two stages:

<u>Stage 1:</u>

a) Choose k so that

$$CR(\tilde{\underline{p}},\underline{0}) = \min \{CR(\underline{p},\underline{0}) \mid \underline{p} = (\underbrace{1,\ldots,1}_{i \text{ times}},0,\ldots,0)', \quad i = 0,1,\ldots,P\},$$

where $\tilde{\underline{p}} = (\underbrace{1,\ldots,1}_{k \text{ times}},0,\ldots,0)'$.

b) Choose n so that

$$CR(\tilde{\underline{p}},\tilde{\underline{q}}) = \min \{CR(\tilde{\underline{p}},\underline{q}) \mid \underline{q} = (\underbrace{1,\ldots,1}_{i \text{ times}},0,\ldots,0)', \quad i = 0,1,\ldots,P+1\},$$

where $\tilde{\underline{q}} = (\underbrace{1,\ldots,1}_{n \text{ times}},0,\ldots,0)'$.

Obviously, Stage 1, is identical to Steps 1 and 2 of Hsiao's procedure discussed above. In the second stage the remaining parameters are eliminated if they do not contribute to reducing the specification criterion. More precisely, the first equation of the system is estimated with $\delta_{12,n-2}$ replaced by zero (providing $n \geq 2$). If the resulting value of CR is lower than the CR value of the model with $\delta_{12,n-2}$ included in the equation, this parameter is deleted. Otherwise it is retained. Then the next parameter is checked in the same manner and so on down to $\delta_{11,1}$ (or the first parameter on the right-hand side of the first equation in (2.5.11)). Formally this procedure can be written as follows.

<u>Stage 2:</u>

a) Set $q_{n-i} = 0$ if

$$CR[\tilde{p},(1,\ldots,1,0,q_{n-i+1},\ldots,q_{n-1},0,\ldots,0)']$$

$$\leq CR[\tilde{p},(1,\ldots,1,1,q_{n-i+1},\ldots,q_{n-1},0,\ldots,0)']$$

and $q_{n-i} = 1$ otherwise, for $i = 2,\ldots,n$. The resulting q vector is denoted by $\hat{q}$.

b) Set $p_{k-i} = 0$ if

$$CR[(1,\ldots,1,0,p_{k-i+1},\ldots,p_k,0,\ldots 0)' , \hat{q}]$$

$$\leq CR[(1,\ldots,1,1,p_{k-i+1},\ldots,p_k,0,\ldots,0)' , \hat{q}]$$

and $p_{k-i} = 1$ otherwise, for $i = 0,\ldots, k-1$. The resulting p vector is denoted by $\hat{p}$.

The vectors $\hat{p}$ and $\hat{q}$ specify the zero restrictions placed upon the coefficients of the first equation. In other words, the zeros in $\hat{p}$ and $\hat{q}$ indicate the coefficients to be deleted from the first equation.

In the second equation the optimal lag length for x_{1t} is determined first, when no lagged values of x_{2t} are present. Then the obtained lag length of x_{1t} is fixed and the optimal lag length for x_{2t} is determined conditionally on the fixed lag length of x_{1t}. Then the individual coefficients are checked.

If the system consists of more than two variables, for each equation all the variables are added into the model in Stage 1 in the order $x_1, x_2, \ldots, x_K$. Then the significance of individual coefficients of the equation with all variables included is checked in Stage 2 starting with the lags of x_K. The treatment of the univariate case is obvious.

In determining the criterion values it will be necessary to estimate various different models. Therefore, as in the case of full AR models the first P values of the original sample are treated as presample values. If in the final equation the greatest lag, say s, is smaller than P, only s observations of each component series are treated as presample values in a final estimation round.

In the empirical analyses in later chapters AIC, SC, and HQ are used as specification criteria in appropriately modified form. For instance, for the first equation of the bivariate system (2.5.11) these criteria are defined as

$$AIC(p,q) = \ln \hat{\sigma}_1^2 + \frac{2}{T-P}\left(\sum_{i=1}^{P} p_i + \sum_{j=0}^{P} q_j\right) \tag{2.5.14}$$

$$SC(\underline{p},\underline{q}) = \ln \hat{\sigma}_1^2 + \frac{\ln(T-P)}{T-P}\left(\sum_{i=1}^{P} p_i + \sum_{j=0}^{P} q_j\right) \tag{2.5.15}$$

and

$$HQ(\underline{p},\underline{q}) = \ln \hat{\sigma}_1^2 + \frac{2\ln\ln(T-P)}{T-P}\left(\sum_{i=1}^{P} p_i + \sum_{j=0}^{P} q_j\right), \tag{2.5.16}$$

where $\hat{\sigma}_1^2$ is the estimator of the variance of v_{1t} without degrees of freedom correction (see (2.4.31)) when a model is fitted with restrictions defined by $\underline{p}$ and $\underline{q}$. A detailed description of the computer program used for subset AR model fitting and forecasting is given by Lütkepohl & Dornbusch (1983).

As in Section 2.5.1, the U.S. investment data with maximal lag length P = 14 have been used again to provide an example. The resulting models are for the AIC criterion

$$x_{1t} = \underset{(0.27)}{0.93} + \underset{(0.10)}{0.41}x_{1,t-1} - \underset{(0.10)}{0.20}x_{1,t-2} - \underset{(0.09)}{0.22}x_{1,t-4}$$

$$+ \underset{(0.05)}{0.10}x_{2t} + \underset{(0.05)}{0.22}x_{2,t-1} + v_{1t}, \quad \tilde{\sigma}_{v_1}^2 = 4.71,$$

$$x_{2t} = \underset{(0.50)}{-0.21} + \underset{(0.18)}{0.37}x_{1,t-1} - \underset{(0.10)}{0.24}x_{2,t-1} - \underset{(0.10)}{0.41}x_{2,t-4} + v_{2t},$$

$$\tilde{\sigma}_{v_2}^2 = 18.6, \tag{2.5.17}$$

for the HQ criterion

$$x_{1t} = \underset{(0.27)}{0.62} + \underset{(0.09)}{0.40}x_{1,t-1} + \underset{(0.05)}{0.17}x_{2,t-1} + v_{1t}, \quad \tilde{\sigma}_{v_1}^2 = 5.64,$$

$$x_{2t} = \underset{(0.48)}{0.13} - \underset{(0.10)}{0.20}x_{2,t-1} - \underset{(0.10)}{0.43}x_{2,t-4} + v_{2t}, \quad \tilde{\sigma}_{v_2}^2 = 19.4, \tag{2.5.18}$$

and for the SC criterion

$$x_{1t} = \underset{(0.27)}{0.62} + \underset{(0.09)}{0.40}x_{1,t-1} + \underset{(0.05)}{0.17}x_{2,t-1} + v_{1t}, \quad \tilde{\sigma}_{v_1}^2 = 5.64,$$

$$x_{2t} = \underset{(0.49)}{0.12} - \underset{(0.10)}{0.46}x_{2,t-4} + v_{2t}, \quad \tilde{\sigma}_{v_2}^2 = 20.1, \tag{2.5.19}$$

where the numbers in parentheses underneath the estimates are estimates of their standard errors and the $\tilde{\sigma}_{v_i}^2$ are estimates of the variance $\sigma_{v_i}^2$

of v_{it} with a correction for degrees of freedom.

2.5.3 The Box-Jenkins Approach

The AR methods presented previously are the only multiple time series methods used in this study. For univariate time series, in some cases, the Box-Jenkins approach will be used in constructing models for forecasting. This procedure is well documented (see e.g. Box & Jenkins (1976), Pankratz (1983), Judge et al. (1982, Chapter 25)) and therefore only a brief summary will be provided here.

The objective of the procedure is to find a parsimonious ARIMA representation (see Section 2.3.2) for the generating process of a given time series. In the first stage a tentative model is specified on the basis of the estimated autocorrelations and partial autocorrelations of the series. Then the model parameters are estimated by an asymptotically efficient method and in a third stage diagnostic checks are carried out to determine the adequacy of the model. The checks usually involve an examination of the plot of the residuals and their autocorrelations as well as Portmanteau tests for whiteness of the residuals. Also the significance of the parameters is usually checked. If a model is rejected an alternative specification is set up, estimated, and exposed to a series of adequacy checks. Often various cycles are required to find an adequate model. An important difference between the previously described AR procedures and the Box-Jenkins approach is the subjective nature of the latter. The final model is not chosen on the basis of a specific selection criterion but results from a series of judgemental decisions by the researcher. All models constructed by the Box-Jenkins approach in the following chapters have been estimated by the ML procedure available in GENSTAT. A nonzero mean term is always kept in the model, regardless of its significance, if such a term is also used in comparable AR models.

2.6 SUMMARY

In this chapter some notation has been introduced and estimation and specification results have been discussed. In order to forecast future values of a set of time series variables a model for the data generation process is usually constructed and its parameters are estimated on the basis of the available data. In this study the models are chosen from the class of discrete-time vector stoahastic processes. Special cases of interest have been considered in this chapter. Primary attention has been given to stationary processes. Their moving average (MA), autoregressive (AR) and, where applicable, ARMA representations have been considered. The estimation problem has been discussed in detail only for AR processes since these will be of primary importance in the remainder of the study whenever the data generation process is not assumed known. Criteria for determining the AR order and a procedure for imposing zero constraints on the AR coefficients have been presented. In the next chapter it will be shown how the processes can be used for prediction.

CHAPTER 3.

FORECASTING VECTOR STOCHASTIC PROCESSES

In this chapter prediction formulas will be given and the corresponding mean squared errors (MSEs) will be derived for the processes discussed in Chapter 2. The general strategy for forecasting or prediction (the two terms will be used interchangeably) is to assume that a model for the generation process of a set of variables of interest $\underline{x} = (x_1, \ldots, x_K)'$ and an information set, say J_t, containing the available information up to time t are given. For example, the data generation process could be an AR or MA process as introduced in Chapter 2 and J_t may contain all current and previous values of the $\underline{x}$ variables, i.e., $J_t = \{\underline{x}_s | s \leq t\}$. If forecasts are desired for a particular purpose a specific cost function may be associated with the possible forecast errors. Then a forecast will be optimal if it minimizes the cost or expected cost. Thus, it will depend on the particular cost function which forecast is optimal.

On the other hand, forecasts of economic variables are often published for general use. In that case the specific cost functions of all potential users cannot be taken into account. Then the statistical properties of the forecasts and perhaps forecast intervals are of interest to enable the user to draw propper conclusions for his or her particular situation. Also it is desirable to choose the forecast such that it minimizes a wide range of plausible cost functions if possible.

In connection with the linear models introduced in Chapter 2, forecasts that minimize the forecast MSE under the assumption that the data generating process is completely known are the most widely used ones. Arguments in favour of choosing forecasts that minimize the MSE are given by Granger (1969a) and Granger & Newbold (1977). They show that minimum MSE forecasts also minimize a range of cost functions other then the MSE. Moreover, for many cost functions the optimal predictors are simple functions of minimum MSE predictors. Furthermore, for an unbiased predictor, the MSE is the variance of the forecast error and it is useful in setting up forecast intervals. Therefore the forecast MSEs will be of major interest in this and subsequent chapters.

In the first section of this chapter it will be assumed that the process used for prediction (including its coefficients) is known and the information set consists of all present and past values of the variables of interest. In practice, however, the data generation process is usually not completely known. In Section 3.2 it is therefore assumed that its coefficients are estimated while its orders are known. Again this assumption is not realistic and therefore forecasting of AR processes of unknown, possibly infinite order is considered in Section 3.3. An extension to certain nonstationary processes is discussed in Section 3.4. In many of the following chapters different forecasts will be compared on the basis of simulation studies. A statistic that is useful in such comparisons is given in Section 3.5. Finally, a summary is provided in Section 3.6.

3.1 FORECASTING KNOWN PROCESSES

3.1.1 Predictors Based on the Moving Average Representation

Consider the K-dimensional, zero mean, stationary stochastic process $\underline{x}_t = (x_{1t},\dots,x_{Kt})'$ with MA representation

$$\underline{x}_t = \sum_{i=o}^{\infty} \Phi_i \underline{u}_{t-i} \quad , \quad \Phi_o = I_K \quad , \tag{3.1.1}$$

where the Φ_i are (KxK) coefficient matrices such that

$$\det\left(\sum_{i=o}^{\infty} \Phi_i z^i\right) \neq 0 \quad \text{for } |z| < 1, \tag{3.1.2}$$

that is, the MA operator has no roots inside the complex unit circle and $\underline{u}_t$ is zero mean white noise with nonsingular covariance matrix $\underline{\Sigma}_u$. The optimal (linear minimum mean squared error (MSE)) predictor h steps ahead based on the information set $J_t = \{\underline{u}_s | s \leq t\}$ is

$$\underline{x}_t(h) = \sum_{i=o}^{\infty} \Phi_{h+i} \underline{u}_{t-i} = \sum_{i=h}^{\infty} \Phi_i \underline{u}_{t+h-i} \; . \tag{3.1.3}$$

This predictor will often be referred to as <u>optimal h-step predictor at origin t</u> and it is in fact the predictor most often used in practice when the data are assumed to be generated by the process (3.1.1). The step length h is often called the <u>forecast horizon</u>.

The forecast error associated with the predictor (3.1.3) is

$$\underline{x}_{t+h} - \underline{x}_t(h) = \sum_{i=o}^{\infty} \Phi_i \underline{u}_{t+h-i} - \sum_{i=h}^{\infty} \Phi_i \underline{u}_{t+h-i} = \sum_{i=o}^{h-1} \Phi_i \underline{u}_{t+h-i} \tag{3.1.4}$$

and thus the predictor is unbiased, that is,

$$E[\underline{x}_{t+h} - \underline{x}_t(h)] = \underline{0} \; , \tag{3.1.5}$$

and the corresponding MSE matrix is

$$\begin{aligned} \not{\Sigma}_{\underline{x}}(h) &= E[\underline{x}_{t+h} - \underline{x}_t(h)][\underline{x}_{t+h} - \underline{x}_t(h)]' \\ &= E[\sum_{i=o}^{h-1} \Phi_i \underline{u}_{t+h-i}][\sum_{i=o}^{h-1} \Phi_i \underline{u}_{t+h-i}]' \\ &= \sum_{i=o}^{h-1} \Phi_i \not{\Sigma}_{\underline{u}} \Phi_i' = \not{\Sigma}_{\underline{x}}(h-1) + \Phi_{h-1} \not{\Sigma}_{\underline{u}} \Phi_{h-1}' \end{aligned} \tag{3.1.6}$$

To see that $\underline{x}_t(h)$ is indeed the optimal linear h-step predictor based on $J_t = \{\underline{u}_s | s \leq t\}$ consider any other linear h-step predictor based on this information set, say

$$\bar{\underline{x}}_t(h) = \sum_{i=o}^{\infty} B_i \underline{u}_{t-i} .$$

The associated forecast error is

$$\begin{aligned} \underline{x}_{t+h} - \bar{\underline{x}}_t(h) &= \sum_{i=o}^{\infty} \Phi_i \underline{u}_{t+h-i} - \sum_{i=h}^{\infty} B_{i-h} \underline{u}_{t+h-i} \\ &= \sum_{i=o}^{h-1} \Phi_i \underline{u}_{t+h-i} + \sum_{i=h}^{\infty} (\Phi_i - B_{i-h}) \underline{u}_{t+h-i} . \end{aligned}$$

Hence, the corresponding MSE matrix is

$$\begin{aligned} \bar{\not{\Sigma}}_{\underline{x}}(h) &= E[\underline{x}_{t+h} - \bar{\underline{x}}_t(h)][\underline{x}_{t+h} - \bar{\underline{x}}_t(h)]' \\ &= \sum_{i=o}^{h-1} \Phi_i \not{\Sigma}_{\underline{u}} \Phi_i' + \sum_{i=h}^{\infty} (\Phi_i - B_{i-h}) \not{\Sigma}_{\underline{u}} (\Phi_i - B_{i-h})' . \end{aligned}$$

Since $\not{\Sigma}_u$ is nonsingular and thus, positive definite, the second sum on the right-hand side of this expression is a positive semidefinite matrix which is nonzero unless $B_{i-h} = \Phi_i$ for $i \geq h$. Thus, $\bar{\not{\Sigma}}_{\underline{x}}(h) - \not{\Sigma}_{\underline{x}}(h)$ is a nonzero positive semidefinite matrix unless $\bar{\underline{x}}_t(h) = \underline{x}_t(h)$. This demonstrates the optimality of $\underline{x}_t(h)$.

An immediate consequence of (3.1.6) is that the forecast MSEs are monotonically nondecreasing with growing forecast horizon h, that is,

$$\underline{\Sigma}_x(h) \geq \underline{\Sigma}_x(r) \quad \text{for } h \geq r, \tag{3.1.7}$$

where the inequality sign between the matrices means as usual that $\underline{\Sigma}_x(h) - \underline{\Sigma}_x(r)$ is positive semidefinite. As the forecast horizon h approaches infinity, the forecast MSE matrix $\underline{\Sigma}_x(h)$ converges to

$$\underline{\Sigma}_x = \sum_{i=o}^{\infty} \Phi_i \underline{\Sigma}_u \Phi_i' , \tag{3.1.8}$$

which is the covariance matrix of $\underline{x}_t$ (see Chapter 2, Section 2.1.2). Thus, the variances of the components of $\underline{x}_t$ are upper bounds for the forecast MSEs. The upper bounds are attained for $h \to \infty$, that is, $\underline{\Sigma}_x(h) \xrightarrow[h\to\infty]{} \underline{\Sigma}_x$. As mentioned in Chapter 2, Section 2.1.1, processes with this property are called nondeterministic. In turn, if $\underline{x}_t$ is a stationary, discrete time stochastic process and $\underline{x}_t(h)$ is the optimal linear h-step predictor based on $\{\underline{x}_s | s \leq t\}$ with corresponding MSE matrix $\underline{\Sigma}_x(h)$, then, by Wold's Decomposition Theorem, $\underline{x}_t$ has a moving average representation of the form (3.1.1) if $\underline{\Sigma}_x(h) \xrightarrow[h\to\infty]{} \underline{\Sigma}_x$. That is, $\underline{x}_t$ has an MA representation if it is nondeterministic.

If $\underline{u}_t$ is Gaussian white noise and hence $\underline{x}_t$ is a Gaussian process, the forecast error vector (3.1.4) has a multivariate normal distribution with mean zero and covariance matrix $\underline{\Sigma}_x(h)$,

$$\underline{x}_{t+h} - \underline{x}_t(h) \sim N(\underline{0}, \underline{\Sigma}_x(h)). \tag{3.1.9}$$

This fact can be used to construct confidence intervals for the forecasts. For instance, for the k-th component of $\underline{x}_t$, a $(1-\alpha)100$ % confidence interval for the h-step forecast is

$$x_{k,t}(h) - \sigma_k(h) z_{\alpha/2} \leq x_{k,t+h} \leq x_{k,t}(h) + \sigma_k(h) z_{\alpha/2}, \tag{3.1.10}$$

where $x_{k,t}(h)$ is the k-th component of $\underline{x}_t(h)$, $\sigma_k^2(h)$ is the k-th diagonal element of $\underline{\Sigma}_x(h)$, and $z_{\alpha/2}$ is the critical value of a standard normal distribution, i.e.,

$$P(z \leq z_{\alpha/2}) = 1 - \frac{\alpha}{2}$$

for a standard normal random variable z.

If $\underline{x}_t$ is a K-dimensional, stationary stochastic process with nonzero mean vector $\underline{\mu} = E(\underline{x}_t)$, define $\underline{z}_t = \underline{x}_t - \underline{\mu}$. In this case the optimal h-step predictor of $\underline{x}_t$ at origin t is easily seen to be

$$\underline{x}_t(h) = \underline{\mu} + \underline{z}_t(h), \qquad (3.1.11)$$

where $\underline{z}_t(h)$ is the optimal h-step predictor of the zero mean process $\underline{z}_t$. That is, the mean vector is simply added to the optimal predictor of the zero mean part. The MSE matrix of $\underline{x}_t(h)$ is not affected, that is,

$$\Sigma_{\underline{x}}(h) = \Sigma_{\underline{z}}(h), \qquad (3.1.12)$$

where $\Sigma_{\underline{z}}(h)$ is the MSE matrix of $\underline{z}_t(h)$.

Sometimes the joint MSE matrix of a number of forecasts for different horizons is of interest. Denoting the vector of all forecasts up to h steps ahead by

$$\underline{X}_t(h) = [\underline{x}_t(1)',\ldots,\underline{x}_t(h)']' \qquad (3.1.13)$$

and

$$\underline{X}_{t+1}^h = [\underline{x}_{t+1}',\ldots,\underline{x}_{t+h}']' \qquad (3.1.14)$$

it follows that

$$\Sigma_{\underline{X}}(h) = E[\underline{X}_{t+1}^h - \underline{X}_t(h)][\underline{X}_{t+1}^h - \underline{X}_t(h)]'$$

$$= E\begin{bmatrix} \sum_{i=o}^{o} \Phi_i \underline{u}_{t+1-i} \\ \sum_{i=o}^{1} \Phi_i \underline{u}_{t+2-i} \\ \vdots \\ \sum_{i=o}^{h-1} \Phi_i \underline{u}_{t+h-i} \end{bmatrix} \begin{bmatrix} \sum_{i=o}^{o} \Phi_i \underline{u}_{t+1-i} \\ \sum_{i=o}^{1} \Phi_i \underline{u}_{t+2-i} \\ \vdots \\ \sum_{i=o}^{h-1} \Phi_i \underline{u}_{t+h-i} \end{bmatrix}'$$

$$= \begin{bmatrix} \Sigma_{\underline{u}} & \Sigma_{\underline{u}}\Phi_1' & \cdots & \Sigma_{\underline{u}}\Phi_{h-1}' \\ \Phi_1\Sigma_{\underline{u}} & \sum_{i=o}^{1} \Phi_i\Sigma_{\underline{u}}\Phi_i' & \cdots & \sum_{i=o}^{1} \Phi_i\Sigma_{\underline{u}}\Phi_{h-2+i}' \\ \vdots & \vdots & \ddots & \vdots \\ \Phi_{h-1}\Sigma_{\underline{u}} & \sum_{i=o}^{1} \Phi_{h-2+i}\Sigma_{\underline{u}}\Phi_i' & \cdots & \sum_{i=o}^{h-1} \Phi_i\Sigma_{\underline{u}}\Phi_i' \end{bmatrix}. \qquad (3.1.15)$$

This matrix can be used to obtain the joint MSE matrix of any two forecasts $\underline{x}_t(r)$ and $\underline{x}_t(s)$, where r, s $\leq$ h, by simply collecting the corresponding blocks from (3.1.15). For example, if r = h - 1 and s = h,

$$E\begin{bmatrix} \underline{x}_{t+h-1} - \underline{x}_t(h-1) \\ \underline{x}_{t+h} - \underline{x}_t(h) \end{bmatrix}\begin{bmatrix} \underline{x}_{t+h-1} - \underline{x}_t(h-1) \\ \underline{x}_{t+h} - \underline{x}_t(h) \end{bmatrix}'$$

$$= \begin{bmatrix} \sum_{i=o}^{h-2} \Phi_i \Sigma_{\underline{u}} \Phi_i' & \sum_{i=o}^{h-2} \Phi_i \Sigma_{\underline{u}} \Phi_{1+i}' \\ \sum_{i=o}^{h-2} \Phi_{1+i} \Sigma_{\underline{u}} \Phi_i' & \sum_{i=o}^{h-1} \Phi_i \Sigma_{\underline{u}} \Phi_i' \end{bmatrix}$$

$$= F \Sigma_{\underline{x}}(h) F',$$

where

$$F = \begin{bmatrix} 0 & \dots & 0 & I_K & 0 \\ 0 & \dots & 0 & 0 & I_K \end{bmatrix}$$

is a (2KxhK) matrix.

3.1.2 Predictors Based on the Autoregressive Representation

If the MA representation (3.1.1) of $\underline{x}_t$ is invertible, that is, the determinant of the MA operator has no roots in and on the unit circle,

$$\det\left(\sum_{i=o}^{\infty} \Phi_i z^i\right) \neq 0 \quad \text{for} \quad |z| \leq 1,$$

optimal forecasts may be computed using the autoregressive (AR) representation

$$\underline{x}_t = \sum_{i=1}^{\infty} A_i \underline{x}_{t-i} + \underline{u}_t, \tag{3.1.16}$$

where the A_i are (KxK) coefficient matrices (see Section 2.1.3). The optimal 1-step predictor at origin t, based on $J_t = \{\underline{u}_s | s \leq t\}$ or, equivalently, $J_t = \{\underline{x}_s | s \leq t\}$, is

$$x_t(1) = \sum_{i=1}^{\infty} \Phi_i \underline{u}_{t+1-i} = \underline{x}_{t+1} - \underline{u}_{t+1} = \sum_{i=1}^{\infty} A_i \underline{x}_{t+1-i}.$$

Similarly, the optimal 2-step forecast at origin t is

$$\underline{x}_t(2) = \sum_{i=2}^{\infty} \Phi_i \underline{u}_{t+2-i} = \underline{x}_{t+2} - \underline{u}_{t+2} - \Phi_1 \underline{u}_{t+1}$$

$$= \sum_{i=1}^{\infty} A_i \underline{x}_{t+2-i} + \underline{u}_{t+2} - \underline{u}_{t+2} - A_1 \underline{u}_{t+1}$$

$$= A_1 \underline{x}_t(1) - A_1 \underline{x}_{t+1} + \sum_{i=1}^{\infty} A_i \underline{x}_{t+2-i}$$

$$= A_1 \underline{x}_t(1) + \sum_{i=2}^{\infty} A_i \underline{x}_{t+2-i},$$

where $\Phi_1 = A_1$ and $-\underline{u}_{t+1} = \underline{x}_t(1) - \underline{x}_{t+1}$ have been used. Proceeding in a similar way for $h > 2$ results in

$$\underline{x}_t(h) = \sum_{i=1}^{h-1} A_i \underline{x}_t(h-i) + \sum_{i=h}^{\infty} A_i \underline{x}_{t+h-i} \tag{3.1.17}$$

which can be used for recursively computing forecasts. Here and in the following a sum is defined to be zero if for the summation index the upper bound is lower than its lower bound. Thus, (3.1.17) can also be used for $h = 1$.

If $\underline{u}_t$ is <u>independent</u> white noise, the formula (3.1.17) can be obtained alternatively by taking the conditional expectation of

$$\underline{x}_{t+h} = \sum_{i=1}^{\infty} A_i \underline{x}_{t+h-i} + \underline{u}_{t+h}$$

given $J_t = \{\underline{x}_s | s \leq t\}$,

$$E(\underline{x}_{t+h}|J_t) = \sum_{i=1}^{h-1} A_i E(\underline{x}_{t+h-i}|J_t) + \sum_{i=h}^{\infty} A_i \underline{x}_{t+h-i}. \tag{3.1.18}$$

Using induction with respect to h it is easy to see that $E(\underline{x}_{t+h}|J_t) = \underline{x}_t(h)$. On the other hand, $E(\underline{x}_{t+h}|J_t)$ is easily seen to be the minimum MSE predictor. Let $\bar{\underline{x}}_t(h)$ be any h-step predictor based on J_t, then

$$E[\underline{x}_{t+h} - \bar{\underline{x}}_t(h)][\underline{x}_{t+h} - \bar{\underline{x}}_t(h)]'$$

$$= E[\underline{x}_{t+h} - E(\underline{x}_{t+h}|J_t) + E(\underline{x}_{t+h}|J_t) - \overline{\underline{x}}_t(h)]$$

$$\cdot\ [\underline{x}_{t+h} - E(\underline{x}_{t+h}|J_t) + E(\underline{x}_{t+h}|J_t) - \overline{\underline{x}}_t(h)]'$$

$$= E[\underline{x}_{t+h} - E(\underline{x}_{t+h}|J_t)][\underline{x}_{t+h} - E(\underline{x}_{t+h}|J_t)]'$$

$$+ E[E(\underline{x}_{t+h}|J_t) - \overline{\underline{x}}_t(h)][E(\underline{x}_{t+h}|J_t) - \overline{\underline{x}}_t(h)]' . \qquad (3.1.19)$$

This result follows since the term $\underline{x}_{t+h} - E(\underline{x}_{t+h}|J_t)$ is a weighted sum of $\underline{u}_s$'s with $s > t$, while $E(\underline{x}_{t+h}|J_t) - \overline{\underline{x}}_t(h)$ is a weighted sum of $\underline{u}_s$'s, $s \leq t$ and thus the two terms are uncorrelated. Hence,

$$E[\underline{x}_{t+h} - E(\underline{x}_{t+h}|J_t)][E(\underline{x}_{t+h}|J_t) - \overline{\underline{x}}_t(h)]' = 0.$$

Consequently, the expression in (3.1.19) is minimized if $\overline{\underline{x}}_t(h) = E(\underline{x}_{t+h}|J_t)$. It follows that $\underline{x}_t(h)$ is optimal among all and not only linear predictors based on J_t if $\underline{u}_t$ is an independent white noise process.

To demonstrate that the independence assumption is critical, an example may be helpful (see Judge et al. (1985, p. 236)). Consider the univariate AR(1) process $x_t = \alpha x_{t-1} + u_t$, where $|\alpha| < 1$,

$$u_t = \begin{cases} e_t & \text{for } t = 0, \pm 2, \pm 4, \ldots \\ \dfrac{e_{t-1}^2 + 1}{\sqrt{2}} & \text{for } t = \pm 1, \pm 3, \ldots \end{cases}$$

and the e_t are independent $N(0,1)$ random variables. Clearly u_t is uncorrelated but not independent white noise. In accordance with the preceeding discussion, the optimal <u>linear</u> 1-step predictor of x_t based on $J_t = \{x_s | s \leq t\}$ is $x_t(1) = \alpha x_t$. This however, is in general not the conditional expected value of x_{t+1} given J_t. For even t,

$$E(x_{t+1}|J_t) = E(\alpha x_t + u_{t+1}|J_t) = \alpha x_t + \frac{e_t^2 - 1}{\sqrt{2}}.$$

If $\underline{x}_t$ is a K-dimensional process with nonzero mean vector $\underline{\mu} = E(\underline{x}_t)$ and such that

$$(\underline{x}_t - \underline{\mu}) = \sum_{i=1}^{\infty} A_i(\underline{x}_{t-i} - \underline{\mu}) + \underline{u}_t$$

and thus,

$$\underline{x}_t = \underline{\nu} + \sum_{i=1}^{\infty} A_i \underline{x}_{t-i} + \underline{u}_t, \tag{3.1.20}$$

where

$$\underline{\nu} = (I_K - \sum_{i=1}^{\infty} A_i)\underline{\mu}.$$

Using (3.1.11) and (3.1.17) the optimal predictor of $\underline{x}_t$ is

$$\underline{x}_t(h) = \underline{\mu} + (\underline{x}_t(h) - \underline{\mu}) = \underline{\mu} + \sum_{i=1}^{h-1} A_i(\underline{x}_t(h-i) - \underline{\mu}) + \sum_{i=h}^{\infty} A_i(\underline{x}_{t+h-i} - \underline{\mu})$$

$$= \underline{\nu} + \sum_{i=1}^{h-1} A_i \underline{x}_t(h-i) + \sum_{i=h}^{\infty} A_i \underline{x}_{t+h-i}. \tag{3.1.21}$$

So far a potentially infinite information set J_t has been assumed. In practice only time series of finite length are available, say $\underline{x}_1, \ldots, \underline{x}_T$. If T is not very small and the determinant of the MA operator has no roots close to the unit circle,

$$\underline{x}_T^*(h) = \sum_{i=1}^{h-1} A_i \underline{x}_T^*(h-i) + \sum_{i=h}^{T+h-1} A_i \underline{x}_{T+h-i} \tag{3.1.22}$$

will be a good approximation to $\underline{x}_T(h)$ in (3.1.17) since the A_i approach zero for $i \to \infty$. As this does not make much difference from a practical point of view it is convenient to allow for an infinite information set in theoretical considerations. The unrealistic assumption of knowing the data generation process is probably in most cases the more serious problem.

3.1.3 Forecasting Known Vector ARMA Processes

If $\underline{x}_t$ is a zero mean, K-dimensional, stationary stochastic process with ARMA representation

$$\underline{x}_t = \sum_{i=1}^{p} \Theta_i \underline{x}_{t-i} + \underline{u}_t + \sum_{i=1}^{q} M_i \underline{u}_{t-i}, \tag{3.1.23}$$

where

$$\det(I_K - \sum_{i=1}^{p} \Theta_i z^i) \neq 0 \quad \text{for} \quad |z| \leq 1$$

and

$$\det(I_K + \sum_{i=1}^{q} M_i z^i) \neq 0 \quad \text{for} \quad |z| \leq 1,$$

then the optimal linear predictor can be computed recursively using

$$\underline{x}_t(h) = \sum_{i=1}^{h-1} \Theta_i \underline{x}_t(h-i) + \sum_{i=h}^{p} \Theta_i \underline{x}_{t+h-i} + \sum_{i=h}^{q} M_i \underline{u}_{t+h-i}, \tag{3.1.24}$$

where $\Theta_i = 0$ for $i > p$. As mentioned earlier, a sum is defined to be zero if the lower bound for the summation index exceeds its upper bound.

A nonzero mean can again be handled as in the pure MA or AR cases. That is, the mean is simply added to the optimal predictor of the zero mean part as in (3.1.11) or an intercept term is included in the forecast formula as in (3.1.21).

If only a time series of finite length, $\underline{x}_1, \ldots \underline{x}_T$, is given, the $\underline{u}_t$ can in general not be obtained exactly. Approximations $\underline{u}_t^*$, to be used in (3.1.24), may be obtained using the recursion

$$\underline{u}_t^* = \underline{x}_t - \sum_{i=1}^{p} \Theta_i \underline{x}_{t-1} - \sum_{i=1}^{q} M_i \underline{u}_{t-i}^*, \quad t = p+1, p+2, \ldots, T, \tag{3.1.25}$$

where $\underline{u}_t^* = \underline{0}$ for $t \leq p$. In practice, the $\underline{u}_t$ in (3.1.24) will often be replaced by estimation residuals.

In all of the foregoing, processes with finite variance have been considered. Prediction of ARMA processes with infinite variance is discussed by Cline & Brockwell (1985).

In the next section the unrealistic assumption of knowing the generation process of the time series under investigation is replaced by the assumption that its coefficients are estimated and an attempt is made to find approximations to the forecast MSE matrices that take into account that estimators rather than true parameters are used in the prediction formulas.

3.2 FORECASTING VECTOR ARMA PROCESSES WITH ESTIMATED COEFFICIENTS

3.2.1 The General Case

In this section it is assumed that $\underline{x}_t$ is a K-dimensional, Gaussian, stationary and invertible vector ARMA process like (3.1.23) with known orders p and q. Its coefficients are assumed to be estimated by a maximum likelihood (ML) procedure. As in Chapter 2, Section 2.4.1, the vector of all parameters (except the elements of Σ_u) is denotet by $\underline{\theta} = (\theta_1, \ldots, \theta_N)'$ and the corresponding ML estimator is $\hat{\underline{\theta}}$. This estimator has an asymptotic normal distribution,

$$\sqrt{T}(\hat{\underline{\theta}} - \underline{\theta}) \xrightarrow{d} N(\underline{0}, \Sigma_{\hat{\underline{\theta}}}), \qquad (3.2.1)$$

where T is the sample size used for estimation and $\Sigma_{\hat{\underline{\theta}}}$ is the inverse information matrix (see Chapter 2).

In deriving asymptotic results it will be assumed troughout this study that estimation and forecasting are based on independent processes with identical stochastic structure. This again is a simplifying assumption that will be violated in practice where usually the same multiple time series is used for estimation and forecasting. If this assumption is replaced by the assumption that the forecast origin is the last period used for estimation many results derived in the following will still hold (see Reinsel (1980), Fuller & Hasza (1981)). The assumption of using independent processes for estimation and forecasting is nevertheless made here in order to simplify some arguments. Such an assumption is justified if it provides asymptotic results that are good approximations to the finite sample properties relevant for applied work. It will be seen in some Monte Carlo studies reported in later chapters that the asymptotic distribution theory developed here is in many cases indeed a useful indicator for small sample properties. Small sample investigations relevant for the results of this section are reported by Reinsel (1980), Fuller & Hasza (1980), and Spitzer & Baillie (1983). They indicate that, for moderate sample sizes, the assumption of having independent processes is a reasonable working hypothesis.

The predictor $\hat{\underline{x}}_t(h)$, obtained by replacing the true parameters in (3.1.24) by their ML estimators, is a consistent estimator of $\underline{x}_t(h)$ and

$$\sqrt{T}[\hat{\underline{x}}_t(h) - \underline{x}_t(h)] \xrightarrow{d} N(\underline{0}, \Omega_{\underline{x}}(h)), \qquad (3.2.2)$$

where

$$\Omega_{\underline{x}}(h) = E\left(\frac{\partial \underline{x}_t(h)}{\partial \underline{\theta}'} \Sigma_{\hat{\underline{\theta}}} \frac{\partial \underline{x}_t(h)'}{\partial \underline{\theta}}\right), \qquad (3.2.3)$$

$$\frac{\partial \underline{x}_t(h)}{\partial \underline{\theta}'} = \left[\frac{\partial x_{kt}(h)}{\partial \theta_n}\right] \quad k = 1, \ldots, K; \; n = 1, \ldots, N$$

is a (K x N) matrix, and

$$\frac{\partial \underline{x}_t(h)'}{\partial \underline{\theta}} = \left[\frac{\partial \underline{x}_t(h)}{\partial \underline{\theta}'}\right]'.$$

To see (3.2.2) define

$$\underline{x}_t^u = (\underline{x}_t', \underline{x}_{t-1}', \ldots, \underline{x}_{t-p+1}', \underline{u}_t', \ldots, \underline{u}_{t-q+1}')'$$

and note that

$$\begin{bmatrix} \sqrt{T}(\hat{\underline{\theta}} - \underline{\theta}) \\ \underline{x}_t^u \end{bmatrix} \qquad (3.2.3a)$$

converges in distribution to a multivariate normal random variable. Since $\sqrt{T}[\hat{\underline{x}}_t(h) - \underline{x}_t(h)]$ is a differentiable function of (3.2.3a) it also converges in distribution to a random vector, say $\underline{y}$. It follows from Theorem A of Serfling (1980, p. 122) that the distribution of $\underline{y}$ given a realization of $\underline{x}_t^u$ is

$$N\left[\underline{0}, \frac{\partial \underline{x}_t(h)}{\partial \underline{\theta}'} \Sigma_{\hat{\underline{\theta}}} \frac{\partial \underline{x}_t(h)'}{\partial \underline{\theta}}\right],$$

provided none of the rows of $\partial \underline{x}_t(h)/\partial \underline{\theta}'$ is identically zero. Thus, the limiting normal distribution holds for almost all realizations of $\underline{x}_t^u$. Since $\underline{x}_t^u$ is also multivariate normal, the joint distribution of $\underline{y}$ and $\underline{x}_t^u$ is multivariate normal and consequently, the marginal distribution of $\underline{y}$ is normal with mean zero and covariance matrix (3.2.3).

Note that

$$\begin{aligned} \underline{x}_{t+h} - \hat{\underline{x}}_t(h) &= \underline{x}_{t+h} - \underline{x}_t(h) + \underline{x}_t(h) - \hat{\underline{x}}_t(h) \\ &= \sum_{i=0}^{h-1} \Phi_i \underline{u}_{t+h-i} + \underline{x}_t(h) - \hat{\underline{x}}_t(h) \end{aligned}$$

and thus, the assumption of independence of the processes used for estimation and forecasting allows to write the <u>asymptotic</u> MSE matrix of $\hat{\underline{x}}_t(h)$ as

$$\begin{aligned} \hat{\Sigma}_{\underline{x}}(h) &= E[\underline{x}_{t+h} - \hat{\underline{x}}_t(h)][\underline{x}_{t+h} - \hat{\underline{x}}_t(h)]' \\ &= E[\underline{x}_{t+h} - \underline{x}_t(h)][\underline{x}_{t+h} - \underline{x}_t(h)]' \\ &\quad + E[\underline{x}_t(h) - \hat{\underline{x}}_t(h)][\underline{x}_t(h) - \hat{\underline{x}}_t(h)]' \\ &= \Sigma_{\underline{x}}(h) + \frac{1}{T}\Omega_{\underline{x}}(h), \end{aligned} \qquad (3.2.4)$$

where the last expectation is taken with respect to the asymptotic distribution of

$$\sqrt{T}[\hat{\underline{x}}_t(h) - \underline{x}_t(h)]. \tag{3.2.5}$$

In other words, it is pretended that (3.2.5) has indeed the distribution $N(\underline{0}, \Omega_{\underline{x}}(h))$ for a given sample size T. Thus, the expression in (3.2.4) is really only an approximation to the actual MSE matrix of $\hat{\underline{x}}_t(h)$. In the following, whenever the expectation is evaluated for a term for which only the asymptotic distribution is known, it will be understood that the expectation is evaluated with respect to the asymptotic distribution. Again, this procedure is only justified if it leads to reasonable small sample approximations to the quantities of interest. In later chapters simulation studies will be used to check this point.

The result in (3.2.4) shows that under the prevailing assumptions the contribution of the estimation variability to the forecast MSE matrix vanishes as T approaches infinity. Given that the parameters are estimated consistently, this result is of course not surprising. Another conclusion from (3.2.4) is that the forecast efficiency can be improved upon (i.e., the MSEs can be reduced) if the efficiency of the estimator for $\underline{\theta}$ is improved. For instance, if a priori constraints for some elements of $\underline{\theta}$ are available and a restricted ML estimator, say $\underline{\theta}^*$, is used for which

$$\sqrt{T}(\underline{\theta}^* - \underline{\theta}) \xrightarrow{d} N(\underline{0}, \Sigma_{\underline{\theta}^*}) \tag{3.2.6}$$

and $\Sigma_{\hat{\underline{\theta}}} - \Sigma_{\underline{\theta}^*}$ is positive semidefinite, then, denoting by $\Omega^*_{\underline{x}}(h)$, the asymptotic covariance matrix of $\sqrt{T}(\underline{x}^*_t(h) - \underline{x}_t(h))$, where in $\underline{x}^*_t(h)$, the parameters are replaced by $\underline{\theta}^*$, the difference

$$\Omega_{\underline{x}}(h) - \Omega^*_{\underline{x}}(h) = E\left[\frac{\partial \underline{x}_t(h)}{\partial \underline{\theta}'}(\Sigma_{\hat{\underline{\theta}}} - \Sigma_{\underline{\theta}^*})\frac{\partial \underline{x}_t(h)'}{\partial \underline{\theta}}\right]$$

will also be positive semidefinite. Hence,

$$\hat{\Sigma}_{\underline{x}}(h) - \Sigma^*_{\underline{x}}(h) = \frac{1}{T}(\Omega_{\underline{x}}(h) - \Omega^*_{\underline{x}}(h))$$

is positive semidefinite. Here $\Sigma^*_{\underline{x}}(h)$ is the MSE matrix when $\underline{\theta}^*$ is used as parameter estimator, that is, $\Sigma^*_{\underline{x}}(h)$ is obtained by replacing $\Omega_{\underline{x}}(h)$ in (3.2.4) with $\Omega^*_{\underline{x}}(h)$.

It is perhaps worth noting that the assumption of $\underline{x}_t$ being a Gaussian process is not necessary to obtain the asymptotic MSE matrix (3.2.4). It suffices to assume that $\underline{x}_t$ is a stationary and invertible vector ARMA process such that $\underline{\theta}$ can be estimated consistently and the estimator has the asymptotic distribution given in (3.2.1), where $\underline{\Sigma}_{\hat{\theta}}$ is not necessarily the inverse information matrix but simply the asymptotic covariance matrix of $\hat{\underline{\theta}}$.

In practice, to actually compute the asymptotic forecast MSE matrix $\hat{\Sigma}_{\underline{x}}(h)$ it is necessary to know $\Omega_{\underline{x}}(h)$. For the general case of a vector ARMA(p,q) process this matrix has a rather complicated structure (see Yamamoto (1980, 1981), Baillie (1980, 1981), Barone & Roy (1983)). Since in the following chapters of this study the explicit structure of $\Omega_{\underline{x}}(h)$ is only needed for finite order AR processes, the matrix will be derived for this special case in Section 3.2.2. Before this is done some further comments for the present, more general situation are in order.

In the following chapters the joint asymptotic MSE matrices of predictors for different forecast horizons will in some cases be of interest. These can be derived analogously to the asymptotic MSE matrices for h-step forecasts. Defining $\underline{X}_t(h)$ and $\underline{X}_{t+1}^h$ as in (3.1.13) and (3.1.14) respectively and denoting by $\hat{\underline{X}}_t(h)$ the (hK x 1) forecast vector with estimated coefficients corresponding to $\underline{X}_t(h)$, it follows that

$$\sqrt{T}[\hat{\underline{X}}_t(h) - \underline{X}_t(h)] \xrightarrow{d} N(\underline{0}, \underline{\Omega}_{\underline{X}}(h)), \tag{3.2.7}$$

where

$$\underline{\Omega}_{\underline{X}}(h) = E\left[\frac{\partial \underline{X}_t(h)}{\partial \underline{\theta}'} \underline{\Sigma}_{\hat{\underline{\theta}}} \frac{\partial \underline{X}_t(h)'}{\partial \underline{\theta}}\right]. \tag{3.2.8}$$

The joint asymptotic MSE matrix of the 1- to h-step predictors is therefore, under the assumptions of this section,

$$\begin{aligned}\hat{\underline{\Sigma}}_{\underline{X}}(h) &= E[\underline{X}_{t+1}^h - \hat{\underline{X}}_t(h)][\underline{X}_{t+1}^h - \hat{\underline{X}}_t(h)]' \\ &= \underline{\Sigma}_{\underline{X}}(h) + \frac{1}{T}\underline{\Omega}_{\underline{X}}(h),\end{aligned} \tag{3.2.9}$$

where $\underline{\Sigma}_{\underline{X}}(h)$ is as defined in (3.1.15). For later reference this result will be summarized in the following proposition.

PROPOSITION 3.1.

Let $\underline{x}_t$ be a Gaussian vector ARMA process as in (3.1.23) and let $\underline{\theta}$ denote the vector of all AR and MA coefficients. Further, let $\hat{\underline{\theta}}$ be a consistent estimator of $\underline{\theta}$ with asymptotic normal distribution,

$$\sqrt{T}(\hat{\underline{\theta}} - \underline{\theta}) \xrightarrow{d} N(\underline{0}, \Sigma_{\hat{\underline{\theta}}}), \tag{3.2.10}$$

and suppose that the process used for estimating $\underline{\theta}$ is independent of $\underline{x}_t$ and has the same stochastic structure. Moreover, let $\underline{X}^h_{t+1}$, $\underline{X}_t(h)$, and $\hat{\underline{X}}_t(h)$ be as defined earlier (see (3.1.13), (3.1.14)).

Then $\hat{\underline{X}}_t(h)$ is a consistent estimator of $\underline{X}_t(h)$, i.e.,

$$\operatorname*{plim}_{T\to\infty} \hat{\underline{X}}_t(h) = \underline{X}_t(h), \tag{3.2.11}$$

and

$$\sqrt{T}[\hat{\underline{X}}_t(h) - \underline{X}_t(h)] \xrightarrow{d} N(\underline{0}, \Omega_{\underline{X}}(h)), \tag{3.2.12}$$

where $\Omega_{\underline{X}}(h)$ is as defined in (3.2.8). The asymptotic MSE matrix of $\hat{\underline{X}}_t(h)$ is

$$\hat{\Sigma}_{\underline{X}}(h) = \Sigma_{\underline{X}}(h) + \frac{1}{T}\Omega_{\underline{X}}(h), \tag{3.2.13}$$

where $\Sigma_{\underline{X}}(h)$ is as defined in (3.1.15).

Although the predictor $\underline{x}_t(h)$ is optimal when the underlying process $\underline{x}_t$ is known, this does not imply that $\hat{\underline{x}}_t(h)$ is the optimal predictor for a process with estimated coefficients. Yamamoto (1982) discusses possible improvements. Nevertheless, in practice the predictor $\hat{\underline{x}}_t(h)$ is still the most widely used choice and therefore it is useful to study its properties.

If the data generation process $\underline{x}_t$ has a nonzero expectation vector $\underline{\mu}$, this vector can be estimated by the sample mean vector

$$\bar{\underline{x}} = \frac{1}{T}\sum_{t=1}^{T} \underline{x}_t , \tag{3.2.14}$$

where T is again the sample size (length of time series). The parameter vector $\underline{\theta}$ containing all the ARMA coefficients, may then be estimated by ML using the mean adjusted data $(\underline{x}_1 - \bar{\underline{x}}),\ldots(\underline{x}_T - \bar{\underline{x}})$. It has been pointed out in Chapter 2, Section 2.4, that $\bar{\underline{x}}$ is a consistent estimator of $\underline{\mu}$ with

$$\sqrt{T}(\bar{\underline{x}} - \underline{\mu}) \xrightarrow{d} N(\underline{0}, \Sigma_{\bar{\underline{x}}}). \tag{3.2.15}$$

Furthermore, $\bar{\underline{x}}$ is asymptotically independent of $\hat{\underline{\theta}}$. Thus, the asymptotic MSE matrix of the predictor $\hat{\underline{x}}_t(h)$ is

$$\hat{\Sigma}_{\underline{x}}(h) = \Sigma_{\underline{x}}(h) + \frac{1}{T}\Omega_{\underline{x}}(h) + \frac{1}{T}G_{\underline{x}}(h) \tag{3.2.16}$$

where the assumption is maintained that independent processes are used for estimation and prediction and

$$G_{\underline{x}}(h) = E\left[\frac{\partial \underline{x}_t(h)}{\partial \underline{\mu}'} \Sigma_{\bar{\underline{x}}} \frac{\partial \underline{x}_t(h)'}{\partial \underline{\mu}}\right]. \tag{3.2.17}$$

This can be seen by noting that the asymptotic covariance matrix of $\sqrt{T}[\hat{\underline{x}}_t(h) - \underline{x}_t(h)]$ is now

$$E\left[\left[\frac{\partial \underline{x}_t(h)}{\partial \underline{\mu}'}, \frac{\partial \underline{x}_t(h)}{\partial \underline{\theta}'}\right]\begin{bmatrix} \Sigma_{\bar{\underline{x}}} & 0 \\ 0 & \Sigma_{\hat{\underline{\theta}}} \end{bmatrix}\begin{bmatrix} \dfrac{\partial \underline{x}_t(h)'}{\partial \underline{\mu}} \\ \dfrac{\partial \underline{x}_t(h)'}{\partial \underline{\theta}} \end{bmatrix}\right]$$

$$= E\left[\frac{\partial \underline{x}_t(h)}{\partial \underline{\mu}'} \Sigma_{\bar{\underline{x}}} \frac{\partial \underline{x}_t(h)'}{\partial \underline{\mu}}\right] + E\left[\frac{\partial \underline{x}_t(h)}{\partial \underline{\theta}'} \Sigma_{\hat{\underline{\theta}}} \frac{\partial \underline{x}_t(h)'}{\partial \underline{\theta}}\right].$$

Hence, a nonzero mean term merely changes the asymptotic MSE matrix by a term that vanishes as the sample size T goes to infinity.

If forecasts of $\underline{x}_t$ one to h steps ahead are considered jointly, the asymptotic MSE matrix becomes

$$\underline{\Sigma}_{\underline{X}}(h) + \frac{1}{T}\underline{\Omega}_{\underline{X}}(h) + \frac{1}{T}\underline{G}_{\underline{X}}(h) = \hat{\underline{\Sigma}}_{\underline{X}}(h), \tag{3.2.18}$$

where

$$\underline{G}_{\underline{X}}(h) = E\left[\frac{\partial \underline{X}_t(h)}{\partial \underline{\mu}'} \Sigma_{\bar{\underline{x}}} \frac{\partial \underline{X}_t(h)'}{\partial \underline{\mu}}\right]. \tag{3.2.19}$$

In the next subsection explicit expressions for the asymptotic MSEs of predictors based on finite order AR processes are derived.

3.2.2 Finite Order AR Processes

As mentioned previously, that part of the asymptotic forecast MSE matrix of a vector ARMA process that is due to estimation variability has a rather complicated form in general. For illustrative purposes, only the special case of a finite order AR process is therefore considered here. In later chapters knowing the explicit form of $\hat{\underline{\Sigma}}_{\underline{x}}(h)$ for this case will be sufficient. Similar results have been derived previously by Yamamoto (1976), Reinsel (1980), Baillie (1979, 1981), Schmidt (1974), and others.

Suppose $\underline{x}_t$ is a K-dimensional stationary AR(p) process of the type (2.1.14),

$$\underline{x}_t = \sum_{i=1}^{p} A_i \underline{x}_{t-i} + \underline{u}_t. \tag{3.2.20}$$

In deriving the asymptotic MSE matrix $\hat{\underline{\Sigma}}_{\underline{x}}(h)$ of the 1- to h-step predictors given in (3.2.9) the following representation of the process is convenient:

$$\underline{X}_t = \underline{A}\underline{X}_{t-1} + \underline{U}_t, \tag{3.2.21}$$

where

$$\underset{(Kp \times 1)}{\underline{X}_t} = \begin{bmatrix} \underline{x}_t \\ \underline{x}_{t-1} \\ \vdots \\ \underline{x}_{t-p+1} \end{bmatrix}, \qquad \underset{(Kp \times Kp)}{\underline{A}} = \begin{bmatrix} A_1 & A_2 & \dots & A_{p-1} & A_p \\ I_K & 0 & \dots & 0 & 0 \\ 0 & I_K & \dots & 0 & 0 \\ \vdots & \vdots & \ddots & \vdots & \vdots \\ 0 & 0 & \dots & I_K & 0 \end{bmatrix}$$

and

$$\underset{(Kp \times 1)}{\underline{U}_t} = \begin{bmatrix} \underline{u}_t \\ \underline{0} \\ \vdots \\ \underline{0} \end{bmatrix}.$$

For constructing $\underline{\Sigma}_{\underline{x}}(h)$, the first term of $\hat{\underline{\Sigma}}_{\underline{x}}(h)$ in (3.2.9), the coefficient matrices Φ_i of the MA representation of $\underline{x}_t$ are needed (see (3.1.15)). They can be obtained easily by noting that the MA representation of $\underline{X}_t$ is

$$\underline{X}_t = \sum_{i=0}^{\infty} \underline{A}^i \underline{U}_{t-i}. \tag{3.2.22}$$

Premultiplying by the (K x Kp) matrix $J = (I_K \; 0 \; \dots \; 0)$ gives the MA representation of $\underline{x}_t$,

$$\underline{x}_t = \sum_{i=0}^{\infty} J\underline{A}^i \underline{U}_{t-i} = \sum_{i=0}^{\infty} J\underline{A}^i J'J\underline{U}_{t-i} = \sum_{i=0}^{\infty} \Phi_i \underline{u}_{t-i}, \tag{3.2.23}$$

where $\Phi_i = J\underline{A}^i J'$. Note that $J'J\underline{U}_t = \underline{U}_t$, while $J\underline{U}_t = \underline{u}_t$.

Using the notation of Chapter 2, Section 2.4.2, and assuming that $\hat{\underline{\alpha}}$ is a consistent estimator of the K^2p-vector $\underline{\alpha} = \text{vec}[A_1, \dots, A_p]'$ which contains all AR coefficients and

$$\sqrt{T}(\hat{\underline{\alpha}} - \underline{\alpha}) \xrightarrow{d} N(\underline{0}, \Sigma_{\underline{u}} \otimes \Gamma_p^{-1}), \tag{3.2.24}$$

it follows that

$$\underline{\Omega}_{\underline{X}}(h) = E\left[\frac{\partial \underline{X}_t(h)}{\partial \underline{\alpha}'} (\Sigma_{\underline{u}} \otimes \Gamma_p^{-1}) \frac{\partial \underline{X}_t(h)'}{\partial \underline{\alpha}}\right]. \tag{3.2.25}$$

Thus, $\partial \underline{X}_t(h)/\partial \underline{\alpha}'$ has to be evaluated. This can be done by noting that the optimal h-step forecast of $\underline{x}_t$ at origin t can be written as

$$\underline{x}_t(h) = J\underline{A}^h \underline{X}_t \tag{3.2.26}$$

since $\underline{A}^h \underline{X}_t$ is the optimal h-step predictor of $\underline{X}_t$. In determining the derivative

$$\frac{\partial \underline{x}_t(h)'}{\partial \underline{\alpha}} = \frac{\partial (J\underline{A}^h \underline{X}_t)'}{\partial \underline{\alpha}} = \frac{\partial [\text{vec}(J\underline{A}^h \underline{X}_t)']'}{\partial \underline{\alpha}} \tag{3.2.27}$$

the following results given by Neudecker (1969) (see also Yamamoto (1976, 1980)) are useful.

LEMMA 3.1

Suppose A is a square matrix whose elements depend on a vector $\underline{\alpha}$. Then

$$\frac{\partial [\text{vec}(A'^h)]'}{\partial \underline{\alpha}} = \frac{\partial [\text{vec}(A')]'}{\partial \underline{\alpha}} \left(\sum_{i=0}^{h-1} (A')^i \otimes A^{h-1-i} \right). \tag{3.2.28}$$

If B and C are conformable matrices independent of $\underline{\alpha}$, then

$$\frac{\partial[\mathrm{vec}(BAC)']'}{\partial\underline{\alpha}} = \frac{\partial[\mathrm{vec}(A')]'}{\partial\underline{\alpha}}(B'\otimes C). \qquad (3.2.29)$$

This lemma makes it easy to obtain an explicit expression for (3.2.27).

$$\frac{\partial[\mathrm{vec}(J\underline{A}^{h}\underline{X}_t)']'}{\partial\underline{\alpha}} = \frac{\partial[\mathrm{vec}(\underline{A}'^{h})]'}{\partial\underline{\alpha}}(J'\otimes\underline{X}_t) \qquad \text{(by (3.2.29))}$$

$$= \frac{\partial[\mathrm{vec}(\underline{A}')]'}{\partial\underline{\alpha}}\Big(\sum_{i=0}^{h-1}(\underline{A}')^{i}\otimes\underline{A}^{h-1-i}\Big)(J'\otimes\underline{X}_t) \qquad \text{(by (3.2.28))}$$

$$= (J\otimes I_{Kp})\Big(\sum_{i=0}^{h-1}(\underline{A}')^{i}\otimes\underline{A}^{h-1-i}\Big)(J'\otimes\underline{X}_t)$$

$$= \sum_{i=0}^{h-1} J(\underline{A}')^{i}J'\otimes\underline{A}^{h-1-i}\underline{X}_t$$

$$= \sum_{i=0}^{h-1} \Phi_i'\otimes\underline{A}^{h-1-i}\underline{X}_t. \qquad (3.2.30)$$

Note that the rule $(A\otimes B)(C\otimes D) = AC\otimes BD$ for conformable matrices A,B,C, and D has been applied in this derivation. Using (3.2.30) and (3.2.27) gives

$$\underline{\Omega}_{\underline{X}}(h) =$$

$$= E\left[\begin{bmatrix} \sum_{i=0}^{0}\Phi_i\otimes\underline{X}_t'(\underline{A}')^{0-i} \\ \vdots \\ \sum_{i=0}^{h-1}\Phi_i\otimes\underline{X}_t'(\underline{A}')^{h-1-i}\end{bmatrix}(\Sigma_{\underline{u}}\otimes\Gamma_p^{-1})\begin{bmatrix} \sum_{i=0}^{0}\Phi_i\otimes\underline{X}_t'(\underline{A}')^{0-i} \\ \vdots \\ \sum_{i=0}^{h-1}\Phi_i\otimes\underline{X}_t'(\underline{A}')^{h-1-i}\end{bmatrix}'\right]$$

$$= E\left[\sum_{j=0}^{l-1}\sum_{i=0}^{k-1}\Phi_j\Sigma_{\underline{u}}\Phi_i'\otimes\underline{X}_t'(A')^{l-1-j}\Gamma_p^{-1}\underline{A}^{k-1-i}\underline{X}_t\right]_{l,k\,=\,1,\dots,h}$$

$$= \left[\sum_{j=0}^{l-1}\sum_{i=0}^{k-1}\Phi_j\Sigma_{\underline{u}}\Phi_i'\otimes E\,\mathrm{tr}[\underline{X}_t'(\underline{A}')^{l-1-j}\Gamma_p^{-1}\underline{A}^{k-1-i}\underline{X}_t]\right]_{l,k\,=\,1,\dots,h}$$

$$= \left[\sum_{j=0}^{l-1}\sum_{i=0}^{k-1}\Phi_j\Sigma_{\underline{u}}\Phi_i'\otimes \mathrm{tr}[(\underline{A}')^{l-1-j}\Gamma_p^{-1}\underline{A}^{k-1-i}\Gamma_p]\right]_{l,k\,=\,1,\dots,h}$$

$$= \left[\sum_{j=0}^{l-1}\sum_{i=0}^{k-1}\mathrm{tr}[(\underline{A}')^{l-1-j}\Gamma_p^{-1}\underline{A}^{k-1-i}\Gamma_p]\Phi_j\Sigma_{\underline{u}}\Phi_i'\right]_{l,k\,=\,1,\dots,h}. \qquad (3.2.31)$$

From this asymptotic covariance matrix the corresponding expression for any r-step forecast, r = 1,...,h, can be obtained,

$$\Omega_{\underline{x}}(r) = \sum_{j=0}^{r-1} \sum_{i=0}^{r-1} \mathrm{tr}[(\underline{A}')^{r-1-j}\Gamma_p^{-1}\underline{A}^{r-1-i}\Gamma_p]\Phi_j \Sigma_{\underline{u}} \Phi_i'. \tag{3.2.32}$$

Stationarity of $\underline{x}_t$ requires that the characteristic roots of $\underline{A}$ are all less than one in obsolute value. An immediate implication is that $\underline{A}^i$ approaches the zero matrix for $i \to \infty$. Since also the Φ_i go to zero as $i \to \infty$ the covariance matrix $\Omega_{\underline{x}}(h)$ approaches zero as the forecast horizon h goes to infinity. This result is not limited to finite order AR processes. It obtains since the forecast $\hat{\underline{x}}_t(h)$ goes to $\underline{0}$ (the mean of $\underline{x}_t$) for $h \to \infty$ and consequently the impact of the estimation variability vanishes with growing forecast horizon.

One effect of this result is that the asymptotic forecast MSE matrices $\hat{\Sigma}_{\underline{x}}(h)$ are not necessarily monotonically nondecreasing for growing h, that is, $\hat{\Sigma}_{\underline{x}}(h) - \hat{\Sigma}_{\underline{x}}(r)$ is not necessarily positive semidefinite for $h > r$ while this is always true for $\Sigma_{\underline{x}}(h) - \Sigma_{\underline{x}}(r)$ (see Section 3.1.1, (3.1.7)). As an easy example consider the univariate AR(1) process $x_t = \alpha x_{t-1} + u_t$ with MA representation $x_t = \sum_{i=0}^{\infty} \alpha^i u_{t-i}$, where u_t is univariate white noise with variance $E(u_t^2) = \sigma_u^2$. For this process, using (3.2.32),

$$\Omega_x(1) = \sigma_u^2$$

and

$$\Omega_x(2) = \sum_{j=0}^{1} \sum_{i=0}^{1} (\alpha^{1-j}\alpha^{1-i})(\alpha^j \sigma_u^2 \alpha^i)$$

$$= 4\alpha^2\sigma_u^2$$

so that

$$\hat{\Sigma}_x(1) = (1 + \tfrac{1}{T})\sigma_u^2$$

and

$$\hat{\Sigma}_x(2) = \sigma_u^2(1 + \alpha^2) + \tfrac{4}{T}\alpha^2\sigma_u^2$$

$$= (1 + (1 + \tfrac{4}{T})\alpha^2)\sigma_u^2. \tag{3.2.33}$$

Thus, $\hat{\Sigma}_x(1) > \hat{\Sigma}_x(2)$ if

$\alpha^2 < \frac{1}{T+4}$.

For example, if T = 20 and α = 0.2 this inequality is satisfied.

In practice the matrices Φ_i, $\underline{A}$, Γ_p, and Σ_u in (3.2.31) will usually be unknown. Replacing them by consistent estimators gives a consistent estimator of $\Omega_{\underline{x}}(h)$ and of $\Sigma_{\underline{x}}(h)$.

As a further comment, it may be worth pointing out that the asymptotic MSE matrix of a 1-step predictor has a particularly easy form for any K-dimensional AR(p) process $\underline{x}_t$. This follows immediately from (3.2.32),

$$\Omega_{\underline{x}}(1) = tr(\Gamma_p^{-1}\Gamma_p)\Sigma_{\underline{u}} = Kp\Sigma_{\underline{u}}. \qquad (3.2.34)$$

Hence,

$$\begin{aligned} \hat{\Sigma}_{\underline{x}}(1) &= \Sigma_{\underline{x}}(1) + \frac{Kp}{T}\Sigma_{\underline{u}} \\ &= (1 + \frac{Kp}{T})\Sigma_{\underline{u}} \end{aligned} \qquad (3.2.35)$$

since $\Sigma_{\underline{x}}(1) = \Sigma_{\underline{u}}$ (see (3.1.6)). This result has been used by Akaike (1969, 1971) in developing his FPE (final prediction error) criterion for choosing the order of an autoregressive process. If a given time series is indeed generated by an AR(p) process and an AR(s) with s > p is fitted for forecasting, the asymptotic 1-step MSE matrix of the latter will be greater than the one obtained by fitting an AR(p). In other words,

$$(1 + \frac{Ks}{T})\Sigma_{\underline{u}} \geq (1 + \frac{Kp}{T})\Sigma_{\underline{u}}$$

for s > p. Akaike replaces the unobserved matrix $\Sigma_{\underline{u}}$ by its ML estimator adjusted for degrees of freedom (see (2.4.16)) and suggests to choose an estimator $\hat{p}$ for the order p so as to minimize the determinant of the resulting matrix, that is, he suggests to minimize

$$\begin{aligned} FPE(p) &= \det\left[(1 + \frac{Kp}{T}) \frac{T}{T-Kp} \hat{\Sigma}_p\right] \\ &= \det\left[(\frac{T+Kp}{T-Kp}) \hat{\Sigma}_p\right] \\ &= (\frac{T+Kp}{T-Kp})^K \det\hat{\Sigma}_p. \end{aligned} \qquad (3.2.36)$$

Note that the covariance estimator differs from the one given in (2.4.16) as it is assumed now that the effectively available sample size is T rather than T - p.

The FPE criterion is very similar to the AIC criterion given in Chapter 2, (2.5.1), which was proposed later by Akaike. To see this, note that

$$\frac{T + pK}{T - pK} = 1 + \frac{2pK}{T} + O(\frac{1}{T^2}), \qquad (3.2.37)$$

where $O(1/T^2)$ denotes a sequence which is bounded when multiplied by T^2 (i.e., a sequence of order $1/T^2$). Assuming an effective sample size of T and using (3.2.37),

$$\begin{aligned} \ln FPE(p) &= \ln \det\hat{\Sigma}_p + K \ln (\frac{T + Kp}{T - Kp}) \\ &= \ln \det\hat{\Sigma}_p + K \ln\left[1 + \frac{2pK}{T} + O(\frac{1}{T^2})\right] \\ &= \ln \det\hat{\Sigma}_p + K \frac{2pK}{T} + O(\frac{1}{T^2}) \\ &= AIC(p) + O(\frac{1}{T^2}). \end{aligned}$$

Thus, for moderate samples, FPE and AIC are almost identical criteria and AIC may be interpreted as a criterion for minimizing the 1-step prediction MSE.

If $\underline{x}_t$ has nonzero mean $\underline{\mu}$, $\underline{\Omega}_{\underline{x}}(h)$ remains unchanged. Since

$$\underline{x}_t(j) = \underline{\mu} + [I_K \quad 0 \quad \dots \quad 0]\,\underline{A}^j \begin{bmatrix} \underline{x}_t - \underline{\mu} \\ \underline{x}_{t-1} - \underline{\mu} \\ \vdots \\ \underline{x}_{t-p+1} - \underline{\mu} \end{bmatrix},$$

the partial derivatives with respect to $\underline{\mu}$ are

$$\frac{\partial \underline{x}_t(j)}{\partial \underline{\mu}'} = I_K - [I_K \quad 0 \quad \dots \quad 0]\,\underline{A}^j \underset{(Kp \times K)}{\begin{bmatrix} I_K \\ \vdots \\ I_K \end{bmatrix}}. \qquad (3.2.38)$$

Hence,

$$\underline{G}_{\underline{x}}(h) = \left[\begin{bmatrix} I_K \\ \vdots \\ I_K \end{bmatrix} - \begin{bmatrix} [I_K & 0 & \dots & 0]\underline{A} \\ [I_K & 0 & \dots & 0]\underline{A}^2 \\ & \vdots & & \\ [I_K & 0 & \dots & 0]\underline{A}^h \end{bmatrix} \begin{bmatrix} I_K \\ I_K \\ \vdots \\ I_K \end{bmatrix}\right] \Sigma_{\bar{\underline{x}}} \times$$

$$\times \left[\begin{bmatrix} I_K \\ \vdots \\ I_K \end{bmatrix} - \begin{bmatrix} [I_K & 0 & \dots & 0] \underline{A} \\ & \vdots & & \\ [I_K & 0 & \dots & 0] \underline{A}^h \end{bmatrix} \begin{bmatrix} I_K \\ \vdots \\ I_K \end{bmatrix} \right]' \qquad (3.2.39)$$

For example, for h = 1,

$$G_{\underline{X}}(h) = G_{\underline{x}}(1) = \Sigma_{\underline{u}} , \qquad (3.2.40)$$

since

$$\Sigma_{\bar{\underline{x}}} = (I_K - A_1 - \dots - A_p)^{-1} \Sigma_{\underline{u}} (I_K - A_1 - \dots - A_p)'^{-1}. \qquad (3.2.41)$$

To illustrate the results of this section an example may be helpful. In Chapter 2, Section 2.5.1, estimation results for U.S. investment data are given using a sample size of T = 87. Assuming that the data are actually generated by the AR(1) process (2.5.10),

$$\underline{\nu} = \begin{bmatrix} 0.62 \\ -0.32 \end{bmatrix} , \quad \underline{A} = A_1 = \begin{bmatrix} 0.40 & 0.17 \\ 0.48 & -0.30 \end{bmatrix} = \Phi_1 ,$$

$$\Gamma_p = \Gamma_1 = \Sigma_{\underline{x}} = \frac{1}{T} \sum_{t=1}^{T} (\underline{x}_t - \bar{\underline{x}})(\underline{x}_t - \bar{\underline{x}})' = \begin{bmatrix} 7.75 & 2.66 \\ 2.66 & 23.9 \end{bmatrix},$$

$$\Sigma_{\underline{u}} = \begin{bmatrix} 5.64 & 2.58 \\ 2.58 & 21.8 \end{bmatrix} \text{ and } \underline{x}_{87} = \begin{bmatrix} 4.3 \\ -1.6 \end{bmatrix}. \qquad (3.2.42)$$

Consequently, using (3.1.21),

$$\underline{x}_{87}(1) = \underline{\nu} + A_1 \underline{x}_{87} = \begin{bmatrix} 2.068 \\ 2.224 \end{bmatrix} \qquad (3.2.43)$$

and

$$\underline{x}_{87}(2) = \underline{\nu} + A_1 \underline{x}_{87}(1) = \begin{bmatrix} 1.825 \\ 0.005 \end{bmatrix}. \qquad (3.2.44)$$

Furthermore, by (3.2.34),

$$\Omega_{\underline{x}}(1) = Kp\Sigma_{\underline{u}} = 2\Sigma_{\underline{u}} = \begin{bmatrix} 11.28 & 5.16 \\ 5.16 & 43.6 \end{bmatrix} \qquad (3.2.45)$$

and, by (3.2.32),

$$\Omega_{\underline{x}}(2) = tr(\underline{A}'\Gamma_p^{-1}\underline{A}\Gamma_p)\Sigma_{\underline{u}} + tr(\underline{A}'\Gamma_p^{-1}\Gamma_p)\Sigma_{\underline{u}}\Phi_1'$$
$$+ tr(\Gamma_p^{-1}\underline{A}\Gamma_p)\Phi_1\Sigma_{\underline{u}} + tr(\Gamma_p^{-1}\Gamma_p)\Phi_1\Sigma_{\underline{u}}\Phi_1'$$
$$= \begin{bmatrix} 6.78 & 1.54 \\ 1.54 & 13.6 \end{bmatrix}. \tag{3.2.46}$$

Also,

$$\sum_{i=0}^{1} tr(\underline{A}'\Gamma_p^{-1}\underline{A}^{1-i}\Gamma_p)\Sigma_{\underline{u}}\Phi_i' = tr(\underline{A}'\Gamma_p^{-1}\underline{A}\Gamma_p)\Sigma_{\underline{u}} + tr(\underline{A}'\Gamma_p^{-1}\Gamma_p)\Sigma_{\underline{u}}\Phi_1'$$
$$= \begin{bmatrix} 2.75 & 1.33 \\ 1.61 & 9.08 \end{bmatrix}$$

and thus, by (3.2.31),

$$\Omega_{\underline{X}}(2) = \begin{bmatrix} 11.28 & 5.16 & 2.75 & 1.33 \\ 5.16 & 43.6 & 1.61 & 9.08 \\ 2.75 & 1.61 & 6.78 & 1.54 \\ 1.33 & 9.08 & 1.54 & 13.6 \end{bmatrix}. \tag{3.2.47}$$

Furthermore, by (3.1.15),

$$\Sigma_{\underline{X}}(2) = \begin{bmatrix} \Sigma_{\underline{u}} & \Sigma_{\underline{u}}A_1' \\ A_1\Sigma_{\underline{u}} & \Sigma_{\underline{u}} + A_1\Sigma_{\underline{u}}A_1' \end{bmatrix} = \begin{bmatrix} 5.64 & 2.58 & 2.69 & 1.93 \\ 2.58 & 21.8 & 4.74 & -5.30 \\ 2.69 & 4.74 & 7.52 & 2.45 \\ 1.93 & -5.30 & 2.45 & 24.3 \end{bmatrix} \tag{3.2.48}$$

and, by (2.4.43),

$$\Sigma_{\overline{\underline{x}}} = (I_2 - A_1)^{-1}\Sigma_{\underline{u}}(I_2 - A_1)'^{-1}$$
$$= \begin{bmatrix} 23.07 & 16.29 \\ 16.29 & 21.87 \end{bmatrix} \tag{3.2.49}$$

Moreover,

$$\underline{G}_{\underline{X}}(2) = \left[\begin{bmatrix} I_2 \\ I_2 \end{bmatrix} - \begin{bmatrix} A_1 \\ A_1^2 \end{bmatrix}\right](I_2 - A_1)^{-1}\Sigma_{\underline{u}}(I_2 - A_1)'^{-1}\left[(I_2-A_1)', (I_2-A_1^2)'\right]$$

$$= \begin{bmatrix} \Sigma_u & \Sigma_u (I_2-A_1)'^{-1}(I_2-A_1^2)' \\ \cdot & (I_2-A_1^2)(I_2-A_1)^{-1}\Sigma_u(I_2-A_1)'^{-1}(I_2-A_1^2)' \end{bmatrix}$$

$$= \begin{bmatrix} 5.64 & 2.58 & 8.32 & 4.53 \\ 2.58 & 21.8 & 7.26 & 16.5 \\ 8.32 & 7.26 & 12.9 & 9.10 \\ 4.53 & 16.5 & 9.10 & 13.8 \end{bmatrix} \tag{3.2.50}$$

Hence, with T = 87,

$$\hat{\Sigma}_x(2) = \Sigma_x(2) + \frac{1}{T}\Omega_x(2) + \frac{1}{T}G_x(2)$$

$$= \begin{bmatrix} 5.83 & 2.67 & 2.82 & 2.00 \\ 2.67 & 22.6 & 4.84 & -5.01 \\ 2.82 & 4.84 & 7.75 & 2.57 \\ 2.00 & -5.01 & 2.57 & 24.6 \end{bmatrix} \tag{3.2.51}$$

Of course, all these quantities are based on estimates and are therefore also estimates and the results are conditional an p = 1 being the correct AR order. It should not be forgotten, however, that p is only an estimate of the AR order. The case of an unknown AR order is considered next.

3.3 FORECASTING AUTOREGRESSIVE PROCESSES OF UNKNOWN ORDER

Given a multiple time series that is generated by a finite order ARMA-(p,q) process with unknown orders, the theory of the previous section is relevant if finite upper bounds for the orders can be given and if the orders are estimated consistently (see Chapter 2, Section 2.5.1). In that case the asymptotic forecast MSE matrices will be the same as if the orders were known. In practice, however, finite upper bounds for the ARMA orders are not always known and in many cases they may not exist, that is, the data generating process may not possess a finite order ARMA representation. In that case an approximation to the forecast MSE matrix can still be derived if the conditions of Section 2.4.3 are satisfied. The asymptotic estimation theory of that section will be used in the following. In particular, it will be assumed that the AR orders of the processes fitted to the data approach infinity with the sample size. An alternative approach would be to determine the MSE matrix if an AR process with some fixed and possibly incorrect order is fitted (see Bhansali (1981) and Kunitomo & Yamamoto (1985)). Since the former approach can be applied more easily in the following chapters it is presented here.

3.3.1 The Asymptotic MSE Matrix

It is assumed that $\underline{x}_t$ is a zero mean, stationary Gaussian AR process of possibly infinite order,

$$\underline{x}_t = \sum_{i=1}^{\infty} A_i \underline{x}_{t-i} + \underline{u}_t \tag{3.3.1}$$

which satisfies the conditions of Theorem 2.1 in Chapter 2, $\underline{u}_t$ is Gaussian white noise and $\underline{x}_t$ has an invertible MA representation,

$$\underline{x}_t = \sum_{i=0}^{\infty} \Phi_i \underline{u}_{t-i} \quad , \quad \Phi_0 = I_K \; , \tag{3.3.2}$$

where

$$\sum_{i=1}^{\infty} \sqrt{tr(\Phi_i' \Phi_i)} \; < \infty. \tag{3.3.3}$$

It is permitted that $\underline{x}_t$ actually has a finite but unknown order p. In that case $A_i = 0$ for $i > p$.

Moreover, it is assumed that AR processes of order p(T) are fitted to a realization of a process that is independent of $\underline{x}_t$ and has the same stochastic structure. The order p(T) depends on the sample size T and meets the conditions underlying Theorem 2.1. As in the previous section the independence assumption ensures that an asymptotic forecast MSE, based on an estimated process, consists of two parts, the MSE for the known process plus a term due to sampling variability of the parameter estimators.

To state the result formally, the following notation is handy.

$$\underset{(Kp \times Kp)}{\underline{A}_p} = \begin{bmatrix} A_1 & A_2 & \cdots & A_{p-1} & A_p \\ I_K & 0 & \cdots & 0 & 0 \\ 0 & I_K & \cdots & 0 & 0 \\ \vdots & \vdots & \ddots & \vdots & \vdots \\ 0 & 0 & \cdots & I_K & 0 \end{bmatrix} , \quad \underset{(Kp \times 1)}{\underline{X}_{t,p}} = \begin{bmatrix} \underline{x}_t \\ \underline{x}_{t-1} \\ \vdots \\ \underline{x}_{t-p+1} \end{bmatrix}$$

and

$$\underset{(K \times Kp)}{J_p} = [I_K \;\; 0 \;\; \cdots \;\; 0] \; . \tag{3.3.4}$$

Here $\underline{A}_p$ and $\underline{X}_{t,p}$ are as in (3.2.21) the only difference being the subscript p, which now makes explicit their dependence on the AR order of the process that is fitted to the data. Recall that if $\underline{x}_t$ were in fact a finite order AR(p) process, then the optimal h-step predictor would be

$$\underline{x}_{t,p}(h) = J_p \underline{A}_p^h \underline{X}_{t,p} \tag{3.3.5}$$

(see (3.2.26)). Thus, if an AR(p) is fitted to the data, the predictor

$$\tilde{\underline{x}}_{t,p}(h) = J_p \tilde{\underline{A}}_p^h \underline{X}_{t,p}\ , \tag{3.3.6}$$

where $\tilde{\underline{A}}_p$ is obtained by replacing the A_i in $\underline{A}_p$ by multivariate least squares estimates, will be entertained in practice. Let

$$\tilde{\underline{X}}_{t,p}(h) = \left[\tilde{\underline{x}}_{t,p}(1)', \ldots, \tilde{\underline{x}}_{t,p}(h)'\right]' \tag{3.3.7}$$

and let $\underline{X}_t(h) = [\underline{x}_t(1)',\ldots,\underline{x}_t(h)']'$ and $\underline{X}_{t+1}^h = (\underline{x}_{t+1}',\ldots,\underline{x}_{t+h}')'$ as before. Using this notation the main result of this section can be stated.

PROPOSITION 3.2

Let $\underline{x}_t$ be a K-dimensional, zero mean, stationary Gaussian AR process as in (3.3.1) satisfying the conditions of Theorem 2.1 and let p(T) be also as in Theorem 2.1. Further assume that independent processes with identical stochastic structures are used for estimation and forecasting. Then

$$\sqrt{\frac{T}{p(T)}}\left[\tilde{\underline{X}}_{t,p(T)}(h) - \underline{X}_t(h)\right] \xrightarrow{d} N(\underline{0},\ K\underline{\Sigma}_X(h)), \tag{3.3.8}$$

where $\underline{\Sigma}_X(h)$ is as defined in (3.1.15). The asymptotic MSE matrix of $\tilde{\underline{X}}_{t,p(T)}(h)$ is

$$\begin{aligned}\tilde{\underline{\Sigma}}_X(h) &= E[\underline{X}_{t+1}^h - \tilde{\underline{X}}_{t,p(T)}(h)][\underline{X}_{t+1}^h - \tilde{\underline{X}}_{t,p(T)}(h)]' \\ &= (1 + \frac{Kp(T)}{T})\underline{\Sigma}_X(h). \end{aligned} \tag{3.3.9}$$

The MSE matrix results since

$$E[\underline{X}_{t+1}^h - \tilde{\underline{X}}_{t,p(T)}(h)][\underline{X}_{t+1}^h - \tilde{\underline{X}}_{t,p(T)}(h)]'$$

$$= E[\underline{x}_{t+1}^{h} + \underline{x}_t(h)][\underline{x}_{t+1}^{h} - \underline{x}_t(h)]'$$

$$+ E[\underline{x}_t(h) - \tilde{\underline{x}}_{t,p(T)}(h)][\underline{x}_t(h) - \tilde{\underline{x}}_{t,p(T)}(h)]' \qquad (3.3.10)$$

(see also (3.2.4)). The result (3.3.8) will be proved in Section 3.3.2. Before that proof is given some comments are in order.

An explicit expression for the asymptotic MSE matrix

$$\tilde{\Sigma}_{\underline{x}}(h) = E[\underline{x}_{t+h} - \tilde{\underline{x}}_{t,p(T)}(h)][\underline{x}_{t+h} - \tilde{\underline{x}}_{t,p(T)}(h)]'$$

for any h follows directly from (3.3.9). Given the structure of $\Sigma_{\underline{x}}(h)$ in (3.1.15) it is obvious that

$$\tilde{\Sigma}_{\underline{x}}(h) = (1 + \frac{Kp(T)}{T})\Sigma_{\underline{x}}(h). \qquad (3.3.11)$$

Unlike for processes with known orders and estimated coefficients that part of the MSE that is due to estimation variability does not vanish with growing forecast horizon h. The explanation for this result is that the AR order increases with the sample size so that, for any h, the sampling variability will, for large T, have an impact on the overall forecast uncertainty. In other words, asymptotically the forecast $\tilde{\underline{x}}_t(h)$ will not become zero for any given h since for large T also p(T) will become large.

It follows from (3.1.7) that $\tilde{\Sigma}_{\underline{x}}(h)$ is a monotonically nondecreasing function of h, that is,

$$\tilde{\Sigma}_{\underline{x}}(h) \geq \tilde{\Sigma}_{\underline{x}}(r) \quad \text{for} \quad h \geq r. \qquad (3.3.12)$$

Another interesting feature of the asymptotic forecast MSE matrix (3.3.11) is that it coincides, for h = 1, with the asymptotic 1-step MSE matrix obtained under the assumption of a known order and estimated coefficients if p(T) = p (see (3.2.35)). This does not hold for h > 1. It remains questionable how accurately the large sample theory approximates the samll sample MSEs. Suppose, for instance, that the actual data generating process is the univariate AR(1), $x_t = \alpha x_{t-1} + u_t$. One might expect that knowledge of the true AR order helps to reduce the asymptotic forecast MSE. If however p(T) = 1 this is in general not the case. To see this note that

$$\hat{\Sigma}_x(2) = \sigma_u^2(1 + \alpha^2 + \frac{4}{T}\alpha^2),$$

where σ_u^2 is the variance of u_t (see (3.2.33)). On the other hand,

$$\tilde{\Sigma}_x(2) = (1 + \frac{1}{T})\sigma_u^2(1 + \alpha^2).$$

Thus, $\tilde{\Sigma}_x(2)$ will be smaller than $\hat{\Sigma}_x(2)$ if $4\alpha^2 > (1+\alpha^2)$ or $\alpha > \sqrt{1/3}$. Of course, this result does not mean that something is wrong with the asymptotic theory. That theory requires p(T) to go to infinity with T and, for p(T) large enough, $\tilde{\Sigma}_x(2)$ will eventually exceed $\hat{\Sigma}_x(2)$. The example only shows that for a small sample size T, when a particular p(T) is chosen, the asymptotic theory has to be used cautiously when conclusions are drawn for the small sample situation.

If $\underline{x}_t$ is a process with nonzero mean $\underline{\mu}$, the sample mean may be subtracted from the original data and the AR coefficient matrices may be estimated from the mean adjusted data. Alternatively, an intercept term may be included in the model to be estimated. If an estimated mean term is involved the following approximate MSE matrix of an h-step predictor will be used:

$$\tilde{\Sigma}_{\underline{x}}(h) = (1 + \frac{Kp(T)}{T})\Sigma_{\underline{x}}(h) + \frac{1}{T}G_{\underline{x}}(h), \qquad (3.3.13)$$

where $G_x(h)$ is the lower right-hand (K x K) submatrix of $\underline{G}_{\underline{x}}(h)$ in (3.2.19). For the vector of 1- to h-step forecasts the approximate MSE matrix

$$(1 + \frac{Kp(T)}{T})\underline{\Sigma}_{\underline{x}}(h) + \frac{1}{T}\underline{G}_{\underline{x}}(h) \qquad (3.3.14)$$

is used. In the following subsection Proposition 3.2 is proved.

3.3.2 Proof of Proposition 3.2

This subsection is rather technical and may be omitted without loss of continuity. Proposition 3.2 generalizes a result due to Lewis & Reinsel (1982) and was given by Lütkepohl (1985b). The following proof closely follows that of Lewis & Reinsel. The main purpose of presenting the proof in some detail is to present the technique, and to show where the assumptions enter that are made in the foregoing. Also, to the best of my knowledge, a detailed proof is only available in working paper form. The notation of Section 3.3.1 is used. For simplicity p(T) is replaced by p, it being understood that this quantity depends on the sample size T. In the course of the proof some intermediate results are stated as lemmas. These will be proved at the end of the section.

Note that

$$\sqrt{\frac{T}{p}}[\underline{\tilde{X}}_{t,p}(h) - \underline{X}_t(h)] =$$

$$= \sqrt{\frac{T}{p}}[\underline{\tilde{X}}_{t,p}(h) - \underline{X}_{t,p}(h)] - \sqrt{\frac{T}{p}}[\underline{X}_t(h) - \underline{X}_{t,p}(h)]. \qquad (3.3.15)$$

The proof of Proposition 3.2 proceeds by showing that the second term on the right-hand side converges to zero in quadratic mean and the limiting distribution of the first term is the normal distribution given in (3.3.8). The latter result is obtained using Theorem 2.1 and the former result follows from Assumption (iii) in Section 2.4.3,

$$\sqrt{T}\left[\sum_{i=p+1}^{\infty} \sqrt{tr(A_i'A_i)}\right] \rightarrow 0 \quad \text{as } T \text{ and thus } p \rightarrow \infty. \qquad (3.3.16)$$

This result is summarized in the following lemma that will be proved later.

LEMMA 3.2

Under the conditions of Proposition 3.2,

$$E\{\frac{T}{p}[\underline{X}_t(h) - \underline{X}_{t,p}(h)]'[\underline{X}_t(h) - \underline{X}_{t,p}(h)]\} \xrightarrow[T\to\infty]{} 0. \qquad (3.3.17)$$

The next step is to show that

$$\sqrt{\frac{T}{p}}[\underline{\tilde{X}}_{t,p}(h) - \underline{X}_{t,p}(h)] \xrightarrow[T\to\infty]{d} N(\underline{0}, K\underline{\Sigma}_{\underline{X}}(h)). \qquad (3.3.18)$$

To see this, the following lemma is useful.

LEMMA 3.3

$$\underline{\tilde{x}}_{t,p}(h) - \underline{x}_{t,p}(h) = J_p(\underline{\tilde{A}}_p^h - \underline{A}_p^h)\underline{X}_{t,p}$$

$$= \sum_{i=0}^{h-1} (\underline{X}_{t,p}' \, \underline{A}_p'^{\,h-i-1} \otimes \Phi_i)(\underline{\tilde{a}}(p) - \underline{a}(p))$$

$$+ \sum_{i=0}^{h-1} [\underline{X}_{t,p}'\underline{A}_p'^{\,h-i-1} \otimes (\tilde{\Phi}_{i,p} - \Phi_i)](\underline{\tilde{a}}(p) - \underline{a}(p)), \qquad (3.3.19)$$

where $\tilde{\Phi}_{i,p} = J_p\underline{\tilde{A}}_p^i J_p'$ (see (3.2.23)), $\underline{a}(p) = vec(A_1,\ldots,A_p)$, and $\underline{\tilde{a}}(p) = vec(\tilde{A}_{1,p},\ldots,\tilde{A}_{p,p})$.

Multiplying the last sum in (3.3.19) by $\sqrt{T/p}$, it converges to zero in probability. This follows by noting that

$$\sqrt{\frac{T}{p}}\sum_{i=0}^{h-1}[\underline{X}_{t,p}'\underline{A}_p'^{\,h-i-1}\otimes(\tilde{\Phi}_{i,p}-\Phi_i)](\tilde{\underline{a}}(p)-\underline{a}(p))$$

$$=\sum_{i=0}^{h-1}(\tilde{\Phi}_{i,p}-\Phi_i)\sqrt{\frac{T}{p}}(\underline{X}_{t,p}'\underline{A}_p'^{\,h-i-1}\otimes I_K)(\tilde{\underline{a}}(p)-\underline{a}(p)) \tag{3.3.20}$$

and

$$\operatorname{plim}(\tilde{\Phi}_{i,p}-\Phi_i)=0 \tag{3.3.21}$$

(see Serfling (1980, Theorem A, p. 122)), while

$$\sqrt{\frac{T}{p}}(\underline{X}_{t,p}'\underline{A}_p'^{\,h-i-1}\otimes I_K)(\tilde{\underline{a}}(p)-\underline{a}(p)) \tag{3.3.22}$$

has a limiting normal distribution by Theorem 2.1 (see also the proof of (3.3.23) below). Thus, (3.3.20) converges to zero in distribution and hence in probability. Consequently, it remains to show that

$$\sqrt{\frac{T}{p}}\begin{bmatrix}\sum_{i=0}^{0}(\underline{X}_{t,p}'\underline{A}_p'^{\,0-i}\otimes\Phi_i)\\ \vdots\\ \sum_{i=0}^{h-1}(\underline{X}_{t,p}'\underline{A}_p'^{\,h-i-1}\otimes\Phi_i)\end{bmatrix}[\tilde{\underline{a}}(p)-\underline{a}(p)]\xrightarrow{d}N(\underline{0},K\underline{\Sigma}_X(h)) \tag{3.3.23}$$

This result follows from Theorem 2.1. Define

$$\mathcal{I}(p)=\frac{1}{\sqrt{p}}\begin{bmatrix}\sum_{i=0}^{0}(\underline{X}_{t,p}'\underline{A}_p'^{\,0-i}\otimes\Phi_i)\\ \vdots\\ \sum_{i=0}^{h-1}(\underline{X}_{t,p}'\underline{A}_p'^{\,h-i-1}\otimes\Phi_i)\end{bmatrix}$$

and $\underline{\ell}(p)'=\underline{f}'\mathcal{I}(p)$, where $\underline{f}=(\underline{f}_1',\ldots,\underline{f}_h')'\neq 0$ is an arbitrary (Kh x 1) vector while the $\underline{f}_i$, i = 1,...,h, are (K x 1) vectors. The following result is easy to prove.

LEMMA 3.4

Under the conditions of Proposition 3.2, $\underline{\ell}(p)'\underline{\ell}(p)$ converges almost surely to a positive constant.

Hence, for almost all realizations of the process $\underline{x}_t$, $\underline{\ell}(p)$ satisfies condition (2.4.53) of Theorem 2.1 and therefore, conditional on a particular realization of $\underline{x}_t$, the theorem implies

$$\frac{\sqrt{T}\ \underline{\ell}(p)'(\underline{\tilde{a}}(p) - \underline{a}(p))}{\sqrt{\underline{\ell}(p)'(\Gamma_p^{-1}\otimes\Sigma_{\underline{u}})\underline{\ell}(p)}} \xrightarrow[T\to\infty]{d} N(0,1) \tag{3.3.24}$$

since $(T - p)/T \xrightarrow[T\to\infty]{} 1$, by Condition (iii) of Section 2.4.3. This result holds for almost all realizations of $\underline{x}_t$ and the limiting distribution does not depend on the particular realization. Therefore it holds unconditionally. Now

$$\operatorname*{plim}_{p\to\infty} \underline{\ell}(p)'(\Gamma_p^{-1}\otimes\Sigma_{\underline{u}})\underline{\ell}(p) = K\underline{f}'\Sigma_{\underline{x}}(h)\underline{f} \tag{3.3.25}$$

and the proposition follows (e.g. Serfling (1980, Theorem, p. 18)). The result (3.3.25) is a consequence of the following lemma.

LEMMA 3.5

Under the conditions of Proposition 3.2,

$$\operatorname*{plim}_{p\to\infty} \frac{1}{p}\underline{X}_{t,p}'\underline{A}_p'^{\,i}\Gamma_p^{-1}\underline{A}_p^{j}\underline{X}_{t,p} = \begin{cases} K & \text{if } i = j \\ 0 & \text{otherwise.} \end{cases} \tag{3.3.26}$$

Noting that

$$\underline{\ell}(p)'(\Gamma_p^{-1}\otimes\Sigma_{\underline{u}})\underline{\ell}(p)$$

$$= \left[\sum_{m=1}^{h}\sum_{i=0}^{m-1}\left(\frac{1}{\sqrt{p}}\underline{X}_{t,p}'\underline{A}_p'^{\,m-1-i}\otimes\underline{f}_m'\Phi_i\right)\right](\Gamma_p^{-1}\otimes\Sigma_{\underline{u}}) \times \left[\sum_{n=1}^{h}\sum_{j=0}^{n-1}\left(\frac{1}{\sqrt{p}}\underline{A}_p^{n-1-j}\underline{X}_{t,p}\otimes\Phi_j'\underline{f}_n\right)\right]$$

$$= \sum_{m=1}^{h}\sum_{n=1}^{h}\sum_{i=0}^{m-1}\sum_{j=0}^{n-1}\left(\frac{1}{p}\underline{X}_{t,p}'\underline{A}_p'^{\,m-1-i}\Gamma_p^{-1}\underline{A}_p^{n-1-j}\underline{X}_{t,p}\right)(\underline{f}_m'\Phi_i\Sigma_{\underline{u}}\Phi_j'\underline{f}_n) \tag{3.3.27}$$

it follows from Lemma 3.5 that

$$\operatorname*{plim}_{p\to\infty} \underline{\ell}'(p)(\Gamma_p^{-1}\otimes\Sigma_{\underline{u}})\underline{\ell}(p)$$

$$= \sum_{m=1}^{h}\sum_{n=m}^{h}\sum_{i=0}^{m-1} K\underline{f}_m'\Phi_i\Sigma_{\underline{u}}\Phi_{n-m+i}'\underline{f}_n$$

$$+ \sum_{n=1}^{h}\sum_{m=n+1}^{h}\sum_{j=0}^{n-1} K\underline{f}_m'\Phi_{m-n+j}\Sigma_{\underline{u}}\Phi_j'\underline{f}_n$$

$$= K\underline{f}'\Sigma_{\underline{x}}(h)\underline{f}. \tag{3.3.28}$$

Thereby Proposition 3.2 is proved. Q.E.D.

It remains to prove the lemmas stated in the foregoing.

Proof of Lemma 3.2

Note that

$$\underline{x}_t(1) - \underline{x}_{t,p}(1) = \sum_{i=p+1}^{\infty} A_i\underline{x}_{t+1-i}\ . \tag{3.3.29}$$

Hence,

$$E(\tfrac{T}{p}[\underline{x}_t(1) - \underline{x}_{t,p}(1)]'[\underline{x}_t(1) - \underline{x}_{t,p}(1)])$$

$$= \frac{T}{p}E\left[\sum_{i=p+1}^{\infty}\sum_{j=p+1}^{\infty}\underline{x}_{t+1-i}'A_i'A_j\underline{x}_{t+1-j}\right]$$

$$= \frac{T}{p}\sum_{i=p+1}^{\infty}\sum_{j=p+1}^{\infty}\operatorname{tr}[(A_i'A_j)\Gamma_{\underline{x}}(j-i)]$$

(where $\Gamma_{\underline{x}}(j-i) = E[\underline{x}_{t+1-j}\underline{x}_{t+1-i}']$ as before)

$$\leq \frac{T}{p}\sum_{i=p+1}^{\infty}\sum_{j=p+1}^{\infty}\sqrt{\operatorname{tr}(A_i'A_i)}\ \sqrt{\operatorname{tr}(A_j'A_j)}\ \sqrt{\operatorname{tr}[\Gamma_{\underline{x}}(j-i)'\Gamma_{\underline{x}}(j-i)]}$$

(by the Schwarz inequality, e.g., Lang (1969,p.150))

$$\leq \text{constant} \times \frac{T}{p}\sum_{i=p+1}^{\infty}\sum_{j=p+1}^{\infty}\sqrt{\operatorname{tr}(A_i'A_i)}\ \sqrt{\operatorname{tr}(A_j'A_j)}$$

(since the terms $\operatorname{tr}[\Gamma_{\underline{x}}(j-i)'\Gamma_{\underline{x}}(j-i)]$ are bounded)

$$= \text{constant} \times \frac{T}{p}\Big[\sum_{i=p+1}^{\infty}\sqrt{\operatorname{tr}(A_i'A_i)}\ \Big]^2$$

$$\leq \text{constant} \times \left(\sqrt{T} \sum_{i=p+1}^{\infty} \sqrt{tr(A_i'A_i)}\ \right)^2 \xrightarrow[T\to\infty]{} 0 \qquad (3.3.30)$$

by condition (3.3.16). It follows by induction, using (3.1.17), that

$$\sqrt{\frac{T}{p}}\ [\underline{x}_t(h) - \underline{x}_{t,p}(h)] \xrightarrow{q.m.} 0,$$

where $\xrightarrow{q.m.}$ stands for convergence in quadratic mean. This result implies (3.3.17). Q.E.D.

Proof of Lemma 3.3

First note that, for square matrices B and C, the relation

$$B^h - C^h = \sum_{i=0}^{h-1} B^i(B - C)C^{h-i-1} \qquad (3.3.31)$$

holds. This can be seen by simply writing out the sum on the right-hand side. Furthermore,

$$J_p\tilde{\underline{A}}_p^i(\tilde{\underline{A}}_p - \underline{A}_p) = J_p\tilde{\underline{A}}^i J_p' J_p(\tilde{\underline{A}}_p - \underline{A}_p). \qquad (3.3.32)$$

This equality follows since for the (Kp x Kp) matrix $D=\tilde{\underline{A}}_p-\underline{A}_p$ and i = 0,

$$J_p\tilde{\underline{A}}_p^i D = J_p D = J_p J_p' J_p D = J_p\tilde{\underline{A}}_p^i J_p' J_p D.$$

For i > 0 it follows by assuming its validity for i - 1,

$$J_p\tilde{\underline{A}}_p^i D = J_p\tilde{\underline{A}}_p^{i-1} J_p' J_p\tilde{\underline{A}}_p D = J_p\tilde{\underline{A}}^{i-1} J_p' J_p\tilde{\underline{A}}_p J_p' J_p D$$

$$= J_p\tilde{\underline{A}}_p^i J_p' J_p D$$

and thus (3.3.32) holds by induction. Hence, using

$$\text{vec}(BCF) = (F'\otimes B)\text{vec}(C) \qquad (3.3.33)$$

for conformable matrices B, C, and F (e.g., Judge et al. (1985, Appendix A)), it follows that

$$J_p(\tilde{\underline{A}}_p^h - \underline{A}_p^h)\underline{x}_{t,p} = \text{vec}[J_p(\tilde{\underline{A}}^h - \underline{A}_p^h)\underline{x}_{t,p}]$$

$$= \text{vec}\{J_p[\sum_{i=0}^{h-1} \tilde{\underline{A}}_p^i(\tilde{\underline{A}}_p - \underline{A}_p)\underline{A}_p^{h-i-1}]\underline{X}_{t,p}\}$$

$$= \sum_{i=0}^{h-1} (\underline{X}'_{t,p}\underline{A}'^{h-i-1}_p \otimes J_p\tilde{\underline{A}}_p^i J'_p)\,\text{vec}[J_p(\tilde{\underline{A}}_p - \underline{A}_p)]$$

$$= \sum_{i=0}^{h-1} (\underline{X}'_{t,p}\underline{A}'^{h-i-1}_p \otimes \tilde{\Phi}_{i,p})(\tilde{\underline{a}}(p) - \underline{a}(p)).$$

This proves Lemma 3.3. Q.E.D.

Proof of Lemma 3.4

In analogy with the notation in (3.3.4) define the infinite dimensional matrix and vectors

$$\underline{A}_\infty = \begin{bmatrix} A_1 & A_2 & A_3 & \cdots \\ I_K & 0 & 0 & \cdots \\ 0 & I_K & 0 & \cdots \\ \vdots & \ddots & \ddots & \end{bmatrix}, \quad \underline{X}_{t,\infty} = \begin{bmatrix} \underline{x}_t \\ \underline{x}_{t-1} \\ \underline{x}_{t-2} \\ \vdots \end{bmatrix}, \quad \underline{U}_{t,\infty} = \begin{bmatrix} u_t \\ \underline{0} \\ \underline{0} \\ \vdots \end{bmatrix}.$$

Using this notation,

$$\underline{X}_{t,\infty} = \underline{A}_\infty \underline{X}_{t-1,\infty} + \underline{U}_{t,\infty} \tag{3.3.34}$$

and thus,

$$\underline{A}_\infty^i \underline{X}_{t,\infty} = \underline{X}_{t+i,\infty} - \underline{U}_{t+i,\infty} - \underline{A}_\infty \underline{U}_{t+i-1,\infty} - \cdots - \underline{A}_\infty^{i-1}\underline{U}_{t+1,\infty}. \tag{3.3.35}$$

Further note that

$$\frac{1}{p}\sum_{k=1}^{p} \underline{x}_{t+i+k}\underline{x}'_{t+j+k} \xrightarrow[p\to\infty]{a.s.} \Gamma_{\underline{x}}(j-i), \tag{3.3.36}$$

where $\xrightarrow{a.s.}$ denotes almost sure convergence. (In Chapter 2, Section 2.4.2, only convergence in probability is claimed. However, the more general result holds and is shown, e.g., in Hannan (1970, Chapter IV, Theorem 2).) Since

$$\underline{X}'_{t+i,p}\underline{X}_{t+j,p} = \text{tr} \sum_{k=0}^{p-1} \underline{x}_{t+i-k}\underline{x}'_{t+j-k}$$

and, using (3.3.35),

$$\frac{1}{p}(\underline{X}'_{t+i,p}\underline{X}_{t+j,p} - \underline{X}'_{t,p}\underline{A}'^{i}_{p}\underline{A}^{j}_{p}\underline{X}_{t,p}) \xrightarrow[p\to\infty]{a.s.} 0,$$

it follows that

$$\frac{1}{p}\underline{X}'_{t,p}\underline{A}'^{i}_{p}\underline{A}^{j}_{p}\underline{X}_{t,p} \xrightarrow[p\to\infty]{a.s.} \mathrm{tr}\Gamma_{\underline{x}}(j-i). \tag{3.3.37}$$

Now

$$\begin{aligned}\underline{\ell}(p)' &= \sum_{m=1}^{h}\frac{1}{\sqrt{p}}\underline{f}'_m\sum_{i=0}^{m-1}(\underline{X}'_{t,p}\underline{A}'^{m-1-i}_{p}\otimes\Phi_i)\\ &= \sum_{m=1}^{h}\sum_{i=0}^{m-1}(\frac{1}{\sqrt{p}}\underline{X}'_{t,p}\underline{A}'^{m-1-i}_{p}\otimes\underline{f}'_m\Phi_i)\end{aligned}$$

and consequently,

$$\begin{aligned}\underline{\ell}(p)'\underline{\ell}(p) &= \sum_{m=1}^{h}\sum_{n=1}^{h}\sum_{i=0}^{m-1}\sum_{j=0}^{n-1}\frac{1}{p}(\underline{X}'_{t,p}\underline{A}'^{m-1-i}_{p}\underline{A}^{n-1-j}_{p}\underline{X}_{t,p})\otimes\underline{f}'_m\Phi_i\Phi'_j\underline{f}_n\\
&\xrightarrow[p\to\infty]{a.s.} \sum_{m=1}^{h}\sum_{n=1}^{h}\sum_{i=0}^{m-1}\sum_{j=0}^{n-1}\mathrm{tr}[\Gamma_{\underline{x}}(n-j-(m-i))](\underline{f}'_m\Phi_i\Phi'_j\underline{f}_n) \quad \text{(by (3.3.37))}\\
&= \sum_{m=1}^{h}\sum_{n=1}^{h}\underline{f}'_m\left[\sum_{i=0}^{m-1}\sum_{j=0}^{n-1}\mathrm{tr}[\Gamma_{\underline{x}}(n-m+i-j)]\Phi_i\Phi'_j\right]\underline{f}_n\\
&= \underline{f}'\left[\left[\sum_{i=0}^{m-1}\sum_{j=0}^{n-1}E[\underline{x}'_{t+m-1-i}\underline{x}_{t+n-1-j}]\Phi_i\Phi'_j\right]_{n,m\,=\,1,\dots,h}\right]\underline{f}\\
&= \underline{f}'E\begin{bmatrix}\sum_{i=0}^{0}\underline{x}'_{t-i}\otimes\Phi_i\\ \vdots\\ \sum_{i=0}^{h-1}\underline{x}'_{t+h-1-i}\otimes\Phi_i\end{bmatrix}\begin{bmatrix}\sum_{i=0}^{0}\underline{x}'_{t-i}\otimes\Phi_i\\ \vdots\\ \sum_{i=0}^{h-1}\underline{x}'_{t+h-1-i}\otimes\Phi_i\end{bmatrix}'\underline{f}.\end{aligned}$$

This, of course, is a positive constant because it is an expectation of a square of a nondegenerate random variable. Q.E.D.

Proof of Lemma 3.5

Using (3.3.35),

$$\operatorname*{plim}_{p\to\infty}\frac{1}{p}(\underline{X}'_{t+i,p}\Gamma_p^{-1}\underline{X}_{t,p} - \underline{X}'_{t,p}\underline{A}'^{i}_{p}\Gamma_p^{-1}\underline{X}_{t,p}) = 0$$

and thus,

$$\operatorname*{plim}_{p\to\infty} \frac{1}{p}(\underline{X}'_{t+i,p}\Gamma_p^{-1}\underline{X}_{t+j,p} - \underline{X}'_{t,p}\underline{A}_p'^{i}\Gamma_p^{-1}\underline{A}^j\underline{X}_{t,p})$$

$$= \operatorname{plim} \frac{1}{p}[(\underline{X}'_{t+i,p} - \underline{X}'_{t,p}\underline{A}_p'^{i})\Gamma_p^{-1}(\underline{X}_{t+j,p} - \underline{A}_p^j\underline{X}_{t,p})] = 0. \qquad (3.3.38)$$

Therefore it suffices to show that

$$\operatorname*{plim}_{p\to\infty} \frac{1}{p}\underline{X}'_{t+i,p}\Gamma_p^{-1}\underline{X}_{t+j,p} = \begin{cases} K & \text{if } i = j \\ 0 & \text{otherwise.} \end{cases} \qquad (3.3.39)$$

For $i = j$ the result is trivial since $\underline{X}'_{t+i,p}\Gamma_p^{-1}\underline{X}_{t+i,p}$ is a χ^2 random variable with Kp degrees of freedom so that, upon multiplication by $1/p$, the mean is K and the variance is $2K/p$ which approaches zero for $p \to \infty$. For $i \neq j$,

$$E(\frac{1}{p}\underline{X}'_{t+i,p}\Gamma_p^{-1}\underline{X}_{t+j,p}) = \frac{1}{p}\operatorname{tr}[\Gamma_p^{-1}E(\underline{X}_{t+i,p}\underline{X}'_{t+j,p})]$$

$$= \frac{1}{p}\operatorname{tr}(\Gamma_p^{-1}\Gamma_p(i-j))$$

where $\Gamma_p(j-i) = E(\underline{X}_{t,p}\underline{X}'_{t+(j-i),p})$, that is,

$$\Gamma_p^{-1}\Gamma_p(j-i) = E(\underline{X}_{t,p}\underline{X}'_{t,p})^{-1}E(\underline{X}_{t,p}\underline{X}'_{t+(j-i),p}).$$

For $j < i$, the last $K(p+(j-i))$ columns of this matrix are equal to the first $K(p+(j-i))$ columns of I_{Kp}. Consequently,

$$\frac{1}{p}\operatorname{tr}\Gamma_p^{-1}\Gamma_p(j-i) \xrightarrow[p\to\infty]{} 0 \qquad \text{for } i \neq j.$$

Furthermore, the variance of $\underline{X}'_{t+i,p}\Gamma_p^{-1}\underline{X}_{t+j,p}$ is of order p (see Hannan (1970, pp. 208 - 211)), and thus,

$$\operatorname{var}(\frac{1}{p}\underline{X}'_{t+i,p}\Gamma^{-1}\underline{X}_{t+j,p}) = \frac{1}{p^2}\operatorname{var}(\underline{X}'_{t+i,p}\Gamma_p^{-1}\underline{X}_{t+j,p}) \xrightarrow[p\to\infty]{} 0.$$

Hence, (3.3.39) and thereby Lemma 3.5 is proved. Q.E.D.

3.4 FORECASTING NONSTATIONARY PROCESSES

As in Chapter 2 only very special nonstationary processes will be discussed here, namely those which can be made stationary by differencing. Following the pattern of the previous discussion in this chapter, forecasting known processes will be treated first. Then forecasting processes with unknown orders and/or estimated coefficients will be considered in Sections 3.4.2 and 3.4.3.

3.4.1 Known Processes

Suppose $\underline{x}_t$ is a K-dimensional process that is stationary after differencing once, that is,

$$\underline{x}_t - \underline{x}_{t-1} = \underline{x}_t^s \quad \text{or} \quad \underline{x}_t = \underline{x}_{t-1} + \underline{x}_t^s \tag{3.4.1}$$

where $\underline{x}_t^s$ is a K-dimensional stationary process with MA representation

$$\underline{x}_t^s = \sum_{i=0}^{\infty} \Phi_i \underline{u}_{t-i} \quad , \quad \Phi_0 = I_K \ , \tag{3.4.2}$$

with

$$\det\left(\sum_{i=0}^{\infty} \Phi_i z^i\right) \neq 0 \quad \text{for} \quad |z| < 1 \tag{3.4.3}$$

and $\underline{u}_t$ is K-dimensional white noise with covariance matrix $\underline{\Sigma}_u$ as before. The starting point of $\underline{x}_t$ is assumed to be $t_o > -\infty$ which is prior to the forecast origin but is otherwise of little importance for the present discussion. However, the starting value $\underline{x}_{t_o}$ can be of importance for forecasting purposes (see Niemi (1984)). Here it is assumed to be $\underline{x}_{t_o}^s$, that is, $\underline{x}_{t_o} = \underline{x}_{t_o}^s$, and the stationary process $\underline{x}_t^s$ is assumed to have been started at $-\infty$.

Writing

$$\underline{x}_{t+h} = \underline{x}_t + \sum_{j=1}^{h} \underline{x}_{t+j}^s \ , \tag{3.4.4}$$

the optimal h-step forecast of the process $\underline{x}_t$ based on $J_t = \{\underline{u}_s | s \leq t\}$ is

$$\underline{x}_t(h) = \underline{x}_t + \sum_{j=1}^{h} \underline{x}_t^s(j) \ , \tag{3.4.5}$$

where $\underline{x}_t^s(j)$ is the optimal j-step forecast of $\underline{x}_t^s$, that is,

$$\underline{x}_t^s(j) = \sum_{i=0}^{\infty} \Phi_{j+i} \underline{u}_{t-i} \tag{3.4.6}$$

(see Section 3.1.1) and it should be noted that $\underline{x}_t$ can be represented as a linear function of the $\underline{u}_s$, $s \leq t$. The forecast error is the sum of forecast errors of the $\underline{x}_t^s$ process,

$$\underline{x}_{t+h} - \underline{x}_t(h) = \sum_{j=1}^{h} (\underline{x}_{t+j}^s - \underline{x}_t^s(j))$$

$$= H_h[\underline{x}_{t+1}^{s,h} - \underline{x}_t^s(h)], \qquad (3.4.7)$$

where, in accordance with earlier notation,

$$\underline{x}_{t+1}^{s,h} = \begin{bmatrix} \underline{x}_{t+1}^s \\ \vdots \\ \underline{x}_{t+h}^s \end{bmatrix}, \quad \underline{x}_t^s(h) = \begin{bmatrix} \underline{x}_t^s(1) \\ \vdots \\ \underline{x}_t^s(h) \end{bmatrix},$$

and $H_h = (I_K \; I_K \; \dots \; I_K)$ is a $(K \times Kh)$ matrix. This representation of the forecast error provides the forecast MSE matrix

$$\Sigma_{\underline{x}}(h) = H_h \Sigma_{\underline{x}^s}(h) H_h', \qquad (3.4.8)$$

where $\Sigma_{\underline{x}^s}(h)$ is the matrix given in (3.1.15). It may be worth noting that

$$\underline{x}_t(1) = \underline{x}_t + \underline{x}_t^s(1) \text{ and } \Sigma_{\underline{x}}(1) = \Sigma_{\underline{x}^s}(1) = \Sigma_{\underline{u}}. \qquad (3.4.9)$$

Defining

$$\underline{x}_{t+1}^h = \begin{bmatrix} \underline{x}_{t+1} \\ \vdots \\ \underline{x}_{t+h} \end{bmatrix} \text{ and } \underline{X}_t(h) = \begin{bmatrix} \underline{x}_t(1) \\ \vdots \\ \underline{x}_t(h) \end{bmatrix}$$

it is also easy to determine the MSE matrix of the vector of forecasts $\underline{X}_t(h)$. Obviously,

$$\underline{x}_{t+1}^h - \underline{X}_t(h) = D_h\left[\underline{x}_{t+1}^{s,h} - \underline{x}_t^s(h)\right], \qquad (3.4.10)$$

where

$$D_h = \begin{bmatrix} I_K & 0 & \dots & 0 \\ I_K & I_K & \dots & 0 \\ \vdots & \vdots & \ddots & \vdots \\ I_K & I_K & \dots & I_K \end{bmatrix}$$

is a lower triangular (Kh x Kh) matrix. Consequently the MSE matrix of $\underline{x}_t(h)$ is

$$\underline{\Sigma}_{\underline{x}}(h) = D_h \underline{\Sigma}_{\underline{x}^s}(h) D_h' \ . \qquad (3.4.11)$$

If the stationary part $\underline{x}_t^s$ of $\underline{x}_t$ has a nonzero mean, i.e.,

$$\underline{x}_t^s = \underline{\mu} + \sum_{i=0}^{\infty} \Phi_i \underline{u}_{t-i} \ , \qquad (3.4.12)$$

the forecast formula in (3.4.5) is unchanged. It suffices to add the mean term in (3.4.6) in the usual way. As the mean $\underline{\mu}$ is assumed known, the MSE matrices for the predictors also remain unchanged.

To illustrate the foregoing results consider again the U.S. investment data that were modeled and estimated in Chapter 2, Section 2.5.1, and suppose the estimated AR(1) process (2.5.10) is in fact the true generation process for the first differences of the original data. Thus, using the notation of this section,

$$\underline{x}_t^s = \underline{\nu} + A_1 \underline{x}_{t-1}^s + \underline{u}_t \ , \qquad (3.4.13)$$

where

$$\underline{\nu} = \begin{bmatrix} 0.62 \\ -0.32 \end{bmatrix}, \quad A_1 = \begin{bmatrix} 0.40 & 0.17 \\ 0.48 & -0.30 \end{bmatrix}, \quad \text{and } \underline{\Sigma}_{\underline{u}} = \begin{bmatrix} 5.64 & 2.58 \\ 2.58 & 21.8 \end{bmatrix}. \qquad (3.4.14)$$

Also, using the data from the Appendix of the book,

$$\underline{x}_{88} = \begin{bmatrix} 155 \\ 7.6 \end{bmatrix} \quad \text{and } \underline{x}_{88}^s = \begin{bmatrix} 4.3 \\ -1.6 \end{bmatrix}. \qquad (3.4.15)$$

Hence,

$$\underline{x}_{88}(1) = \underline{x}_{88} + \underline{\nu} + A_1 \underline{x}_{88}^s = \begin{bmatrix} 157 \\ 9.8 \end{bmatrix} \qquad (3.4.16)$$

and

$$\underline{x}_{88}(2) = \underline{x}_{88} + \underline{x}_{88}^s(1) + \underline{x}_{88}^s(2) = \underline{x}_{88}(1) + \underline{\nu} + A_1 \underline{x}_{88}^s(1)$$

$$= \begin{bmatrix} 159 \\ 9.8 \end{bmatrix}. \qquad (3.4.17)$$

The forecast MSE matrices are

$$\underline{\Sigma}_{\underline{x}}(1) = \Sigma_{\underline{u}} = \begin{bmatrix} 5.64 & 2.58 \\ 2.58 & 21.8 \end{bmatrix} \qquad (3.4.18)$$

(see (3.4.9)) and

$$\Sigma_{\underline{x}}(2) = [I_2 \ I_2]\underline{\Sigma}_{\underline{x}^s}(2)\begin{bmatrix} I_2 \\ I_2 \end{bmatrix} = \begin{bmatrix} 18.5 & 11.7 \\ 11.7 & 35.5 \end{bmatrix} , \qquad (3.4.19)$$

where (3.2.48) has been used. Furthermore,

$$\underline{\Sigma}_{\underline{x}}(2) = \begin{bmatrix} I_2 & 0 \\ I_2 & I_2 \end{bmatrix} \underline{\Sigma}_{\underline{x}^s}(2) \begin{bmatrix} I_2 & I_2 \\ 0 & I_2 \end{bmatrix} = \begin{bmatrix} 5.64 & 2.58 & 8.33 & 4.51 \\ 2.58 & 21.8 & 7.32 & 16.5 \\ 8.33 & 7.32 & 18.5 & 11.7 \\ 4.51 & 16.5 & 11.7 & 35.5 \end{bmatrix} \qquad (3.4.20)$$

If $\underline{x}_t^s$ has a finite order AR representation as in the previous example, say

$$\underline{x}_t^s = A_1\underline{x}_{t-1}^s + \dots + A_p\underline{x}_{t-p}^s + \underline{u}_t , \qquad (3.4.21)$$

then $\underline{x}_t$ also has a finite order AR representation,

$$\underline{x}_t = \Theta_1\underline{x}_{t-1} + \dots + \Theta_{p+1}\underline{x}_{t-p-1} + \underline{u}_t , \quad t > t_o + p , \qquad (3.4.22)$$

where

$$\Theta(L) = I_K - \sum_{i=1}^{p+1} \Theta_i L^i = (I_K - \sum_{i=1}^{p} A_i L^i)(I_K - I_K L) . \qquad (3.4.23)$$

This representation may be used alternatively to compute optimal h-step forecasts recursively using the recursions of Section 3.1. In other words,

$$\underline{x}_t(h) = \sum_{i=1}^{h-1} \Theta_i\underline{x}_t(h-i) + \sum_{i=h}^{p+1} \Theta_i\underline{x}_{t+h-i} , \qquad (3.4.24)$$

where $\Theta_i = 0$ for $i > p + 1$ (see (3.1.24)). Similarly, if $\underline{x}_t^s$ has an ARMA representation, a recursive formula of the type (3.1.24) may be used to compute the optimal forecasts of $\underline{x}_t$. More precisely, if

$$\underline{x}_t^s = A_1\underline{x}_{t-1}^s + \dots + A_p\underline{x}_{t-p}^s + \underline{u}_t + M_1\underline{u}_{t-1} + \dots + M_q\underline{u}_{t-q}, \qquad (3.4.25)$$

where the determinant of the MA operator is assumed to have no roots inside the complex unit circle, the optimal h-step predictor is

$$\underline{x}_t(h) = \sum_{i=1}^{h-1} \Theta_i \underline{x}_t(h-i) + \sum_{i=h}^{p+1} \Theta_i \underline{x}_{t+h-i} + \sum_{i=h}^{q} M_i \underline{u}_{t+h-i} \qquad (3.4.26)$$

If the process $\underline{x}_t$ has a nonzero mean vector, an intercept term may be added to this expression. The intercept term is precisely the same as that of the stationary process $\underline{x}_t^s$.

The previous discussion is easy to generalize to higher order differencing. Suppose, for instance, that $\underline{z}_t$ is a K-dimensional process which is stationary after differencing twice,

$$\underline{z}_t - \underline{z}_{t-1} = \underline{x}_t \ , \qquad (3.4.27)$$

where $\underline{x}_t$ is as in (3.4.1). Defining

$$\underline{z}_t(h) = \underline{z}_t + \sum_{j=1}^{h} \underline{x}_t(j) \ , \qquad (3.4.28)$$

it follows from the previous discussion that the forecast error is a linear function of the forecast errors associated with $\underline{x}_t^s(h)$,

$$\underline{z}_{t+h} - \underline{z}_t(h) = H_h[\underline{x}_{t+1}^h - \underline{x}_t(h)] = H_h D_h[\underline{x}_{t+1}^{s,h} - \underline{x}_t^s(h)] \ , \qquad (3.4.29)$$

and the forecast MSE matrices of $\underline{z}_t$ are

$$\not{\Sigma}_{\underline{z}}(h) = H_h \not{\Sigma}_{\underline{x}}(h) H_h' = H_h D_h \not{\Sigma}_{\underline{x}^s}(h) D_h' H_h' \ . \qquad (3.4.30)$$

In general, if higher order differences or different differences for the individual components of $\underline{x}_t$ are required to obtain stationarity, the forecast errors are linear transformations of the forecast errors of the stationary part, $[\underline{x}_{t+1}^{s,h} - \underline{x}_t^s(h)]$, and thus the MSE matrices are easily obtainable. If the stationary process $\underline{x}_t^s$ is obtained by applying some differencing operator D(L) of degree d to $\underline{x}_t$, say

$$\underline{x}_t^s = D(L)\underline{x}_t \ , \qquad (3.4.31)$$

and $\underline{x}_t^s$ has an ARMA representation (3.4.25), then $\underline{x}_t$ has an ARMA(p+d,q) representation

$$\underline{x}_t = \sum_{i=1}^{p+d} \Theta_i \underline{x}_{t-i} + \underline{u}_t + \sum_{i=1}^{q} M_i \underline{u}_{t-i}, \tag{3.4.32}$$

where the Θ_i are such that

$$(I_K - \sum_{i=1}^{p+d} \Theta_i L^i) = (I_K - \sum_{i=1}^{p} A_i L^i) D(L) .$$

This ARMA representation can be used analogously to (3.4.26) to compute the h-step predictors $\underline{x}_t(h)$. Since it is not ruled out that the determinant of the MA operator of $\underline{x}_t^s$ has roots on the unit circle (only roots inside the unit circle are prohibited) it is not really necessary at this point to consider the case where different components of $\underline{x}_t$ are differenced a different number of times. All components may simply be differenced simultaneously as many times as is necessary to make them all stationary. At worst this procedure will result in a stationary $\underline{x}_t^s$ process with noninvertible MA representation. As shown in Section 3.1.1 this is no serious problem as long as the MA coefficients are assumed known and the information set consists of past and present $\underline{u}_t$. In practice, however, the process coefficients will be estimated and then invertibility of the MA representation is highly desirable (see Section 3.2).

Before turning to processes with estimated coefficients it may be useful to mention that seasonal differences can also be handled in the manner described in the foregoing. Suppose $\underline{x}_t$ is a K-dimensional, nonstationary process such that

$$\underline{x}_t - \underline{x}_{t-s} = \underline{x}_t^s \quad \text{or} \quad \underline{x}_t = \underline{x}_{t-s} + \underline{x}_t^s \tag{3.4.33}$$

and $\underline{x}_t^s$ is as given in (3.4.2). Here s is some positive integer. In practice it will usually be the seasonal period. In this case,

$$\begin{aligned} \underline{x}_{t+h} &= \underline{x}_{t+h-ns} + \sum_{j=1}^{n} \underline{x}^s_{t+h-ns+js} \\ &= \underline{x}_{t+h-ns} + \sum_{j=1}^{n} \underline{x}^s_{t+h+(j-n)s} , \end{aligned} \tag{3.4.34}$$

where

$$n = \min\{j \in \mathbb{N} | js \geq h\} ,$$

and the h-step forecast is

$$\underline{x}_t(h) = \underline{x}_{t+h-ns} + \sum_{j=1}^{n} \underline{x}_t^s(h+(j-n)s). \tag{3.4.35}$$

Again the forecast errors are linear functions of the forecast errors of the stationary process $\underline{x}_t^s$,

$$\underline{x}_{t+h} - \underline{x}_t(h) = H_h^s[\underline{X}_{t+1}^{s,h} - \underline{X}_t^s(h)] , \tag{3.4.36}$$

where H_h^s is a (K x Kh) matrix containing n (K x K) identity matrices and zeros otherwise. For example, for s = 4 (e.g. quarterly data) and h = 5, it follows that n = 2 and

$$H_h^s = [0 \; I_K \; 0 \; 0 \; 0 \; I_K] .$$

The MSE matrix can be obtained straightforwardly. The important result to remember is that also in this case the forecast errors can be written as a linear transformation of the forecast errors of the stationary process $\underline{x}_t^s$.

3.4.2 Estimated Coefficients

Under the assumptions of the previous subsection it is easy to derive the forecast MSE matrices even if the coefficients of the stationary process $\underline{x}_t^s$ are replaced by estimators. Suppose that the process $\underline{x}_t^s$ satisfies the assumptions stated in Proposition 3.1 and let $\underline{x}_t$ be a process from which $\underline{x}_t^s$ is obtained by differencing. Further suppose that the vector of forecast errors satisfies

$$\underline{X}_{t+1}^h - \underline{X}_t(h) = D[\underline{X}_{t+1}^{s,h} - \underline{X}_t^s(h)] ,$$

where D is an appropriate (Kh x Kh) matrix. The matrix D is assumed known. In other words, it is assumed known which difference operator has to be applied to obtain stationarity. Replacing the process coefficients by estimators as in Proposition 3.1 and using the notation of Section 3.2, it follows that the asymptotic forecast MSE matrix of the vector of 1- to h-step forecasts of $\underline{x}_t$ is

$$\hat{\underline{\Sigma}}_{\underline{X}}(h) = D\hat{\underline{\Sigma}}_{\underline{X}^s}(h)D' = \underline{\Sigma}_{\underline{X}}(h) + \frac{1}{T}D\underline{\Omega}_{\underline{X}^s}(h)D', \tag{3.4.37}$$

where $\Omega_{\underline{X}^s}(h)$ is the covariance matrix of the asymptotic distribution of $\sqrt{T}\,[\hat{\underline{X}}_t^s(h) - \underline{X}_t^s(h)]$ and T is the sample size used for estimation. From this matrix, forecast MSEs for individual forecasts or groups of forecasts can be obtained. For instance,

$$\hat{\Sigma}_{\underline{x}}(h) = \Sigma_{\underline{x}}(h) + \frac{1}{T}F\Omega_{\underline{X}^s}(h)F' , \tag{3.4.38}$$

where the (K x Kh) matrix F consists of the last K rows of D.

If $\underline{x}_t^s$ has a nonzero mean, under assumptions as in Section 3.2.1, a further term enters the asymptotic MSE matrix. Denoting by $\bar{\underline{x}}^s$ the vector of sample means of $\underline{x}_t^s$ and by $\Sigma_{\bar{\underline{x}}^s}$ the corresponding asymptotic covariance matrix, then, by (3.2.18),

$$\hat{\Sigma}_{\underline{x}}(h) = \Sigma_{\underline{x}}(h) + \frac{1}{T}D\Omega_{\underline{X}^s}(h)D' + \frac{1}{T}DG_{\underline{X}^s}(h)D' , \tag{3.4.39}$$

where $G_{\underline{X}^s}(h)$ is as defined in (3.2.19) with $\underline{X}$ replaced by $\underline{X}^s$.

The U.S. investment data are used again to illustrate these results. Assuming that their first differences are indeed generated by an AR(1) process and $\hat{\Sigma}_{\underline{X}^s}(2)$ is the matrix given in (3.2.51), the following MSE matrices are obtained. For h = 1, D = I_2 and hence,

$$\hat{\Sigma}_{\underline{x}}(1) = \hat{\Sigma}_{\underline{x}^s}(1) = \begin{bmatrix} 5.83 & 2.67 \\ 2.67 & 22.6 \end{bmatrix} \tag{3.4.40}$$

is the upper left-hand (2 x 2) block of (3.2.51). For h = 2,

$$\hat{\Sigma}_{\underline{X}}(2) = \begin{bmatrix} I_2 & 0 \\ I_2 & I_2 \end{bmatrix} \hat{\Sigma}_{\underline{X}^s}(2) \begin{bmatrix} I_2 & I_2 \\ 0 & I_2 \end{bmatrix}$$

$$= \begin{bmatrix} 5.83 & 2.67 & 8.65 & 4.67 \\ 2.67 & 22.6 & 7.51 & 17.6 \\ 8.65 & 7.51 & 19.2 & 12.1 \\ 4.67 & 17.6 & 12.1 & 37.2 \end{bmatrix} \tag{3.4.41}$$

Note that, although data for 88 quarters are originally available, only T = 87 (differenced) data for each of the variables have been used for estimation. Hence, the matrix (3.2.51) may be used in the above computations.

3.4.3 Unknown Order

Like in the case of processes with estimated coefficients, under suitable assumptions, the asymptotic forecast MSE matrices for the nonstationary process $\underline{x}_t$ investigated in the previous subsection can be obtained easily if $\underline{x}_t^s$ has an AR representation of unknown and possibly infinite order. Assuming that the conditions of Proposition 3.2 are satisfied for $\underline{x}_t^s$ and the order $p(T)$ of the AR process fitted to the data, the approximate MSE matrix of $\underline{\tilde{x}}_{t,p(T)}(h)$ is easily seen to be

$$\tilde{\underline{\Sigma}}_{\underline{x}}(h) = (1 + \frac{Kp(T)}{T})D\underline{\Sigma}_{\underline{x}^s}(h)D'$$

$$= (1 + \frac{Kp(T)}{T})\underline{\Sigma}_{\underline{x}}(h) \quad . \qquad (3.4.42)$$

Here $\underline{\tilde{x}}_{t,p}(h)$ is as defined in (3.3.7) and D is as specified in the previous subsection.

3.5 COMPARING FORECASTS

In the previous sections of this chapter predictors are introduced for different representations of the data generation process. In the following chapters these predictors will be used to construct and compare various different forecasts for aggregated variables. The criterion for comparing these predictors will be the forecast MSE or MSE matrix. Since only asymptotic MSEs are available if the process orders and/or coefficients are unknown and have to be estimated, Monte Carlo studies will be carried out for comparing the small sample MSEs. In this section a statistic will be introduced that is useful in assessing the significance of differences in small sample MSEs. The discussion of this section is based on Section 8.3 of Granger & Newbold (1977).

Suppose $e^{(1)}$ and $e^{(2)}$ are forecast errors obtained by using two specific unbiased predictors and assume that $(e^{(1)}, e^{(2)})$ has a bivariate normal distribution with variances (mean squared forecasting errors) MSE_1 and MSE_2. Furthermore suppose that a random sample $(e_r^{(1)}, e_r^{(2)})$, $r = 1,\ldots,R$, of pairs of forecast errors from the distribution of $(e^{(1)}, e^{(2)})$ is available. Defining

$$\hat{\rho} = \frac{\sum_{r=1}^{R} (e_r^{(1)} + e_r^{(2)})(e_r^{(1)} - e_r^{(2)})}{\left[\sum_{r=1}^{R} (e_r^{(1)} + e_r^{(2)})^2 \sum_{r=1}^{R} (e_r^{(1)} - e_r^{(2)})^2\right]^{1/2}} \qquad (3.5.1)$$

it can be shown that, asymptotically as R goes to infinity, $\sqrt{R}\,\hat{\rho}$ has a standard normal distribution,

$$\sqrt{R}\,\hat{\rho} \xrightarrow[R\to\infty]{d} N(0,1), \tag{3.5.2}$$

if $MSE_1 = MSE_2$. Thus, $\sqrt{R}\hat{\rho}$ is useful as a test statistic for testing the null hypothesis

$$H_0 : MSE_1 = MSE_2 \text{ against } H_1 : MSE_1 \neq MSE_2 . \tag{3.5.3}$$

In later chapters, where the statistic $\sqrt{R}\,\hat{\rho}$ is used to assess the significance of differences in MSEs of different predictors, the errors $(e^{(1)}, e^{(2)})$ will usually not have an exact bivariate normal distribution. For instance, if predictors are based on estimated AR processes, the prediction errors will only have an asymptotic normal distribution as T, the sample size used for estimation, approaches infinity. Thus, both T and R (number of replications of the Monte Carlo experiment) have to go to infinity to obtain a standard normal distribution of $\sqrt{R}\,\hat{\rho}$. Nevertheless, this statistic will be used as a rough check of significant differences between MSEs of different predictors.

3.6 SUMMARY

In this chapter the basic forecasting concepts have been introduced that will be used in the following chapters of this study. Optimal prediction under the assumption of having a known stochastic process has been considered first. The forecast MSE matrix has been used as optimality criterion. Then an asymptotic theory has been presented that permits to take into account the sampling variability induced by using estimated rather than known coefficients for the processes on which the predictors are based. A different asymptotic theory has also been introduced that does not require knowledge of the order of the underlying process. In fact, this process may be of infinite AR order. Finally the theory has been extended to nonstationary processes that can be made stationary by differencing.

It must be admitted, however, that the asymptotic theories involve some unrealistic assumptions like, for instance, that estimation and forecasting are based on independent processes with identical stochastic structures. Also, either the ARMA orders of the underlying processes are assumed known or the AR order approaches infinity at a certain rate with growing sample size. Of course, in practice usually only one sample of a fixed size T is available and a specific AR order must be chosen. Therefore simulation experiments will be conducted in later chapters to see whether or not the results based on asymptotic theory are good approximations to small sample results. A statistic has been introduced that is useful for comparing forecast MSEs in Monte Carlo studies.

In the following chapters a pattern similar to the one of this chapter will be adopted. For instance, forecasting contemporaneously aggregated variables will be discussed first under the assumption of known data generation processes in the next chapter and the case of estimated processes will be considered in Chapter 5.

CHAPTER 4. FORECASTING CONTEMPORANEOUSLY AGGREGATED KNOWN PROCESSES

A contemporaneous aggregate of the variables $x_{1t},\ldots,x_{Kt}$ at time t is their sum or weighted sum, $y_t = f_1x_{1t} + \ldots + f_Kx_{Kt}$, where the f_k, $k = 1,\ldots,K$, are the aggregation weights. Examples are numerous in economics. For instance, the Gross National Product (y) is the sum of Private Consumption Expenditures (x_1), Gross Private Domestic Investment (x_2), Government Expenditures (x_3) and Net Exports (x_4), that is, in this case the aggregation weights are all equal to one, $f_1 = f_2 = f_3 = f_4 = 1$. Also price indices are weighted sums of prices of different commodities. In fact, practically all macroeconomic variables and many micro economic variables as well are contemporaneous aggregates of some sort. Therefore systems of contemporaneous aggregates are often of interest. Such a system, say $\underline{y} = (y_1,\ldots,y_M)'$, can be written as a linear transformation of the disaggregate components $\underline{x} = (x_1,\ldots,x_K)'$, that is $\underline{y} = F\underline{x}$, where F is a suitable (M x K) transformation matrix. Thus, if analyzing a contemporaneously aggregated vector stochastic process $\underline{x}_t$ is the aim, linear transformations $\underline{y}_t = F\underline{x}_t$ must be considered. Therefore linear transformations of vector stochastic processes are the subject of this chapter. It will be assumed that the aggregation matrix F is the same for all periods, that is, F does not depend on t.

The main objective of this chapter is to compare forecasts for the linearly transformed process $\underline{y}_t = F\underline{x}_t$ under the assumption that the processes $\underline{x}_t$ and $\underline{y}_t$ are completely known. There are three obvious possibilities for predicting $\underline{y}_t$:

(1) An optimal predictor for $\underline{x}_t$ may be obtained and the resulting forecasts are transformed.

(2) An optimal predictor based directly on the process $\underline{y}_t$ may be used.

(3) Optimal univariate predictors for the individual components of $\underline{x}_t$ may be obtained and these are then transformed in order to forecast $\underline{y}_t$.

The first predictor is based on the largest information set and will turn out to be optimal. In practice it involves constructing a multiple time series model which may be more expensive than modelling the possibly lower dimensional process $\underline{y}_t$ directly. The third predictor involves only univariate time series models and will often be relatively cheap. It turns out, however, that there are processes for which this predictor is inferior to the second one.

The results of this chapter are also of interest in analyzing phenomena other than contemporaneous aggregation. For instance, any subprocess $\underline{y}_t$ of a stochastic process $\underline{x}_t$ can be regarded as a linear transformation of the latter. Assuming that $\underline{y}_t$ consists of the last M components of $\underline{x}_t$ it can be represented as $\underline{y}_t = F\underline{x}_t$, where $F = (0\ I_M)$ is a $(M \times K)$ matrix and I_M denotes the $(M \times M)$ identity matrix as before. As a further example consider a set of variables z_{kt}, $k = 1,\ldots,M$, that are measured with error so that the observed variables are $y_{kt} = z_{kt} + u_{kt}$, $k = 1,\ldots,M$, where the u_{kt} represent the measurement errors. Then $\underline{y}_t = (y_{1t},\ldots,y_{Mt})'$ is again a linear transformation of a process $\underline{x}_t = (z_{1t},\ldots,z_{Mt},u_{1t},\ldots,u_{Mt})'$ with transformation matrix $F = (I_M\ I_M)$. These examples demonstrate the wide range of problems that can be handled in the framework of this chapter.

The organization of the chapter is as follows. After a brief introduction of the notation and basic assumptions, the forecasting problem for linearly transformed stationary and nonstationary processes is discussed in Sections 4.2 and 4.3. Some interesting consequences for vector ARMA processes are considered in Section 4.4 and a summary and concluding remarks are provided in Section 4.5. This chapter is to a large extent based on results given by Kohn (1982) and Lütkepohl (1984a). Related work and special case results can be found in articles by Granger & Morris (1976), Rose (1977), Ansley, Spivey & Wrobleski (1977), Tiao & Guttman (1980), Wei & Abraham (1981) and others. Further references will be given throughout the chapter.

4.1 LINEAR TRANSFORMATIONS OF VECTOR STOCHASTIC PROCESSES

Let $\underline{x}_t$ be a zero mean K-dimensional, stationary, nondeterministic stochastic process with MA representation as in (2.1.2),

$$\underline{x}_t = \sum_{i=0}^{\infty} \Phi_i \underline{u}_{t-i} = \Phi(L)\underline{u}_t \quad , \quad \Phi_0 = I_K \; , \tag{4.1.1}$$

where $\underline{u}_t$ is white noise with nonsingular covariance matrix $\Sigma_{\underline{u}}$ and

$$\det(\Phi(z)) \neq 0 \quad \text{for} \quad |z| < 1. \tag{4.1.2}$$

Note that $\det(\Phi(z))$ may have roots on the complex unit circle so that $\underline{x}_t$ is not necessarily invertible.

It is assumed that interest centers on a linear transformation $\underline{y}_t$ of $\underline{x}_t$,

$$\underline{y}_t = F\underline{x}_t \ , \tag{4.1.3}$$

where F is an (M x K) matrix of rank M. It is easy to see that $\underline{y}_t$ is also stationary and nondeterministic (for the latter property see the discussion below (4.2.3)) and has zero mean. Thus, it has an MA representation, say

$$\underline{y}_t = \sum_{i=0}^{\infty} \Psi_i \underline{v}_{t-i} = \Psi(L)\underline{v}_t \ , \quad \Psi_0 = I_M \ , \tag{4.1.4}$$

where $\underline{v}_t$ is M-dimensional white noise with covariance matrix $\Sigma_{\underline{v}}$ and

$$\det(\Psi(z)) \neq 0 \quad \text{for} \quad |z| < 1. \tag{4.1.5}$$

The spectral density matrix of $\underline{y}_t$ is (see Section 2.1.4)

$$\begin{aligned} \underline{f}_{\underline{y}}(\omega) &= \frac{1}{2\pi}\Psi(e^{i\omega})\Sigma_{\underline{v}}\Psi(e^{-i\omega})' \\ &= \frac{1}{2\pi}\sum_{h=-\infty}^{\infty} e^{-i\omega h}\Gamma_{\underline{y}}(h) \\ &= \frac{1}{2\pi}\sum_{h=-\infty}^{\infty} e^{-i\omega h}F\Gamma_{\underline{x}}(h)F' \\ &= \frac{1}{2\pi}F\Phi(e^{i\omega})\Sigma_{\underline{u}}\Phi(e^{-i\omega})'F' \\ &= F\underline{f}_{\underline{x}}(\omega)F' \ , \qquad -\pi \leq \omega \leq \pi, \end{aligned} \tag{4.1.6}$$

where $\Gamma_{\underline{y}}(h) = E(\underline{y}_t\underline{y}'_{t+h})$ and $\Gamma_{\underline{x}}(h) = E(\underline{x}_t\underline{x}'_{t+h})$, as before. Thus, if $\det(\Phi(z))$ has no roots on the complex unit circle the same must hold for $\det(\Psi(z))$ because F is assumed to be of full rank M and $\underline{f}_{\underline{x}}(\omega)$ is positive definite for all $\omega\varepsilon[-\pi,\pi]$. Therefore, if $\underline{x}_t$ has an AR representation, the same holds for $\underline{y}_t$.

Note that this result relies on $\Sigma_{\underline{u}}$ and thus $\Sigma_{\underline{x}}$ being nonsingular. If this condition is not assumed a counterexample to the aforementioned result can easily be constructed. Consider the bivariate MA(1) process

$$\underline{x}_t = \begin{bmatrix} x_{1t} \\ x_{2t} \end{bmatrix} = \begin{bmatrix} u_t \\ u_t \end{bmatrix} + \begin{bmatrix} 0 & -1 \\ 0 & 0 \end{bmatrix}\begin{bmatrix} u_{t-1} \\ u_{t-1} \end{bmatrix}$$

which has the AR(1) representation

$$\underline{x}_t = \begin{bmatrix} 0 & -1 \\ 0 & 0 \end{bmatrix} \underline{x}_{t-1} + \begin{bmatrix} u_t \\ u_t \end{bmatrix}.$$

However, $y_t = (1 \quad 0)\underline{x}_t = x_{1t} = u_t - u_{t-1}$ has no AR representation. Of course, the crucial violation of our assumptions is that

$$\Sigma_{\underline{u}} = \begin{bmatrix} \sigma_u^2 & \sigma_u^2 \\ \sigma_u^2 & \sigma_u^2 \end{bmatrix}$$

is singular. Here $\sigma_u^2 = E(u_t^2)$.

If $\det(\Phi(z_o)) = 0$ for some z_o with $|z_o| = 1$, then $\det(\Psi(z_o))$ may still be nonzero. This is easily seen by considering a bivariate process $\underline{x}_t = (x_{1t}, x_{2t})'$ with

$$\Phi(L) = \begin{bmatrix} 1-L & 0 \\ 0 & 1-\phi L \end{bmatrix},$$

where $0 < |\phi| < 1$. Clearly, $\det(\Phi(1)) = 0$ while, for $F = (0 \quad 1)$, $y_t = F\underline{x}_t = (1 - \phi L)u_{2t}$ has an invertible MA operator.

4.2 FORECASTING LINEARLY TRANSFORMED STATIONARY VECTOR STOCHASTIC PROCESSES

In this section the three predictors of interest will be introduced formally. Then a comparison on the basis of their MSE matrices is performed and conditions for equality are given and discussed. As a by-product characterizations of Granger-causality are obtained.

4.2.1 The Predictors

Let $\underline{x}_t$, F, and $\underline{y}_t$ be as in Section 4.1. It is assumed now that interest centers on forecasts of $\underline{y}_t$. The optimal (linear minimum MSE) h-step predictor based on the information set $\{\underline{u}_s | s \leq t\}$ can be determined as in Chapter 3, Section 3.1. Denoting the optimal predictor by

$$\underline{y}_t^o(h) = \sum_{i=0}^{\infty} H_i \underline{u}_{t-i}$$

its MSE matrix is

$$\Sigma_{\underline{y}}^{o}(h) = E[\underline{y}_t^o(h) - \underline{y}_{t+h}][\underline{y}_t^o(h) - \underline{y}_{t+h}]'$$
$$= F(\sum_{i=0}^{h-1} \Phi_i \Sigma_{\underline{u}} \Phi_i')F' + \sum_{i=0}^{\infty} (H_i - F\Phi_{h+i})\Sigma_{\underline{u}}(H_i - F\Phi_{h+i})'$$

which is minimized for $H_i = F\Phi_{h+i}$. Therefore the optimal h-step predictor is

$$\underline{y}_t^o(h) = F\sum_{i=0}^{\infty} \Phi_{h+i}\underline{u}_{t-i} = F\underline{x}_t(h), \tag{4.2.1}$$

where the "o" stands for "optimal", and its MSE matrix is

$$\Sigma_{\underline{y}}^{o}(h) = F(\sum_{i=0}^{h-1} \Phi_i \Sigma_{\underline{u}} \Phi_i')F' = F\Sigma_{\underline{x}}(h)F'. \tag{4.2.2}$$

Here $\underline{x}_t(h)$ is the optimal h-step predictor of $\underline{x}_t$ at origin t and $\Sigma_{\underline{x}}(h)$ is the corresponding MSE matrix (see (3.1.3) and (3.1.6)).

From $\Sigma_{\underline{x}}(h) \xrightarrow[h\to\infty]{} \Sigma_{\underline{x}} = E(\underline{x}_t\underline{x}_t')$ it follows that

$$\Sigma_{\underline{y}}^{o}(h) \xrightarrow[h\to\infty]{} F\Sigma_{\underline{x}}F' = \Sigma_{\underline{y}} = E(\underline{y}_t\underline{y}_t') \tag{4.2.3}$$

This fact can be used to show that $\underline{y}_t$ is nondeterministic. Suppose that $\underline{x}_t$ has an AR representation. Then $\underline{y}_t^o(h)$ can be written in terms of past and present $\underline{x}_s$, $s \le t$, rather than the $\underline{u}_s$ (see (3.1.17)). Since $\underline{y}_t^o(h)$ is optimal, the MSE matrix $\Sigma_{\underline{y}}(h)$ of a predictor based on $\underline{y}_s = F\underline{x}_s$, $s \le t$, must also converge to $\Sigma_{\underline{y}}$ as $h \to \infty$. In fact, the result remains valid even if $\underline{x}_t$ has no AR representation. Using Hilbert space theory it can be shown that $F\underline{x}_t(h)$ is the optimal predictor based on a Hilbert space $\mathcal{H}_t$ generated by the $\underline{x}_s$, $s \le t$. Since the $\underline{y}_s$, $s \le t$, generate only a subspace of $\mathcal{H}_t$ the predictor based on that subspace cannot be better than $F\underline{x}_t(h)$.

The optimal h-step predictor of $\underline{y}_t$ based on $\{\underline{v}_s | s \le t\}$ is

$$\underline{y}_t(h) = \sum_{i=0}^{\infty} \Psi_{h+i}\underline{v}_{t-i} \tag{4.2.4}$$

and its MSE matrix is

$$\Sigma_{\underline{y}}(h) = \sum_{i=0}^{h-1} \Psi_i \Sigma_{\underline{v}} \Psi_i' . \tag{4.2.5}$$

Both predictors, $\underline{y}_t^o(h)$ and $\underline{y}_t(h)$ are based on multivariate processes if $M > 1$. Since building multivariate time series models may be more expensive than univariate ones, a predictor based on univariate models is a plausible alternative that has been used in practice (e.g., Dunn, Williams & DeChaine (1976), Kang (1986)). Also, if univariate models for the components x_{kt} of $\underline{x}_t$ are used, more information may be utilized than in the predictor $\underline{y}_t(h)$ which is based on the transformed process only.

The univariate component x_{kt} is also a linear transformation of $\underline{x}_t$ with (1 x K) transformation matrix $(0,\dots,0,1,0,\dots,0)$, where the 1 appears as the k-th component. Therefore the x_{kt} have MA representations, say

$$x_{kt} = \sum_{i=0}^{\infty} \xi_{ki} w_{k,t-i} = \xi_k(L) w_{kt} \quad , \quad \xi_{k0} = 1 \quad , \quad k = 1,\dots,K, \qquad (4.2.6)$$

where

$$\xi_k(z) \neq 0 \quad \text{for} \quad |z| < 1 \qquad (4.2.7)$$

and the w_{kt} are univariate white noise processes. Note that $\underline{w}_t = (w_{1t},\dots,w_{Kt})'$ is in general not K-dimensional white noise. Writing (4.2.6) compactly gives

$$\underline{x}_t = \sum_{i=0}^{\infty} \Xi_i \underline{w}_{t-i} = \Xi(L)\underline{w}_t \, , \qquad (4.2.8)$$

where the Ξ_i are diagonal matrices with $\xi_{1i},\dots,\xi_{Ki}$ on the diagonals. The process $\underline{w}_t$ is nondeterministic and stationary and thus has an MA representation, say

$$\underline{w}_t = \sum_{i=0}^{\infty} M_i \bar{\underline{u}}_{t-i} = M(L)\bar{\underline{u}}_t \quad , \quad M_0 = I_K \, , \qquad (4.2.9)$$

where $\bar{\underline{u}}_t = \underline{u}_t$ and

$$M(L) = \Xi(L)^{-1}\Phi(L), \qquad (4.2.10)$$

if $\Xi(L)$ is invertible, i.e., $\det(\Xi(z)) \neq 0$ for $|z| \leq 1$.

The optimal h-step predictor of x_{kt} based on $\{w_{ks} | s \leq t\}$ is

$$x_{kt}^u(h) = \sum_{i=0}^{\infty} \xi_{k,h+i} w_{k,t-i} \quad , \quad k = 1,\dots,K \, , \qquad (4.2.11)$$

where the superscript "u" stands for "univariate" and indicates that the predictor is based on the univariate component $w_{k,t}$ only. Compactl (4.2.11) can be written as

$$\underline{x}_t^u(h) = \sum_{i=0}^{\infty} \Xi_{h+i}\underline{w}_{t-i} \tag{4.2.12}$$

and an h-step predictor for $\underline{y}_t$ is obtained as

$$\underline{y}_t^u(h) = F\underline{x}_t^u(h) \ . \tag{4.2.13}$$

The forecast error is

$$\underline{y}_{t+h} - \underline{y}_t^u(h) = F(\underline{x}_{t+h} - \underline{x}_t^u(h))$$

$$= F \sum_{i=0}^{h-1} \Xi_i \underline{w}_{t+h-i} = F[I_K \Xi_1 \cdots \Xi_{h-1}] \begin{bmatrix} \underline{w}_{t+h} \\ \underline{w}_{t+h-1} \\ \vdots \\ \underline{w}_{t+1} \end{bmatrix} . \tag{4.2.14}$$

Hence, the MSE matrix of $\underline{y}_t^u(h)$ is

$$\Sigma_{\underline{y}}^u(h) = E[\underline{y}_{t+h} - \underline{y}_t^u(h)][\underline{y}_{t+h} - \underline{y}_t^u(h)]'$$

$$= F[I_K \Xi_1 \ \cdots \ \Xi_{h-1}] E\left[\begin{bmatrix} \underline{w}_{t+h} \\ \vdots \\ \underline{w}_{t+1} \end{bmatrix}\begin{bmatrix} \underline{w}_{t+h} \\ \vdots \\ \underline{w}_{t+1} \end{bmatrix}'\right] \begin{bmatrix} I_K \\ \Xi_1' \\ \vdots \\ \Xi_{h-1}' \end{bmatrix} F'$$

$$= F[I_K \Xi_1 \ \cdots \ \Xi_{h-1}] \begin{bmatrix} \Gamma_{\underline{w}}(0) & \Gamma_{\underline{w}}(-1) & \cdots & \Gamma_{\underline{w}}(-h+1) \\ \Gamma_{\underline{w}}(1) & \Gamma_{\underline{w}}(0) & \cdots & \Gamma_{\underline{w}}(-h+2) \\ \vdots & \vdots & \ddots & \vdots \\ \Gamma_{\underline{w}}(h-1) & \Gamma_{\underline{w}}(h-2) & \cdots & \Gamma_{\underline{w}}(0) \end{bmatrix} \begin{bmatrix} I_K \\ \Xi_1' \\ \vdots \\ \Xi_{h-1}' \end{bmatrix} F', \tag{4.2.15}$$

where

$$\Gamma_{\underline{w}}(j) = E(\underline{w}_t \underline{w}_{t+j}') = \sum_{i=0}^{\infty} M_i \Sigma_{\underline{u}} M_{i+j}'$$

in accordance with notation used earlier.

4.2.2 Comparison of the Predictors

From the discussion of the previous subsection it is already clear that out of the three predictors $\underline{y}_t^o(h)$ is the optimal one, that is,

$$\Sigma_{\underline{y}}(h) \geq \Sigma_{\underline{y}}^o(h) \quad \text{and} \quad \Sigma_{\underline{y}}^u(h) \geq \Sigma_{\underline{y}}^o(h) \;, \tag{4.2.16}$$

where "$\geq$" means as usual that the difference between the right-hand matrix and the left-hand matrix is positive semidefinite. If $\Phi(L)$ is invertible this can be seen directly by noting that also $\Psi(L)$ and $\Xi(L)$ are invertible (see Section 4.1). Consequently, $\underline{v}_t = \Psi(L)^{-1}F\underline{x}_t$ and $\underline{w}_t = \Xi(L)^{-1}\underline{x}_t$ and hence, both $\underline{y}_t(h)$ and $\underline{y}_t^u(h)$ are linear predictors based on $J_t = \{\underline{u}_s | s \leq t\}$ that cannot be better than the optimal predictor $\underline{y}_t^o(h)$. If $\Phi(L)$ is noninvertible, (4.2.16) follows from a Hilbert space argument.

In any case, all three prediction MSE matrices approach $\Sigma_{\underline{y}}$, the covariance matrix of $\underline{y}_t$, if $h \to \infty$. Thus, the difference between the predictors vanishes for long range forecasting.

Whether or not $\Sigma_{\underline{y}}(h) \geq \Sigma_{\underline{y}}^u(h)$ depends on the structure of the disaggregate process $\underline{x}_t$ and the aggregation matrix F. This fact was pointed out by Wei & Abraham (1981) and can be seen, for instance, by considering the following example. Let $\underline{x}_t$ be the bivariate MA(1) process

$$\begin{bmatrix} x_{1t} \\ x_{2t} \end{bmatrix} = \begin{bmatrix} u_{1t} \\ u_{2t} \end{bmatrix} + \begin{bmatrix} 0 & 1 \\ 0 & 0 \end{bmatrix} \begin{bmatrix} u_{1,t-1} \\ u_{2,t-1} \end{bmatrix} \tag{4.2.17}$$

with $\Sigma_{\underline{u}} = I_2$. The univariate subprocesses are both white noise processes,

$$x_{1t} = w_{1t} \quad \text{with} \quad w_{1t} = u_{1t} + u_{2,t-1}$$

and

$$x_{2t} = w_{2t} \quad \text{with} \quad w_{2t} = u_{2t} \;.$$

Consequently, for $F = (1, 1)$, i.e., $y_t = x_{1t} + x_{2t}$,

$$\Sigma_y^u(1) = E(w_{1t}^2) + E(w_{2t}^2) = E(u_{1t}^2) + E(u_{2,t-1}^2) + E(u_{2t}^2) = 3$$

while $\Sigma_y(1) = 2.618$. The latter can be seen by noting that y_t is an MA(1) process (see Section 4.4.1),

$$y_t = v_t + \psi v_{t-1} \,,$$

where the parameters ψ and $\sigma_v^2 = E(v_t^2)$ are obtained by solving the system of equations

$$(1 + \psi^2)\sigma_v^2 = E(y_t^2) = E(u_{1t} + u_{2t} + u_{2,t-1})^2 = 3$$

$$\psi\sigma_v^2 = E(y_t y_{t-1}) = 1$$

under the constraint $|\psi| \leq 1$. Thus, $\psi = (3 - \sqrt{5})/2$ and $\sigma_v^2 = 1/\psi = 2.618$. Since $\Sigma_y(1) = \sigma_v^2$ the foregoing claim is confirmed. Hence, in this case, $\Sigma_y(1) < \Sigma_y^u(1)$. The process in Table 5.7 in Chapter 5 is another example of this type. On the other hand, if $\Phi(L)$ is diagonal, $\underline{y}_t^u(h)$ is identical to the optimal predictor (see also Proposition 4.1 and Corollary 4.1.2) and it is easy to construct examples where $\Sigma_{\underline{y}}(1) > \Sigma_{\underline{y}}^u(1)$. In fact, it suffices to choose a diagonal $\Phi(L)$ operator with different elements on the diagonal and F a vector of ones (see Corollary 4.1.2).

In the following subsection conditions for equality of the predictors are provided and some interesting consequences are pointed out.

4.2.3 Equality of the Predictors

In the previous subsection it has been pointed out that the predictors become equivalent for long range forecasting ($h \to \infty$). For some processes and aggregation matrices they are identical for any forecast horizon $h = 1,2,...$. This situation is explored now. Conditions for equality of the predictors are summarized in the following proposition which was given earlier partly by Kohn (1982) and by Lütkepohl (1984a).

PROPOSITION 4.1

Let $\underline{x}_t$ be a K-dimensional stochastic process as in (4.1.1) with univariate subprocesses as in (4.2.6). Also, let F be an $(M \times K)$ matrix of rank M, $\underline{y}_t = F\underline{x}_t$ as in (4.1.4) and the predictors $\underline{y}_t^o(h)$, $\underline{y}_t(h)$, and $\underline{y}_t^u(h)$ as in (4.2.1), (4.2.4), and (4.2.13), respectively. Then

(i) $\underline{y}_t^o(1) = \underline{y}_t(1) \iff F\Phi(L) = \Psi(L)F$;

(ii) $\underline{y}_t^u(1) = \underline{y}_t(1) \iff F\Xi(L) = \Psi(L)F$;

(iii) provided $\Phi(L)$ and $\Xi(L)$ are invertible,
$\underline{y}_t^o(1) = \underline{y}_t^u(1) \iff F\Phi(L)^{-1} = F\Xi(L)^{-1}$.

Proof.

To prove (i) note that

$$\underline{y}_{t+1} - \underline{y}^o_t(1) = F\underline{u}_{t+1} \qquad (4.2.18)$$

and

$$\underline{y}_{t+1} - \underline{y}_t(1) = \underline{v}_{t+1} \,. \qquad (4.2.19)$$

Thus, $\underline{y}^o_t(1) = \underline{y}_t(1)$ implies $F\underline{u}_t = \underline{v}_t$ and, consequently,

$$F\Phi(L)\underline{u}_t = \underline{y}_t = \Psi(L)\underline{v}_t = \Psi(L)F\underline{u}_t \,.$$

Hence, $F\Phi(L) = \Psi(L)F$ follows from $\not{\Sigma}_u$ being nonsingular. In turn, $F\Phi(L) = \Psi(L)F$ implies $F\underline{u}_t = \underline{v}_t$ and therefore (i) follows from (4.2.18) and (4.2.19).

Furthermore, using (4.2.19) and

$$\underline{y}_{t+1} - \underline{y}^u_t(1) = F\underline{w}_{t+1} \,, \qquad (4.2.20)$$

the equality $\underline{y}^u_t(1) = \underline{y}_t(1)$ implies

$$F\Xi(L)\underline{w}_t = \underline{y}_t = \Psi(L)\underline{v}_t = \Psi(L)F\underline{w}_t$$

and thereby $F\Xi(L) = \Psi(L)F$. This equality in turn implies

$$\Psi(L)\underline{v}_t = \underline{y}_t = F\Xi(L)\underline{w}_t = \Psi(L)F\underline{w}_t = \Psi(L)FM(L)\bar{\underline{u}}_t \,, \qquad (4.2.21)$$

where it has been used that $\underline{w}_t$ is nondeterministic and stationary and therefore has the MA representation (4.2.9). From (4.2.21) it follows that $\underline{v}_t = F\bar{\underline{u}}_t = F\underline{w}_t$ and $M_i = 0$ for $i > 0$. Thus (ii) follows from (4.2.19) and (4.2.20).

Finally,

$$\underline{y}^o_t(1) = F\Phi(L)\underline{u}_{t+1} - F\underline{u}_{t+1} \qquad (4.2.22)$$

and

$$\begin{aligned}\underline{y}^u_t(1) &= F\Xi(L)\underline{w}_{t+1} - F\underline{w}_{t+1} \\ &= F\Xi(L)\Xi(L)^{-1}\Phi(L)\underline{u}_{t+1} - F\Xi(L)^{-1}\Phi(L)\underline{u}_{t+1} \,,\end{aligned} \qquad (4.2.23)$$

where $\underline{w}_t = \Xi(L)^{-1}\Phi(L)\underline{u}_t$ has been used (see (4.2.10)). Now (iii) follows immediately from (4.2.22) and (4.2.23). Q.E.D.

The proposition has a number of interesting implications that will be stated as corollaries in the following.

COROLLARY 4.1.1

Under the conditions of Proposition 4.1,

$$\text{(i)}\quad \underline{y}_t^o(h) = \underline{y}_t(h) \quad \text{for } h = 1,2,\ldots \quad \Longleftrightarrow \quad F\Phi(L) = \Psi(L)F\ ;$$

$$\text{(ii)}\quad \underline{y}_t^u(h) = \underline{y}_t(h) \quad \text{for } h = 1,2,\ldots \quad \Longleftrightarrow \quad F\Xi(L) = \Psi(L)F\ ;$$

$$\text{(iii)}\quad \underline{y}_t^o(h) = \underline{y}_t^u(h) \quad \text{for } h = 1,2,\ldots \quad \Longleftrightarrow \quad F\Phi(L)^{-1} = F\Xi(L)^{-1}.$$

This result follows readily from the defining formulas of the three predictors (4.2.1), (4.2.4), and (4.2.13). These formulas show that equality of the 1-step predictors implies equality of the corresponding h-step predictors for $h > 1$. The following result was given by Rose (1977) and can be regarded as in illustration of Proposition 4.1(i).

COROLLARY 4.1.2

Let the components of $\underline{x}_t$ be independent processes with MA representations as in (4.2.6) and let F be a (1 x K) vector with no zero element. Then

$$y_t(1) = y_t^o(1) \Longleftrightarrow \text{all } \xi_k(L) \text{ are identical} \quad \text{for } k = 1,2,\ldots,K.$$

Independence of the components of $\underline{x}_t$ implies a diagonal MA operator

$$\Phi(L) = \begin{bmatrix} \xi_1(L) & & 0 \\ & \ddots & \\ 0 & & \xi_K(L) \end{bmatrix}$$

and hence, the corollary is an immediate consequence of Proposition 4.1 (i). Using $F = I_K$, Proposition 4.1 (iii) implies the following result.

COROLLARY 4.1.3

The univariate forecasts of all components of the invertible process $\underline{x}_t$ are as efficient as the multivariate predictor $\underline{x}_t(h)$, i.e., $\Sigma_{\underline{x}}(h) = \Sigma_{\underline{x}}^u(h)$ for all h, if and only if, $\Phi(L)$ is a diagonal matrix operator.

The following corollary was proved by Tiao & Guttman (1980, Theorem 1) and is also a special case of Proposition 4.1 (i) (see also Corollary 4.1.1)..

COROLLARY 4.1.4

Let F be a (1 x K) vector and $\underline{x}_t$ and y_t as before. The MSEs of the linear combinations

$$c_1 y_t^o(1) + \ldots + c_m y_t^o(m)$$

and

$$c_1 y_t(1) + \ldots + c_m y_t(m)$$

are identical for arbitrary constants $c_1, \ldots, c_m$, if and only if, $F\Phi(L) = \Psi(L)F$.

Kohn (1982) notes another interesting consequence of Proposition 4.1 (i).

COROLLARY 4.1.5

Let $\underline{x}_t$ be a K-dimensional, stationary AR(p) process,

$$\underline{x}_t - \sum_{i=1}^{p} A_i \underline{x}_{t-i} = A(L)\underline{x}_t = \underline{u}_t ,$$

and F an (M x K) matrix of rank M as before. Then $\underline{y}_t^o(1) = \underline{y}_t(1)$ implies that $\underline{y}_t = F\underline{x}_t$ is an AR(p*) process with $p^* \leq p$.

Proof.

The rank of F being M implies that F contains an (M x M) submatrix $\bar{F}$ of rank M. From $\underline{y}_t^o(1) = \underline{y}_t(1)$ it follows by Proposition 4.1 (i) that $FA(L)^{-1} = \Psi(L)F$ and thus, $FA(L) = \Psi(L)^{-1}F$. Denoting $\Psi(L)^{-1}$ by $B(L) = I_M + B_1 L + \ldots$ it follows that $B_i F = 0$ for $i > p$ and hence, $B_i \bar{F} = 0$ which implies $B_i = 0$ for $i > p$. Q.E.D.

Proposition 4.1 also implies characterizations of Granger-causality. This concept is discussed next.

4.2.4 Granger-Causality

Roughly speaking the variables $\underline{z}_t$ are called Granger-causal for the variables $\underline{y}_t$ if the information in the $\underline{z}_t$ process helps to improve the forecasts of $\underline{y}_t$ (Granger (1969 b)). In order to formalize this rough description let J_t contain all the information in the universe available up to period t and let $\Sigma_{\underline{y}}(1|J_t)$ denote the MSE matrix of the optimal 1-step predictor of $\underline{y}_t$ at origin t given that all the information in J_t is taken into account. The vector of variables $\underline{z}_t$ is called Granger-causal for $\underline{y}_t$ if

$$\Sigma_{\underline{y}}(1|J_t) \neq \Sigma_{\underline{y}}(1|J_t \setminus \{\underline{z}_s | s \leq t\}) , \tag{4.2.24}$$

where $J_t \setminus \{\underline{z}_s | s \leq t\}$ is the set containing all the information in the universe except the information in the present and past of the process $\underline{z}_t$. Of course, in (4.2.24) the inequality sign could be replaced by "$\leq$ and $\neq$" because J_t contains at least as much information about the future of $\underline{y}_t$ as $J_t \setminus \{\underline{z}_s | s \leq t\}$.

In practice the foregoing definition is too general to be operational since usually only a fraction of all information in the universe will be available. Therefore the information set is often limited to contain only the available information on the variables of the system, that is,

$$J_t = \{(\underline{y}_s', \underline{z}_s')' | s \leq t\}. \tag{4.2.25}$$

Furthermore, in practice, usually only linear predictors are compared.

If $\underline{x}_t = (\underline{y}_t', \underline{z}_t')'$ is as in (4.1.1) with invertible MA representation partitioned accordingly,

$$\underline{x}_t = \begin{bmatrix} \underline{y}_t \\ \underline{z}_t \end{bmatrix} = \begin{bmatrix} \Phi_{11}(L) & \Phi_{12}(L) \\ \Phi_{21}(L) & \Phi_{22}(L) \end{bmatrix} \underline{u}_t \tag{4.2.26}$$

then, assuming $\underline{y}_t$ is M-dimensional, $\underline{y}_t = F\underline{x}_t$ with $F = (I_M \quad 0)$. Therefore the optimal linear 1-step predictor based on J_t (as given in (4.2.25)) is $\underline{y}_t^o(1) = F\underline{x}_t(1)$. Invertibility of $\Phi(L)$ implies that $\underline{y}_t$ has the invertible MA representation $\underline{y}_t = \Psi(L)\underline{v}_t$ and the optimal predictor based on $\{\underline{y}_s | s \leq t\} = J_t \setminus \{\underline{z}_s | s \leq t\}$ is $\underline{y}_t(1)$.

By Proposition 4.1 (i) equality of $\underline{y}_t^o(1)$ and $\underline{y}_t(1)$ (i.e. noncausality) is equivalent to

$$F\Phi(L) = [\Phi_{11}(L) \quad \Phi_{12}(L)] = \Psi(L)F = [\Psi(L) \quad 0].$$

Therefore, $\underline{z}_t$ is not Granger-causal for $\underline{y}_t$ if and only if $\Phi_{12}(L) = 0$ and $\underline{z}_t$ is Granger-causal for $\underline{y}_t$ if and only if $\Phi_{12}(L) \neq 0$. If

$$\begin{bmatrix} A_{11}(L) & A_{12}(L) \\ A_{21}(L) & A_{22}(L) \end{bmatrix} \begin{bmatrix} \underline{y}_t \\ \underline{z}_t \end{bmatrix} = \underline{u}_t$$

is the correspondingly partitioned AR representation of $\underline{x}_t$ this result implies that $\underline{z}_t$ is not Granger-causal for $\underline{y}_t$ if and only if $A_{12}(L) = 0$.

The fact that the restrictions for noncausality are easily testable, to some extent explains the popularity of the concept of Granger-causality although it must be admitted that a bit of the original concept has been sacrificed on the way from the original definition to the practical, testable concept underlying the simple constraints for the MA and AR coefficients. For an extensive and detailed discussion of the pros and cons of the concept the reader is referred to Kirchgässner (1981), Tjøstheim (1981), Geweke (1982), Newbold (1982), Lütkepohl (1982 b), Engle, Hendry & Richard (1983) among many others. Tests for Granger-noncausality are described and compared, for instance, by Geweke, Meese & Dent (1983).

The fact that the equality of the predictors $\underline{y}_t(1)$ and $\underline{y}_t^o(1)$ can be checked easily by testing zero constraints if $F = (I_M \;\; 0)$ can be exploited to construct a simple test for predictor equality also for more general F matrices. Since the (M x K) matrix F is assumed to have rank M, there exists a ((K - M) x K) matrix C such that

$$\mathcal{F} = \begin{bmatrix} F \\ C \end{bmatrix}$$

is nonsingular. Defining $\underline{z}_t = \mathcal{F}\underline{x}_t$ it is easy to verify that $\underline{z}_t$ has an MA representation $\underline{z}_t = \tilde{\underline{u}}_t + \tilde{\Phi}_1\tilde{\underline{u}}_{t-1} + \ldots$, where $\tilde{\underline{u}}_t = \mathcal{F}\underline{u}_t$ and $\tilde{\Phi}_i = \mathcal{F}\Phi_i\mathcal{F}^{-1}$ and $\underline{z}_t(h) = \underline{z}_t^o(h) (= \mathcal{F}\underline{x}_t(h))$. Since $\underline{y}_t = (I_M \;\; 0)\underline{z}_t$, it suffices to test zero constraints on the $\tilde{\Phi}_i$ in order to check the hypothesis that $\underline{y}_t(1) = \underline{y}_t^o(1)$.

4.3 FORECASTING LINEARLY TRANSFORMED NONSTATIONARY PROCESSES

For the types of nonstationary processes discussed in Chapters 2 and 3 the treatment of linear transformations does not pose any serious additional problems. For illustrative purposes let $\underline{x}_t$ be such that it is stationary after differencing once, that is,

$$\underline{x}_t = \underline{x}_{t-1} + \underline{x}_t^s, \tag{4.3.1}$$

where $\underline{x}_t^s$ is a stationary process with MA representation

$$\underline{x}_t^s = \Phi(L)\underline{u}_t \tag{4.3.2}$$

and $\Phi(L)$ is as in (4.1.1). Note that $\det(\Phi(z))$ may have roots on the unit circle. These roots may be induced by overdifferencing, that is, it is possible that $\underline{x}_t$ is stationary without differencing all of its components. The starting period of $\underline{x}_t$ is assumed to be $t_o > -\infty$ whereas $\underline{x}_t^s$ is assumed to be started at $-\infty$ and $\underline{x}_{t_o} = \underline{x}_{t_o}^s$.

Let F be again an (M x K) matrix of rank M and suppose that interest centers on

$$\underline{y}_t = F\underline{x}_t = F\underline{x}_{t-1} + F\underline{x}_t^s = \underline{y}_{t-1} + \underline{y}_t^s , \tag{4.3.3}$$

where $\underline{y}_t^s$ is a stationary process with MA representation

$$\underline{y}_t^s = \Psi(L)\underline{v}_t \tag{4.3.4}$$

and $\Psi(L)$ is as in (4.1.4).

Now the following forecasts may be compared:

$$\underline{y}_t^o(h) = \underline{y}_t + \sum_{j=1}^{h} \underline{y}_t^{so}(j) , \tag{4.3.5}$$

$$\underline{y}_t(h) = \underline{y}_t + \sum_{j=1}^{h} \underline{y}_t^{s}(j) , \tag{4.3.6}$$

and

$$\underline{y}_t^u(h) = \underline{y}_t + \sum_{j=1}^{h} \underline{y}_t^{su}(j) , \tag{4.3.7}$$

where $\underline{y}_t^{so}(j) = F\underline{x}_t^s(j)$ and $\underline{y}_t^{su}(j) = F\underline{x}_t^{su}(j)$, $\underline{x}_t^{su}(j)$ being the j-step predictor based on the univariate components of $\underline{x}_t^s$ (see (4.2.12)). Furthermore, let

$$\underline{\Sigma}_{\underline{X}^s}(h) , \quad \underline{\Sigma}_{\underline{Y}^s}(h) , \quad \text{and} \quad \underline{\Sigma}^u_{\underline{X}^s}(h) \tag{4.3.8}$$

denote the MSE matrices of

$$\begin{bmatrix} \underline{x}_t^s(1) \\ \vdots \\ \underline{x}_t^s(h) \end{bmatrix} , \quad \begin{bmatrix} \underline{y}_t^s(1) \\ \vdots \\ \underline{y}_t^s(h) \end{bmatrix} , \quad \text{and} \quad \begin{bmatrix} \underline{x}_t^{su}(1) \\ \vdots \\ \underline{x}_t^{su}(h) \end{bmatrix}$$

respectively (see Chapter 3, Section 3.1).

With this notation the MSE matrix of $\underline{y}_t^o(h)$ is easily seen to be

$$\Sigma_{\underline{y}}^o(h) = FH_h^K \Sigma_{\underline{x}^s}(h) H_h^{K\prime} F' , \tag{4.3.9}$$

where $H_h^K = [I_K \; I_K \; \dots \; I_K]$ is a (K x Kh) matrix. Also,

$$\Sigma_{\underline{y}}(h) = H_h^M \Sigma_{\underline{y}^s}(h) H_h^{M\prime} \tag{4.3.10}$$

and

$$\Sigma_{\underline{y}}^u(h) = FH_h^K \Sigma_{\underline{x}^s}^u(h) H_h^{K\prime} F' . \tag{4.3.11}$$

From the results in Sections 4.2.1 and 4.2.2 it follows that

$$\Sigma_{\underline{y}}(h) \geq \Sigma_{\underline{y}}^o(h) \quad \text{and} \quad \Sigma_{\underline{y}}^u(h) \geq \Sigma_{\underline{y}}^o(h) , \tag{4.3.12}$$

so that $\underline{y}_t^o(h)$ is still optimal, while it depends on the particular structure of the process $\underline{x}_t$ and the transformation matrix F which one of the predictors $\underline{y}_t(h)$ and $\underline{y}_t^u(h)$ is to be preferred.

A deviation from the stationary case is that the differences between the three MSE matrices will not vanish with increasing forecast horizon h. In the present nonstationary case the variance - covariance matrix of $\underline{y}_t$ will increase for growing t and will in general approach infinity as $t \to \infty$. Therefore the forecast MSEs will also increase without bounds for $h \to \infty$.

The conditions for equality of the predictors are the same as for the stationary case given in Proposition 4.1. For the condition $F\Phi(L)^{-1} = F\Xi(L)^{-1}$ in Proposition 4.1 (iii) to be meaningful, invertibility of $\Phi(L)$ and $\Xi(L)$ (containing the univariate MA operators of the components of $\underline{x}_t^s$) must be assumed so that overdifferencing will be a problem. Of course, it is easy to extend the foregoing discussion to handle cases where different differencing operators have to be applied for different components of $\underline{x}_t$. However, it should be noted that even if the differenced components of $\underline{x}_t$ have invertible univariate MA representations this does not guarantee that the same differences may be applied in the multivariate system if invertibility of the multivariate MA representation is crucial (see Chapter 2, Section 2.2).

4.4 LINEARLY TRANSFORMED VECTOR ARMA PROCESSES

When the parameters of a process have to be estimated a representation with only a finite number of parameters is needed. Therefore it is important that a linearly transformed finite order vector ARMA process also has an ARMA representation with finite orders. A detailed discussion of this result is the subject of this section. In the first subsection it is shown that a linearly transformed MA(q) process is again an MA process with order not greater than q. This result is used in the second subsection to obtain an ARMA representation of a linear transformation of a vector ARMA(p,q) process.

4.4.1 Finite Order MA Processes

Let $\underline{x}_t$ be a K-dimensional finite order MA(q) process,

$$\underline{x}_t = \underline{u}_t + M_1\underline{u}_{t-1} + \dots + M_q\underline{u}_{t-q} = M(L)\underline{u}_t \tag{4.4.1}$$

with $\det(M(z)) \neq 0$ for $|z| < 1$ and positive definite white noise covariance matrix $\Sigma_{\underline{u}}$. Further let F be an (M x K) matrix of rank M. Since $\underline{y}_t = F\underline{x}_t$ is nondeterministic it has an MA representation

$$\underline{y}_t = \underline{v}_t + \Psi_1\underline{v}_{t-1} + \dots = \Psi(L)\underline{v}_t \tag{4.4.2}$$

with $\det(\Psi(z)) \neq 0$ for $|z| < 1$ and nonsingular covariance matrix $\Sigma_{\underline{v}}$ of $\underline{v}_t$ (see Section 4.1). Now the relation $\Sigma_{\underline{y}}(h) \geq \Sigma^o_{\underline{y}}(h)$ implies that $\Psi_i = 0$ for $i > q$. This can be seen by noting that

$$\Sigma^o_{\underline{y}}(h) = F\Sigma_{\underline{x}}(h)F' = F\Sigma_{\underline{x}}F' = \Sigma_{\underline{y}} \quad \text{for} \quad h > q \tag{4.4.3}$$

because $\underline{x}_t$ has a finite order MA representation (see Chapter 3, (3.1.6) and (3.1.8)). Consequently,

$$\Sigma_{\underline{y}}(h) = \sum_{i=0}^{h-1} \Psi_i\Sigma_{\underline{v}}\Psi_i' = \Sigma_{\underline{y}} \quad \text{for} \quad h > q .$$

In other words,

$$\sum_{i=q+1}^{h-1} \Psi_i\Sigma_{\underline{v}}\Psi_i' = 0$$

and hence, $\Psi_i = 0$ for $i > q$ since $\Sigma_{\underline{v}}$ is positive definite. This result has some interesting consequences and is therefore stated as a proposition.

PROPOSITION 4.2

Let $\underline{x}_t$ be a K-dimensional MA(q) process and F an (M x K) matrix of rank M. Then the process $\underline{y}_t = F\underline{x}_t$ has an MA(q*) representation with $q^* \leq q$.

It is easy to construct examples where q* is strictly less than q. Consider, for instance, the process (4.2.17) with F = (0, 1). The proposition is also an immediate consequence of the properties of the spectral representations of $\underline{x}_t$ and $\underline{y}_t$ (see Lütkepohl (1986 a, Kapitel 2, 2.A.1)). Also, it may be worth noting that the requirements that $\Sigma_{\underline{u}}$ be positive definite and rank F = M, so that $\underline{x}_t$ and $\underline{y}_t$ have no linearly dependent components, are not really necessary for Proposition 4.2 to hold. These conditions are stated here merely for convenience. The result in the proposition and special cases have been proved and discussed, for instance, by T.W. Anderson (1971, pp. 224 - 225), O.D. Anderson (1975 a, b, 1978), Granger & Morris (1976), Box & Jenkins (1976), Rose (1977), Ansley, Spivey & Wrobleski (1977), Teräsvirta (1977), Tiao & Guttman (1980), and Lütkepohl (1984 a).

4.4.2 ARMA Processes

Suppose now that $\underline{x}_t$ is a K-dimensional ARMA(p,q) process as in Chapter 2, (2.3.5),

$$\Theta(L)\underline{x}_t = M(L)\underline{u}_t , \tag{4.4.4}$$

where $\underline{u}_t$ is as in (4.4.1),

$$\begin{aligned}\Theta(L) &= I_K - \Theta_1 L - \dots - \Theta_p L^p \\ &= [\theta_{ij}(L)]_{i,j} = \left[\sum_{n=0}^{p_{ij}} \theta_{ij,n} L^n\right]_{i,j = 1,\dots,K} ,\end{aligned} \tag{4.4.5}$$

where $p = \max\{p_{ij} \mid i,j = 1,\dots,K\}$, and

$$\begin{aligned}M(L) &= I_K + M_1 L + \dots + M_q L^q \\ &= [\mu_{ij}(L)]_{i,j} = \left[\sum_{n=0}^{q_{ij}} \mu_{ij,n} L^n\right]_{i,j = 1,\dots,K} ,\end{aligned} \tag{4.4.6}$$

where $q = \max\{q_{ij} | i,j = 1,\ldots,K\}$ and $\det(M(z)) \neq 0$ for $|z| < 1$. At this point it is not assumed that $\underline{x}_t$ is stationary, that is, $\det(\Theta(z))$ may have roots on the unit circle. With this notation the following corollary is an easy consequence of Proposition 4.2.

COROLLARY 4.2.1

Let F be an (M x K) matrix of rank M. Then $\underline{y}_t = F\underline{x}_t$ has an ARMA-(p^*, q^*) representation with

$$p^* \leq \deg\det(\Theta(L)) = g \tag{4.4.7}$$

and

$$q^* \leq \max\{[\deg\Theta_{ij}(L)] - (g-p^*) + q_{in} \mid i,j,n = 1,\ldots,K\}, \tag{4.4.8}$$

where deg(•) denotes the degree of a polynomial and $\Theta_{ij}(L)$ is the ij-th cofactor of $\Theta(L)$.

Proof.

Multiplying (4.4.4) by the adjoint $\Theta(L)^*$ of $\Theta(L)$ gives an ARMA representation

$$\det(\Theta(L))\underline{x}_t = \Theta(L)^*M(L)\underline{u}_t \tag{4.4.9}$$

(see Chapter 2, (2.3.8)). Thus, $\underline{y}_t = F\underline{x}_t$ has an ARMA representation

$$\det(\Theta(L))\underline{y}_t = F\Theta(L)^*M(L)\underline{u}_t , \tag{4.4.10}$$

where the AR operator has the order $g = \deg\det(\Theta(L))$. By Proposition 4.2 the order of the MA operator is not greater than

$$\max\{[\deg\Theta_{ij}(L)] + q_{in} \mid i,j,n = 1,\ldots,K\}$$

because

$$\Theta(L)^*M(L) = \left[\sum_{i=1}^{K} \Theta_{ij}(L)\mu_{in}(L)\right]_{j,n=1,\ldots,K} .$$

The corollary follows since cancellation of factors in the AR and MA operators is possible. Q.E.D.

It should be understood that Corollary 4.2.1 gives but one set of upper bounds for an ARMA representation of $\underline{y}_t$. In Chapter 2, Section 2.3, it has been pointed out that the vector ARMA representation is not unique unless certain constraints are imposed. Thus, in general, there will be different ARMA representations of $\underline{y}_t$ with orders possibly smaller than those in (4.4.7) and (4.4.8). As a trivial example consider the case where F is a nonsingular matrix. Then $\underline{y}_t$ has also an ARMA(p,q) representation (see Section 2.3.1) while the bounds in (4.4.7) and (4.4.8) may be as large as Kp and (K - 1)p + q, respectively.

As another example consider an M-dimensional subprocess of $\underline{x}_t$, say $\underline{y}_t = \underline{x}_{1t} = (x_{1t},\ldots,x_{Mt})' = F\underline{x}_t$ with $F = (I_M \quad 0)$. Defining $\underline{x}_{2t} = (x_{M+1,t},\ldots,x_{Kt})'$ and partitioning $\underline{u}_t$, $\Theta(L)$, and $M(L)$ appropriately, the system $\underline{x}_t = (\underline{x}_{1t}', \underline{x}_{2t}')'$ can be written as

$$\Theta_{11}(L)\underline{x}_{1t} + \Theta_{12}(L)\underline{x}_{2t} = M_{11}(L)\underline{u}_{1t} + M_{12}(L)\underline{u}_{2t} \qquad (4.4.11)$$

$$\Theta_{21}(L)\underline{x}_{1t} + \Theta_{22}(L)\underline{x}_{2t} = M_{21}(L)\underline{u}_{1t} + M_{22}(L)\underline{u}_{2t} \,. \qquad (4.4.12)$$

Multiplying the second equation by the adjoint $\Theta_{22}(L)^*$ of $\Theta_{22}(L)$ gives

$$\det(\Theta_{22}(L))\underline{x}_{2t} = -\Theta_{22}(L)^*\Theta_{21}(L)\underline{x}_{1t} + \Theta_{22}(L)^*M_{21}(L)\underline{u}_{1t} + \\ + \Theta_{22}(L)^*M_{22}(L)\underline{u}_{2t} \,. \qquad (4.4.13)$$

Furthermore, multiplying (4.4.11) by $\det(\Theta_{22}(L))$ and replacing $\det(\Theta_{22}(L))\underline{x}_{2t}$ by the right-hand side of (4.4.13) results in

$$[\det(\Theta_{22}(L))\Theta_{11}(L) - \Theta_{12}(L)\Theta_{22}(L)^*\Theta_{21}(L)]\underline{x}_{1t}$$

$$= [\det(\Theta_{22}(L))M_{11}(L) - \Theta_{12}(L)\Theta_{22}(L)^*M_{21}(L)]\underline{u}_{1t}$$

$$+ [\det(\Theta_{22}(L))M_{12}(L) - \Theta_{12}(L)\Theta_{22}(L)^*M_{22}(L)]\underline{u}_{2t} \,. \qquad (4.4.14)$$

Using this representation Proposition 4.2 implies that $\underline{y}_t = \underline{x}_{1t}$ has an ARMA(p*,q*) representation with

$$p^* \leq \max\{(K-M)p + p,\ (K-M-1)p + p + p\} = (K-M+1)p \qquad (4.4.15)$$

and

$$q^* \leq \max\{(K-M)p + q,\ p + (K-M-1)p + q\} = (K-M)p + q \qquad (4.4.16)$$

These upper bounds may be smaller than those in Corollary 4.2.1 and they can be used for an arbitrary (M x K) transformation matrix F of rank M. Defining

$$\mathcal{F} = \begin{bmatrix} F \\ C \end{bmatrix},$$

where C is such that $\mathcal{F}$ is a nonsingular (K x K) matrix, the process $\underline{z}_t = \mathcal{F}\underline{x}_t$ has a vector ARMA(p,q) representation. Hence, by the foregoing considerations, $\underline{y}_t = (I_M \; 0)\underline{z}_t = F\underline{x}_t$ has an ARMA(p*, q*) representation, where p* and q* are as in (4.4.15) and (4.4.16) respectively. Thereby the following result is established.

COROLLARY 4.2.2

Let F be an (M x K) matrix of rank M. Then $\underline{y}_t = F\underline{x}_t$ has an ARMA(p*, q*) representation with

$$p^* \leq (K-M+1)p \tag{4.4.17}$$

and

$$q^* \leq (K-M)p + q . \tag{4.4.18}$$

These results will be useful in the empirical studies in the next chapter and it should be remembered that stationarity and invertibility of $\underline{x}_t$ has not been assumed here.

4.5 SUMMARY AND COMMENTS

In this chapter forecasting linearly transformed processes has been considered. Three predictors have been compared: (1) the optimal predictor of the original process is transformed linearly; (2) the transformed process is forecast directly; (3) the univariate component series of the original process are predicted based on their own past only and the predictors are then transformed. The first predictor is based on the disaggregate, original process and hence uses the greatest information set and is therefore optimal under a mean squared error criterion. A generally valid ranking of the second and third alternatives cannot be given, that is, it depends on the original process and the transformation matrix which of the two predictors has smaller MSEs. Necessary and sufficient conditions for equality of the predictors have been given and, as an immediate consequence, characterizations of Granger-causality have been obtained. Furthermore, extensions to such nonstationary processes that can be made stationary by differencing have been discussed. Finally, linear transformations of vector ARMA processes have been considered. It was found that a linear transformation of a finite order vector ARMA process is again an ARMA process and different sets of upper bounds for the orders of the latter have been derived.

In practice the considered processes will often have a nonzero mean vector $\underline{\mu}$. As long as $\underline{\mu}$ is assumed known there will be no additional problems. All the results of this chapter hold for the zero mean parts of the considered processes. For instance, if $\underline{x}_t = \underline{\mu} + \underline{z}_t$, where $\underline{z}_t$ is a zero mean process, then the linearly transformed process $F\underline{x}_t = F\underline{\mu} + F\underline{z}_t$ consists also of a zero mean part $F\underline{z}_t$ and the transformed mean term $F\underline{\mu}$. Thus, the interesting part is really the zero mean part which has been discussed in this chapter.

Another problem arising in practice is more serious, namely the involved processes are usually unknown and have to be estimated. In Chapter 3 it has been demonstrated that this has consequences for the forecast MSEs and therefore prediction of contemporaneously aggregated <u>estimated</u> processes is discussed in the next chapter.

CHAPTER 5. FORECASTING CONTEMPORANEOUSLY AGGREGATED ESTIMATED PROCESSES

In the previous chapter three predictors have been compared for a contemporaneously aggregated vector stochastic process. The first predictor is obtained by aggregating the forecasts based on the original process. The second predictor results from forecasting the aggregate process directly based on the aggregate variables. Finally, the third predictor is obtained from aggregating univariate forecasts of the individual components of the disaggregate process. The comparison has been carried out under the assumption that the predictors are based on known processes.

In this chapter this unrealistic assumption will be replaced by the assumption that the process orders and/or parameters are unknown and have to be estimated. For simplicity it will be assumed that a weighted sum of the components of the disaggregate process is considered so that the aggregate process is univariate. The discussion can easily be generalized to other types of contemporaneous aggregation. However, the notation will be somewhat more cumbersome in the general case where a multivariate aggregate is considered without providing more insight into the problems of interest.

In the first section the required notation and some basic results from the previous chapter will be summarized and in Section 5.2 predictors based on processes with estimated coefficients will be discussed. In Section 5.3 the case of unknown orders and estimated coefficients is considered and some comments on nonstationary processes with estimated orders and/or coefficients are provided in Section 5.4. The small sample properties of the three predictors are studied by means of a Monte Carlo experiment in the fifth section and an empirical example is discussed in detail in Section 5.6. Conclusions are contained in Section 5.7. Some of the results of this chapter have been previously published (see Lütkepohl (1984b, 1985c, 1986a)).

5.1 SUMMARY OF ASSUMPTIONS AND PREDICTORS

In this chapter contemporaneous aggregation will be considered in a slightly more special setting than in Chapter 4. It is now assumed that $\underline{x}_t$ is a K-dimensional Gaussian (normally distributed) stationary stochastic process with MA representation

$$\underline{x}_t = \underline{\mu}_x + \sum_{i=0}^{\infty} \Phi_i \underline{u}_{t-i} = \underline{\mu}_x + \Phi(L)\underline{u}_t \tag{5.1.1}$$

where $\Phi_0 = I_K$, $\underline{\mu}_x = (\mu_1,\ldots,\mu_K)' = E(\underline{x}_t)$, $\underline{u}_t$ is Gaussian white noise with nonsingular covariance matrix $\Sigma_{\underline{u}}$,

$$\det(\Phi(z)) \neq 0 \quad \text{for } |z| \leq 1 \quad , \tag{5.1.2}$$

and

$$\sum_{i=0}^{\infty} \sqrt{tr(\Phi_i'\Phi_i)} < \infty \quad . \tag{5.1.3}$$

Consequently, $\underline{x}_t$ also has an AR representation,

$$\underline{x}_t - \sum_{i=1}^{\infty} A_i \underline{x}_{t-i} = A(L)\underline{x}_t = \underline{\nu}_x + \underline{u}_t \tag{5.1.4}$$

with $A(z) = \Phi(z)^{-1}$, $\det(A(z)) \neq 0$ for $|z| \leq 1$ and $\underline{\nu}_x = A(1)\underline{\mu}_x$. These conditions are, for instance, satisfied if $\underline{x}_t$ is a stationary and invertible ARMA process and in much of what follows it is in fact assumed that $\underline{x}_t$ is such a process.

For simplicity it is now assumed that the aggregate process is univariate, that is, F is a (1 x K) nonzero vector and $y_t = F\underline{x}_t$. From Chapter 4 it is known that y_t also has an MA representation,

$$y_t = \mu_y + \sum_{i=0}^{\infty} \psi_i v_{t-i} = \mu_y + \psi(L)v_t \quad , \tag{5.1.5}$$

where $\mu_y = F\underline{\mu}_x$, $\psi_0 = 1$, and $\psi(z) \neq 0$ for $|z| \leq 1$. Furthermore y_t has an AR representation

$$y_t - \sum_{i=1}^{\infty} \theta_i y_{t-i} = \theta(L)y_t = \nu_y + v_t \tag{5.1.6}$$

with $\theta(L) = \psi(L)^{-1}$ and $\theta(z) \neq 0$ for $|z| \leq 1$.

Moreover, the individual components of $\underline{x}_t$ have univariate MA representations,

$$x_{kt} = \mu_k + \sum_{i=0}^{\infty} \xi_{ki} w_{k,t-i} = \mu_k + \xi_k(L) w_{kt} , \qquad k = 1,\dots,K , \quad (5.1.7)$$

or, in matrix notation,

$$\underline{x}_t = \underline{\mu}_x + \sum_{i=0}^{\infty} \Xi_i \underline{w}_{t-i} = \underline{\mu}_x + \Xi(L)\underline{w}_t \quad (5.1.8)$$

with $\xi_k(z) \neq 0$ for $|z| \leq 1$ and $\Xi(L)$ being a diagonal matrix operator with the $\xi_k(L)$ on the diagonal. The component processes also have AR representations

$$x_{kt} - \sum_{i=1}^{\infty} \eta_{ki} x_{k,t-i} = \eta_k(L) x_{kt} = \nu_k + w_{kt} , \qquad k = 1,\dots,K , (5.1.9)$$

where $\nu_k = \eta_k(1)\mu_k$ and $\eta_k(L) = \xi_k(L)^{-1}$.

The three predictors to be compared in the following are summarized in Table 5.1 together with their mean squared errors for known processes. The reader is referred to the previous chapter for a more detailed discussion. A lower case σ^2 is used to denote the MSEs which are now scalars rather than matrices. Also, in the following, if the process is not indicated, it is understood that the MSEs of predictors for y_t are meant. Note that

$$\sigma_o^2(h) , \sigma^2(h) , \sigma_u^2(h) \xrightarrow[h \to \infty]{} \sigma_y^2 , \quad (5.1.10)$$

where σ_y^2 is the variance of y_t . In the following sections interest centers on the MSEs when the processes are estimated rather than known.

5.2 ESTIMATED COEFFICIENTS

In this section it is assumed that the coefficients of the involved processes are estimated and the MSEs can be approximated as in Chapter 3, Section 3.2. The disaggregate process $\underline{x}_t$ is assumed to be a Gaussian vector ARMA process with finite, known orders. Then, using results of the previous chapter, Section 4.4, the component series x_{kt} , $k = 1,\dots,K$ and y_t are also finite order Gaussian vector ARMA processes. In Chapter 4 it was only shown that a linear transformation of a finite order ARMA process is again of finite order ARMA type. The normal distribution follows from the well-known result that linear

Table 5.1. Predictors and Mean Squared Errors

Predictor	Description	Mean Squared Error
$y_t^o(h) = F\underline{x}_t(h) = F(\underline{\mu}_x + \sum_{i=0}^{\infty} \Phi_{h+i}\underline{u}_{t-i})$ $= F(\underline{\nu}_x + \sum_{i=1}^{h-1} A_i\underline{x}_t(h-i) + \sum_{i=h}^{\infty} A_i\underline{x}_{t+h-i})$	prediction of disaggregate process and aggregation of disaggregate **forecasts**	$\sigma_o^2(h) = F\Sigma_{\underline{x}}(h)F'$ $= F(\sum_{i=0}^{h-1} \Phi_i\Sigma_{\underline{u}}\Phi_i')F'$
$y_t(h) = \mu_y + \sum_{i=0}^{\infty} \psi_{h+i}v_{t-i}$ $= \nu_y + \sum_{i=1}^{h-1} \theta_i y_t(h-i) + \sum_{i=h}^{\infty} \theta_i y_{t+h-i}$	prediction based on aggregated process	$\sigma^2(h) = \sigma_v^2 \sum_{i=0}^{h-1} \psi_i^2$
$y_t^u(h) = F\underline{x}_t^u(h) = F(\underline{\mu}_x + \sum_{i=0}^{\infty} \Xi_{h+i}\underline{w}_{t-i})$ $= F\begin{bmatrix} \nu_1 + \sum_{i=1}^{h-1} \eta_{1i}x_{1t}^u(h-i) + \sum_{i=h}^{\infty} \eta_{1i}x_{1,t+h-i} \\ \vdots \\ \nu_K + \sum_{i=1}^{h-1} \eta_{Ki}x_{Kt}^u(h-i) + \sum_{i=h}^{\infty} \eta_{Ki}x_{K,t+h-i} \end{bmatrix}$	univariate prediction of the individual component series and aggregation of forecasts	$\sigma_u^2(h) = F[\,I_K \Xi_1 \ldots \Xi_{h-1}\,]\times$ $\mathbf{E}\left[\begin{bmatrix} \underline{w}_{t+h} \\ \vdots \\ \underline{w}_{t+1} \end{bmatrix} \begin{bmatrix} \underline{w}_{t+h} \\ \vdots \\ \underline{w}_{t+1} \end{bmatrix}'\right] \begin{bmatrix} I_K \\ \Xi_1' \\ \vdots \\ \Xi_{h-1}' \end{bmatrix} F'$

transformations of normal random vectors are normal. The coefficients of all processes are assumed to be estimated with ML procedures using realizations from processes independent of those used for forecasting and with identical stochastic structures. The sample size or time series length used for estimation is denoted by T. A more detailed discussion of the conditions underlying the asymptotic MSEs used in this section is given in Section 3.2.

The predictors obtained by replacing the true parameters in Table 5.1 by ML estimators will be furnished with a caret as in Chapter 3. For example,

$$\hat{y}_t(h) = \hat{\mu}_y + \sum_{i=0}^{\infty} \hat{\psi}_{h+i} v_{t-i} \qquad (5.2.1)$$

is the predictor with estimated coefficients corresponding to $y_t(h)$ and $\hat{\mu}_y$, $\hat{\psi}_i$ are the ML estimators. The asymptotic MSE corresponding to the predictor $\hat{y}_t(h)$ is

$$\hat{\sigma}^2(h) = \sigma^2(h) + \frac{1}{T}(\omega_y(h) + g_y(h)) \quad , \qquad (5.2.2)$$

where $\omega_y(h) + g_y(h)$ is the variance of the asymptotic distribution of $\sqrt{T}(\hat{y}_t(h) - y_t(h))$, $\omega_y(h)$ being the contribution from estimating the ARMA parameters and $g_y(h)$ being due to estimating the mean term. Furthermore, the asymptotic MSE matrix of $\hat{\underline{x}}_t(h)$ is

$$\hat{\Sigma}_{\underline{x}}(h) = \Sigma_{\underline{x}}(h) + \frac{1}{T}(\Omega_{\underline{x}}(h) + G_{\underline{x}}(h)) \quad , \qquad (5.2.3)$$

where $\Omega_{\underline{x}}(h) + G_{\underline{x}}(h)$ is the covariance matrix of the asymptotic distribution of $\sqrt{T}(\hat{\underline{x}}_t(h) - \underline{x}_t(h))$ (see Chapter 3, (3.2.16)). The MSE of $\hat{y}^o_t(h) = F\hat{\underline{x}}_t(h)$ is therefore

$$\hat{\sigma}^2_o(h) = F\hat{\Sigma}_{\underline{x}}(h)F' = \sigma^2_o(h) + \frac{1}{T}F\Omega_{\underline{x}}(h)F' + \frac{1}{T}FG_{\underline{x}}(h)F' \quad . \qquad (5.2.4)$$

Before discussing the MSE of $\hat{y}^u_t(h)$, the MSEs $\hat{\sigma}^2(h)$ and $\hat{\sigma}^2_o(h)$ will now be compared.

5.2.1 Comparison of $\hat{y}^o_t(h)$ and $\hat{y}_t(h)$

As shown in Chapter 4,

$$\sigma^2_o(h) \leq \sigma^2(h) \quad . \qquad (5.2.5)$$

If a strict inequality holds in (5.2.5) the same will hold for $\hat{\sigma}_o^2(h)$ and $\hat{\sigma}^2(h)$ if T is large enough. Therefore a case of primary interest in the following is when $\underline{x}_t$ and F are such that $\sigma_o^2(h) = \sigma^2(h)$, that is, $y_t^o(h) = y_t(h)$ (see Proposition 4.1), so that the estimation variability is the only source of differences in the MSEs. Hence, the difference between $\omega_y(h) + g_y(h)$ and $F\Omega_{\underline{x}}(h)F' + FG_{\underline{x}}(h)F'$ is of interest. The effect of estimating the possibly nonzero process mean will be considered first.

Note that

$$\bar{y} = \frac{1}{T}\sum_{t=1}^{T} y_t = \frac{1}{T}\sum_{t=1}^{T} F\underline{x}_t = F\bar{\underline{x}} . \qquad (5.2.6)$$

If $\bar{y}$ is used as an estimator for μ_y and $\underline{\mu}_x$ is estimated by $\bar{\underline{x}}$, the contribution of the mean term to the forecast MSEs $\hat{\sigma}^2(h)$ and $\hat{\sigma}^2(h)$ is the same provided $y_t^o(h) = y_t(h)$. Since using the sample means is asymptotically equivalent to ML estimation of the mean terms (see Chapter 2, Section 2.4.1) it follows that $g_y(h) = FG_{\underline{x}}(h)F'$ in the present case. Formally this can be seen from the definitions of $g_y(h)$ and $G_{\underline{x}}(h)$ (see (3.2.17)).

$$g_y(h) = \sigma_{\bar{y}}^2 E\left[\frac{\partial y_t(h)}{\partial \mu_y}\right]^2 = F\Sigma_{\bar{\underline{x}}}F' E\left[\frac{\partial y_t(h)}{\partial \mu_y}\right]^2$$

and

$$FG_{\underline{x}}(h)F' = FE\left[\frac{\partial \underline{x}_t(h)}{\partial \underline{\mu}_x'} \Sigma_{\bar{\underline{x}}} \frac{\partial \underline{x}_t(h)'}{\partial \underline{\mu}_x}\right]F'$$

$$= E\left[\frac{\partial y_t(h)}{\partial \underline{\mu}_x'} \Sigma_{\bar{\underline{x}}} \frac{\partial y_t(h)}{\partial \underline{\mu}_x}\right]$$

$$= E\left[\frac{\partial y_t(h)}{\partial (\underline{\mu}_x'F')} \frac{\partial (\underline{\mu}_x'F')}{\partial \underline{\mu}_x'} \Sigma_{\bar{\underline{x}}} \frac{\partial y_t(h)}{\partial (F\underline{\mu}_x)} \frac{\partial (F\underline{\mu}_x)}{\partial \underline{\mu}_x}\right]$$

$$= E\left[\frac{\partial y_t(h)}{\partial \mu_y} F\Sigma_{\bar{\underline{x}}}F' \frac{\partial y_t(h)}{\partial \mu_y}\right] = g_y(h) \qquad (5.2.7)$$

where $y_t(h) = y_t^o(h) = F\underline{x}_t(h)$ has been used. Thus, in the present situation, where $\sigma^2(h) = \sigma_o^2(h)$ is assumed, the relative performance of the two predictors with estimated coefficients depends on the terms $\omega_y(h)$ and $F\Omega_{\underline{x}}(h)F'$ only.

It turns out that if the restrictions implied by $y_t^o(h) = y_t(h)$ (see Proposition 4.1(i)) are taken into account in the parameter estimation,

$$\omega_y(h) \geq F\Omega_{\underline{x}}(h)F' \tag{5.2.8}$$

and a strict inequality will hold in general. Hence, even if the predictors are identical for known processes, it is preferable to use the information in the disaggregate process if the parameters are replaced by estimators. In other words, estimating the parameters from the disaggregate data is preferable to using the aggregate series y_t for estimation, provided the constraints

$$F\Phi(L) = \psi(L)F \tag{5.2.9}$$

implied by $y_t^o(1) = y_t(1)$ are observed. This result follows from properties of ML estimation (Lütkepohl (1986a)). Note that (5.2.9) means that in fact only the parameters in $\psi(L)$ have to be estimated. For example, if $\underline{x}_t$ and hence y_t are ARMA processes, $\psi(L)$ is the ratio of two finite order operators in L and the coefficients of these operators have to be estimated and suffice to obtain an estimator of $F\Phi(L)$ which can then be used to construct the predictor $\hat{y}_t^o(h)$.

To illustrate the result and to demonstrate that in general the inequality in (5.2.8) will be strict the following example is useful. Consider the bivariate AR(1) process

$$\begin{bmatrix} x_{1t} \\ x_{2t} \end{bmatrix} = \begin{bmatrix} \alpha_1 & 0 \\ \alpha_2 & \alpha_3 \end{bmatrix} \begin{bmatrix} x_{1,t-1} \\ x_{2,t-1} \end{bmatrix} + \begin{bmatrix} u_{1t} \\ u_{2t} \end{bmatrix} \tag{5.2.10}$$

with $\Sigma_{\underline{u}}$ nondiagonal. Let $F = (1,0)$. Then

$$y_t = x_{1t} = \alpha_1 x_{1,t-1} + u_{1t} \quad .$$

Estimating α_1 by LS (ML) using the $y_t = x_{1t}$ data only, the resulting estimator is in general asymptotically less efficient than the seemingly unrelated regression (SUR) (generalized least squares) estimator if the zero constraint in the first equation is observed (see Judge et al. (1982, Chapter 11)). In other words, in general $\sigma^2(\text{LS}) > \sigma^2(\text{SUR})$, where

$\sigma^2(LS)$ is the asymptotic variance of the LS estimator of α_1 based only on the y_t data and $\sigma^2(SUR)$ is the asymptotic variance of the SUR estimator of α_1. Consequently,

$$\omega_y(1) = \sigma^2(LS)E\left[\frac{\partial x_{1t}(1)}{\partial \alpha_1}\right]^2 > \sigma^2(SUR)E\left[\frac{\partial x_{1t}(1)}{\partial \alpha_1}\right]^2 = F\Omega_{\underline{x}}(1)F' . \tag{5.2.11}$$

In practice, of course, the restrictions (5.2.9) may be unknown and it is of interest to ask whether (5.2.8) will still hold in that situation. The following simple counterexample shows that the answer to this question is in the negative. Consider the bivariate AR(1) process

$$\begin{bmatrix} 1+\alpha L & 0 \\ 0 & 1+\alpha L \end{bmatrix} \begin{bmatrix} x_{1t} \\ x_{2t} \end{bmatrix} = \begin{bmatrix} u_{1t} \\ u_{2t} \end{bmatrix} \tag{5.2.12}$$

and $F = (1,1)$, that is, the components x_{1t} and x_{2t} are simply added together such that $y_t = x_{1t} + x_{2t}$. Thus,

$$(1+\alpha L)y_t = v_t \tag{5.2.13}$$

is also an AR(1) process and it is easy to see that $y_t(h) = y_t^o(h)$ for all h. Note that $v_t = u_{1t} + u_{2t}$ with $\sigma_v^2 = F\Sigma_{\underline{u}}F'$. However, from Chapter 3, (3.2.34), it follows that $\Omega_{\underline{x}}(1) = 2\Sigma_{\underline{u}}$ and thus

$$F\Omega_{\underline{x}}(1)F' = 2F\Sigma_{\underline{u}}F' \tag{5.2.14}$$

while $\omega_y(1) = \sigma_v^2 = F\Sigma_{\underline{u}}F'$. Therefore, $\omega_y(1) < F\Omega_{\underline{x}}(1)F'$, and hence

$$\hat{\sigma}_o^2(1) > \hat{\sigma}^2(h) . \tag{5.2.15}$$

This result means that the predictor $\hat{y}_t^o(h)$, based on the multivariate process $\underline{x}_t$, may be inferior to the predictor $\hat{y}_t(h)$, based on the univariate aggregated process, when estimated parameters are used. Also, using $F = (1,0)$ and the process in (5.2.12) provides an example where the forecasts of a variable obtained on the basis of its own past only are superior to those based on a multivariate series. In the next subsection the predictors $\hat{y}_t^o(h)$ and $\hat{y}_t^u(h)$ will be compared.

5.2.2 Comparison of $\hat{y}^o_t(h)$ and $\hat{y}^u_t(h)$

When estimated coefficients are used the asymptotic forecast MSEs of the individual components of $\underline{x}_t$ predicted from their own past have the form

$$\hat{\sigma}^2_k(h) = \sigma^2_k(h) + \frac{1}{T}(\omega_k(h) + g_k(h)) \quad , \quad k = 1,\ldots,K \quad , \tag{5.2.16}$$

where $\sigma^2_k(h)$ is the k-th diagonal element of the MSE matrix of $\underline{x}^u_t(h)$,

$$\Sigma^u_{\underline{x}}(h) = [I_K \ \Xi_1 \ \ldots \ \Xi_{h-1}]E\left[\begin{bmatrix}\underline{w}_{t+h}\\ \vdots \\ \underline{w}_{t+1}\end{bmatrix}[\underline{w}'_{t+h},\ldots,\underline{w}'_{t+1}]\right]\begin{bmatrix}I_K\\ \Xi'_1\\ \vdots \\ \Xi'_{h-1}\end{bmatrix} , \tag{5.2.17}$$

$\omega_k(h) + g_k(h)$ is the variance of the asymptotic distribution of $\sqrt{T}(\hat{x}^u_{kt}(h) - x^u_{kt}(h))$, and $\omega_k(h)$ comes from estimating the ARMA parameters, while $g_k(h)$ is contributed by estimating the mean term.

The quantities in (5.2.16) are the diagonal elements of the asymptotic MSE matrix $\hat{\Sigma}^u_{\underline{x}}(h)$ of $\hat{\underline{x}}^u_t(h)$. Of course, for deriving $\hat{\sigma}^2_u(h)$ the off-diagonal elements of this matrix are also required. These are not quite as easily obtainable as for $\hat{\Sigma}_{\underline{x}}(h)$. Remember that the simple structure of the latter matrix follows since in

$$\underline{x}_{t+h} - \hat{\underline{x}}_t(h) = [\underline{x}_{t+h} - \underline{x}_t(h)] + [\underline{x}_t(h) - \hat{\underline{x}}_t(h)]$$

$$= \sum_{i=0}^{h-1} \Phi_i \underline{u}_{t+h-i} + [\underline{x}_t(h) - \hat{\underline{x}}_t(h)] \tag{5.2.18}$$

the two terms after the last equality sign are independent (see Chapter 3, Section 3.2.1). Partitioning the forecast error associated with $\hat{\underline{x}}^u_t(h)$ in a similar way gives

$$\underline{x}_{t+h} - \hat{\underline{x}}^u_t(h) = [\underline{x}_{t+h} - \underline{x}^u_t(h)] + [\underline{x}^u_t(h) - \hat{\underline{x}}^u_t(h)]$$

$$= \sum_{i=0}^{h-1} \Xi_i \underline{w}_{t+h-i} + [\underline{x}^u_t(h) - \hat{\underline{x}}^u_t(h)] \ . \tag{5.2.19}$$

The last two terms will not be independent in general since $\underline{w}_t$ is in general not K-dimensional white noise.

Nevertheless, it is not difficult to see that

$$\hat{\sigma}_u^2(h) > \hat{\sigma}_o^2(h) \text{ if } \sigma_u^2(h) > \sigma_o^2(h) \quad \text{and} \quad T \quad \text{is large.} \tag{5.2.20}$$

This result follows from the consistency of the parameter estimators. Therefore the case where the two predictors are identical for known processes and thus,

$$\sigma_u^2(h) = \sigma_o^2(h) \quad , \tag{5.2.21}$$

is again of interest. In this case $\hat{y}_t^u(h)$ may in fact dominate $\hat{y}_t^o(h)$.

To see this consider again the example process (5.2.12) with $\not{\Sigma}_{\underline{u}} = I_2$ and $F = (1,1)$. Clearly, the component series are $(1+\alpha L)x_{kt} = u_{kt}$, $k = 1,2$, and hence, condition (5.2.21) is satisfied. Now, however, $\underline{w}_t = \underline{u}_t$ is bivariate white noise and

$$\hat{\not{\Sigma}}_{\underline{x}}^u = \begin{bmatrix} \hat{\sigma}_1^2(h) & 0 \\ 0 & \hat{\sigma}_2^2(h) \end{bmatrix}$$

$$= \begin{bmatrix} \sigma_1^2(h) & 0 \\ 0 & \sigma_2^2(h) \end{bmatrix} + \frac{1}{T}\begin{bmatrix} \omega_1(h) & 0 \\ 0 & \omega_2(h) \end{bmatrix} + \frac{1}{T}\begin{bmatrix} g_1(h) & 0 \\ 0 & g_2(h) \end{bmatrix} . \tag{5.2.22}$$

The first and last terms in this last expression are identical to $\not{\Sigma}_{\underline{x}}(h)$ and $\frac{1}{T}G_{\underline{x}}(h)$, respectively. Therefore it remains to compare $F\Omega_{\underline{x}}(h)F'$ and

$$F\begin{bmatrix} \omega_1(h) & 0 \\ 0 & \omega_2(h) \end{bmatrix}F' = \omega_1(h) + \omega_2(h) \quad .$$

From (3.2.34), $F\Omega_{\underline{x}}(1)F' = 2\, F\not{\Sigma}_{\underline{u}}F' = 4$. On the other hand, by the same result of Chapter 3, $\omega_1(1) = \omega_2(1) = 1$. Consequently, $\hat{\sigma}_o^2(1) > \hat{\sigma}_u^2(1)$, meaning that $\hat{y}_t^o(1)$ is inferior to $\hat{y}_t^u(1)$. Like in the comparison of $\hat{y}_t^o(h)$ and $\hat{y}_t(h)$, this result relies on ignoring the restrictions for the coefficients of the multivariate process.

In summary, if estimated parameters are used in the three prediction formulas, in general the relations

$$\hat{\sigma}_o^2(h) \le \hat{\sigma}^2(h \quad , \quad \hat{\sigma}_u^2(h) \tag{5.2.23}$$

will hold for large T and if possible parameter restrictions are taken into account in the estimation procedure. However, due to the variability induced by estimating the process coefficients, $\hat{y}_t^o(h)$ may lose its optimality property and may be inferior to the other predictors if restrictions for the coefficients are unknown and are not enforced in the estimation procedure.

As mentioned in Chapter 4, a general ranking of $\sigma^2(h)$ and $\sigma_u^2(h)$ is not possible. Again, if $\sigma^2(h) > \sigma_u^2(h)$ or $\sigma^2(h) < \sigma_u^2(h)$ the same will hold for $\hat{\sigma}^2(h)$ and $\hat{\sigma}_u^2(h)$ for large T. For the example process (5.2.12) with $F = (1,1)$ it is easy to see that $\sigma^2(h) = \sigma_u^2(h)$ and from the foregoing discussion it is clear that the asymptotic MSEs are also identical, $\hat{\sigma}^2(h) = \hat{\sigma}_u^2(h)$.

Of course these results are based on asymptotic theory and their small sample validity needs to be investigated. This will be done in Section 5.5. In the following section the three predictors will be compared under the assumption that the true process orders are not known in advance and possibly "misspecified" processes are used for estimation and prediction.

5.3 UNKNOWN ORDERS AND ESTIMATED COEFFICIENTS

In practice, the situation assumed in the previous section is still unrealistic because the ML estimators of the process coefficients are only available if the ARMA orders of the processes are known. These orders will usually also be determined on the basis of the available data. If the orders are finite and are estimated consistently (see HQ and SC, Section 2.5.1), the asymptotic forecast MSE matrices are the same as in the case of known process orders. Therefore, in this case, the results of the previous section are relevant.

On the other hand, in practice the actual data generation process may not have a representation with a finite number of parameters or perhaps a pure AR model is fitted to an ARMA time series with infinite AR representation. For this situation an asymptotic theory has been discussed in Chapter 3, Section 3.3, that permits to derive approximate expressions for the forecast MSEs. In the following it will be assumed that the assumptions of Proposition 3.2 hold for the processes discussed here. For instance, $\underline{x}_t$ may be a Gaussian vector ARMA(p,q) process and only pure finite order AR processes are fitted. The order p(T) depends on the sample size (time series length) in such a way that

$$p(T) \to \infty \quad , \quad \frac{p(T)^3}{T} \to 0 \quad , \tag{5.3.1a}$$

$$\sqrt{T}\left[\sum_{i=p(T)+1}^{\infty} \sqrt{\mathrm{tr}(A_i'A_i)}\right] \to 0 \quad , \tag{5.3.1b}$$

$$\sqrt{T}\left[\sum_{i=p(T)+1}^{\infty} |\theta_i|\right] \to 0 \quad , \tag{5.3.1c}$$

and

$$\sqrt{T}\left[\sum_{i=p(T)+1}^{\infty} |\eta_{ki}|\right] \to 0 \quad , \quad \text{for} \quad k = 1,\dots,K \quad , \tag{5.3.1d}$$

when $T \to \infty$. Also, estimation and forecasting are based on independent processes with identical stochastic structures. Since the contribution of estimated mean terms to the approximate forecast MSEs in (3.3.13) and (3.3.14) is the same as in the previous section, zero process means will be assumed in the following.

Using Proposition 3.2 the following asymptotic MSEs for the predictors $\tilde{y}_t^o(h)$ and $\tilde{y}_t(h)$ result:

$$\tilde{\sigma}_o^2(h) = F\tilde{\Sigma}_{\underline{x}}(h)F' = (1 + \frac{Kp(T)}{T})\sigma_o^2(h) \tag{5.3.2}$$

and

$$\tilde{\sigma}^2(h) = (1 + \frac{p(T)}{T})\sigma^2(h) \quad , \tag{5.3.3}$$

where $\tilde{\sigma}_o^2(h)$ is the MSE obtained by fitting finite order vector AR processes to the disaggregate series $\underline{x}_t$ and aggregating the forecasts, while $\tilde{\sigma}^2(h)$ results from fitting univariate AR processes to the aggreate y_t. The MSE of the third predictor, $\tilde{y}_t^u(h)$, based on the estimated univariate components x_{kt}, is again more difficult to obtain. For the univariate components

$$\tilde{\sigma}_k^2(h) = (1 + \frac{p(T)}{T})\sigma_k^2(h) \quad , \quad k = 1,\dots,K \quad , \tag{5.3.4}$$

where $\sigma_k^2(h)$ is the k-th diagonal element of (5.2.17) as before. Thus, if the components are independent,

$$\tilde{\sigma}_u^2(h) = (1 + \frac{p(T)}{T})(f_1^2\sigma_1^2(h) + \dots + f_K^2\sigma_K^2(h)) \quad , \tag{5.3.5}$$

where f_k is the k-th component of F, that is, $F = (f_1,\dots,f_K)$. Here it is assumed that the same AR order p(T) is used for each component series. This assumption is easy to remove and is used for convenience. For the main points stated in the following it is of no consequence.

A comparison of the three asymptotic MSEs shows immediately that

$$\sigma_o^2(h) < \sigma^2(h) \quad , \quad \sigma_u^2(h) \tag{5.3.6}$$

implies

$$\tilde{\sigma}_o^2(h) < \tilde{\sigma}^2(h) \quad , \quad \tilde{\sigma}_u^2(h) \tag{5.3.7}$$

if T is large enough. Note that, by condition (5.3.1a), the ratio p(T)/T approaches zero fast as T goes to infinity. The relation (5.3.6) holds for some h unless the conditions of Proposition 4.1 are satisfied and it is easy to see that (5.3.7) remains valid even if the component series are not independent. In fact, if the component series of $\underline{x}_t$ are independent, $\sigma_o^2(h) = \sigma_u^2(h)$ holds. In view of (5.3.6) and (5.3.7) the case where the predictors are identical for known processes is again of particular interest.

Suppose first that $\sigma_o^2(h) = \sigma^2(h)$. It is easy to see that now $\tilde{y}_t^o(h)$ will be inferior to $\tilde{y}_t(h)$. Clearly, using (5.3.2) and (5.3.3),

$$\tilde{\sigma}_o^2(h) - \tilde{\sigma}^2(h) = (K-1)\,\frac{p(T)}{T}\sigma^2(h) > 0 \quad \text{for} \quad K > 1 \; . \tag{5.3.8}$$

Here again it is assumed that the same order p(T) is used for $\underline{x}_t$ and y_t which may not be so in practice. On the other hand, for the present discussion where the order is a function of the sample size, it seems reasonable to use the same function for the $\underline{x}_t$ and y_t series.

It is perhaps worth noting that the difference beween the forecast MSEs in (5.3.8) increases with the number K of component series of the disaggregate process. In other words, under the foregoing conditions, the predictor based on the multivariate process deteriorates relative to the univariate predictor when the variable of interest is disaggregated in more components. This result is a consequence of increasing the number of coefficients and thereby the estimation uncertainty in the multivariate system when the dimension of the disaggregate process is increased.

If the component series of $\underline{x}_t$ are independent as assumed in (5.3.5), $\underline{x}_t^u(h)$ is the optimal h-step predictor of the $\underline{x}_t$ process, that is, $\underline{x}_t^u(h) = \underline{x}_t(h)$, and consequently, $\sigma_o^2(h) = \sigma_u^2(h)$. Thus, in this situation, using (5.3.2) and (5.3.5),

$$\tilde{\sigma}_o^2(h) - \tilde{\sigma}_u^2(h) = (K-1)\frac{p(T)}{T}\sigma_o^2(h) > 0 \tag{5.3.9}$$

for $K > 1$, meaning that $\tilde{y}_t^o(h)$ is inferior to $\tilde{y}_t^u(h)$. Again the relative efficiency of the aggregated multivariate predictor deteriorates with the number K of disaggregate components.

If the component series of $\underline{x}_t$ are independent and in addition $\sigma^2(h) = \sigma_u^2(h)$ holds, then all three predictors are identical for known processes. Therefore, by (5.3.3) and (5.3.5),

$$\tilde{\sigma}^2(h) = \tilde{\sigma}_u^2(h) , \tag{5.3.10}$$

provided AR processes with the same orders p(T) are fitted.

In summary, the predictor $\tilde{y}_t^o(h)$ remains optimal if finite order AR processes with orders chosen according to (5.3.1) are fitted and the sample size is large. Only in special cases, when the estimation variability is the major source of MSE differences, $\tilde{y}_t(h)$ and $\tilde{y}_t^u(h)$ may outperform $\tilde{y}_t^o(h)$. For instance, if the component series are independent, $\tilde{y}_t^u(h)$ becomes optimal and, in view of Corollary 4.1.2, it strictly dominates $\tilde{y}_t^o(h)$ and $\tilde{y}_t(h)$ if all components of the aggregation matrix F are nonzero and the component series do not have identical MA representations.

As in the previous section these results are based on asymptotic theory. Before performing a small sample comparison in Section 5.5 some brief comments on the nonstationary case are given in the following.

5.4 NONSTATIONARY PROCESSES

Assuming that a stationary and invertible process can be obtained by differencing, the treatment of nonstationary processes does not pose any additional problems, provided the required differencing operator is known. More specifically, the conditions underlying the discussion of the previous sections have to be fulfilled for the differenced series and the coefficients and, if applicable, the process orders are estimated from the stationary series. This is the situation considered in Chapter 3, Sections 3.4.2 and 3.4.3. From the expressions for the asymptotic MSE matrices given in those sections and in Section 4.3 it is obvious that for the nonstationary case the same general conclusions hold as for the predictors based on estimated stationary processes. Briefly, if only the coefficients are estimated whereas the process orders are assumed known, the predictor $\hat{y}_t^o(h)$ will in general be superior to $\hat{y}_t(h)$ and $\hat{y}_t^u(h)$ if T is large. However, there are cases, where the contribution of the estimation variability to the forecast MSEs is greater for multivariate models than for univariate specifications. Therefore, under special circumstances, the predictors $\hat{y}_t(h)$ and/or $\hat{y}_t^u(h)$ may dominate $\hat{y}_t^o(h)$. The same holds if process orders and parameters have been estimated. Again these results follow from asymptotic theory. A small sample comparison of the three predictors for some stationary processes is reported next.

5.5 SMALL SAMPLE RESULTS

In this section I will first describe the general design of the Monte Carlo experiment that was performed in order to investigate the small sample validity of the previous asymptotic results. Then the results for some finite order AR and MA processes will be discussed in detail.

5.5.1 Design of the Monte Carlo Experiment

Realizations of a number of bivariate AR(1) and MA(1) processes were generated and the different predictors and their MSEs were computed. The components of the white noise $\underline{u}_t = (u_{1t}, u_{2t})'$ for the disaggregate processes $\underline{x}_t$ were generated as independent standard normal variates using a NAG library subroutine. Thus, $\underline{u}_t$ is bivariate normal with covariance matrix $\Sigma_u = I_2$. For each process R = 600 realizations were generated and results for three different sample sizes (T = 40, 100, 200) and two different forecast horizons (h = 1 and 5) will be reported. For each realization of a process 100 presample observations were generated to reduce the impact of starting-up values. Presample observations were used for estimation. For example, when an AR(1) was fitted to the data, one presample value, in addition to the T sample observations, was used for each variable. Estimation and forecasting were based on the same sample and the forecast origin is always the last sample period used for estimation. From a practical viewpoint this is a more realistic approach than using independent realizations for estimation and forecasting. Note that in this respect the Monte Carlo design differs from the assumptions underlying the asymptotic theory.

Also, in practice, a single sample of a fixed length T is usually given and an AR order has to be decided upon using the given data. In this situation, rather than specifying an arbitrary function p(T) for the AR order used, it is more plausible to determine the AR order by means of some specification criterion (see Chapter 2, Section 2.5.1). In the Monte Carlo study the three criteria AIC, HQ, and SC defined in (2.5.1), (2.5.2), and (2.5.3), respectively, were applied. The maximum AR order used in the search procedure for an optimal order is $P = 6$ for all processes and sample sizes. This maximum order was not terribly restrictive, that is, $P = 6$ was not chosen very often as AR order estimate. At the same time, using $P = 6$ kept the cost for the simulations in acceptable limits and for the AR processes it left some room for overfitting. More details will be given later. Unlike in the theoretical discussion of Section 5.3 the orders of the processes fitted to the disaggregate series $\underline{x}_t$, its components, and the aggregate y_t were not restricted to be identical for a particular realization. A restriction of equal orders seems somewhat artificial from a practical point of view and was therefore not enforced in the simulation experiment.

In all cases full finite order AR processes without zero constraints for the coefficients were fitted. Rather than subtracting the sample mean, intercept terms were included in the models. Asymptotically the two methods of coping with a nonzero mean are equivalent.

The difference between the forecast MSEs is evaluated using the statistic $\hat{\rho}$ described in Chapter 3, Section 3.5. When statements about the significance of MSE differences are made in the following they relate to a two-sided test using $\hat{\rho}$ as the test statistic. If no significance level is mentioned, a 5% level is presumed. A detailed discussion of some Monte Carlo results follows.

5.5.2 Simulation Results for AR Process I

The first process used in the simulation experiment is a bivariate AR(1) and is given in Table 5.2. It is similar to the example process (5.2.12) with $\alpha = 0.5$ and a nonzero mean term. For this process the univariate components and the aggregate $y_t = x_{1t} + x_{2t}$ are also AR(1) processes and all three predictors are identical if the processes are assumed known, that is,

$$\sigma_o^2(h) = \sigma^2(h) = \sigma_u^2(h) \quad \text{for} \quad h = 1,2,\dots \quad . \tag{5.5.1}$$

The process is especially suited for a simulation comparison of the predictors because MSE differences only result from the estimation uncertainty and not from the structure of the process.

Assuming that the AR orders are known it follows from the discus-

Table 5.2. Forecast Comparison for Aggregated AR Process I

$$\begin{bmatrix} 1+0.5L & 0 \\ 0 & 1+0.5L \end{bmatrix} \begin{bmatrix} x_{1t} \\ x_{2t} \end{bmatrix} = \begin{bmatrix} 1 \\ 1 \end{bmatrix} + \begin{bmatrix} u_{1t} \\ u_{2t} \end{bmatrix} , \quad \Sigma_{\underline{u}} = I \quad , \quad F = (1,1) \Rightarrow \sigma_o^2(1) = 2 \; , \; \sigma_o^2(5) = 2.63$$

$$\left.\begin{aligned} (1+0.5L)x_{1t} &= 1 + w_{1t} \quad , \quad \sigma_{w_1}^2 = 1 \\ (1+0.5L)x_{2t} &= 1 + w_{2t} \quad , \quad \sigma_{w_2}^2 = 1 \end{aligned}\right\} \Rightarrow \sigma_u^2(1) = 2 \; , \; \sigma_u^2(5) = 2.63$$

$$y_t = x_{1t} + x_{2t} \; , \; (1+0.5L)y_t = 2 + v_t \; , \; \sigma_v^2 = 2 \Rightarrow \sigma^2(1) = 2 \; , \; \sigma^2(5) = 2.63$$

Sample size T	forecast horizon h	p=1			p(AIC)			p(HQ)			p(SC)		
		$\hat\sigma_o^2(h)$	$\hat\sigma^2(h)$	$\hat\sigma_u^2(h)$	$\tilde\sigma_o^2(h)$	$\tilde\sigma^2(h)$	$\tilde\sigma_u^2(h)$	$\tilde\sigma_o^2(h)$	$\tilde\sigma^2(h)$	$\tilde\sigma_u^2(h)$	$\tilde\sigma_o^2(h)$	$\tilde\sigma^2(h)$	$\tilde\sigma_u^2(h)$
40	1	2.08	2.01	2.01	2.21	2.14	2.21	2.13	2.06	2.19	2.12	2.01	2.05
	5	2.53	2.53	2.52	2.58	2.55	2.56	2.53	2.53	2.56	2.53	2.52	2.53
100	1	2.01	1.98	2.00	2.03	1.97	2.03	2.02	1.98	2.00	2.01	1.99	2.00
	5	2.61	2.61	2.60	2.63	2.64	2.64	2.63	2.62	2.62	2.61	2.62	2.61
200	1	1.94	1.92	1.91	1.96	1.95	1.92	1.94	1.94	1.92	1.94	1.93	1.92
	5	2.78	2.79	2.78	2.79	2.79	2.78	2.78	2.79	2.78	2.78	2.78	2.78

sion in Section 5.2 that

$$\hat{\sigma}_o^2(1) > \hat{\sigma}^2(1) = \hat{\sigma}_u^2(1) \qquad (5.5.2)$$

since $F\Omega_{\underline{x}}(1)F' = 4$ (see (5.2.14)) and $\omega_y(1) = \sigma_v^2 = 2$. Also, using (3.2.32),

$$\Omega_{\underline{x}}(5) = \sum_{j=0}^{4}\sum_{i=0}^{4} \mathrm{tr}\left[\begin{bmatrix}-0.5 & 0\\ 0 & -0.5\end{bmatrix}^{4-j} \Gamma_{\underline{x}}^{-1} \begin{bmatrix}-0.5 & 0\\ 0 & -0.5\end{bmatrix}^{4-i} \Gamma_{\underline{x}}\right]\begin{bmatrix}-0.5 & 0\\ 0 & -0.5\end{bmatrix}^{j+i}$$

$$= \begin{bmatrix}0.195 & 0\\ 0 & 0.195\end{bmatrix} \qquad (5.5.3)$$

where it has been used that

$$\Gamma_{\underline{x}} = \sum_{i=0}^{\infty}\begin{bmatrix}-0.5 & 0\\ 0 & -0.5\end{bmatrix}^{2i} = \begin{bmatrix}1.33 & 0\\ 0 & 1.33\end{bmatrix}$$

cancels against its inverse. Hence,

$$F\Omega_{\underline{x}}(5)F' = 0.39 \ . \qquad (5.5.4)$$

In contrast,

$$\omega_y(5) = 2\sum_{j=0}^{4}\sum_{i=0}^{4}(-0.5^{4-j}(-0.5)^{4-i}(-0.5)^{j}(-0.5)^{i} = 0.195 \ . \qquad (5.5.5)$$

Therefore,

$$\hat{\sigma}_o^2(5) > \hat{\sigma}^2(5) \qquad (5.5.6)$$

and it is also easy to show that $\hat{\sigma}_u^2(5) = \hat{\sigma}^2(5)$. Note, however, that the difference between $\hat{\sigma}_o^2(5)$ and the other two 5-step MSEs is relatively small.

In Table 5.2 the forecast MSEs obtained in the Monte Carlo study are given. If the true AR order is used for each process ($p = 1$) the MSEs are fully in line with what one would expect on the basis of the foregoing asymptotic considerations. For $T = 40$ and $h = 1$ aggregating multivariate forecasts is indeed inferior to the other two alternatives, that is, (5.5.2) holds and the differences are significant at the 5%

level. Moreover, the differences between $\hat{\sigma}_u^2(1)$ and $\hat{\sigma}^2(1)$ are not significant (even at the 10% level). For sample sizes T = 100 and 200 the differences between the 1-step MSEs of all three predictors are insignificant at the 5% level, the only exception being a significant difference between $\hat{\sigma}_o^2(1)$ and $\hat{\sigma}_u^2(1)$ for T = 200. The fact that the differences disappear for increasing sample size reflects that the contribution of the estimation variability to the MSEs decreases with increasing sample size. In all cases the MSEs of the 5-step predictors are almost identical which is in line with (5.5.4), (5.5.5) and the fact that $\hat{\sigma}_u^2(5) = \hat{\sigma}^2(5)$.

For different sample sizes there are some differences in the MSEs in Table 5.2. This indicates that the sampling variability of the MSEs is relatively great despite the large number of replications (R = 600) of the experiment. To get a rough idea about the standard error of the MSEs note that the forecast errors would be normally distributed if they were computed using known instead of estimated processes. For instance, for $y_t(h)$ the forecast error is

$$y_{t+h} - y_t(h) = v_{t+h} + \psi_1 v_{t+h-1} + \dots + \psi_{h-1} v_{t+1} \quad ,$$

which is normally distributed with mean zero and variance $\sigma^2(h)$. Thus,

$$\frac{(y_{t+h} - y_t(h))^2}{\sigma^2(h)}$$

is distributed as a χ^2 random variable with one degree of freedom and has variance 2. Consequently, the variance of the squared error $(y_{t+h} - y_t(h))^2$ is $2(\sigma^2(h))^2$. Taking the average of R independent squared forecast errors then results in a quantity with standard deviation

$$\sigma^2(h)\sqrt{2/R} \ . \qquad (5.5.7)$$

For the process y_t in Table 5.2 and h = 1 this quantity is $2\sqrt{2/600}$ = 0.115 and similar results are obtained for the other MSEs. Thus, the differences in the MSEs for the different sample sizes are not surprising, in particular since estimated rather than known processes have been used so that the actual standard errors are likely to be even greater than the theoretical ones obtained as in (5.5.7). Of course, the considerations leading to the quantity in (5.5.7) cannot be used to assess the significance of the differences between the MSEs of different predictors for the same sample size because these MSEs are computed on the basis of the same random numbers and consequently are highly correlated. Therefore, in evaluating the significance between these MSEs, the statistic described in Chapter 3, Section 3.5, has been used as mentioned earlier. Of course, these are the differences of interest in this study.

The three predictors were also compared on the basis of models with AR orders estimated by the three criteria AIC, HQ, and SC. The resulting MSEs are also given in Table 5.2. Using a maximum AR order of p = 6 in the search for an optimal order was not restrictive in this case since all criteria have chosen the maximum AR order in less than 5% of the replications for all sample sizes.

Based on the asymptotic considerations of Section 5.3 the relations

$$\tilde{\sigma}_o^2(h) > \tilde{\sigma}^2(h) = \tilde{\sigma}_u^2(h) \qquad (5.5.8)$$

are readily obtained (see (5.3.8) and (5.3.9)). For the AIC criterion a significant difference (at the 5% level) is only obtained in one case. For T = 100, $\tilde{\sigma}_o^2(1)$ is significantly greater than $\tilde{\sigma}^2(1)$. In most cases the inequalities (5.5.8) hold although the differences are not significant.

For the HQ criterion $\tilde{\sigma}_o^2(1)$ is significantly greater than $\tilde{\sigma}^2(1)$ for T = 100 which is again in accordance with asymptotic theory. The only other significant difference is obtained between $\tilde{\sigma}^2(1)$ and $\tilde{\sigma}_u^2(1)$ for T = 40 which is somewhat unexpected and may be spurious. Although not significant, all 1-step MSE differences have the expected sign for T = 100 and 200. There are no significant differences between 5-step MSEs.

The results for SC reflect that this criterion estimates the AR order consistently. For T = 100 and 200 the MSEs are almost identical to those obtained when using the true AR order. In fact, for these sample sizes, the SC criterion has chosen the correct AR order p = 1 for each of the processes in more than 95% of the replications. For T = 40 , $\tilde{\sigma}_o^2(1) > \tilde{\sigma}^2(1)$ is significant at the 1% level while $\tilde{\sigma}_o^2(1) > \tilde{\sigma}_u^2(1)$ is not significant at the 5% level.

For all three criteria none of the differences between the 5-step MSEs is significant at the 5% level. This fact may be explained by noting that, for a low order AR process with characteristic roots not close to the unit circle, the 5-step predictor is approximately the sample mean. Since mostly low order AR processes are chosen by the three criteria the long rang forecasts provided by the three alternative predictors are very similar so that significant differences are not detected in R = 600 replications of the experiment. This deviation from the asymptotic considerations of Section 5.3 results from the assumptions regarding the AR orders of the processes used for prediction. Remember that the idea underlying the asymptotic theory of Section 5.3 is that processes of increasing order are fitted as the sample size T goes to infinity. Therefore, in this framework, for any h the chosen predictor will be different from the sample mean asymptotically.

Except for this slight discrepancy between the asymptotic theory and the small sample results the former seems to be a good indicator for the small sample performance of the three predictors at least for the process in Table 5.2.

5.5.3 Simulation Results for AR Process II

The next process considered in the simulation experiment is also a bivariate AR(1) for the disaggregate series and is given in Table 5.3. Since the bivariate AR operator has diagonal form the univariate subprocesses are also of AR(1) type. The aggregated process $y_t = x_{1t} + x_{2t}$ has an AR(2) representation. This process can be derived by considering the representation (2.3.8) of a vector ARMA process in Chapter 2 (see also Section 4.4.2). For the special case here

$$\det\left[\begin{bmatrix} 1+0.5L & 0 \\ 0 & 1-0.5L \end{bmatrix}\right]\begin{bmatrix} x_{1t} \\ x_{2t} \end{bmatrix} =$$

$$\begin{bmatrix} 1-0.5 \\ 1+0.5 \end{bmatrix} + \begin{bmatrix} 1-0.5L & 0 \\ 0 & 1+0.5L \end{bmatrix}\begin{bmatrix} u_{1t} \\ u_{2t} \end{bmatrix}$$

is obtained. Thus, adding the components gives

$$(1+0.5L)(1-0.5L)y_t = (1-0.25L^2)y_t$$

$$= 2 + (1-0.5L)u_{1t} + (1+0.5L)u_{2t}$$

and it is easy to see that the term on the right-hand side is white noise with variance $\sigma_v^2 = 2.5$.

For the MSEs of the three predictors the relations

Table 5.3 . Forecast Comparison for Aggregated AR Process II

$$\begin{bmatrix} 1+0.5L & 0 \\ 0 & 1-0.5L \end{bmatrix} \begin{bmatrix} x_{1t} \\ x_{2t} \end{bmatrix} = \begin{bmatrix} 1 \\ 1 \end{bmatrix} + \begin{bmatrix} u_{1t} \\ u_{2t} \end{bmatrix}, \quad \Sigma_{\underline{u}} = I, \quad F = (1,1) \rightarrow \sigma_o^2(1) = 2, \ \sigma_o^2(5) = 2.63$$

$$\left.\begin{aligned} (1+0.5L)x_{1t} &= 1 + w_{1t}, \quad \sigma_{w_1}^2 = 1 \\ (1-0.5L)x_{2t} &= 1 + w_{2t}, \quad \sigma_{w_2}^2 = 1 \end{aligned}\right\} \rightarrow \sigma_u^2(1) = 2, \ \sigma_u^2(5) = 2.63$$

$$y_t = x_{1t} + x_{2t}, \quad (1+0.5L)(1-0.5L)y_t = 2 + v_t, \quad \sigma_v^2 = 2.5 \rightarrow \sigma^2(1) = 2.5, \ \sigma^2(5) = 2.67 \approx \sigma_y^2$$

Sample size T	forecast horizon h	actual p (=1 or 2)			p(AIC)			p(HQ)			p(SC)		
		$\hat{\sigma}_o^2(h)$	$\hat{\sigma}^2(h)$	$\hat{\sigma}_u^2(h)$	$\tilde{\sigma}_o^2(h)$	$\tilde{\sigma}^2(h)$	$\tilde{\sigma}_u^2(h)$	$\tilde{\sigma}_o^2(h)$	$\tilde{\sigma}^2(h)$	$\tilde{\sigma}_u^2(h)$	$\tilde{\sigma}_o^2(h)$	$\tilde{\sigma}^2(h)$	$\tilde{\sigma}_u^2(h)$
40	1	2.23	2.61	2.13	2.30	2.71	2.24	2.25	2.65	2.22	2.32	2.60	2.21
	5	2.88	2.87	2.87	2.85	2.92	2.94	2.88	2.89	2.86	2.88	2.86	2.87
100	1	1.89	2.69	1.89	1.91	2.76	1.94	1.88	2.77	1.92	1.89	2.80	1.91
	5	2.71	2.71	2.71	2.70	2.73	2.70	2.71	2.71	2.71	2.71	2.71	2.71
200	1	2.11	2.70	2.10	2.13	2.73	2.13	2.12	2.71	2.12	2.11	2.81	2.11
	5	2.95	2.96	2.95	2.95	2.96	2.94	2.95	2.95	2.94	2.95	2.96	2.95

$$\sigma_o^2(h) = \sigma_u^2(h) < \sigma^2(h) \tag{5.5.9}$$

hold. Note, however, that for h = 5 the three MSEs are almost identical to the variance of y_t , $\sigma_y^2 = 2.67$. If the process orders are assumed known and the coefficients are estimated the predictor $\hat{y}_t^u(h)$ based on the univariate component series becomes optimal,

$$\hat{\sigma}_u^2(h) < \hat{\sigma}_o^2(h) < \hat{\sigma}^2(h) \quad , \tag{5.5.10}$$

where the first inequality is due to estimation variability.

In Table 5.3, when the true AR orders p = 1 or 2 are used, either the MSEs are identical or the relations (5.5.10) hold for all sample sizes and both forecast horizons reported. For h = 1 and T = 40 the differences are significant at the 1% level. Again the differences between $\hat{\sigma}_o^2(h)$ and $\hat{\sigma}_u^2(h)$ tend to vanish with increasing sample size while the differences between $\hat{\sigma}^2(1)$ and the other two MSEs persist, as predicted by the asymptotic theory. Again the MSE differences for the 5-step forecasts tend to be small in accordance with asymptotic theory. In summary, the small sample simulation results are in agreement with the asymptotic theory if the AR orders are assumed known.

If the process orders are specified according to the asymptotic theory of Section 5.3, relations similar to (5.5.10) can be derived,

$$\tilde{\sigma}_u^2(h) < \tilde{\sigma}_o^2(h) < \tilde{\sigma}^2(h) \quad . \tag{5.5.11}$$

The MSEs obtained by specifying the AR order with the criteria AIC, HQ, and SC are also presented in Table 5.3. For T = 40 the relations (5.5.11) are satisfied by the 1-step MSEs in the table. They are significant at the 5% level if the SC criterion is used. On the other hand, $\tilde{\sigma}_o^2(1)$ and $\tilde{\sigma}_u^2(1)$ are not significantly different for AIC and HQ. For all three criteria the differences between $\tilde{\sigma}_o^2(1)$ and $\tilde{\sigma}_u^2(1)$ are not significant at common levels for T = 100 and 200. The 5-step prediction MSEs are again very similar. Overall, for the present process, the asymptotic theories are good indicators for the small sample performance of the predictors. It may be noteworthy that here again the maximum AR order of P = 6 used with the specification criteria for all three sample sizes was not restrictive as it was assumed in less than 5% of the replications for each process and order estimation criterion.

Although the results of this and the previous subsection may suggest the conclusion that the asymptotic theory is generally as useful indicator for the small sample performance of the predictors, such a conclusion has to be drawn with caution because the processes considered are of a very special type. However, simulations with a number of other disaggregate finite order AR processes point in the same direction. More limited simulation results (only two predictors are compared and two criteria for AR order selection are used) for two other AR processes are reported in Lütkepohl (1984b), where the significance of the MSE differences has not been assessed, though.

5.5.4 Simulation Results for MA Process I

The previously considered processes are both of finite order AR type. In practice, processes with infinite AR representations may often be more realistic models for real life data generation processes. Also, the asymptotic theory of Section 5.3 is valid for such processes even if only finite order AR models are fitted to the available data. Therefore simulations with some finite order MA processes with infinite AR representations have been carried out.

The first MA process is a bivariate MA(1) for the disaggregate data and is given in Table 5.4 together with the component processes and the implied generation process for the aggregate $y_t = x_{1t} + x_{2t}$. If the process is assumed known all three predictors are identical for all forecast horizons. Thus differences in the forecasts stem from estimation and specification uncertainty which is of primary interest here. Of course, for h = 2,3,... the MSEs of all predictors are identical to the variance σ_y^2 of y_t if the processes are assumed known. However, if AR processes of potentially increasing order are fitted, it still makes sense to consider the resulting MSEs associated with long range forecasts. Therefore the MSEs for h = 1 and 5 are reported in Table 5.4.

Before discussing these MSEs it may be instructive to look at the AR orders selected by the three criteria AIC, HQ, and SC. Recall that the asymptotic theory used in Section 5.3 requires the AR order to approach infinity with the sample size T. The frequency distributions of the orders obtained in the Monte Carlo study are given in Table 5.5. Although the same maximum AR order P = 6 was used for all sample sizes, the orders selected by the three criteria increase on average with growing T, in accordance with the assumptions underlying the asymptotic theory. The maximum order is not chosen very often by any of the criteria so that P = 6 is not a restrictive upper bound for the sample sizes considered here.

Based on asymptotic theory one would expect that

Table 5.4. Forecast Comparison for Aggregated MA Process I

$$\begin{bmatrix} x_{1t} \\ x_{2t} \end{bmatrix} = \begin{bmatrix} 1 \\ 1 \end{bmatrix} + \begin{bmatrix} 1+0.5L & 0 \\ 0 & 1+0.5L \end{bmatrix} \begin{bmatrix} u_{1t} \\ u_{2t} \end{bmatrix}, \quad \Sigma_{\underline{u}} = I, \quad F = (1,1) \rightarrow \sigma_o^2(1)=2, \quad \sigma_o^2(5) = \sigma_y^2 = 2.5$$

$$\left.\begin{array}{ll} x_{1t} = 1 + (1+0.5L)w_{1t}, & \sigma_{w_1}^2 = 1 \\ x_{2t} = 1 + (1+0.5L)w_{2t}, & \sigma_{w_2}^2 = 1 \end{array}\right\} \rightarrow \sigma_u^2(1)=2, \quad \sigma_u^2(5) = \sigma_y^2 = 2.5$$

$$y_t = x_{1t} + x_{2t}, \quad y_t = 2 + (1+0.5L)v_t, \quad \sigma_v^2 = 2 \rightarrow \sigma^2(1)=2, \quad \sigma^2(5) = \sigma_y^2 = 2.5$$

Sample size T	forecast horizon h	p=0	p(AIC)			p(HQ)			p(SC)		
		$\tilde\sigma_o^2(h) = \tilde\sigma^2(h) = \tilde\sigma_u^2(h)$	$\tilde\sigma_o^2(h)$	$\tilde\sigma^2(h)$	$\tilde\sigma_u^2(h)$	$\tilde\sigma_o^2(h)$	$\tilde\sigma^2(h)$	$\tilde\sigma_u^2(h)$	$\tilde\sigma_o^2(h)$	$\tilde\sigma^2(h)$	$\tilde\sigma_u^2(h)$
40	1	2.43	2.37	2.30	2.23	2.37	2.22	2.20	2.42	2.22	2.23
	5	2.83	3.04	2.96	2.89	2.85	2.83	2.89	2.81	2.83	2.89
100	1	2.59	2.29	2.18	2.21	2.26	2.15	2.22	2.26	2.17	2.22
	5	2.62	2.60	2.63	2.64	2.62	2.63	2.63	2.61	2.61	2.60
200	1	2.58	2.13	2.08	2.09	2.14	2.12	2.08	2.18	2.12	2.10
	5	2.26	2.27	2.28	2.27	2.26	2.28	2.27	2.26	2.27	2.26

Table 5.5. Frequency Distributions of Estimated AR Orders in Percent - Underlying Disaggregate Process: MA Process I*

Sample size	AR	$\underline{x}_t = (x_{1t}, x_{2t})'$			y_t			x_{1t}			x_{2t}		
T	order	p(AIC)	p(HQ)	p(SC)	p(AIC)	p(HQ)	p(SC)	p(AIC)	p(HQ)	p(SC)	p(AIC)	p(HQ)	p(SC)
40	0	8	22	50	7	12	25	7	11	23	7	12	25
	1	38	50	43	32	40	42	30	39	45	30	39	45
	2	35	23	7	37	35	30	34	33	26	35	33	25
	3	7	3	0	8	6	1	9	6	3	9	6	2
	4	6	1	0	9	4	2	10	7	2	10	6	2
	5	3	0	0	4	1	0	5	2	0	4	3	1
	6	4	1	0	4	1	0	5	2	1	5	2	0
100	0	0	0	4	0	0	2	0	0	0	0	0	1
	1	19	52	77	16	32	49	16	29	46	17	29	46
	2	55	45	19	44	49	43	44	51	45	43	53	47
	3	15	3	0	17	11	6	18	12	7	18	11	4
	4	7	1	0	12	6	1	10	5	1	11	4	2
	5	2	0	0	5	2	0	6	1	0	6	2	0
	6	2	0	0	6	1	0	7	1	0	5	1	0
200	0	0	0	0	0	0	0	0	0	0	0	0	0
	1	4	17	61	3	11	27	3	10	23	4	11	27
	2	55	75	39	43	57	58	38	60	64	40	58	60
	3	27	8	1	27	22	13	28	22	11	27	21	12
	4	10	1	0	15	7	2	16	7	2	19	8	2
	5	3	0	0	7	3	0	9	2	0	5	2	0
	6	1	0	0	6	1	0	7	0	0	6	1	0

* Some columns do not sum to 100 due to rounding errors.

$$\tilde{\sigma}_o^2(h) > \tilde{\sigma}^2(h) \approx \tilde{\sigma}_u^2(h) \quad . \tag{5.5.12}$$

It turns out that for all three criteria and sample sizes

$$\tilde{\sigma}_o^2(1) > \tilde{\sigma}(1) \quad , \quad \tilde{\sigma}_u^2(1)$$

and in most cases the differences are significant at the 5% level. Moreover for all three criteria the differences between $\tilde{\sigma}^2(1)$ and $\tilde{\sigma}_u^2(1)$ are not significant at the 5% level. Thus, for h = 1 the simulation results are in full agreement with the asymptotic results of Section 5.3.

For forecast horizon h = 5, the optimal predictor is the process mean (see p = 0 in Table 5.4) and for T = 100 and 200 and all three criteria the differences between the 5-step MSEs are not significant at the 5% level. They are all close to the MSE of the sample mean (p = 0). This result can be explained by the fact that many low order AR processes are fitted (see Table 5.5) so that the 5-step forecasts are close to the means of the y_t series.

For T = 40, three of the 5-step MSEs are significantly different at the 5% level. More precisely, for SC, $\tilde{\sigma}_u^2(5)$ is significantly greater than both $\tilde{\sigma}_o^2(5)$ and $\tilde{\sigma}^2(5)$ and for AIC $\tilde{\sigma}_o^2(5)$ is significantly greater than $\tilde{\sigma}_u^2(5)$. Thus, for T = 40 and h = 5 the small sample results for SC are not quite in line with the asymptotic relation (5.5.12).

5.5.5 Simulation Results for MA Process II

The next processes considered in the present Monte Carlo study are shown in Table 5.6. The disaggregate process is again a bivariate MA(1) and the univariate components are also MA(1) processes. The aggregate $y_t = x_{1t} + x_{2t}$ is white noise. In this case,

$$\sigma_o^2(1) = \sigma_u^2(1) < \sigma^2(1) \quad , \tag{5.5.13}$$

whereas for the asymptotic MSEs

$$\tilde{\sigma}_u^2(1) < \tilde{\sigma}_o^2(1) < \tilde{\sigma}^2(1) \tag{5.5.14}$$

according to the results of Section 5.3. In Table 5.6 it can be seen that (5.5.14) holds indeed in most cases. The only exception is obtained for sample size T = 200 when the AR order is chosen with the

Table 5.6. Forecast Comparison of Aggregated MA Process II

$$\begin{bmatrix} x_{1t} \\ x_{2t} \end{bmatrix} = \begin{bmatrix} 1 \\ 1 \end{bmatrix} + \begin{bmatrix} 1+0.5L & 0 \\ 0 & 1-0.5L \end{bmatrix} \begin{bmatrix} u_{1t} \\ u_{2t} \end{bmatrix}, \quad \Sigma_{\underline{u}} = I, \quad F = (1,1) \rightarrow \sigma_o^2(1)=2, \quad \sigma_o^2(5) = \sigma_y^2 = 2.5$$

$$\left.\begin{aligned} x_{1t} &= 1 + (1+0.5L)w_{1t}, \quad \sigma_{w_1}^2 = 1 \\ x_{2t} &= 1 + (1-0.5L)w_{2t}, \quad \sigma_{w_2}^2 = 1 \end{aligned}\right\} \rightarrow \sigma_u^2(1)=2, \quad \sigma_u^2(5) = \sigma_y^2 = 2.5$$

$$y_t = x_{1t} + x_{2t}, \quad y_t = 2 + v_t, \quad \sigma_v^2 = 2.5 \rightarrow \sigma^2(1)=2.5, \quad \sigma^2(5) = \sigma_y^2 = 2.5$$

Sample size T	forecast horizon h	p = 0	p(AIC)			p(HQ)			p(SC)		
		$\tilde\sigma_o^2(h)=\tilde\sigma^2(h)=\tilde\sigma_u^2(h)$	$\tilde\sigma_o^2(h)$	$\tilde\sigma^2(h)$	$\tilde\sigma_u^2(h)$	$\tilde\sigma_o^2(h)$	$\tilde\sigma^2(h)$	$\tilde\sigma_u^2(h)$	$\tilde\sigma_o^2(h)$	$\tilde\sigma^2(h)$	$\tilde\sigma_u^2(h)$
40	1	2.52	2.37	2.72	2.31	2.33	2.64	2.30	2.49	2.61	2.31
	5	2.62	2.84	2.72	2.78	2.71	2.65	2.73	2.64	2.63	2.65
100	1	2.58	2.22	2.66	2.15	2.24	2.64	2.14	2.25	2.62	2.13
	5	2.64	2.68	2.64	2.66	2.63	2.64	2.67	2.65	2.64	2.65
200	1	2.53	2.15	2.52	2.10	2.14	2.53	2.11	2.10	2.52	2.12
	5	2.55	2.57	2.55	2.59	2.55	2.55	2.58	2.55	2.55	2.55

SC criterion. The differences between $\tilde{\sigma}^2(1)$ and the other two MSEs are in most cases significant at the 1% level.

For h = 5 the predictors are all identical for known processes, while for estimated processes the asymptotic relations

$$\tilde{\sigma}_o^2(5) > \tilde{\sigma}_u^2(5) = \tilde{\sigma}^2(5) \qquad (5.5.15)$$

hold. Thus, the aggregated multivariate predictor $\tilde{y}_t^o(h)$ has changed ranks with the univariate predictor $\tilde{y}_t(h)$ as compared to the situation for h = 1 (see (5.5.14)). This again is reflected by the results in Table 5.6, when T = 40 and the AR order is selected by AIC. In all other cases the MSEs are very similar for h = 5.

5.5.6 Simulation Results for MA Process III

All processes discussed so far in this section are boundary cases in that some of the 1-step predictors are identical for known processes. They are suitable for getting an idea about the impact of the estimation variability. Just for illustrative purposes, the bivariate MA(1) in Table 5.7 has also been simulated. This process is such that

$$\sigma_o^2(1) < \sigma^2(1) < \sigma_u^2(1) . \qquad (5.5.16)$$

As mentioned in Chapter 4, processes for which the aggregated multivariate predictor is optimal may be more typical in practice. The small sample MSEs in Table 5.7 unanimously reflect the relation (5.5.16) for T = 100 and 200 and the relations $\tilde{\sigma}_o^2(1) < \tilde{\sigma}^2(1)$ and $\tilde{\sigma}_o^2(1) < \tilde{\sigma}_u^2(1)$ are significant at the 5% level for all three sample sizes. For T = 40 the differences between $\tilde{\sigma}^2(1)$ and $\tilde{\sigma}_u^2(1)$ are not significant at the 5% level.

For h = 5, all predictors are identical for known processes and for estimated processes

$$\tilde{\sigma}_o^2(5) > \tilde{\sigma}^2(5) = \tilde{\sigma}_u^2(5) . \qquad (5.5.17)$$

Of course, the optimal 5-step predictor is again the process mean. For the present process the relations (5.5.17) do not always hold. However, in most cases the MSE differences are not significant at the 5% level. It is perhaps worth noting that for the multivariate MA process, for large sample sizes, the criteria tend to choose higher order AR processes than in the previous examples. For instance, the maximum AR order

Table 5.7. Forecast Comparison of Aggregated MA Process III

$$\begin{bmatrix} x_{1t} \\ x_{2t} \end{bmatrix} = \begin{bmatrix} 1 \\ 1 \end{bmatrix} + \begin{bmatrix} 1 + 0.3L & -0.66L \\ -0.5L & 1 - 0.5L \end{bmatrix} \begin{bmatrix} u_{1t} \\ u_{2t} \end{bmatrix}, \quad \Sigma_{\underline{u}} = I, \quad F = (1,1) \rightarrow \quad \sigma_o^2(1) = 2, \quad \sigma_o^2(5) = \sigma_y^2 = 3.39$$

$$\left.\begin{array}{l} x_{1t} = 1 + (1+0.205L)w_{1t}, \quad \sigma_{w_1}^2 = 1.46 \\ x_{2t} = 1 + (1-0.382L)w_{2t}, \quad \sigma_{w_2}^2 = 1.31 \end{array}\right\} \rightarrow \quad \sigma_u^2(1) = 2.83, \quad \sigma_u^2(5) = \sigma_y^2 = 3.39$$

$$y_t = x_{1t} + x_{2t}, \quad y_t = 2 + (1-0.504L)v_t, \quad \sigma_v^2 = 2.70 \quad \rightarrow \quad \sigma^2(1) = 2.70, \quad \sigma^2(5) = \sigma_y^2 = 3.39$$

Sample size T	forecast horizon h	p = 0	p(AIC)			p(HQ)			p(SC)		
		$\tilde{\sigma}_o^2(h)=\tilde{\sigma}^2(h)=\tilde{\sigma}_u^2(h)$	$\tilde{\sigma}_o^2(h)$	$\tilde{\sigma}^2(h)$	$\tilde{\sigma}_u^2(h)$	$\tilde{\sigma}_o^2(h)$	$\tilde{\sigma}^2(h)$	$\tilde{\sigma}_u^2(h)$	$\tilde{\sigma}_o^2(h)$	$\tilde{\sigma}^2(h)$	$\tilde{\sigma}_u^2(h)$
40	1	3.61	2.78	3.32	3.15	2.81	3.28	3.10	2.89	3.30	3.11
	5	3.61	3.86	3.74	3.70	3.59	3.74	3.65	3.63	3.64	3.61
100	1	3.15	2.15	2.64	2.80	2.21	2.66	2.76	2.30	2.68	2.77
	5	3.37	3.50	3.44	3.37	3.49	3.43	3.37	3.41	3.39	3.38
200	1	3.47	2.02	2.72	2.89	2.09	2.72	2.91	2.20	2.72	2.89
	5	3.45	3.49	3.51	3.47	3.50	3.48	3.46	3.45	3.45	3.45

of P = 6 was chosen in more than 17% of the cases by AIC for T = 200.

The process in Table 5.7 was also used in a Monte Carlo study reported by Lütkepohl (1984b). In Table 6 of that article the 5-step MSE $\tilde{\sigma}_o^2(5)$ obtained with AIC is considerably greater than $\tilde{\sigma}^2(5)$ for T = 200. This result may be due to a programming error that may have affected the multivariate AIC results for T = 200 in Table 6 of that article.

Some other MA(1) processes were also simulated and the general result is that the asymptotic theory is an excellent indicator for small sample short term forecast performance, while for longer term forecasting, if low order AR processes are fitted, the MSEs will not differ much from the forecast MSE of the sample mean. In the next section a real life example is considered.

5.6 AN EMPIRICAL EXAMPLE

In this section the seasonally adjusted, quarterly U.S. investment data discussed in Chapters 2 and 3 will be used to illustrate the theoretical findings of this and the previous chapter. More precisely, x_{1t} is Fixed Investment and x_{2t} represents Change in Business Inventories so that $y_t = x_{1t} + x_{2t}$ is the Gross Private Domestic Investment (see Figure 5.1). The estimation and specification period is the first quarter of 1947 to the fourth quarter of 1968 and the forecast period is 1969.I to 1972.IV so that the 1973 oil price shock has no impact on the results. For estimation and specification purposes the first differences $(1-L)x_{1t}$, $(1-L)x_{2t}$, and $(1-L)y_t$ of the three original variables are used to obtain stationary series. On the other hand, forecasts are computed for the original variables (see Sections 3.4 and 4.3).

Full and subset AR models are specified using AIC, HQ, and SC and a maximum lag of P = 14. The models are fitted as explained in Chapter 2, Section 2.5. The resulting full AR models for the bivariate series $\underline{x}_t = (x_{1t}, x_{2t})'$ are given in Chapter 2, (2.5.9) and (2.5.10). Note, however, that the x_{1t} and x_{2t} in those formulas are the first differences of the present x_{1t} and x_{2t}. That is, the x_{1t} and x_{2t} in (2.5.9) and (2.5.10) have to be replaced by $(1-L)x_{1t}$ and $(1-L)x_{2t}$, respectively, to obtain the models used in the following.

Fitting univariate full AR models for the first differences of Fixed Investment, $(1-L)x_{1t}$, gives for

$$\text{AIC:}\ (1-\underset{(0.11)}{0.49}L + \underset{(0.12)}{0.14}L^2-\underset{(0.12)}{0.02}L^3+\underset{(0.11)}{0.25}L^4)(1-L)x_{1t} = \underset{(0.30)}{0.83} + w_{1t} \quad ,$$

$$\tilde{\sigma}^2_{w_1} = 5.81 \quad , \qquad (5.6.1)$$

and for

$$\text{HQ, SC:}\quad \underset{(0.10)}{(1 - 0.46L)}(1 - L)x_{1t} = \underset{(0.29)}{0.58} + w_{1t} \quad ,$$

$$\tilde{\sigma}^2_{w_1} = 6.26 \quad , \qquad (5.6.2)$$

where the numbers in parentheses are estimated standard errors. For the first differences of Change in Business Inventories all three criteria choose an AR(4) model:

$$\text{AIC, HQ, SC:}\quad (1+\underset{(0.10)}{0.19}L-\underset{(0.10)}{0.07}L^2-\underset{(0.10)}{0.06}L^3+\underset{(0.10)}{0.43}L^4)(1-L)x_{2t} = \underset{(0.49)}{0.11}+w_{2t} \quad ,$$

$$\tilde{\sigma}^2_{w_2} = 19.7 \; . \qquad (5.6.3)$$

Finally, for the total investment y_t the following models are obtained:

$$\text{AIC, HQ:}\quad (1-\underset{(0.10)}{0.13}L-\underset{(0.10)}{0.11}L^2-\underset{(0.10)}{0.02}L^3+\underset{(0.10)}{0.42}L^4)(1-L)y_t = \underset{(0.64)}{1.17} + v_t \quad ,$$

$$\tilde{\sigma}^2_v = 31.5 \quad , \qquad (5.6.4)$$

$$\text{SC:}\quad (1 - L)y_t = \underset{(0.66)}{1.07} + v_t \quad , \qquad \tilde{\sigma}^2_v = 37.3 \; . \qquad (5.6.5)$$

Using these full AR models, 1-step forecasts with forecast origins 1968.IV, 1969.I,...,1972.III were computed. Similarly 2-step forecasts from 15 origins, 3-step forecasts from 14 origins etc. were determined and the average squared forecast errors for the entire forecast period 1969.I to 1972.IV are given in Table 5.8. Thus, the

$$\tilde{\sigma}^2_o(h) = \frac{1}{17-h}\sum_{i=0}^{16-h} (\tilde{y}^o_{88+i}(h) - y_{88+i+h})^2 \quad , \quad h = 1,\ldots,8 \; , \; (5.6.6)$$

are based on aggregated multivariate forecasts computed with the models (2.5.9) and (2.5.10). Here y_{88} is the total investment of the 88-th quarter of the sample, that is, the value for 1968.IV. Furthermore, the

$$\tilde{\sigma}^2(h) = \frac{1}{17-h}\sum_{i=0}^{16-h} (\tilde{y}_{88+i}(h) - y_{88+i+h})^2 \quad , \quad h = 1,\ldots,8 \; , (5.6.7)$$

are based on the univariate forecasts from the models (5.6.4) and (5.6.5), while the

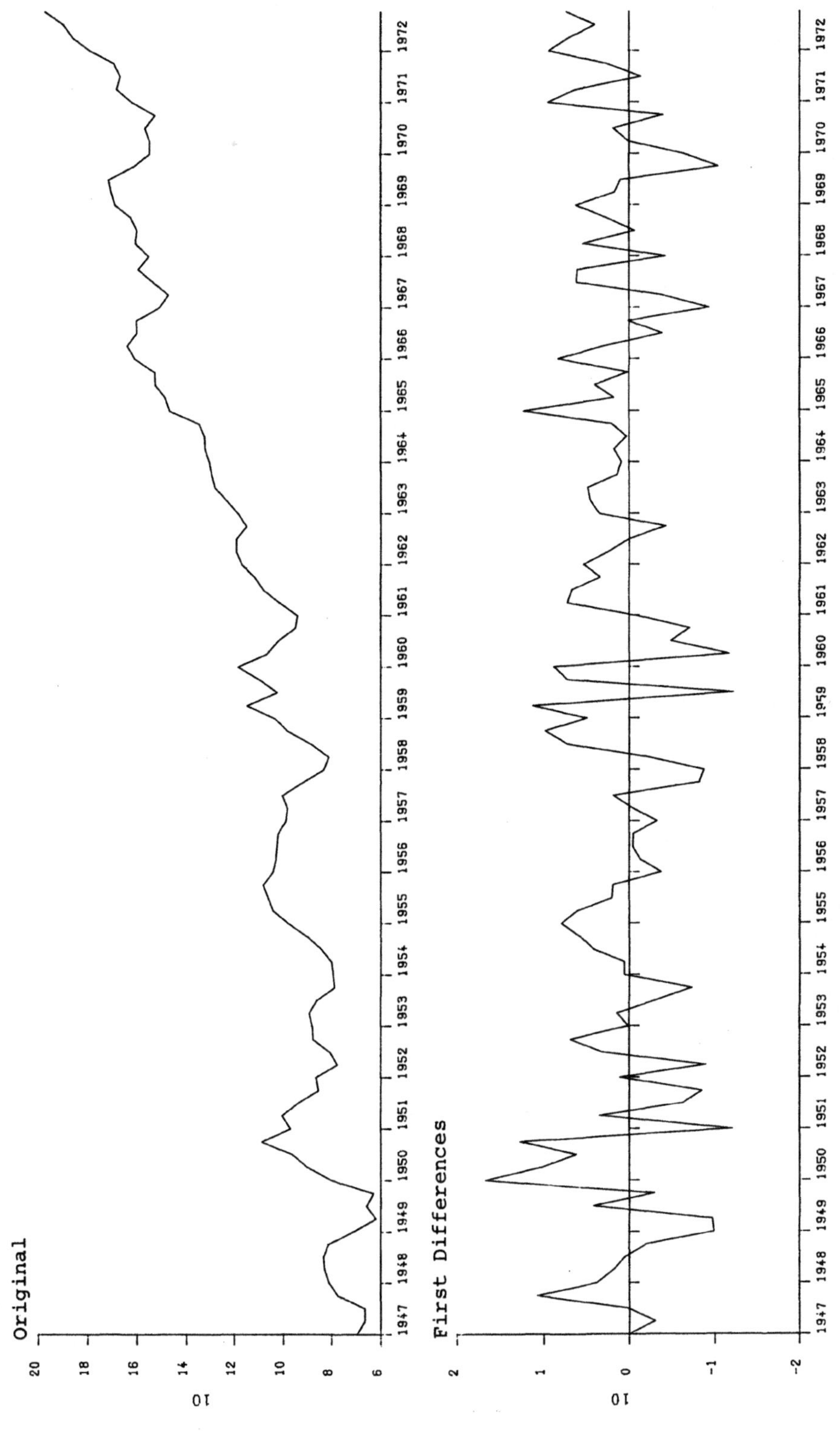

Figure 5.1. Quarterly, Seasonally Adjusted U.S. Gross Private Domestic Investment

Table 5.8. Forecast Results for Seasonally Adjusted Quarterly U.S. Gross Private Domestic Investment

Specification criterion	forecast horizon h	aggregated multivariate forecasts [$\tilde{\sigma}_o^2(h)$]		univariate forecasts [$\tilde{\sigma}^2(h)$]			aggregated univariate forecasts [$\tilde{\sigma}_u^2(h)$]		
		full AR	subset AR	full AR	subset AR	implied ARIMA	full AR	subset AR	implied ARIMA
AIC	1	23	26	34	36	41	30	28	22
	2	62	76	89	93	106	77	71	55
	3	98	120	144	152	136	123	113	88
	4	165	193	217	225	169	197	187	128
	5	238	248	254	263	179	246	237	157
	6	272	263	266	281	181	267	262	170
	7	289	278	284	297	183	288	286	174
	8	323	305	300	305	187	311	309	184
HQ	1	22	27	34	36	34	28	27	23
	2	64	75	89	93	82	72	70	59
	3	111	120	144	152	121	114	111	90
	4	196	195	217	225	166	192	188	137
	5	284	269	254	263	183	266	264	171
	6	333	310	266	281	185	312	312	187
	7	407	354	284	297	189	363	363	189
	8	501	403	300	305	194	418	415	196
SC	1	22	28	32	32	35	28	27	25
	2	64	80	86	86	85	72	73	63
	3	111	126	149	149	129	114	115	101
	4	196	198	220	220	177	192	189	165
	5	284	271	284	284	197	266	263	197
	6	333	310	316	316	205	312	311	213
	7	407	351	361	361	209	363	361	225
	8	501	402	398	398	216	418	415	241
Box-Jenkins	1					34			29
	2					85			65
	3					122			94
	4					168			144
	5					187			181
	6					194			203
	7					200			220
	8					200			234

$$\tilde{\sigma}_u^2(h) = \frac{1}{17-h} \sum_{i=0}^{16-h} (\tilde{y}^u_{88+i}(h) - y_{88+i+h})^2 \quad , \quad h = 1,\ldots,8 \quad ,(5.6.8)$$

are the average squared errors of the aggregated univariate forecasts based on the AR models (5.6.1), (5.6.2), and (5.6.3).

Intuitively it seems plausible to expect that there are intertemporal correlations between Fixed Investment (x_{1t}) and the Change in Business Inventories (x_{2t}). Thus, the MA operator of $(1-L)\underline{x}_t$ is not likely to be diagonal and the conditions in Proposition 4.1(i) and (ii) are not expected to be satisfied for the generation process of the investment data (see also Corollaries 4.1.2 and 4.1.3).

Consequently one would expect that

$$\sigma_o^2(h) < \sigma^2(h), \ \sigma_u^2(h) \ . \qquad (5.6.9)$$

Considering the MSEs from the full AR models only, it turns out that for the AIC models

$$\tilde{\sigma}_o^2(h) < \tilde{\sigma}_u^2(h) < \tilde{\sigma}^2(h) \quad \text{for} \quad h = 1,\ldots,5 \quad , \qquad (5.6.10)$$

and the same holds for HQ and SC for forecast horizons h = 1,2,3. For longer forecast horizons the three predictors provide very similar MSEs for AIC, whereas the aggregated multivariate forecasts based on the more parsimonious HQ/SC models deteriorate substantially relative to univariate and aggregated univariate forecasts.

Forecasts were also computed using subset AR methods. The multivariate subset AR models obtained by AIC, HQ, and SC are given in Chapter 2, (2.5.17), (2.5.18), and (2.5.19), where the x_{it} have to be replaced by $(1-L)x_{it}$ as explained earlier. The univariate models for Fixed Investment obtained with HQ and SC are identical to the full AR model (5.6.2) and for

$$\text{AIC:} \ (1 \underset{(0.10)}{-0.43L} \underset{(0.10)}{+0.26L^4})(1-L)x_{1t} = \underset{(0.30)}{0.79} + w_{1t} \ ,$$

$$\tilde{\sigma}^2_{w_1} = 5.77 \ , \qquad (5.6.11)$$

is obtained. The subset AR models for the Change in Business Inventories are

$$\text{AIC, HQ:} \ (1 \underset{(0.10)}{+0.20L} \underset{(0.10)}{+0.43L^4})(1-L)x_{2t} = \underset{(0.48)}{0.13} + w_{2t} \ ,$$

$$\tilde{\sigma}^2_{w_2} = 19.3 \quad , \qquad (5.6.12)$$

and

$$\text{SC:} \; (1 + \underset{(0.10)}{0.46}L^4)(1 - L)x_{2t} = \underset{(0.49)}{0.12} + w_{2t} \quad ,$$

$$\tilde{\sigma}^2_{w_2} = 20.1 \; . \qquad (5.6.13)$$

The SC subset AR model for the Gross Private Domestic Investment (y_t) is a random walk (see (5.6.5)) and for

$$\text{AIC, HQ:} \; (1 + \underset{(0.10)}{0.41}L^4)(1 - L)y_t = \underset{(0.63)}{1.42} + v_t \quad ,$$

$$\tilde{\sigma}^2_v = 31.6 \quad , \qquad (5.6.14)$$

results.

In Section 5.2 it has been argued that placing constraints on the AR coefficients may improve the forecast efficiency. In Table 5.8, where also the MSEs of the subset AR models are given, it can be seen that the subset AR forecasts are indeed in some cases more efficient than their full AR counterparts. However, in most cases the full AR models provide superior forecasts for short forecast horizons. For HQ and SC this is not surprising given that the full AR models chosen by these criteria are already fairly parsimonious. Moreover, it should be kept in mind that even if a predictor from one model is superior to a predictor from another model under a MSE measure of forecast efficiency, it does not follow that the first predictor provides smaller squared forecast errors for each realization of the underlying data generation process.

If any of the bivariate subset AR models is assumed to be the true data generation process, it is possible to derive the corresponding univariate ARIMA models for x_{1t}, x_{2t}, and y_t using the representation

$$\det(A(L))(1 - L)\underline{x}_t = A(L)^*\underline{u}_t \quad , \qquad (5.6.15)$$

where $A(L)^*$ is the adjoint of the bivariate subset AR operator $A(L)$ (see Chapter 4, (4.4.10)). For instance, for the AIC subset AR model in (2.5.17) ,

$$A(L) = \begin{bmatrix} 1 - 0.41L + 0.20L^2 + 0.22L^4 & -0.10 - 0.22L \\ -0.37L & 1 + 0.24L + 0.41L^4 \end{bmatrix} . \qquad (5.6.16)$$

Hence,

$$\det(A(L)) = \theta(L) = 1 + \theta_1 L + \theta_2 L^2 + \theta_3 L^3 + \theta_4 L^4 + \theta_5 L^5 + \theta_6 L^6 + \theta_8 L^8 , \qquad (5.6.17)$$

where θ_7 is set to zero because L^7 does not appear in the determinant. Further,

$$A(L)^* = \begin{bmatrix} 1 + 0.24L + 0.41L^4 & 0.10 + 0.22L \\ 0.37L & 1 - 0.41L + 0.20L^2 + 0.22L^4 \end{bmatrix} \qquad (5.6.18)$$

so that, by Proposition 4.2 and Corollary 4.2.1, x_{1t}, x_{2t}, and y_t have ARIMA(8,1,4) representations with the AR operator given in (5.6.17). Therefore these "implied ARIMA models" were also estimated using the ML procedure of the GENSTAT package. The estimated models are

$$\underset{}{(1+\underset{(0.48)}{0.11}L+\underset{(0.30)}{0.39}L^2+\underset{(0.32)}{0.21}L^3+\underset{(0.29)}{0.02}L^4+\underset{(0.16)}{0.27}L^5+\underset{(0.21)}{0.14}L^6+\underset{(0.15)}{0.23}L^8)(1-L)x_{1t}}$$

$$= 2.23 + (1+\underset{(0.49)}{0.62}L+\underset{(0.52)}{0.57}L^2+\underset{(0.48)}{0.43}L^3-\underset{(0.46)}{0.22}L^4)w_{1t} ,$$

$$\tilde{\sigma}^2_{w_1} = 5.73 , \qquad (5.6.19)$$

$$(1+\underset{(0.26)}{0.21}L+\underset{(0.21)}{0.11}L^2-\underset{(0.18)}{0.23}L^3-\underset{(0.24)}{0.10}L^4+\underset{(0.18)}{0.02}L^5+\underset{(0.18)}{0.20}L^6+\underset{(0.19)}{0.02}L^8)(1-L)x_{2t}$$

$$= 0.12 + (1-\underset{(0.24)}{0.09}L+\underset{(0.20)}{0.07}L^2-\underset{(0.16)}{0.27}L^3-\underset{(0.22)}{0.72}L^4)w_{2t} ,$$

$$\tilde{\sigma}^2_{w_2} = 17.4 , \qquad (5.6.20)$$

and

$$(1-\underset{(0.18)}{0.07}L+\underset{(0.27)}{0.33}L^2-\underset{(0.18)}{0.03}L^3-\underset{(0.23)}{0.03}L^4+\underset{(0.13)}{0.03}L^5+\underset{(0.17)}{0.35}L^6+\underset{(0.19)}{0.05}L^8)(1-L)y_t$$

$$= 1.70 + (1+\underset{(0.18)}{0.06}L+\underset{(0.25)}{0.37}L^2+\underset{(0.17)}{0.04}L^3-\underset{(0.25)}{0.63}L^4)v_t ,$$

$$\tilde{\sigma}^2_v = 29.3 , \qquad (5.6.21)$$

where the numbers underneath the estimated coefficients are estimated standard errors. Of course, the coefficient estimates are quite meaningless as most of them are much lower in absolute value than their respective standard errors. Thus, the models are grossly overparameterized. Nevertheless, for comparison purposes, they have been used for computing forecasts. The MSEs are also given in Table 5.8. The aggregated univariate forecasts based on the heavily parameterized models (5.6.19) and (5.6.20) are optimal for all forecast horizons. Especially for longer term forecasts the gains in precision are quite dramatic. Also (5.6.21) provides excellent long range forecasts.

In a similar fashion the univariate ARIMA models implied by the bivariate HQ subset AR model (2.5.18) were estimated and used for forecasting. The resulting models are

$$\underset{}{(1} - \underset{(0.16)}{0.14L} + \underset{(0.19)}{0.34L^2} - \underset{(0.18)}{0.27L^4} + \underset{(0.14)}{0.37L^5})(1 - L)x_{1t}$$

$$= 1.24 + (1 + \underset{(0.18)}{0.38L} + \underset{(0.20)}{0.38L^2} + \underset{(0.15)}{0.17L^3} - \underset{(0.18)}{0.65L^4})w_{1t}\,,\quad \tilde{\sigma}^2_{w_1} = 5.61\,, \quad (5.6.22)$$

$$(1 - \underset{(0.11)}{0.64L} - \underset{(0.11)}{0.23L^2} + \underset{(0.11)}{0.50L^4} - \underset{(0.11)}{0.25L^5})(1-L)x_{2t} = 0.04 + (1 - \underset{(0.05)}{1.00L})w_{2t}\,,$$

$$\tilde{\sigma}^2_{w_2} = 16.8\,, \quad (5.6.23)$$

and

$$(1 + \underset{(0.25)}{0.10L} - \underset{(0.22)}{0.24L^2} + \underset{(0.22)}{0.06L^4} + \underset{(0.16)}{0.15L^5})(1-L)y_t$$

$$= 1.12 + (1 + \underset{(0.25)}{0.27L} - \underset{(0.22)}{0.23L^2} + \underset{(0.11)}{0.01L^3} - \underset{(0.22)}{0.51L^4})v_t\,,\quad \tilde{\sigma}^2_v = 29.2\,. \quad (5.6.24)$$

Obviously, also these models would be regarded as overparameterized by common standards. Not only are some of the parameter estimates insignificant but there is also possible cancellation of factors. For example, the MA operator (1-L) in (5.6.23) may be cancelled against the difference operator. Nevertheless these models provide excellent forecasts (see Table 5.8).

Proceeding in the same way for the bivariate subset AR model (2.5.19) obtained with the SC criterion, gives

$$(1 - \underset{(0.30)}{0.13L} - \underset{(0.22)}{0.25L^4} + \underset{(0.17)}{0.36L^5})(1 - L)x_{1t}$$

$$= 0.93 + (1 + \underset{(0.29)}{0.36L} + \underset{(0.17)}{0.11L^2} + \underset{(0.11)}{0.03L^3} - \underset{(0.20)}{0.64L^4})w_{1t}\,,\quad \tilde{\sigma}^2_{w_1} = 5.67\,, \quad (5.6.25)$$

$$(1 + \underset{(0.50)}{0.21L} + \underset{(0.10)}{0.46L^4} + \underset{(0.26)}{0.07L^5})(1 - L)x_{2t} = 0.17 + (1 - \underset{(0.51)}{0.02L})w_{2t}\,,$$

$$\tilde{\sigma}^2_{w_2} = 19.1\,, \quad (5.6.26)$$

and

$$(1 + \underset{(0.25)}{0.07L} - \underset{(0.19)}{0.05L^4} + \underset{(0.16)}{0.13L^5})(1 - L)y_t$$

$$= 1.20 + (1 + \underset{(0.24)}{0.26L} - \underset{(0.11)}{0.04L^2} + \underset{(0.10)}{0.05L^3} - \underset{(0.17)}{0.65L^4})v_t \ , \ \tilde{\sigma}_v^2 = 28.8 \ . \qquad (5.6.27)$$

Again, by usual standards, these models would be regarded as overparameterized given the considerable number of insignificant parameters. As can be seen in Table 5.8, also these models provide excellent forecasts, especially for the long range.

Of course, it is of interest to know why the univariate ARIMA monsters implied by the bivariate subset AR models provide such good forecasts despite their heavy parameterization. There are some possible explanations. First, this result may occur by chance for the particular data set under study. If only the evidence provided by the present example were available this explanation might be acceptable. However, the phenomenon that high order ARIMA models provide very good long range forecasts has been observed for other time series as well (see Lütkepohl (1984b)).

A second explanation could be that including MA terms and thereby considering effectively infinite order AR processes is preferable to using finite order autoregressions for forecasting. In order to check whether this explanation of the splendit forecast performance of the univariate ARIMA models is a reasonable one, more parsimonious ARIMA models were also fitted using the Box-Jenkins methodology (see Chapter 2, Section 2.5.3). The resulting models are

$$(1 - \underset{(0.10)}{0.45L})(1 + \underset{(0.11)}{0.33L^4} + \underset{(0.12)}{0.19L^8})(1 - L)x_{1t} = 0.80 + w_{1t} \ ,$$

$$\tilde{\sigma}_{w_1}^2 = 5.79 \ , \qquad (5.6.28)$$

$$(1 - L)x_{2t} = \underset{(0.09)}{0.11} + (1 - \underset{(0.11)}{0.28L})(1 - \underset{(0.07)}{0.76L^4})w_{2t} \ ,$$

$$\tilde{\sigma}_{w_2}^2 = 16.0 \ , \qquad (5.6.29)$$

and

$$(1 - L)y_t = \underset{(0.25)}{1.06} + (1 - \underset{(0.09)}{0.59L^4})v_t \ , \qquad \tilde{\sigma}_v^2 = 28.9 \ . \qquad (5.6.30)$$

It has been argued by Box & Jenkins (1976) and others that parsimoniously parameterized ARIMA models are better suited for prediction than profligately parameterized specifications. Therefore it is of interest that in most cases the forecast MSEs from the Box-Jenkins models exceed those from the models implied by the bivariate AIC subset AR process (see Table 5.8). Also, for the short term, the Box-Jenkins models predict no better than some of the pure AR models. This sheds some doubt on the second attempt to explain the good performance of the "implied ARIMA models".

A third possible explanation may be that making use of the information in the disaggregate multivariate data is of considerable value in constructing univariate ARIMA models for predicting an aggregate. Of course, in the present context this means that a seemingly overparameterized ARIMA model may well provide better forecasts than a parsimonious candidate. In the present example the ARIMA monsters seem to pick up a little more of the long term movement of the series under study.

In closing this example section some further comments are in order.

(1) Comparing the different predictors it is obvious that their relative performance crucially depends on the method used for model specification.

(2) If only forecasts from full AR models are compared the results are roughly in line with what was to be expected on the basis of the theoretical discussion of the previous sections. At least for short-term prediction aggregating multivariate forecasts ($\tilde{y}_t^o(h)$) is preferable to aggregating univariate forecasts ($\tilde{y}_t^u(h)$) which in turn is superior to forecasting the aggregated series directly.

(3) It must be kept in mind that this is but one example that does not permit to draw general conclusions for other cases, in particular, since some of the conditions of the theoretical sections are not satisfied here. For instance, the forecast MSEs are computed on the basis of only a single realization of the underlying generation process. In contrast a large number of independent realizations was used in the Monte Carlo experiment. Some more examples are discussed in Lütkepohl (1984b).

5.7 CONCLUSIONS

In this and the previous chapter the following three possibilities are compared for predicting a time series variable that is the sum or weighted sum of a number of disaggregate variables: (1) The disaggregate variables are predicted on the basis of their multivariate generation process and the resulting forecasts are then aggregated. (2) The aggregate is predicted directly using a univariate time series model. (3) The individual disaggregate variables are forecast with univariate methods and then these forecasts are aggregated. In the previous chapter the first predictor is shown to be optimal under a mean squared error measure of forecast performance if the data generation process is known. The relative efficiency of the second and third forecasting possibilities depends on the generation process of the disaggregate variables and on the aggregation weights.

In this chapter the situation has been analyzed where the data generation processes are not known and have to be estimated. Two asymptotic theories have been used in deriving asymptotic approximations to the forecast MSEs. The first theory assumes that the ARMA coefficients are estimated. The process orders are assumed to be finite and they are either known or estimated by a consistent criterion. The second asymptotic theory does not assume known ARMA orders but permits that finite order AR processes are fitted when the true underlying AR structure is in fact of infinite order. In the latter theory the AR order is assumed to approach infinity as the sample size (time series length) goes to infinity. Under both scenarios it is possible that the first predictor becomes inferior to both the second and third predictors.

A Monte Carlo experiment has been used to investigate the small sample performance of the three predictors. It turns out that for the processes used in the simulation experiment the asymptotic theories are useful indicators for the small sample behavior of the predictors. In particular, in extreme situations it is indeed possible that the aggregated multivariate forecasts are dominated by univariate forecasts of the aggregate and aggregated univariate forecasts.

Roughly speaking, this situation arises when too many parameters are estimated in the multivariate system. If many parameters are contained in such a system the sampling variability due to estimation may be greater than in the univariate models so that the forecast MSEs of the latter will be smaller than those of the former. This phenomenon has been observed even though only bivariate systems have been considered in the simulation examples. The theoretical results suggest that it becomes even more severe for higher dimensional systems. Consequently, one conclusion from the previous discussion is that when forecasting a contemporaneous aggregate is the aim, it is theoretically useful to get data on the disaggregate components. In practice, however, if the generating process is unknown and has to be specified and estimated from the available data, disaggregation may only be useful to a certain extent. Excessive disaggregation in very many components may even be harmful to the forecast precision.

As a compromise between using a multivariate forecasting model and forecasting the aggregate directly with univariate methods it may sometimes be advantageous to forecast the components with univariate methods and aggregate these forecasts. This prediction possibility has performed well for the U.S. investment data that have served as an example. There are processes, though, for which the predictor based on the univariate component series is inferior to forecasting the aggregate directly. Generally a predictor based on univariate component forecasts can be recommended if the residuals of the individual univariate component processes are multivariate white noise. It has been shown in Chapter 4 that aggregating univariate forecasts is optimal in this situation. In particular, the third predictor is optimal if the univariate components are uncorrelated processes.

So far only contemporaneous aggregation has been considered. In the next chapter it will be demonstrated that the previously obtained results can also be used to investigate different predictors for temporally aggregated time series. In fact, in the framework of the next chapter, temporal and contemporaneous aggregation may be considered jointly.

CHAPTER 6. FORECASTING TEMPORALLY AND CONTEMPORANEOUSLY AGGREGATED KNOWN PROCESSES

A temporal aggregate is a variable obtained by aggregating over time, that is, weighted values associated with consecutive time periods are added up. For instance, the annual Gross National Product (GNP) is the sum of quarterly or monthly GNP values. As another example, the monthly number of unemployed persons may be computed as the average of the daily unemployment figures or, alternatively, the value of a particular key day, e.g., the last working day of the month, may be used. In both cases the unemployment figure is a weighted sum of the daily numbers. While equal weights are associated with each day in the first alternative, the last day gets a weight of one and all other days get zero weights in the second alternative.

The examples mentioned here involve two different types of variables. The GNP is a flow variable whereas the number of unemployed persons is a stock variable. Although there are important differences in the ways temporal aggregates of the two types of variables are computed, there is also a common feature: the temporal aggregate is a weighted sum of consecutive values of disaggregate variables.

Forecasts of temporally aggregated variables are often required. For instance, for investment decisions, monthly, quarterly or annual sales forecasts may be needed, depending on the desired target time of delivery. Also, before a person borrows money with annual interest payments, a forecast of the annual income will be needed. In this chapter it will be shown that forecasts for temporally aggregated variables can be compared in a similar way as those for contemporaneous aggregates. In fact, the framework of this chapter will even permit to jointly analyze temporal and contemporaneous aggregation. As explained in Chapter 1, forecasts of temporally and contemporaneously aggregated variables are often of interest. Both types of aggregation will be treated jointly in this chapter.

To see the different prediction possibilities of a contemporaneously and temporally aggregated variable consider the weekly sales of a retail firm with different branches mentioned in Chapter 1. To stock in for the next week, the total demand in all branches (aggregated contemporaneously) and for all days (aggregated temporally) needs to be predicted. One way to obtain such a forecast is to use the daily sales figures of each individual branch collected during the past weeks, construct a multivariate forecasting model for this data, use that model for forecasting the daily sales of each branch and then aggregate the obtained forecasts. Another approach would be to aggregate the sales figures first and then build a univariate forecasting model for the past total weekly sales. Also it would be possible to use contemporaneously aggregated (i.e. aggregated over all branches) daily data, use a univariate time series model to obtain daily forecasts and aggregate these forecasts temporally. Furthermore one could use temporally aggregated, weekly data for each individual branch, construct a multivariate forecasting model for this data and aggregate the obtained forecasts contemporaneously over all branches. A fifth possibility is to construct univariate forecasting models for the daily sales figures of each of the separate branches, obtain daily univariate forecasts and aggregate these temporally and contemporaneously. Finally, weekly univariate forecasts could be obtained using the temporally aggregated weekly sales figures for each branch. The desired forecast is then obtained by contemporaneously aggregating these forecasts.

The six predictors resulting from these forecast possibilities will be compared in this chapter under the assumption of knowing the true data generation process. Other possible predictors can be analyzed in the same manner and will therefore not be treated here. In the general framework of this chapter results will be derived without distinguishing between temporal aggregation of stock and flow variables. Special results for these two cases will be discussed in the next two chapters.

In Section 6.1 of this chapter, following Lütkepohl (1986a), a framework will be presented in which temporal and contemporaneous aggregation can be treated simultaneously. Also, the presented framework permits the system under investigation to contain both stock and flow variables. In Sections 6.2 and 6.3 the six different predictors are formally defined and compared and Section 6.4 contains a discussion of nonstationary processes. Some results for temporally and contemporaneously aggregated vector ARMA processes are derived in Section 6.5 and concluding remarks are set forth in Section 6.6. Throughout this chapter the assumption is made that the data generating processes are known. The case of estimated processes is treated in Chapters 7 to 9. Parts of this chapter are based on Lütkepohl (1986a).

6.1 MACRO PROCESSES

In this section so-called macro processes will be introduced that will prove useful in considering the aggregation problem in full generality. It will be shown that these processes can be used to represent joint temporal and contemporaneous aggregation in terms of linear transformations of vector stochastic processes. Forecasting linearly transformed processes has been considered in Chapter 4. Hence, the results of that chapter will be useful here.

Consider again a K-dimensional, nondeterministic, zero mean, stationary stochastic process $\underline{x}_t = (x_{1t},\dots,x_{Kt})'$ with MA representation

$$\underline{x}_t = \sum_{i=0}^{\infty} \Phi_i \underline{u}_{t-i} = \Phi(L)\underline{u}_t , \qquad \Phi_0 = I_K , \tag{6.1.1}$$

where $\underline{u}_t = (u_{1t},\dots,u_{Kt})'$ is K-dimensional white noise with nonsingular covariance matrix $\Sigma_{\underline{u}}$ and

$$\det(\Phi(z)) \neq 0 \quad \text{for} \quad |z| < 1 . \tag{6.1.2}$$

As mentioned earlier, stationary vector ARMA processes are examples of processes satisfying these conditions. Thus, $\underline{x}_t$ may be a member of the ARMA class.

Suppose that $\underline{x}_t$ is to be aggregated over m time periods. To provide a framework in which to analyze the resulting aggregate a <u>macro process</u> $\underline{\mathcal{X}}_{\mathcal{t}}$ corresponding to $\underline{x}_t$ and m is defined as

$$\underline{\mathcal{X}}_{\mathcal{t}} = \sum_{i=0}^{\infty} \mathcal{H}_i \underline{a}_{\mathcal{t}-i} , \quad \mathcal{t} = 0, \pm 1, \pm 2, \dots, \tag{6.1.3}$$

where

$$\underline{\mathcal{X}}_{\mathcal{t}} = \underset{(mK \times 1)}{\begin{bmatrix} \underline{x}_{m(\mathcal{t}-1)+1} \\ \underline{x}_{m(\mathcal{t}-1)+2} \\ \vdots \\ \underline{x}_{m(\mathcal{t}-1)+m} \end{bmatrix}} \qquad \underline{a}_{\mathcal{t}} = \underset{(mK \times 1)}{\begin{bmatrix} \underline{u}_{m(\mathcal{t}-1)+1} \\ \underline{u}_{m(\mathcal{t}-1)+2} \\ \vdots \\ \underline{u}_{m(\mathcal{t}-1)+m} \end{bmatrix}} \tag{6.1.4}$$

$$\mathcal{H}_0 = \begin{bmatrix} I_K & 0 & 0 & \dots & 0 \\ \Phi_1 & I_K & 0 & \dots & 0 \\ \Phi_2 & \Phi_1 & I_K & \dots & 0 \\ \vdots & \vdots & \vdots & \ddots & \vdots \\ \Phi_{m-1} & \Phi_{m-2} & \Phi_{m-3} & \dots & I_K \end{bmatrix} , \quad (mK \times mK)$$

$$H_i = \begin{bmatrix} \Phi_{im} & \Phi_{im-1} & \cdots & \Phi_{im-m+1} \\ \Phi_{im+1} & \Phi_{im} & \cdots & \Phi_{im-m+2} \\ \vdots & \vdots & \ddots & \vdots \\ \Phi_{im+m-1} & \Phi_{im+m-2} & \cdots & \Phi_{im} \end{bmatrix} \quad (mK \times mK) , \quad i = 1,2,... \tag{6.1.5}$$

and

$$\Sigma_{\underline{a}} = I_m \otimes \Sigma_{\underline{u}} . \tag{6.1.6}$$

As usual, $\otimes$ denotes the Kronecker product. Defining an mK-dimensional white noise process $\underline{u}_t = H_0\underline{a}_t$ with

$$\Sigma_{\underline{u}} = H_0(I_m \otimes \Sigma_{\underline{u}})H_0' ,$$

and defining $M_i = H_iH_0^{-1}$, $i = 0,1,2,...$, gives a representation

$$\underline{x}_t = \sum_{i=0}^{\infty} M_i\underline{u}_{t-i} = (\sum_{i=0}^{\infty} M_iL^i)\underline{u}_t = M(L)\underline{u}_t , \tag{6.1.7}$$

where $M_0 = I_{mK}$ and L denotes the lag operator defined such that $L^i\underline{u}_t = \underline{u}_{t-i}$, that is, L operates on the macro time index.

The process $\underline{x}_t$ can be used to investigate temporal aggregates of $\underline{x}_t$. For example, if all components of $\underline{x}_t$ are flow variables that are aggregated (added up) over m time periods, then the aggregate $\underline{y}_t$ is simply a linear transformation of $\underline{x}_t$, $\underline{y}_t = F\underline{x}_t$, where $F = (I_K\ I_K\ ...\ I_K)$ is a (K x mK) matrix. If $\underline{x}_t$ is a process of stock variables and the temporal aggregate $\underline{y}_t$ consists of every m-th $\underline{x}_t$ variable, $\underline{y}_t = \underline{x}_{mt} = F\underline{x}_t$, where $F = (0\ I_K)$ is a (K x mK) matrix. Similarly, if $\underline{x}_t$ consists of stock and flow variables and is aggregated temporally and contemporaneously, the aggregate is a linear transformation of the macro process corresponding to $\underline{x}_t$ and m. Before considering various different predictors for such an aggregate, it is useful to mention some properties of macro processes.

Condition (6.1.2) can be shown to imply

$$\det(M(z)) \neq 0 \quad \text{for} \quad |z| < 1. \tag{6.1.8}$$

Moreover, if (6.1.2) holds for $|z| \leq 1$ so that the MA representation (6.1.1) of $\underline{x}_t$ is invertible, the same is true for (6.1.7). In other words, the MA representation (6.1.7) of the macro process $\underline{x}_t$ is also invertible. This can be seen by noting that invertibility of $\underline{x}_t$ implies the existence of an AR representation

$$\underline{x}_t = \sum_{i=1}^{\infty} A_i \underline{x}_{t-i} + \underline{u}_t \qquad (6.1.9)$$

or

$$A(L)\underline{x}_t = \underline{u}_t \, , \qquad (6.1.10)$$

where $A(L) = \Phi(L)^{-1}$. This AR representation can be used to construct an AR representation of the macro process $\underline{\mathcal{x}}_t$,

$$\bar{\mathcal{A}}_0 \underline{\mathcal{x}}_t = \sum_{i=1}^{\infty} \bar{\mathcal{A}}_i \underline{\mathcal{x}}_{t-i} + \underline{a}_t \, , \qquad (6.1.11)$$

where

$$\bar{\mathcal{A}}_0 = \begin{bmatrix} I_K & 0 & 0 & \dots & 0 \\ -A_1 & I_K & 0 & \dots & 0 \\ -A_2 & -A_1 & I_K & & \vdots \\ \vdots & \vdots & \vdots & \ddots & \\ -A_{m-1} & -A_{m-2} & -A_{m-3} & \dots & I_K \end{bmatrix} ,$$

$$\bar{\mathcal{A}}_i = \underset{(mK \times mK)}{\begin{bmatrix} A_{im} & A_{im-1} & \dots & A_{im-m+1} \\ A_{im+1} & A_{im} & \dots & A_{im-m+2} \\ \vdots & \vdots & \ddots & \vdots \\ A_{im+m-1} & A_{im+m-2} & \dots & A_{im} \end{bmatrix}} , \; i = 1,2,\dots \, , \qquad (6.1.12)$$

and $\underline{a}_t$ is white noise as in (6.1.3). Since $A(L)\Phi(L) = I_K$, it is easy to see that $\bar{\mathcal{A}}_0 = H_0^{-1}$ (see (6.1.5)). Therefore, left multiplying (6.1.11) by $\bar{\mathcal{A}}_0^{-1} = H_0$, the AR representation

$$\underline{\mathcal{x}}_t = \sum_{i=1}^{\infty} \mathcal{A}_i \underline{\mathcal{x}}_{t-i} + \underline{u}_t \qquad (6.1.13)$$

or

$$\mathcal{A}(\mathcal{L})\underline{\mathcal{x}}_t = (I_{mK} - \sum_{i=1}^{\infty} \mathcal{A}_i \mathcal{L}^i)\underline{\mathcal{x}}_t = \underline{u}_t \qquad (6.1.14)$$

is obtained. Thus, the macro process has an AR representation if the underlying process $\underline{x}_t$ has one.

In the next section six predictors for a temporal and contemporaneous aggregate will be introduced formally using macro processes.

6.2 SIX PREDICTORS

It will be assumed that temporal and contemporaneous aggregation is expressed by the (N x mK) transformation matrix

$$F = F_2F_1 = F_3(I_m \otimes F_2), \tag{6.2.1}$$

where F_1 is a (K x mK) matrix of rank K representing temporal aggregation (e.g., $F_1 = (I_K \ldots I_K)$ or $F_1 = (0\ I_K))$, F_2 is an (N x K) matrix of rank N representing contemporaneous aggregation and F_3 is an (N x mN) matrix of rank N representing temporal aggregation of the contemporaneously aggregated system.

As an example consider the bivariate system $\underline{x}_t = (x_{1t}, x_{2t})'$ of quarterly Fixed Investment (x_{1t}) and Change in Business Inventories (x_{2t}) and suppose interest centers on the annual total investment (y_t). Thus, m = 4 and the relevant macro process is

$$\underline{x}'_t = (\underline{x}'_{4(t-1)+1}, \underline{x}'_{4(t-1)+2}, \underline{x}'_{4(t-1)+3}, \underline{x}'_{4t}).$$

Defining

$$F = (1\ 1\ \ldots\ 1) \quad (1 \times 8)$$

gives $y_t = F\underline{x}_t$. The transformation matrix F can be written as a product

$$F = F_2F_1 = (1\ 1)(I_2\ I_2\ I_2\ I_2)$$

or

$$F = F_3(I_4 \otimes F_2) = (1\ 1\ 1\ 1)(I_4 \otimes (1\ 1)).$$

Thus, $F_1 = (I_2\ I_2\ I_2\ I_2)$, $F_2 = (1\ 1)$, and $F_3 = (1\ 1\ 1\ 1)$.

Assuming again that $\underline{x}_t$ is K-dimensional, F is (N x mK) as in (6.2.1) and the aggregate $\underline{y}_t$ is N-dimensional there are various possibilities to forecast $\underline{y}_t$, each having advantages in certain situations.

(1) The disaggregate process is forecast and the forecasts are aggregated. This predictor will be denoted by

$$\underline{y}_t^o(h) = F\underline{x}_t(h) = F\sum_{i=0}^{\infty} M_{h+i}\underline{u}_{t-i} \quad . \tag{6.2.2}$$

In Chapter 4 it is shown that $\underline{x}_t(h)$ is the optimal (linear minimum MSE) h-step predictor of $\underline{x}_{t+h}$ based on $\{\underline{u}_s | s \leq t\} = \{\underline{u}_s | s \leq mt\}$ and $\underline{x}_t(h)$ contains the optimal forecasts of $\underline{x}_t$. This predictor is optimal among all the predictors discussed in the following in the sense that it results in the smallest MSEs. The MSE matrix will be denoted by $\Sigma^o(h)$, that is,

$$\begin{aligned} \Sigma^o(h) &= F(\sum_{i=0}^{h-1} M_i \Sigma_{\underline{u}} M_i')F' \\ &= F(\sum_{i=0}^{h-1} M_i H_0 (I_m \otimes \Sigma_{\underline{u}}) H_0' M_i')F' \\ &= F(\sum_{i=0}^{h-1} H_i (I_m \otimes \Sigma_{\underline{u}}) H_i')F' \ , \end{aligned} \tag{6.2.3}$$

where it is understood that this is the MSE matrix of a predictor for the process $\underline{y}_t$.

(2) If only aggregate data is available the predictor $\underline{y}_t^o(h)$ is not feasible. Expressing the aggregated process as

$$\underline{y}_t = N(L)\underline{v}_t = (\sum_{i=0}^{\infty} N_i L^i)\underline{v}_t = \sum_{i=0}^{\infty} N_i \underline{v}_{t-i} \ , \qquad N_0 = I_N \ , \tag{6.2.4}$$

where $\underline{v}_t$ is N-dimensional white noise with covariance matrix $\Sigma_{\underline{v}}$ and

$$\det(N(z)) \neq 0 \quad \text{for} \quad |z| < 1 \ , \tag{6.2.5}$$

the optimal h-step predictor based on $\{\underline{v}_s | s \leq t\}$ is

$$\underline{y}_t(h) = \sum_{i=0}^{\infty} N_{h+i}\underline{v}_{t-i} \quad . \tag{6.2.6}$$

The corresponding MSE matrix will be denoted by $\Sigma(h)$, that is,

$$\Sigma(h) = \sum_{i=0}^{h-1} N_i \Sigma_{\underline{v}} N_i' \quad . \tag{6.2.7}$$

Note that the existence of the representation (6.2.4) follows from results discussed in Chapter 4, Section 4.1.

(3) Instead of building a multiple time series model for $\underline{x}_t$ the

forecaster may want to predict the individual components and then aggregate the univariate forecasts. In order to express this predictor formally, univariate MA representations

$$x_{kt} = \sum_{i=0}^{\infty} \xi_{ki} w_{k,t-i} = \xi_k(L) w_{kt} \quad , \quad \xi_{k0} = 1 \quad , \quad k = 1,\ldots,K, \quad (6.2.8)$$

of the individual components of $\underline{x}_t$ are used (see Chapter 4, (4.2.6)). Here the w_{kt} are univariate white noise processes and the $\xi_k(z)$ have no roots inside the complex unit circle. Thus, the process $\underline{x}_t$ can be written as

$$\underline{x}_t = \sum_{i=0}^{\infty} \Xi_i \underline{w}_{t-i} = \Xi(L) \underline{w}_t \ , \qquad (6.2.9)$$

where $\Xi_i = \text{diag.}(\xi_{1i},\ldots,\xi_{Ki})$ and $\underline{w}_t = (w_{1t},\ldots,w_{Kt})'$. Note that in general $\underline{w}_t$ is not K-dimensional white noise although the w_{kt} are univariate white noise processes. The macro process can be written as

$$\underline{x}_t = \sum_{i=0}^{\infty} H_i^u \underline{a}_{t-i}^u \ ,$$

where the H_i^u are defined analogously to the H_i in (6.1.5) with Φ_i replaced by Ξ_i and $\underline{a}_t^u$ is defined analogously to $\underline{a}_t$ in (6.1.4) replacing the $\underline{u}_t$ by $\underline{w}_t$. Defining $M_i^u = H_i^u(H_0^u)^{-1}, i = 0,1,2,\ldots,$ and $\underline{u}_t^u = H_0^u \underline{a}_t^u$ gives the representation

$$\underline{x}_t = \sum_{i=0}^{\infty} M_i^u \underline{u}_{t-i}^u = M^u(L)\underline{u}_t^u \ . \qquad (6.2.10)$$

The optimal disaggregate univariate forecasts are contained in

$$\underline{x}_t^u(h) = \sum_{i=0}^{\infty} M_{h+i}^u \underline{u}_{t-i}^u \qquad (6.2.11)$$

and

$$\underline{y}_t^u(h) = F\underline{x}_t^u(h) \qquad (6.2.12)$$

is the desired forecast obtained by aggregating the disaggregate univariate predictors. The corresponding MSE matrix will be denoted by $\Sigma^u(h)$, that is,

$$\not{Z}^u(h) = F[I_{mK} M_1^u \dots M_{h-1}^u] E \left[\begin{bmatrix} \underline{u}_{t+h}^u \\ \underline{u}_{t+h-1}^u \\ \vdots \\ \underline{u}_{t+1}^u \end{bmatrix} [\underline{u}_{t+h}^{u'}, \dots, \underline{u}_{t+1}^{u'}] \right] \begin{bmatrix} I_{mK} \\ M_1^{u'} \\ \vdots \\ M_{h-1}^{u'} \end{bmatrix} F'. \quad (6.2.13)$$

(4) As another alternative, a predictor may be based on temporally aggregated data. The temporally aggregated process can be expressed as

$$\bar{\underline{z}}_t = F_1 \underline{x}_t = \sum_{i=0}^{\infty} R_i \bar{\underline{w}}_{t-i} = R(L)\bar{\underline{w}}_t \quad , \quad R_0 = I_K \, , \quad (6.2.14)$$

where $\bar{\underline{w}}_t$ is K-dimensional white noise with covariance matrix $\not{Z}_{\bar{w}}$ and $\det(R(z))$ has no roots inside the complex unit circle. The optimal h-step predictor based on $\{\bar{\underline{w}}_s | s \le t\}$ is

$$\bar{\underline{z}}_t(h) = \sum_{i=0}^{\infty} R_{h+i} \bar{\underline{w}}_{t-i} \, , \quad (6.2.15)$$

and hence an h-step predictor

$$\bar{\underline{y}}_t^o(h) = F_2 \bar{\underline{z}}_t(h)$$

for $\underline{y}_{t+h}$ is obtained. The corresponding MSE matrix is

$$\not{Z}^o(h) = F_2 \left(\sum_{i=0}^{h-1} R_i \not{Z}_{\bar{\underline{w}}} R_i' \right) F_2' \, . \quad (6.2.16)$$

(5) As an alternative to constructing a multivariate model for the temporally aggregated process $\bar{\underline{z}}_t$, the univariate components of this process may be forecast and the forecasts may be aggregated contemporaneously. Let

$$\bar{z}_{kt} = \sum_{i=0}^{\infty} r_{ki} \bar{w}_{k,t-i}^u \quad , \quad r_{k0} = 1 \, , \quad (6.2.17)$$

be the MA representation of the k-th component of $\bar{\underline{z}}_t$, k = 1,...,K. Then

$$\bar{\underline{z}}_t = \sum_{i=0}^{\infty} R_i^u \bar{\underline{w}}_{t-i}^u = R^u(L) \bar{\underline{w}}_t^u \quad (6.2.18)$$

is another representation of $\bar{z}_t$. Here $R_i^u = \text{diag.}(r_{1i},\ldots,r_{Ki})$ and $\bar{w}_t^u = (\bar{w}_{1t}^u,\ldots,\bar{w}_{Kt}^u)'$ is not vector white noise in general. Using this notation the above described h-step predictor is

$$\bar{y}_t^u(h) = F_2\bar{z}_t^u(h) = F_2\sum_{i=0}^{\infty} R_{h+i}^u\bar{w}_{t-i}^u \qquad (6.2.19)$$

and its MSE matrix will be denoted by $\bar{\Sigma}^u(h)$, that is,

$$\bar{\Sigma}^u(h) = F_2(I_K R_1^u \ldots R_{h-1}^u)E\left[\begin{bmatrix}\bar{w}_{t+h}^u\\ \bar{w}_{t+h-1}^u\\ \vdots\\ \bar{w}_{t+1}^u\end{bmatrix}\left[\bar{w}_{t+h}^{u\prime},\ldots,\bar{w}_{t+1}^{u\prime}\right]\right]\begin{bmatrix}I_K\\ R_1^{u\prime}\\ \vdots\\ R_{h-1}^{u\prime}\end{bmatrix}F_2'. \qquad (6.2.20)$$

(6) Finally, if contemporaneously disaggregated data is not available, the contemporaneously aggregated process may be predicted. The desired forecasts are then obtained by temporally aggregating these predictions. To express the resulting predictor formally the "contemporaneously aggregated macro process"

$$z_t = (I_m \otimes F_2)x_t = \mathcal{D}(L)w_t = \sum_{i=0}^{\infty}\mathcal{D}_i w_{t-i}\ , \quad \mathcal{D}_0 = I_{mN}\ , \qquad (6.2.21)$$

is used, where w_t is mN-dimensional white noise with covariance matrix Σ_w and $\det(\mathcal{D}(z))$ has no roots inside the complex unit circle. The optimal h-step predictor based on $\{w_s|s \le t\}$ is

$$z_t(h) = \sum_{i=0}^{\infty}\mathcal{D}_{h+i}w_{t-i} \qquad (6.2.22)$$

and

$$y_t^*(h) = F_3 z_t(h) \qquad (6.2.23)$$

is a predictor for y_t with MSE matrix

$$\Sigma^*(h) = F_3\left(\sum_{i=0}^{h-1}\mathcal{D}_i\Sigma_w\mathcal{D}_i'\right)F_3'\ . \qquad (6.2.24)$$

The processes defined in the foregoing are listed in Table 6.1 and the predictors for the aggregate y_t are summarized in Table 6.2. They have all been used in practice. Often no reasons are given why a particular candidate is employed. For instance, if quarterly data is used

Table 6.1. Processes Used for Prediction

Disaggregate process:

$$\underline{x}_t = \Phi(L)\underline{u}_t = \sum_{i=0}^{\infty} \Phi_i \underline{u}_{t-i} \quad , \quad \Phi_0 = I_K$$

$$= \Xi(L)\underline{w}_t = \sum_{i=0}^{\infty} \Xi_i \underline{w}_{t-i} \quad , \quad \Xi(L) \text{ diagonal}$$

corresponding macro process:

$$\underline{\mathcal{X}}_{\mathcal{t}} = M(L)\underline{u}_{\mathcal{t}} = \sum_{i=0}^{\infty} M_i \underline{u}_{\mathcal{t}-i} \quad , \quad M_0 = I_{mK}$$

$$= M^u(L)\underline{u}^u_{\mathcal{t}} = \sum_{i=0}^{\infty} M^u_i \underline{u}^u_{\mathcal{t}-i}$$

Temporally and contemporaneously aggregated process:

$$\underline{y}_{\mathcal{t}} = F\underline{x}_{\mathcal{t}} = N(L)\underline{v}_{\mathcal{t}} = \sum_{i=0}^{\infty} N_i \underline{v}_{\mathcal{t}-i} \quad , \quad N_0 = I_N$$

Temporally aggregated process:

$$\underline{\overline{z}}_{\mathcal{t}} = F_1\underline{x}_{\mathcal{t}} = R(L)\underline{\overline{w}}_{\mathcal{t}} = \sum_{i=0}^{\infty} R_i \underline{\overline{w}}_{\mathcal{t}-i} \quad , \quad R_0 = I_K$$

$$= R^u(L)\underline{\overline{w}}^u_{\mathcal{t}} = \sum_{i=0}^{\infty} R^u_i \underline{\overline{w}}^u_{\mathcal{t}-i} \quad , \quad R^u(L) \text{ diagonal}$$

Contemporaneously aggregated process:

$$\underline{z}_t = F_2\underline{x}_t$$

corresponding macro process:

$$\underline{z}_{\mathcal{t}} = (I_m \otimes F_2)\underline{x}_{\mathcal{t}} = D(L)\underline{w}_{\mathcal{t}} = \sum_{i=0}^{\infty} D_i \underline{w}_{\mathcal{t}-i} \quad , \quad D_0 = I_{mN}$$

Table 6.2. Predictors for Aggregated Process

Predictor	Description	MSE matrix
$\underline{y}_t^o(h) = F\underline{x}_t(h) = F\sum_{i=0}^{\infty} M_{h+i}\underline{u}_{t-i}$	Prediction of the disaggregate process and aggregation of the predictions	$\Sigma^o(h)$
$\underline{y}_t(h) = \sum_{i=0}^{\infty} N_{h+i}\underline{v}_{t-i}$	Direct prediction of the aggregated process	$\Sigma(h)$
$\underline{y}_t^u(h) = F\underline{x}_t^u(h) = F\sum_{i=0}^{\infty} M_{h+i}^u\underline{u}_{t-i}^u$	Prediction of the univariate components of the disaggregate process and aggregation of the univariate predictions	$\Sigma^u(h)$
$\overline{\underline{y}}_t^o(h) = F_2\overline{\underline{z}}_t(h) = F_2\sum_{i=0}^{\infty} R_{h+i}\overline{\underline{w}}_{t-i}$	Prediction of the temporally aggregated process and contemporaneous aggregation of the predictions	$\overline{\Sigma}^o(h)$
$\overline{\underline{y}}_t^u(h) = F_2\overline{\underline{z}}_t^u(h) = F_2\sum_{i=0}^{\infty} R_{h+i}^u\overline{\underline{w}}_{t-i}^u$	Prediction of the univariate components of the temporally aggregated process and contemporaneous aggregation of the univariate predictions	$\overline{\Sigma}^u(h)$
$\underline{y}_t^*(h) = F_3\underline{z}_t(h) = F_3\sum_{i=0}^{\infty} D_{h+i}\underline{w}_{t-i}$	Prediction of the contemporaneously aggregated process and temporal aggregation of the predictions	$\Sigma^*(h)$

for quarterly predictions often no arguments are provided why a monthly model has not been considered for forecasting. Of course, lack of appropriate data may be one reason. In such a situation the consequences for the forecast precision will be of interest and in the next section some relevant results will be provided.

There are various other reasonable possibilities to forecast y_{t+h} that will not be discussed in the following but can be treated in a similar fashion. For example, if only aggregated data is available the individual components of y_t could be predicted instead of the N-dimensional process (provided $N > 1$). Also, the contemporaneous and temporal aggregation could be done in various steps. This procedure is very common in practice. For instance, annual sales figures are obtained by summing the monthly figures which are themselves sums of daily values. The different stages of aggregation can be expressed by writing the aggregation matrix F as a product of a number of "partial aggregation matrices" analogously to (6.2.1). The properties of the various possible predictors can be investigated using the tools presented in this chapter. In the next section the MSEs of the predictors summarized in Table 6.2 will be compared and conditions for their equivalence will be given.

6.3 COMPARISON OF PREDICTORS

Using the framework of the previous two sections it is easy to derive a number of relations between the MSE matrices of the various predictors from results given in Chapter 4. In Table 6.3 some relations between the predictors and their MSE matrices are summarized.

In Table 6.3(a) the inequality sign "$\leq$" between matrices means as usual that the differences between the right-hand and the left-hand matrices are positive semidefinite. All the relations in (1) - (3) follow from (4.2.16) in Chapter 4 by noting that only different linear transformations of vector stochastic processes are considered. The first result means that the predictor based on a multivariate model for the fully disaggregated data is optimal among all considered predictors. Relation (2) means that contemporaneous aggregation of the predictions of the temporally aggregated univariate components is inferior to both the predictor based on the temporally aggregated multivariate process and the predictor based on univariate forecasts of the fully disaggregated components. Furthermore, relation (3) in Table 6.3(a) states that the predictor based on the fully aggregated process is inferior to temporally aggregating the predictor based on the contemporaneously aggre-

Table 6.3. Relations Between Predictors and MSE Matrices

(a) Comparison of some MSE matrices

(1) $\Sigma^{o}(h) \leq \Sigma(h),\ \Sigma^{u}(h),\ \bar{\Sigma}^{o}(h),\ \bar{\Sigma}^{u}(h),\ \Sigma^{*}(h)$

(2) $\bar{\Sigma}^{o}(h),\ \Sigma^{u}(h) \leq \bar{\Sigma}^{u}(h)$

(3) $\bar{\Sigma}^{o}(h),\ \Sigma^{*}(h) \leq \Sigma(h)$

(4) $\Sigma^{o}(h),\ \Sigma(h),\ \Sigma^{u}(h),\ \bar{\Sigma}^{o}(h),\ \bar{\Sigma}^{u}(h),\ \Sigma^{*}(h) \xrightarrow[h\to\infty]{} \Sigma_{\mathbf{y}} = E(\mathbf{y}_t\mathbf{y}_t')$

(b) Conditions for equality of predictors

$\mathbf{y}^{o}_t(1) = \mathbf{y}_t(1)$	$\iff$	$FM(L)$	$= N(L)F$
$\mathbf{y}^{o}_t(1) = \mathbf{y}^{u}_t(1)$	$\iff$	$FM(L)^{-1}$	$= FM^{u}(L)^{-1}$
$\mathbf{y}^{o}_t(1) = \bar{\mathbf{y}}^{o}_t(1)$	$\iff$	$FM(L)^{-1}$	$= F_2R(L)^{-1}F_1$
$\mathbf{y}^{o}_t(1) = \bar{\mathbf{y}}^{u}_t(1)$	$\iff$	$FM(L)^{-1}$	$= F_2R^{u}(L)^{-1}F_1$
$\mathbf{y}^{o}_t(1) = \mathbf{y}^{*}_t(1)$	$\iff$	$FM(L)^{-1}$	$= F_3\mathcal{D}(L)^{-1}(I_m \otimes F_2)$
$\mathbf{y}_t(1) = \mathbf{y}^{u}_t(1)$	$\iff$	$FM^{u}(L)$	$= N(L)F$
$\mathbf{y}_t(1) = \bar{\mathbf{y}}^{o}_t(1)$	$\iff$	$F_2R(L)$	$= N(L)F_2$
$\mathbf{y}_t(1) = \bar{\mathbf{y}}^{u}_t(1)$	$\iff$	$F_2R^{u}(L)$	$= N(L)F_2$
$\mathbf{y}_t(1) = \mathbf{y}^{*}_t(1)$	$\iff$	$F_3\mathcal{D}(L)$	$= N(L)F_3$
$\mathbf{y}^{u}_t(1) = \bar{\mathbf{y}}^{o}_t(1)$	$\iff$	$FM^{u}(L)^{-1}$	$= F_2R(L)^{-1}F_1$
$\mathbf{y}^{u}_t(1) = \bar{\mathbf{y}}^{u}_t(1)$	$\iff$	$FM^{u}(L)^{-1}$	$= F_2R^{u}(L)^{-1}F_1$
$\mathbf{y}^{u}_t(1) = \mathbf{y}^{*}_t(1)$	$\iff$	$FM^{u}(L)^{-1}$	$= F_3\mathcal{D}(L)^{-1}(I_m \otimes F_2)$
$\bar{\mathbf{y}}^{o}_t(1) = \bar{\mathbf{y}}^{u}_t(1)$	$\iff$	$F_2R(L)^{-1}$	$= F_2R^{u}(L)^{-1}$

---

gated process and to contemporaneously aggregating the predictor based on the temporally aggregated multivariate process. The result in Table 6.3(a)(4) follows from $\underline{x}_t$ being nondeterministic and means that for long range prediction all predictors approach the process mean of zero.

It may also be of interest for which predictors a generally valid ranking cannot be given. Here again a result mentioned in Chapter 4 is useful. It is noted in Section 4.2.2 that if $\underline{y}_t$ is a linear transformation of $\underline{x}_t$, that is, $\underline{y}_t = F\underline{x}_t$, a general ranking of $\underline{y}_t(h)$ and $\underline{y}_t^u(h)$ is not possible. This result implies that the rankings of $\underline{\mathcal{y}}_t(h)$ and $\underline{\mathcal{y}}_t^u(h)$, $\underline{\mathcal{y}}_t(h)$ and $\overline{\underline{\mathcal{y}}}_t^u(h)$, and of $\underline{\mathcal{y}}_t^*(h)$ and $\overline{\underline{\mathcal{y}}}_t^u(h)$ depend on the structure of the basic process $\underline{x}_t$ and the aggregation matrix F. Also, a general ranking of $\overline{\underline{\mathcal{y}}}_t^o(h)$ and $\underline{\mathcal{y}}_t^*(h)$ cannot be given because in cases with no contemporaneous aggregation ($F_2 = I$) $\overline{\underline{\mathcal{y}}}_t^o(h)$ will be dominated by $\underline{\mathcal{y}}_t^*(h)$, whereas the converse will be true if there is no temporal aggregation ($F_1 = I$, $F_3 = I$).

All the conditions for equality of the different predictors given in Table 6.3(b) follow straightforwardly from Proposition 4.1 in Chapter 4 and the proof of that proposition. For example, the condition for equality of $\underline{\mathcal{y}}_t^o(1)$ and $\underline{\mathcal{y}}_t(1)$ is merely a restatement of the condition in Proposition 4.1(i). Also the second equivalence is merely a restatement of the corresponding condition in Proposition 4.1(iii). Of course, whenever inverse operators are involved, they are assumed to exist. The third equivalence follows by noting that $\underline{\mathcal{y}}_t^o(1) = \overline{\underline{\mathcal{y}}}_t^o(1)$ implies

$$F\underline{u}_{t+1} = \underline{\mathcal{y}}_{t+1} - \underline{\mathcal{y}}_t^o(1) = \underline{\mathcal{y}}_{t+1} - \overline{\underline{\mathcal{y}}}_t^o(1) = F_2\overline{\underline{w}}_{t+1} . \qquad (6.3.1)$$

Furthermore, by the definition of $\overline{\underline{z}}_t$,

$$R(L)\overline{\underline{w}}_t = F_1\underline{x}_t = F_1M(L)\underline{u}_t$$

so that

$$\overline{\underline{w}}_t = R(L)^{-1}F_1M(L)\underline{u}_t .$$

Hence, by (6.3.1),

$$F = F_2R(L)^{-1}F_1M(L)$$

or

$$FM(L)^{-1} = F_2R(L)^{-1}F_1 .$$

In turn, if the latter condition is satisfied,

$$\begin{aligned}\overline{y}^{o}_{t}(1) &= F_2 R(L)\overline{w}_{t+1} - F_2\overline{w}_{t+1} \\ &= F_2 R(L) R(L)^{-1} F_1 M(L) u_{t+1} - F_2 R(L)^{-1} F_1 M(L) u_{t+1} \\ &= F M(L) u_{t+1} - F M(L)^{-1} M(L) u_{t+1} \\ &= y^{o}_{t}(1) \ .\end{aligned}$$

The fourth and fifth equivalences follow by similar arguments while the sixth result is a restatement of Proposition 4.1(ii), and so on.

Note that invertibility of the underlying processes is not required where the inverse operators are not involved in the conditions for predictor equivalence in Table 6.3(b). Moreover, equality of the 1-step forecasts implies equality of the h-step forecasts for h = 2,3,... . These results are of some importance in practice because if two predictors are identical the forecaster can choose the most convenient one without losing forecast efficiency. Of course, in practice the structure of the involved processes will usually be unknown prior to the analysis so that an a priori choice of the best (minimum MSE and most convenient) predictor will be difficult. Nevertheless, some information on the data generation process may sometimes be available, indicating that certain processes are more likely than others. To illustrate in which cases the conditions for equality of the different predictors will be satisfied, some examples will be discussed now.

Suppose x_t is as in (6.1.1). If all the Φ_i are diagonal matrices then it is easy to see that $M(L) = M^u(L)$. Thus, the predictors $y^o_t(h)$ and $y^u_t(h)$ will be identical for any aggregation matrix F. Furthermore, the temporally aggregated process $\overline{z}_t$ will have diagonal coefficient matrices R_i and thus, $\overline{y}^o_t(h) = \overline{y}^u_t(h)$. If the Φ_i in (6.1.1) are diagonal matrices with identical diagonal elements, that is,

$$\Phi_i = \begin{bmatrix} \phi_i & & 0 \\ & \ddots & \\ 0 & & \phi_i \end{bmatrix} \qquad (6.3.2)$$

then $y^*_t(h) = y^o_t(h)$, that is, $y^*_t(h)$ is optimal for all aggregation matrices F (see Corollary 4.1.2). Moreover, if

$$x_t = \sum_{i=0}^{\infty} \Phi_{im} u_{t-im} \ , \qquad (6.3.3)$$

i.e., $\Phi_i = 0$ unless i is an integer multiple of m, then all predictors will be identical for any F matrix if the Φ_{im}, $i = 0,1,2,\ldots$, are diagonal with identical diagonal elements as in (6.3.2). In this case the macro process corresponding to $\underline{x}_t$ and m has the form

$$\underline{x}_t = M(L)\underline{u}_t = \begin{bmatrix} \Phi(L) & 0 & \cdots & 0 \\ 0 & \Phi(L) & \cdots & 0 \\ \vdots & \vdots & \ddots & \vdots \\ 0 & 0 & \cdots & \Phi(L) \end{bmatrix} \underline{u}_t \qquad (6.3.4)$$

$$= \phi(L)\underline{u}_t ,$$

where

$$\Phi(L) = \sum_{i=0}^{\infty} \Phi_{im} L^i$$

and

$$\phi(L) = \sum_{i=0}^{\infty} \phi_{im} L^i .$$

It is easy to check that in this situation all the conditions in Table 6.3 (b) are satisfied for any aggregation matrix F. A process of the special type (6.3.3) may arise if strong seasonal factors are present and m is equal to the seasonal period and if furthermore all the components to be aggregated are independent and have the same stochastic structure.

So far only examples have been discussed where equality of the predictors results from the special structure of $\underline{x}_t$ regardless of F. In the next example the form of F is crucial. Suppose $\underline{x}_t$ has the form (6.3.3) where the Φ_{im} are not necessarily diagonal matrices. If all components of $\underline{x}_t$ are flow variables and there is only temporal aggregation, i.e., $F = (I_K \ldots I_K)$ is a $(K \times mK)$ matrix, then it follows immediately from (6.3.3) and (6.3.4) that $FM(L) = N(L)F$ and thus, $\underline{y}_t^o(h)$ and $\underline{y}_t(h)$ are identical. The same holds, if $\underline{x}_t$ consists of stock variables only and $F = (0 \ I_K)$. However, if $\underline{x}_t$ contains stock and flow variables, $\underline{y}_t^o(h)$ will in general be superior to $\underline{y}_t(h)$. To see this suppose that $\underline{x}_t = (x_{1t}, x_{2t})'$ is a bivariate process, x_{1t} is a flow variable, x_{2t} is a stock variable and $F = (G_1 \ G_2)$, where

$$G_1 = \begin{bmatrix} 1 & 0 \\ 0 & 0 \end{bmatrix}, \quad G_2 = I_2 ,$$

so that there is only temporal aggregation over two periods (m = 2).

Using (6.3.1) and

$$\underline{y}_{t+1} - \underline{y}_t(1) = \underline{v}_{t+1} , \tag{6.3.5}$$

equality of $\underline{y}^o_t(1)$ and $\underline{y}_t(1)$ implies $F\underline{u}_t = \underline{v}_t$. Consequently,

$$\begin{aligned}\underline{y}_t &= \sum_{i=0}^{\infty} N_i \underline{v}_{t-i} = \sum_{i=0}^{\infty} N_i F\underline{u}_{t-i} \\ &= F\underline{x}_t = \sum_{i=0}^{\infty} FM_i \underline{u}_{t-i} = \sum_{i=0}^{\infty} (G_1\Phi_{im} \;\; G_2\Phi_{im})\underline{u}_{t-i} .\end{aligned}$$

Comparing corresponding coefficients gives

$$(N_iG_1 \;\; N_iG_2) = N_iF = (G_1\Phi_{im} \;\; G_2\Phi_{im}) .$$

Hence,

$$N_i = \Phi_{im} \quad \text{and} \quad N_iG_1 = G_1\Phi_{im} , \quad i = 0,1,2,\ldots , \tag{6.3.6}$$

where $G_2 = I_2$ has been used. Clearly, (6.3.6) holds only for special Φ_{im} matrices. For instance, if

$$N_1 = \Phi_m = \begin{bmatrix} \phi_{11} & \phi_{12} \\ \phi_{21} & \phi_{22} \end{bmatrix} ,$$

then

$$G_1\Phi_m = \begin{bmatrix} \phi_{11} & \phi_{12} \\ 0 & 0 \end{bmatrix}$$

and

$$\Phi_m G_1 = \begin{bmatrix} \phi_{11} & 0 \\ \phi_{21} & 0 \end{bmatrix} .$$

Thus, equality of the latter two matrices requires $\phi_{12} = \phi_{21} = 0$.

This example demonstrates the importance of having a framework in which to analyze systems with both stock and flow variables. Even if equality of the predictors $\underline{y}^o_t(h)$ and $\underline{y}_t(h)$ holds for systems consisting either of stock variables or of flow variables only, predictor equality will in general not hold if both types of variables are involved. Further situations where some predictors are identical will be discussed in subsequent chapters.

So far stationary processes have been considered. In the following section extensions to certain nonstationary processes are noted.

6.4 NONSTATIONARY PROCESSES

6.4.1 Differencing to Obtain Stationarity

In the context of contemporaneous aggregation it was demonstrated that nonstationary processes do not create additional problems if they can be transformed to stationarity by applying the same differencing operator to each component. In this case the same differencing operator can be used for the aggregate. In the following it will be investigated whether a similar result holds for temporally aggregated processes.

Suppose the same differencing operator is applied to each component of the K-dimensional disaggregate process $\underline{x}_t$ to obtain stationarity, that is,

$$\Delta(L)\underline{x}_t = \underline{x}_t^s \qquad (6.4.1)$$

is stationary, where, for instance,

$$\Delta(L) = (1 - L)^d \qquad (6.4.2)$$

or

$$\Delta(L) = (1 - L^s)^D \qquad (6.4.3)$$

or

$$\Delta(L) = (1 - L^s)^D(1 - L)^d \ . \qquad (6.4.4)$$

Here d and D are nonnegative integers and s is a positive integer that will usually represent a seasonal period like s = 4 for quarterly data and s = 12 for monthly data.

Given the assumptions of the previous sections, applying the same differencing operator to each component series is not restrictive because unit roots in the MA operator of the stationary process $\underline{x}_t^s$ are permitted. On the other hand, in practice, when estimated processes are considered, the existence of an AR representation of $\underline{x}_t^s$ is usually assumed. Therefore it is perhaps worth noting that somewhat more general situations (i.e., different differencing operators for different components) can be handled in a similar way and the following is meant to be an illustration of how to proceed.

As before, let m be the number of periods of temporal aggregation and $\underline{x}_t$ denotes the macro process corresponding to $\underline{x}_t$ and m. If $\Delta(L) = (1 - L)^d$ as in (6.4.1), then $(1 - L)^d \underline{x}_t$ is also stationary. Here L is again the lag operator operating on the macro time index t. This result follows by noting that

$$(1 - L)^d \underline{x}_t = \begin{bmatrix} (1 - L^m)^d \underline{x}_{(t-1)m+1} \\ (1 - L^m)^d \underline{x}_{(t-1)m+2} \\ \vdots \\ (1 - L^m)^d \underline{x}_{(t-1)m+m} \end{bmatrix} \qquad (6.4.5)$$

and

$$(1 - L^m)^d \underline{x}_t = (1 + L + \dots + L^{m-1})^d (1 - L)^d \underline{x}_t \quad ,$$

which is the sum (linear transformation) of stationary processes of the type $(1 - L)^d \underline{x}_t$ and is therefore stationary (see Chapter 4). Thus, in order to obtain a stationary macro process, the ordinary difference operator $(1 - L)$ has to be applied to $\underline{x}_t$ as many times as $(1 - L)$ is applied to the disaggregate process $\underline{x}_t$.

The situation is a bit different if $\Delta(L)$ is a seasonal differencing operator as in (6.4.3). In practice it is often reasonable to assume that s is an integer multiple of m. For example, if $\underline{x}_t$ consists of monthly (s = 12) variables that are aggregated over m = 3 periods to obtain quarterly variables, s/m = 4. In that case $(1 - L^{s/m})^D \underline{x}_t$ will be stationary. This result follows immediately by writing the macro process as in (6.4.5) with the differencing operator modified appropriately. Thus, when the seasonal differencing operator is applied to the macro process, the operator has to be adjusted for the change in the seasonal period.

Combining the two situations considered in the foregoing gives the result that

$$(1 - L^{s/m})^D (1 - L)^d \underline{x}_t$$

is stationary if the same holds for

$$(1 - L^s)^D (1 - L)^d \underline{x}_t \; .$$

This result can be used to determine the differencing operator to be applied to the processes in Table 6.1 in order to obtain stationarity.

For instance, it follows from the discussion in Chapter 4, Section 4.3, that the aggregate $\underline{y}_t = F\underline{x}_t$, where F is an (N x Km) aggregation matrix, can also be transformed to stationarity by applying the differencing operator $(1 - L^{s/m})^D(1 - L)^d$. In summary, to induce stationarity in a temporally and contemporaneously aggregated process, the simple difference operator is applied as many times as for the original, disaggregate process while the seasonal difference operator is adjusted for the change in the seasonal period caused by temporal aggregation. For instance, if $\underline{x}_t$ is a monthly process and $\underline{y}_t$ is a quarterly process, the seasonal difference operator $(1 - L^{12})$ for $\underline{x}_t$ has to be changed to $(1 - L^4)$ for $\underline{y}_t$. Of course, this result is in complete agreement with intuition. Analogous results hold for the other processes used in Section 6.2.

6.4.2 Forecasting Aggregated Nonstationary Processes

Unlike contemporaneous aggregation, a forecast comparison for nonstationary temporally aggregated processes cannot simply be performed by considering the stationary parts of the different processes. To illustrate the potential problems, consider the univariate process x_t which is assumed to be stationary after differencing once,

$$x_t = x_{t-1} + x_t^s = x_{t-m} + \sum_{j=1}^{m} x_{t-m+j}^s , \qquad (6.4.6)$$

where x_t^s is the stationary part. If this process is aggregated over m periods by adding consecutive variables, the aggregate is

$$\begin{aligned} y_t &= x_{mt} + \dots + x_{mt-m+1} \\ &= (x_{mt-m} + \sum_{j=1}^{m} x_{mt-m+j}^s) + \dots + (x_{mt-m+1-m} + \sum_{j=1}^{m} x_{mt-m+1-m+j}^s) \\ &= y_{t-1} + y_t^s , \end{aligned}$$

where

$$y_t^s = \sum_{i=0}^{m-1} \sum_{j=1}^{m} x_{mt-m-i+j}^s \qquad (6.4.7)$$

is the stationary part of the aggregate y_t. The process y_t^s is obviously distinct from the process

$$x^s_{mt} + \dots + x^s_{mt-m+1}$$

obtained by temporally aggregating the stationary process x^s_t. Therefore, in order to compare the forecasts $y_t(h)$ and $y^o_t(h)$ it does not suffice to compare the stationary part forecasts. In particular the conditions for predictor equivalence given in Table 6.3(b) will no longer be valid if the MA operators of the stationary part processes are used.

Rather than discussing the problem in full generality it is more instructive to investigate the consequences of special types of temporal aggregation separately. This will be done in the following chapters.

General results worth noting in the present general context are that (i) also for nonstationary processes the precictor $\underline{y}^o_t$ based on the fully disaggregated process $\underline{x}_t$ will still be optimal, that is, the relations in Table 6.3(a)(1) remain valid, and (ii) also the relations in Table 6.3(a)(2) and (3) continue to hold. On the other hand, the MSE matrices do not converge for increasing forecast horizon. In other words, the differences between the forecast MSEs will in general not disappear for long range forecasts.

6.5 TEMPORALLY AND CONTEMPORANEOUSLY AGGREGATED VECTOR ARMA PROCESSES

Since the parameters of the considered processes are assumed known in this chapter, there is no need to restrict the discussion to finite parameterizations. In the following chapters estimated processes will also be treated and then it will sometimes be useful to restrict the generation process of the disaggregate data to the class of finite order vector ARMA processes. Following Lütkepohl (1984c) it will be demonstrated in this section that temporally and contemporaneously aggregated vector ARMA processes are again members of the ARMA class. Given that macro processes have already been introduced in Section 6.1 this is certainly no surprising result. Nevertheless a brief discussion of the topic may be instructive.

Suppose that $\underline{x}_t$ is a K-dimensional vector ARMA(p,q) process,

$$\underline{x}_t = \Theta_1\underline{x}_{t-1} + \dots + \Theta_p\underline{x}_{t-p} + \underline{u}_t + M_1\underline{u}_{t-1} + \dots + M_q\underline{u}_{t-q} \qquad (6.5.1)$$

or, in lag operator notation,

$$\Theta(L)\underline{x}_t = M(L)\underline{u}_t , \qquad (6.5.2)$$

where $\underline{u}_t$ is white noise with nonsingular covariance matrix $\Sigma_{\underline{u}}$,

$$\Theta(L) = I_K - \Theta_1 L - \ldots - \Theta_p L^p ,$$

and

$$M(L) = I_K + M_1 L + \ldots + M_q L^q ,$$

as in the previous chapters. It is not necessary at this point to assume stationarity and invertibility.

For any positive integer m, the macro process $\underline{x}_t$ corresponding to $\underline{x}_t$ and m has an ARMA(P,Q) representation

$$\bar{A}_0 \underline{x}_t = \bar{A}_1 \underline{x}_{t-1} + \ldots + \bar{A}_P \underline{x}_{t-P} + H_0 \underline{a}_t + H_1 \underline{a}_{t-1} + \ldots + H_Q \underline{a}_{t-Q} \quad (6.5.3)$$

or

$$\bar{A}(L) \underline{x}_t = H(L) \underline{a}_t , \quad (6.5.4)$$

where $\underline{x}_t$ and $\underline{a}_t$ are as in (6.1.4), $\bar{A}(L)$ and $H(L)$ are defined in the obvious way, the (mK x mK) matrices $\bar{A}_i$, i = 0,...,P, have a similar form as in (6.1.12) replacing the A_j by Θ_j for j = 1,...,p and by zero for j > p, and the H_i, i = 0,1,...,Q, are similar as in (6.1.5) where the Φ_j have to be replaced by M_j for j = 1,...,q, and by zero for j > q. The order P is chosen to be the smallest number so that $\bar{A}_i = 0$ for i > P, that is,

$$P = \min\{n \in \mathbb{N} \mid nm \geq p\} , \quad (6.5.5)$$

and Q is the smallest number such that $H_i = 0$ for i > Q, that is,

$$Q = \min\{n \in \mathbb{N} \mid nm \geq q\} , \quad (6.5.6)$$

where $\mathbb{N}$ denotes the nonnegative integers.

As an example consider the ARMA(2,1) process

$$\underline{x}_t = \Theta_1 \underline{x}_{t-1} + \Theta_2 \underline{x}_{t-2} + \underline{u}_t + M_1 \underline{u}_{t-1} \quad (6.5.7)$$

and m = 3. The corresponding macro process $\underline{x}_t$ is an ARMA(1,1) process,

$$\bar{A}_0 \underline{x}_t = \bar{A}_1 \underline{x}_{t-1} + H_0 \underline{a}_t + H_1 \underline{a}_{t-1} , \quad (6.5.8)$$

where

$$\bar{A}_0 = \begin{bmatrix} I_K & 0 & 0 \\ -\Theta_1 & I_K & 0 \\ -\Theta_2 & -\Theta_1 & I_K \end{bmatrix} , \quad \bar{A}_1 = \begin{bmatrix} 0 & \Theta_2 & \Theta_1 \\ 0 & 0 & \Theta_2 \\ 0 & 0 & 0 \end{bmatrix} ,$$

$$H_0 = \begin{bmatrix} I_K & 0 & 0 \\ M_1 & I_K & 0 \\ 0 & M_1 & I_K \end{bmatrix} , \quad H_1 = \begin{bmatrix} 0 & 0 & M_1 \\ 0 & 0 & 0 \\ 0 & 0 & 0 \end{bmatrix} .$$

Using the ARMA representation of the macro process it follows from Proposition 4.2 in Chapter 4 that the aggregate $\underline{y}_t$ also has an ARMA representation. More precisely, the following proposition can be shown (Lütkepohl (1984c)).

PROPOSITION 6.1

Let $\underline{x}_t$ be a vector ARMA(p,q) process as in (6.5.1), let m be a positive integer and let $\underline{\mathcal{X}}_t$ be the macro process associated with $\underline{x}_t$ and m. Further let F be an (N x mK) aggregation matrix of rank N. Then $\underline{y}_t = F\underline{\mathcal{X}}_t$ has an ARMA(P*,Q*) representation with

$$P^* \leq Kp \tag{6.5.9}$$

and

$$Q^* \leq \begin{cases} Kp & \text{for } m \geq p \geq q , \\ Kp + 1 & \text{for } m \geq q > p , \\ Kp + Q & \text{otherwise} . \end{cases} \tag{6.5.10}$$

Proof.

Using the representation

$$\det(\bar{A}(L))\underline{\mathcal{X}}_t = \bar{A}(L)^* H(L)\underline{a}_t \tag{6.5.11}$$

of the macro process, where $\bar{A}(L)^*$ is the adjoint of $\bar{A}(L)$, it follows that

$$\det(\bar{A}(L))\underline{y}_t = F\bar{A}(L)^* H(L)\underline{a}_t \tag{6.5.12}$$

is an ARMA representation of the aggregate $\underline{y}_t$.

To determine the degree of the AR operator note that $Pm \geq p$ by (6.5.5) and hence there exists a nonnegative integer s such that Pm = p + s and thus, P = (p+s)/m. Since the last Ks rows of $\bar{A}_P$ are zero, the operators in the last Ks rows of $\bar{A}(L)$ have a degree not greater than P - 1. Noting that the determinant is the sum of all products of precisely one element from each row and each column (appropriately multiplied by 1 or -1) gives

$$\deg \det(\bar{A}(L)) \leq K(m-s)P + Ks(P-1) = Kp . \tag{6.5.13}$$

Thereby (6.5.9) is demonstrated.

By Proposition 4.2, the degree Q* of the MA part of (6.5.12) is less than or equal to the degree of $\bar{A}(L)^*H(L)$. Thus,

$$Q^* \leq \max\{\deg \bar{A}_{ij}(L) + Q_{in} | i,j,n = 1,\dots,mK\} , \tag{6.5.14}$$

where $\bar{A}_{ij}(L)$ is the ij-th cofactor of $\bar{A}(L)$ and Q_{in} is the order of the in-th operator in $H(L)$ in (6.5.4). From $\deg \bar{A}_{ij}(L) \leq Kp$ and $Q_{in} \leq Q$ it follows that $Q^* \leq Kp + Q$. For $p,q \leq m$,

$$\deg \bar{A}_{ij}(L) \leq Kp - 1 \quad \text{for } i \leq Kp$$

and

$$Q_{in} \begin{cases} \leq 1 & \text{for } i \leq Kq \\ = 0 & \text{for } i > Kq . \end{cases}$$

Thus,

$$\deg A_{ij}(L) + Q_{in} \leq \begin{cases} Kp , & \text{if} \quad Kq \leq Kp \text{ and } p,q \leq m \\ Kp + 1 , & \text{if} \quad p < q \leq m . \end{cases} \qquad \text{Q.E.D.}$$

Special cases of Proposition 6.1 have been discussed by many authors. In many cases it is possible to provide bounds for the ARMA orders of y_t that are lower than those given in (6.5.9) and (6.5.10). For example, Quenouille (1958), Tiao (1972), Amemiya & Wu (1972), Brewer (1973), Wei (1978a, 1981), Stram & Wei (1986), Ahsanullah & Wei (1984a, b) and Weiss (1984) consider temporally aggregated univariate processes and Werner (1982) gives smaller bounds for the ARMA orders assuming a (K x mK) aggregation matrix $F = (0 \; I_K)$ (see also Schönfeld (1980)). Brewer also treats certain bivariate processes. A more detailed discussion of special cases is given by Lütkepohl (1986a). In the following it suffices to know that a temporally and contemporaneously aggregated vector ARMA process has again a finite order ARMA representation.

Proposition 6.1 also implies that the other processes in Table 6.1 are finite order ARMA processes if the disaggregate process $\underline{x}_t$ is from this class.

6.6 CONCLUSIONS AND COMMENTS

In this chapter it has been demonstrated that joint temporal and contemporaneous aggregates of vector stochastic processes can be interpreted as linear transformations of so-called macro processes. Using this general result, six predictors for temporally and contemporaneously aggregated systems have been compared. The predictor obtained by aggregating forecasts from the fully disaggregated original process is optimal in the sense that it has the smallest forecast MSEs. Thus, based on this result, the recommendation is that forecasts should be obtained from the disaggregate process if possible.

In practice, however, there are some problems with this suggestion. First, disaggregate data may not be available and it may be expensive to get them. Second, the optimality of the predictor based on the disaggregate process is derived on the assumption that the data generation process is known. This assumption is not realistic and constructing a model for the generation process of the disaggregate data may be more expensive than obtaining a model for aggregate data. Also, as for the case of pure contemporaneous aggregation, it needs to be investigated whether the optimality of the predictor is maintained if the estimation and modelling uncertainty is taken into account in deriving the forecast MSEs. For that purpose, special forms of temporal aggregation will be considered in the following chapters.

CHAPTER 7. TEMPORAL AGGREGATION OF STOCK VARIABLES - SYSTEMATICALLY MISSING OBSERVATIONS

The subject of this chapter is temporal aggregation of stock variables where the aggregate consists of every m-th variable (or vector of variables) of the original, full process. In other words, forecasting time series with systematically (or periodically) missing observations will be discussed. Treating this special form of aggregation separately is useful in order to demonstrate the implications of the general results of the previous chapter for this special case.

Moreover, questions related to forecasting time series with systematically missing observations are of independent interest. For instance, to determine the shelf space that has to be allocated to a certain product the responsible manager of a supermarket may only be interested in the demand for the product during the weekly peak times. Let us assume that interest centers on the Saturday demand. In this situation, is it better to build a time series model based on the daily sales figures for every day of the past weeks, or is it better to construct a model based only on the past Saturday data? A similar question is relevant when forecasts are desired only for $h (h > 1)$ periods ahead. For example, for planning purposes , at the end of a particular year, the government may desire a forecast of an investment variable that is recorded quarterly, for the last quarter of the following year. In that situation one could ask the question whether using only the investment figures for the fourth quarters of previous years for computing the required forecast is better than using data for all previous quarters. More generally, should the full series be used for forecasting or is it better to use only an incomplete, partial series with systematically missing observations?

If the data generation processes are assumed known, this question can be answered in the framework of the previous chapter. For instance, for the first example, denoting the daily sales by x_t and assuming the supermarket is opened seven days a week, a macro process $\underline{x}_t = (x_{7t-6}, x_{7t-5},\ldots,x_{7t})'$ can be specified so that the Saturday demand is $y_t = x_{7t} = F\underline{x}_t$, where $F = (0, 0, 0, 0, 0, 0, 1)$. Hence, assuming that x_t is generated by a process of the type considered in Chapter 6, the results of that chapter imply that the forecasts obtained from the daily series x_t are at least as good as those from the weekly partial series y_t. The intuitive reason is that the full series x_t contains at least as much information about the future of y_t as the partial series. In Section 7.1 this result is stated formally for the present special case and conditions for the equivalence of the two predictors are provided that are easier to interpret than those given in general form in Chapter 6.

In Sections 7.2 and 7.3 it is assumed that the orders and/or coefficients of the full and partial processes are unknown and have to be determined from the available data. In that case, under special circumstances the forecasts from the partial process may become superior to those from the full process. The nonstationary case is treated in Section 7.4 and the results of a Monte Carlo experiment investigating the small sample validity of the asymptotic results are discussed in Section 7.5. Empirical examples are considered in Section 7.6 and conclusions are given in the last section. Parts of this chapter are taken from Lütkepohl (1986b).

The recent literature on missing observations and aggregation of stock variables is quite extensive. In time series analysis some authors have focussed on the change in the ARMA structure due to systematically missing observations (e.g., Quenouille (1958), Brewer (1973), Wei (1981), Werner (1982), Weiss (1984)). Others have treated the problem of estimating the spectrum (Jones (1962), Parzen (1963)) or ARMA parameters (Zellner (1966), Jones (1980), Harvey & Pierse (1984), Palm & Nijman (1984), Nijman (1985)) of the full process when observations are missing. Also estimating the missing observations has been of interest (Chow & Lin (1971), Ginsburgh (1973), Fernândez (1981), Litterman (1983), Harvey & Pierse (1984), Nijman & Palm (1986)). In the econometrics literature the discussion has also centered on estimating a model for the full series from an incomplete, partial sample. Varying assumptions have been made regarding the variables for which observations are missing and whether or not they are missing periodically. For an extensive list of references see Nijman (1985). In contrast to these studies the forecasting problem is of primary interest in this chapter. Furthermore the case of multiple time series is considered and observations are assumed to be missing for all variables of the system simultaneously.

7.1 FORECASTING KNOWN PROCESSES WITH SYSTEMATICALLY MISSING OBSERVATIONS

In this section the forecasts based on the full and the partial series are formally introduced and compared under the assumption of knowing the data generation processes. Necessary and sufficient conditions for equality of the forecasts are given.

Suppose $\underline{x}_t = (x_{1t},\ldots,x_{Kt})'$ is a K-dimensional process with MA representation

$$\underline{x}_t = \underline{\mu} + \sum_{i=0}^{\infty} \Phi_i \underline{u}_{t-i} = \underline{\mu} + \Phi(L)\underline{u}_t \ , \ \Phi_0 = I_K \ , \tag{7.1.1}$$

where $\underline{\mu} = E(\underline{x}_t)$, $\underline{u}_t = (u_{1t},\ldots,u_{Kt})'$ is K-dimensional, zero mean white noise with nonsingular covariance matrix $\Sigma_{\underline{u}}$ and $\det(\Phi(z))$ has no roots inside the complex unit circle,

$$\det(\Phi(z)) \neq 0 \quad \text{for } |z| < 1 \ . \tag{7.1.2}$$

At this point it is not assumed that $\underline{x}_t$ has an AR representation. The optimal h-step predictor of $\underline{x}_t$ based on $\{\underline{u}_s | s \leq t\}$ is

$$\underline{x}_t(h) = \underline{\mu} + \sum_{i=0}^{\infty} \Phi_{h+i}\underline{u}_{t-i} \tag{7.1.3}$$

and the corresponding MSE matrix is

$$\Sigma_{\underline{x}}(h) = \sum_{i=0}^{h-1} \Phi_i \Sigma_{\underline{u}} \Phi_i' \ . \tag{7.1.4}$$

The process $\underline{y}_t = (y_{1t},\ldots,y_{Kt})'$ consisting of every m-th variable of the $\underline{x}_t$ process, that is, $\underline{y}_t = \underline{x}_{mt}$, is also stationary and nondeterministic and has an MA representation

$$\underline{y}_t = \underline{\mu} + \sum_{i=0}^{\infty} N_i \underline{v}_{t-i} \ , \ N_0 = I_K \ , \tag{7.1.5}$$

where $\underline{\mu} = E(\underline{y}_t) = E(\underline{x}_t)$, $\underline{v}_t$ is K-dimensional white noise with nonsingular covariance matrix $\Sigma_{\underline{v}}$ and

$$\det(N(z)) \neq 0 \quad \text{for } |z| < 1 \tag{7.1.6}$$

(see Chapter 6). The optimal h-step forecast of $\underline{y}_t$ based on $\{\underline{v}_s | s \leq t\}$

is

$$\underline{y}_t(h) = \underline{\mu} + \sum_{i=0}^{\infty} N_{h+i}\underline{v}_{t-i} \tag{7.1.7}$$

and the corresponding MSE matrix is

$$\Sigma(h) = \sum_{i=0}^{h-1} N_i \Sigma_{\underline{v}} N_i' . \tag{7.1.8}$$

Using the full process, $\underline{x}_{mt}(mh)$ is also a forecast of the vector $\underline{y}_{t+h}$. This predictor will be denoted by $\underline{y}_t^o(h)$, i.e.,

$$\underline{y}_t^o(h) = \underline{x}_{mt}(mh) , \tag{7.1.9}$$

in accordance with the notation used in the previous chapter. The MSE matrix of $\underline{y}_t^o(h)$ is

$$\Sigma^o(h) = \sum_{i=0}^{mh-1} \Phi_i \Sigma_{\underline{u}} \Phi_i' . \tag{7.1.10}$$

From Chapter 6 it is known that $\Sigma^o(h) \le \Sigma(h)$, that is, the difference $\Sigma(h) - \Sigma^o(h)$ is positive semidefinite (see Table 6.3). Furthermore, the difference between the two MSE matrices converges to zero as the forecast horizon increases because

$$\Sigma(h),\ \Sigma^o(h) \xrightarrow[h\to\infty]{} \Sigma_{\underline{y}} = E(\underline{y}_t\underline{y}_t') = \Sigma_{\underline{x}} . \tag{7.1.11}$$

Moreover, necessary and sufficient conditions for equality of $\underline{y}_t^o(1)$ and $\underline{y}_t(1)$ are given in Table 6.3(b). For the special case of temporal aggregation of stock variables the conditions can be stated in the following simple form.

PROPOSITION 7.1

Let $\underline{x}_t$ be as in (7.1.1) and $\underline{y}_t(h)$ and $\underline{y}_t^o(h)$ as in (7.1.7) and (7.1.9) respectively. Then $\underline{y}_t(1) = \underline{y}_t^o(1)$ if and only if

$$\Phi(z) = \left(\sum_{i=0}^{\infty} \Phi_{im} z^{im}\right)\left(\sum_{i=0}^{m-1} \Phi_i z^i\right) . \tag{7.1.12}$$

Proof.

Equality of the two predictors is equivalent to

$$\underline{v}_t = \underline{y}_t - \underline{y}_{t-1}(1) = \underline{y}_t - \underline{y}^o_{t-1}(1) = \underline{x}_{mt} - \underline{x}_{m(t-1)}(m) =$$

$$= \underline{u}_{mt} + \Phi_1\underline{u}_{mt-1} + \dots + \Phi_{m-1}\underline{u}_{mt-m+1} \, . \quad (7.1.13)$$

If (7.1.12) holds, $\underline{y}_t$ has the MA representation

$$\underline{y}_t = \underline{\mu} + \sum_{i=0}^{\infty} \Phi_{im}\underline{v}_{t-i}$$

with $\underline{v}_t = \sum_{i=0}^{m-1} \Phi_i\underline{u}_{mt-i}$. Thus, the "if"-part of the proposition follows from (7.1.13).

Also, if (7.1.13) holds,

$$\underline{y}_t = \underline{\mu} + \sum_{i=0}^{\infty} N_i\underline{v}_{t-i} = \underline{\mu} + \sum_{i=0}^{\infty} N_i\left(\sum_{j=0}^{m-1} \Phi_j\underline{u}_{m(t-i)-j}\right). \quad (7.1.14)$$

On the other hand,

$$\underline{y}_t = \underline{x}_{mt} = \underline{\mu} + \sum_{j=0}^{\infty} \Phi_j\underline{u}_{mt-j} \, . \quad (7.1.15)$$

Comparing the coefficient matrices of $\underline{u}_{mt-mi}$ in (7.1.14) and (7.1.15) shows that $N_i = \Phi_{mi}$ for $i = 0,1,2,\dots$. Q.E.D.

The condition (7.1.12) is useful because it is often very easy to check. It implies that the two predictors are identical if $\underline{x}_t$ is a finite order MA(q) process with $q < m$ and if $\underline{x}_t$ is a purely periodic or purely seasonal process like

$$\underline{x}_t = \underline{\mu} + \sum_{i=0}^{\infty} \Phi_{im}\underline{u}_{t-im} \, . \quad (7.1.16)$$

Also, if $\underline{x}_t$ is a stationary AR(1) process, $\underline{x}_t = A_1\underline{x}_{t-1} + \underline{u}_t$, the condition (7.1.12) is satisfied since the MA operator of such a process is

$$\sum_{i=0}^{\infty} \Phi_i z^i = \left(\sum_{i=0}^{\infty} A_1^{im} z^{im}\right)\left(\sum_{i=0}^{m-1} A_1^i z^i\right) . \quad (7.1.17)$$

Hence, if $\underline{x}_t$ is an AR(1) process, the two pedictors $\underline{y}_t(h)$ and $\underline{y}^o_t(h)$ will be identical for any given m and any h. Note that equality of the h-step predictors follows from equality of the 1-step predictors (see Chapter 6).

These results are based on the unrealistic assumption that the involved processes are known. In the next section processes with estimated coefficients are considered.

7.2 PROCESSES WITH ESTIMATED COEFFICIENTS

In this section the asymptotic theory of Section 3.2 will be applied to investigate the consequences of using processes with estimated coefficients for prediction. The conditions of that section are assumed to hold. In particular, the full process $\underline{x}_t$ is a Gaussian vector ARMA(p,q) process with known orders. It follows from Section 6.5 that in this case the partial process $\underline{y}_t$ is also a finite order Gaussian vector ARMA process. The coefficients of the processes are assumed to be estimated by maximum likelihood and estimation and forecasting are based on independent processes as explained in Section 3.2. Under these conditions the asymptotic MSE matrix of the h-step predictor for $\underline{x}_t$ is

$$\hat{\Sigma}_{\underline{x}}(h) = \Sigma_{\underline{x}}(h) + \frac{1}{T}(\Omega_{\underline{x}}(h) + G_{\underline{x}}(h)) , \qquad (7.2.1)$$

where T is the sample size used for estimation and $\Omega_{\underline{x}}(h) + G_{\underline{x}}(h)$ is the covariance matrix of the asymptotic distribution of $\sqrt{T}(\hat{\underline{x}}_t(h) - \underline{x}_t(h))$. Here and in the following, predictors are furnished with a caret when true coefficients are replaced by estimators. For instance, $\hat{\underline{x}}_t(h)$ is the predictor $\underline{x}_t(h)$ with estimated coefficients.

For the predictor $\hat{\underline{y}}_t^o(h)$ it is assumed that the coefficients are estimated on the basis of the full series and thus, its asymptotic MSE matrix is

$$\hat{\Sigma}^o(h) = \hat{\Sigma}_{\underline{x}}(mh) = \Sigma_{\underline{x}}(mh) + \frac{1}{T}(\Omega_{\underline{x}}(mh) + G_{\underline{x}}(mh))$$

$$= \Sigma^o(h) + \frac{1}{T}(\Omega_{\underline{x}}(mh) + G_{\underline{x}}(mh)) . \qquad (7.2.2)$$

Using only the partial process $\underline{y}_t$ for estimation, the asymptotic MSE matrix of $\hat{\underline{y}}_t(h)$ is

$$\hat{\Sigma}(h) = \Sigma(h) + \frac{1}{\mathcal{T}}(\Omega_{\underline{y}}(h) + G_{\underline{y}}(h)) \qquad (7.2.3)$$

where $\mathcal{T}$ is the sample size of the partial process used for estimation and $\Omega_{\underline{y}}(h) + G_{\underline{y}}(h)$ is the covariance matrix of the asymptotic distribution of $\sqrt{\mathcal{T}}(\hat{\underline{y}}_t(h) - \underline{y}_t(h))$. In the following it will be assumed that $\mathcal{T} = T/m$ unless otherwise noted. Hence,

$$\hat{\Sigma}(h) = \Sigma(h) + \frac{1}{T}(m\Omega_{y}(h) + mG_{y}(h)).$$

The asymptotic MSE matrices of the two predictors under investigation consist of the MSE matricesfor known processes($\Sigma^{o}(h)$ and $\Sigma(h)$) and a component that is due to estimation and approaches zero if T (and hence T) goes to infinity. Thus, if $y_t^{o}(h)$ strictly dominates $y_t(h)$ (i.e., $\Sigma(h) - \Sigma^{o}(h)$ is positive definite) the same will hold for the estimated predictors if the sample size T is large. Since the relation between $\Sigma(h)$ and $\Sigma^{o}(h)$ has been treated in the previous section the MSE components due to estimation will be of primary interest in the following.

To simplify matters it is assumed for the moment that the two predictors are identical for known processes, that is, $y_t(h) = y_t^{o}(h)$ for all h and (7.1.12) is satisfied. Let us consider $G_{x}(mh)$ and $G_{y}(h)$ first. Recall that these terms are due to estimating the mean term μ. In Section 3.2 it is shown that under the prevailing conditions

$$G_{x}(mh) = E\left[\frac{\partial x_t(mh)}{\partial \mu'} \Sigma_{\bar{x}} \frac{\partial x_t(mh)'}{\partial \mu}\right] \tag{7.2.4}$$

and

$$G_{y}(h) = E\left[\frac{y_t(h)}{\partial \mu'} \Sigma_{\bar{y}} \frac{y_t(h)'}{\partial \mu}\right], \tag{7.2.5}$$

where $\Sigma_{\bar{x}}$ and $\Sigma_{\bar{y}}$ are the covariance matrices of the asymptotic distributions of $\sqrt{T}(\bar{x} - \mu)$ and $\sqrt{T}(\bar{y} - \mu)$ respectively. As usual $\bar{x}$ denotes the vector of sample means of the full x_t series while $\bar{y}$ denotes the sample means of the partial series with systematically missing observations. It is noted in Section 2.4.1 that $\bar{x}$ is asymptotically equivalent to the ML estimator of μ. Thus, since the ML estimator is asymptotically efficient , the asymptotic covariance matrix of $\sqrt{T}(\bar{y} - \mu) = \sqrt{m}\sqrt{T}(\bar{y} - \mu)$ cannot be smaller than $\Sigma_{\bar{x}}$. In other words,

$$\Sigma_{\bar{x}} \leq m\Sigma_{\bar{y}} \ . \tag{7.2.6}$$

Furthermore, since $y_t(h) = y_t^{o}(h) = x_{mt}(mh)$ is assumed, it follows from (7.1.12) that

$$\frac{\partial y_t(h)}{\partial \mu'} = \frac{\partial x_{mt}(mh)}{\partial \mu'} \ .$$

Consequently,

$$G_{\underline{x}}(mh) \leq m\, G_{\underline{y}}(h) \ . \tag{7.2.7}$$

In other words, even if the predictors are identical, the mean term can be estimated more efficiently using the full sample rather than a partial sample with systematically missing observations and hence the contribution of the estimated mean term to the asymptotic MSE matrix is smaller when the full process is used. Actually, so far it is only shown that $G_{\underline{x}}(mh)$ is not greater than $mG_{\underline{y}}(h)$. However, it is easy to see that in general the two are not equal. For instance, if x_t is a univariate MA(1) process, $x_t = \mu + u_t + \phi u_{t-1}$,

$$\Sigma_{\bar{x}} = (1 + \phi)^2 \sigma_u^2 \ , \tag{7.2.8}$$

where σ_u^2 is the variance of u_t (see (2.4.6)). On the other hand, for $m = 2$, the partial process $y_t = x_{2t} = \mu + v_t$ is white noise with $v_t = u_{2t} + \phi u_{2t-1}$ and thus, $\sigma_v^2 = (1 + \phi^2)\sigma_u^2$ is the variance of v_t. Furthermore, $\Sigma_{\bar{y}} = \sigma_v^2$. Consequently, $\Sigma_{\bar{x}} < 2\, \Sigma_{\bar{y}}$ for $0 < |\phi| < 1$. Thus, there is a real gain from using the full process for estimating the mean.

Let us now compare $\Omega_{\underline{x}}(mh)$ and $\Omega_{\underline{y}}(h)$, assuming again that $\underline{y}_t(h) = \underline{y}_t^o(h)$. These terms come from estimating the ARMA parameters and all situations are possible: (1) $\Omega_{\underline{x}}(mh)$ may strictly dominate $m\Omega_{\underline{y}}(h)$; (2) $m\Omega_{\underline{y}}(h)$ may be strictly superior to $\Omega_{\underline{x}}(mh)$; and (3) the two terms may be identical. The three possibilities will be illustrated by examples.

The third possibility can be seen by considering an MA(q) process $\underline{x}_t$ with $q < m$. In that case, the optimal predictor $\underline{x}_t(mh) = \underline{\mu}$ for $h = 1,2,\ldots$. Thus, the MA coefficients are not involved in the prediction formula and $\Omega_{\underline{x}}(mh) = 0$. The same holds for the partial process $\underline{y}_t$ which is white noise, that is, $\Omega_{\underline{y}}(h) = 0$ for $h = 1,2,\ldots$.

An example in which $m\Omega_{\underline{y}}(h) < \Omega_{\underline{x}}(mh)$ is obtained by considering the bivariate AR(1) process $\underline{x}_t = A_1\underline{x}_{t-1} + \underline{u}_t$ with

$$A_1 = \begin{bmatrix} 0 & \alpha \\ 0 & 0 \end{bmatrix} .$$

Using $m = 2$, the partial process

$$\underline{y}_t = A_1^2 \underline{y}_{t-1} + \underline{v}_t = \underline{v}_t$$

is white noise with $\underline{v}_t = \underline{u}_{2t} + A_1\underline{u}_{2t-1}$ because $A_1^2 = 0$ (see also (7.1.17)). Consequently $\Omega_{\underline{y}}(h) = 0$ while $\Omega_{\underline{x}}(2)$ is easily seen to be nonzero for $\alpha \neq 0$ provided $\underline{x}_t$ is estimated as an unconstrained AR(1). In that case, using (3.2.32),

$$\Omega_{\underline{x}}(2) = \sum_{i,j=0}^{1} \operatorname{tr}((A_1^{1-j})'\Sigma_{\underline{x}}^{-1}A_1^{1-i}\Sigma_{\underline{x}})A_1^j\Sigma_{\underline{u}}A_1'^{i} \quad . \tag{7.2.9}$$

Assuming $\Sigma_{\underline{u}} = I_2$ and using

$$\Sigma_{\underline{x}} = E(\underline{x}_t\underline{x}_t') = I_2 + A_1A_1' = \begin{bmatrix} 1+\alpha^2 & 0 \\ 0 & 1 \end{bmatrix}$$

gives

$$\begin{aligned}\Omega_{\underline{x}}(2) &= \operatorname{tr}(A_1'\Sigma_{\underline{x}}^{-1}A_1\Sigma_{\underline{x}})I_2 + \operatorname{tr}(\Sigma_{\underline{x}}^{-1}A_1\Sigma_{\underline{x}})A_1 \\ &\quad + \operatorname{tr}(A_1'\Sigma_{\underline{x}}^{-1}\Sigma_{\underline{x}})A_1' + \operatorname{tr}(\Sigma_{\underline{x}}^{-1}\Sigma_{\underline{x}})A_1A_1' \\ &= \frac{\alpha^2}{1+\alpha^2}I_2 + 2\begin{bmatrix} \alpha^2 & 0 \\ 0 & 0 \end{bmatrix} \\ &= \begin{bmatrix} \frac{\alpha^2}{1+\alpha^2} + 2\alpha^2 & 0 \\ 0 & \frac{\alpha^2}{1+\alpha^2} \end{bmatrix} .\end{aligned} \tag{7.2.10}$$

This result relies an $\underline{x}_t$ being estimated without constraints. If α were known to be the only nonzero element in A_1, the matrix $\Omega_{\underline{x}}(2)$ would be zero because in that case the optimal 2-step predictor based on the full process is $\hat{\underline{x}}_t(2) = \hat{A}_1^2\underline{x}_t = \underline{0}$. Thus, the gain in forecast efficiency obtained from using the incomplete series $\underline{y}_t$, results from estimating too many parameters for the full process. In practice, if $\underline{y}_t$ is recognized to be zero mean white noise, the zero vector is known to be the optimal predictor and consequently should be used. In general, even if parameter restrictions are ignored, $\Omega_{\underline{x}}(mh)$ may be smaller than $m\Omega_{\underline{y}}(h)$. This is demonstrated by the following example.

Suppose that $\underline{x}_t$ is a stationary AR(m) process for which all coefficient matrices but the m-th are zero, that is,

$$\underline{x}_t = A_m\underline{x}_{t-m} + \underline{u}_t \ . \tag{7.2.11}$$

This process has the MA representation

$$\underline{x}_t = \sum_{i=0}^{\infty} \Phi_{im} \underline{u}_{t-im} \tag{7.2.12}$$

with $\Phi_{im} = A_m^i$ and thus, $\mathcal{Z}_{\underline{y}}(h) = \mathcal{Z}_{\underline{y}}^o(h)$ for all h by Proposition 7.1. If $\underline{x}_t$ is estimated as a full AR(m) process,

$$\underline{x}_t = A_1 \underline{x}_{t-1} + \ldots + A_m \underline{x}_{t-m} + \underline{u}_t ,$$

where $A_1, \ldots, A_{m-1}$ are not set to zero in the ML(LS) estimation, the forecast MSE part due to parameter estimation is, by (3.2.32),

$$\Omega_{\underline{x}}(mh) = \sum_{i,j=0}^{mh-1} tr((\underline{A}')^{mh-1-j} \Gamma^{-1} \underline{A}^{mh-1-i} \Gamma) \Phi_j \mathcal{Z}_{\underline{u}} \Phi_i' , \tag{7.2.13}$$

where

$$\underline{A} = \begin{bmatrix} 0 & 0 & \ldots & 0 & A_m \\ I_K & 0 & \ldots & 0 & 0 \\ 0 & I_K & \ldots & 0 & 0 \\ \vdots & \vdots & \ddots & \vdots & \vdots \\ 0 & 0 & \ldots & I_K & 0 \end{bmatrix} \text{ so that } \underline{A}^{mh-1} = \begin{bmatrix} 0 & A_m^h & 0 & \ldots & 0 \\ 0 & 0 & A_m^h & \ldots & 0 \\ \vdots & \vdots & \vdots & \ddots & \vdots \\ 0 & 0 & 0 & \ldots & A_m^h \\ A_m^{h-1} & 0 & 0 & \ldots & 0 \end{bmatrix}$$

(mK x mK)

(7.2.14)

and

$$\Gamma = \begin{bmatrix} \mathcal{Z}_{\underline{x}} & 0 & \ldots & 0 \\ 0 & \mathcal{Z}_{\underline{x}} & \ldots & 0 \\ \vdots & \vdots & \ddots & \vdots \\ 0 & 0 & \ldots & \mathcal{Z}_{\underline{x}} \end{bmatrix} . \quad (mK \times mK)$$

Note that

$$(\underline{A}')^{mh-1} \Gamma^{-1} \underline{A}^{mh-1} \Gamma = \begin{bmatrix} A_m'^{h-1} \mathcal{Z}_{\underline{x}}^{-1} A_m^{h-1} \mathcal{Z}_{\underline{x}} & 0 & \ldots & 0 \\ 0 & A_m'^{h} \mathcal{Z}_{\underline{x}}^{-1} A_m^{h} \mathcal{Z}_{\underline{x}} & \ldots & 0 \\ \vdots & \vdots & \ddots & \\ 0 & 0 & \ldots & A_m'^{h} \mathcal{Z}_{\underline{x}}^{-1} A_m^{h} \mathcal{Z}_{\underline{x}} \end{bmatrix}$$

(mK x mK)

(7.2.15)

and

$$\Omega_{\underline{x}}(mh) = \sum_{i,j=0}^{h-1} tr((\underline{A}')^{mh-1-mj}\Gamma^{-1}\ \underline{A}^{mh-1-mi}\Gamma) A_m^j \Sigma_{\underline{u}} A_m'^i \ . \tag{7.2.16}$$

Thus, for h = 1,

$$\Omega_{\underline{x}}(m) = tr(\underline{A}'^{m-1}\Gamma^{-1}\ \underline{A}^{m-1}\Gamma)\Sigma_{\underline{u}} \ . \tag{7.2.17}$$

It is shown in the Appendix to this chapter that

$$tr(\underline{A}'^{m-1}\Gamma^{-1}\ \underline{A}^{m-1}\Gamma) < mK \ . \tag{7.2.18}$$

On the other hand $\underline{y}_t$ is an AR(1) process,

$$\underline{y}_t = A_m \underline{y}_{t-1} + \underline{v}_t \tag{7.2.19}$$

with $\underline{v}_t = \underline{u}_{mt}$ and hence,

$$\Omega_{\underline{y}}(1) = K\Sigma_{\underline{v}} = K\Sigma_{\underline{u}} \tag{7.2.20}$$

(see (3.2.34)) so that

$$m\Omega_{\underline{y}}(1) > \Omega_{\underline{x}}(m)$$

for m > 1. Of course, if the restrictions $A_1 = \dots = A_{m-1} = 0$ were known and enforced in the estimation procedure the efficiency gain from using the full process for estimation would be even greater. In summary, the examples show that all three situations

$$m\Omega_{\underline{y}}(h) > \Omega_{\underline{x}}(mh) \ , \ m\Omega_{\underline{y}}(h) < \Omega_{\underline{x}}(mh) \ , \text{ and } m\Omega_{\underline{y}}(h) = \Omega_{\underline{x}}(mh) \tag{7.2.21}$$

are possible.

For the foregoing examples the MSE differences for known processes are zero. It is also of interest to investigate the consequences of using processes with estimated coefficients if the condition (7.1.12) in Proposition 7.1 is not satisfied. The analysis of this case is complicated by the fact that the ARMA structure of the partial process $\underline{y}_t$ can be quite different from that of $\underline{x}_t$ (see Section 6.5). I have not found any evidence that the situation here is different from that for processes satisfying (7.1.12).

In summary, if processes with estimated coefficients and known orders are used for forecasting, then using the series with missing observations, the difference in the MSE matrices may be unchanged or increased or decreased, depending on the structure of the full process $\underline{x}_t$ and the aggregation period m. However, it seems that situations where $\hat{\underline{y}}_t(h)$ dominates $\hat{\underline{y}}^o_t(h)$ can be avoided by taking into account all possible parameter restrictions for the full process in the estimation procedure.

In practice it is usually unrealistic to assume that the orders of the involved data generation processes are known. Therefore it is perhaps worth noting that the previous results remain valid if the orders are estimated consistently. In the next section a different asymptotic theory is used to investigate the consequences of forecasting with estimated processes.

7.3 PROCESSES WITH UNKNOWN ORDERS AND ESTIMATED COEFFICIENTS

Assuming that the full process $\underline{x}_t$ and the partial process $\underline{y}_t$ both satisfy the conditions of Section 3.3, an approximate MSE matrix of $\tilde{\underline{y}}^o_t(h)$ is

$$\tilde{\Sigma}^o(h) = (1 + \frac{Kp(T)}{T})\Sigma_{\underline{x}}(mh) = (1 + \frac{Kp(T)}{T})\Sigma^o(h) \qquad (7.3.1)$$

and $\tilde{\underline{y}}_t(h)$ has approximate MSE matrix

$$\tilde{\Sigma}(h) = (1 + \frac{Kp(T)}{T})\Sigma(h) \quad . \qquad (7.3.2)$$

In order to obtain these MSE matrices it is assumed, in accordance with Section 3.3, that only finite order AR processes are fitted although the actual data generation processes may have infinite AR order. The resulting predictors and MSEs are furnished with a tilde. The orders p of the AR processes fitted to the data are assumed to be functions of the sample size (time series length) used for estimation with the following properties:

$$p(T) \to \infty \quad , \quad \frac{p(T)^3}{T} \to 0 \quad , \quad \text{and } \sqrt{T}\Big[\sum_{j=p(T)+1}^{\infty} \sqrt{tr(A_j'A_j)}\Big] \to 0 \text{ as } T \to \infty \qquad (7.3.3a)$$

and

$$p(T) \to \infty \quad , \quad \frac{p(T)^3}{T} \to 0 \quad , \quad \text{and } \sqrt{T}\Big[\sum_{j=p(T)+1}^{\infty} \sqrt{tr(\Theta_j'\Theta_j)}\Big] \to 0 \text{ as } T \to \infty \qquad (7.3.3b)$$

where the A_j and Θ_j are the coefficient matrices of the AR representations of the full process $\underline{x}_t$ and the partial process $\underline{y}_t$, respectively. For simplicity it is assumed in this section that all processes have zero mean and a mean term is not estimated. The consequences of estimating the mean terms have been analyzed in the previous section.

From (7.3.1) and (7.3.2) it follows that the difference $\tilde{\Sigma}(h) - \tilde{\Sigma}^o(h)$ will be positive definite if the same holds for $\Sigma(h) - \Sigma^o(h)$ and the sample size T is large because, by (7.3.3), p(T)/T and $p(\mathcal{T})/\mathcal{T}$ approach zero fast as T goes to infinity. If any of the MSEs of the two predictors are identical for known processes the difference for estimated processes will be

$$K\left(\frac{p(\mathcal{T})}{\mathcal{T}} - \frac{p(T)}{T}\right)\Sigma(h)$$

which is likely to be positive definite if the conditions (7.3.3) are satisfied. For instance, if $p(T) = T^{1/(3+\delta)}$, where δ is some positive number, and $\mathcal{T} = T/m$, then

$$\frac{p(\mathcal{T})}{\mathcal{T}} - \frac{p(T)}{T} = T^{(1/(3+\delta))-1}(m^{1-1/(3+\delta)} - 1) > 0 \qquad (7.3.4)$$

for positive integers T and m > 1. Thus, it appears that even under the most favorable conditions for the partial process $\underline{y}_t$, when the two forecasts are identical for known processes, the forecast precision will deteriorate if observations are missing systematically. In other words, under these conditions, the forecasts based on the partial process $\underline{y}_t$ will be inferior to those based on the full process $\underline{x}_t$ if estimated processes are used.

This result is likely to depend upon the particular asymptotic theory used here, since in practice the orders of the processes $\underline{x}_t$ and $\underline{y}_t$ will be chosen on the basis of a single realization of the processes so that the conditions for p(.) stated in (7.3.3) are of little relevance. Suppose, for instance, that the actual data generation process $\underline{x}_t$ is an MA(q), with q < m so that $\underline{y}_t$ is white noise and condition (7.1.12) of Proposition 7.1 is satisfied and $\Sigma(h) = \Sigma^o(h)$. In this situation one may fit an AR(p) with $p \neq 0$ to $\underline{x}_t$ while $\underline{y}_t$ is recognized to be an AR(0). Assuming that the formulas (7.3.1) and (7.3.2) are still approximately valid gives

$$\tilde{\Sigma}(h) - \tilde{\Sigma}^o(h) = \Sigma(h) - (1 - \frac{Kp}{T})\Sigma(h) = -\frac{Kp}{T}\Sigma(h) < 0 . \qquad (7.3.5)$$

This result is intuitively plausible since the forecast $\tilde{\underline{y}}_t(h)$ is now based on the true process $\underline{y}_t$ while $\tilde{\underline{y}}^o(h)$ is based on a model which only approximates the true process $\underline{x}_t$ and in addition uses estimated parameters. As a practical rule this result suggests that if the incomplete series with missing observations is found to be white noise, the process mean should be used as forecast. Of course, if in this example an MA(q) is fitted to the full series $\underline{x}_t$, the optimal mh-step forecast $\underline{x}_t(mh)$ is the zero vector for $h \geq 1$ and thus, $\tilde{\not{Z}}^o(h) = \not{Z}^o(h) = \not{Z}(h)$. In Section 7.5 Monte Carlo simulations are used to investigate whether the asymptotic theory is a good indicator for the small sample behavior of the forecast MSEs. In the following section some comments on nonstationary processes will be made.

7.4 NONSTATIONARY TIME SERIES WITH SYSTEMATICALLY MISSING OBSERVATIONS

Some results for stationary processes carry over to the nonstationary case if it is assumed that the nonstationarity can be removed by differencing. In particular, the predictor $\underline{y}_t^o(h)$ based on the full nonstationary process is generally superior to the predictor $\underline{y}_t(h)$ which is based on the partial process, that is,

$$\not{Z}^o(h) \leq \not{Z}(h) \ . \tag{7.4.1}$$

However, the difference between the two predictors will in general not approach zero with growing forecast horizon. Moreover, care has to be exercised when conditions for equality of the two predictors are considered. To see this, suppose that all components of the full process $\underline{x}_t$ are stationary after differencing once, that is

$$\underline{x}_t^s = \underline{x}_t - \underline{x}_{t-1}$$

is stationary. It is assumed that $\underline{x}_t^s$ has the infinite MA representation

$$\underline{x}_t^s = \sum_{i=0}^{\infty} \Phi_i \underline{u}_{t-i} = \Phi(L)\underline{u}_t \ , \quad \Phi_0 = I_K \ , \tag{7.4.2}$$

and $\det(\Phi(z)) \neq 0$ for $|z| < 1$. As in the previous sections, forecasts of $\underline{y}_t = \underline{x}_{mt}$ are of interest. Obviously,

$$\underline{y}_t^s = \underline{y}_t - \underline{y}_{t-1} = \underline{x}_{mt} - \underline{x}_{mt-m}$$

$$= \underline{x}_{mt}^s + \underline{x}_{mt-1}^s + \dots + \underline{x}_{mt-m+2}^s + \underline{x}_{mt-m+1} - \underline{x}_{mt-m}$$

$$= \underline{x}^s_{m\ell} + \dots + \underline{x}^s_{m\ell-m+1} \qquad (7.4.3)$$

is the sum of m stationary processes and is therefore also stationary (see also Section 6.4.1).

The two 1-step predictors of interest are

$$\underline{y}_\ell(1) = \underline{y}_\ell + \underline{y}^s_\ell(1) , \qquad (7.4.4)$$

where $\underline{y}^s_\ell(1)$ is the optimal 1-step predictor based on the process $\underline{y}^s_\ell$, and

$$\underline{y}^o_\ell(1) = \underline{x}_{m\ell}(m) = \underline{x}_{m\ell} + \sum_{j=1}^{m} \underline{x}^s_{m\ell}(j) , \qquad (7.4.5)$$

where $\underline{x}^s_{m\ell}(j)$ is the optimal j-step predictor based on the process $\underline{x}^s_t$. The two predictors in (7.4.4) and (7.4.5) are identical if

$$\underline{y}^s_\ell(1) = \sum_{j=1}^{m} \underline{x}^s_{m\ell}(j) . \qquad (7.4.6)$$

Thus, Proposition 7.1 cannot be used for the stationary parts of the nonstationary full and partial processes. In other words, even if condition (7.1.12) is satisfied, $\underline{y}_\ell(1)$ may differ from $\underline{y}^o_\ell(1)$.

On the other hand it is easy to see that there are nonstationary processes for which the predictors are identical. For instance, if $\underline{x}_t$ is such that $\underline{x}^s_t$ has an MA representation of the type (7.1.16),

$$\underline{x}^s_t = \sum_{i=0}^{\infty} \Phi_{im} \underline{u}_{t-im} , \qquad (7.4.7)$$

then (7.4.6) holds and hence, $\underline{y}^o_\ell(1) = \underline{y}_\ell(1)$. This follows because $\underline{x}^s_t$ having the representation (7.4.7) implies, using (7.4.3),

$$\underline{y}^s_\ell = \underline{x}^s_{m\ell} + \dots + \underline{x}^s_{m\ell-m+1}$$

$$= \sum_{i=0}^{\infty} \Phi_{im} (\underline{u}_{m\ell-im} + \underline{u}_{m\ell-1-im} + \dots + \underline{u}_{m\ell-m+1-im})$$

$$= \sum_{i=0}^{\infty} \Phi_{im} \underline{v}_{\ell-i} , \qquad (7.4.8)$$

where

$$\underline{v}_{\ell-i} = \underline{u}_{m(\ell-i)} + \underline{u}_{m(\ell-i)-1} + \dots + \underline{u}_{m(\ell-i)-m+1} . \qquad (7.4.9)$$

On the other hand,

$$\underline{v}_t = \underline{y}_t - \underline{y}_{t-1}(1) \tag{7.4.10}$$

and

$$\begin{aligned}\underline{y}_t - \underline{y}^o_{t-1}(1) &= \underline{x}_{mt} - \underline{x}_{m(t-1)}(m)\\ &= \underline{x}_{m(t-1)} + \sum_{j=1}^{m} \underline{x}^s_{m(t-1)+j} - (\underline{x}_{m(t-1)} + \sum_{j=1}^{m} \underline{x}^s_{m(t-1)}(j))\\ &= \underline{u}_{mt} + \underline{u}_{mt-1} + \dots + \underline{u}_{mt-m+1} .\end{aligned} \tag{7.4.11}$$

Consequently, (7.4.9) is equivalent to $\underline{y}^o_t(1) = \underline{y}_t(1)$.

Note that in this example the stationary part of the partial process is a temporal aggregate of the stationary part of the full process where variables associated with consecutive time periods are added. This type of temporal aggregation will be treated in detail in the next chapter. Also, processes that require other types of differencing to obtain stationarity can be analyzed in a similar manner. Of course, in order to derive conditions for equality of the two predictors, the relationship between the stationary parts of the full and the partial process has to be considered.

If estimated rather than known nonstationary processes are used for prediction the analysis can proceed similarly as in the previous sections if only the stationary parts of the involved processes are assumed to be estimated. In other words, it has to be assumed that the type of differencing required for stationarity is known. Also, the stationary parts have to satisfy the conditions of the previous two sections. In particular, they have to have AR representations so that overdifferencing is not permitted. In addition, it must be taken into account in the analysis that the relationship between the differenced full and partial processes is different from the relationship of the original processes. The case where the relationship between $\underline{y}^s_t$ and $\underline{x}^s_t$ is as in (7.4.3) is discussed in more detail in the next chapter. It turns out that using estimated processes will in general increase the efficiency of the predictor based on the full process over the one based on a series with systematically missing observations (see Sections 8.2 and 8.3). In the next section the small sample MSEs of predictors based on estimated processes are considered.

7.5 MONTE CARLO RESULTS

In the following the results of a Monte Carlo study are discussed to assess the relative efficiency of the two predictors $\underline{y}_t(h)$ and $\underline{y}_t^o(h)$ in small samples. The design of the simulation experiment is essentially the same as in Chapter 5, Section 5.5. In particular, the white noise errors and components of white noise vectors for each of the processes considered are independent pseudo standard normal random numbers generated by a NAG subroutine. The MSEs of 1-step and 5-step ahead forecasts of the partial process with systematically missing observations will be reported for three different sample sizes. For each process R = 600 realizations were generated and for each realization 50 presample values were discarded to reduce the impact of starting-up values. Presample values for lagged variables were used for estimation in addition to the sample values. All processes were estimated without zero restrictions for the coefficients. Although some of the processes discussed in the following are MA processes, only pure AR processes were fitted to the data in accordance with the large sample theory of Section 7.3. The three criteria AIC, HQ, and SC were used to determine the orders p of the fitted processes and the statistic introduced in Section 3.5 is used to assess the significance of differences in the estimated MSEs. Since interest centers on the MSE differences due to estimation variability, only processes are considered that satisfy (7.1.12). Thus, all MSE differences result from estimating and specifying the processes from the given data.

7.5.1 Univariate AR Processes

The first process investigated is the univariate AR(2)

$$x_t = 1 + 0.5x_{t-2} + u_t \quad \text{with} \quad \Sigma_u = 1 \qquad (7.5.1)$$

which is similar to (7.2.11). If every second observation is missing (m = 2), the partial process

$$y_t = x_{2t} = 1 + 0.5y_{t-1} + v_t \quad \text{with} \quad v_t = u_{2t} \qquad (7.5.2)$$

is obtained. For these processes

$$\Sigma^o(1) = \Sigma_x(2) = 1 = \Sigma(1) \ . \qquad (7.5.3)$$

and

$$\Sigma^{o}(5) = \Sigma_x(10) = \sum_{i=0}^{4} 0.5^{2i} = 1.316 = \Sigma(5) \qquad (7.5.4)$$

since x_t has the MA representation

$$x_t = \frac{1}{1-0.5} + \frac{1}{1-0.5L^2} u_t = 2 + \sum_{i=0}^{\infty} 0.5^i u_{t-2i} \,. \qquad (7.5.5)$$

Of course, since (7.1.12) is satisfied, the MSEs $\Sigma(h)$ and $\Sigma^{o}(h)$ are identical for all h. It is also easy to derive the other pieces of the asymptotic MSEs when the AR orders are assumed known.

Using (7.2.15) and (7.2.16) with

$$\underline{A} = \begin{bmatrix} 0 & \alpha \\ 1 & 0 \end{bmatrix},$$

where $\alpha = 0.5$ in the present case, and noting that Σ_x cancels against Σ_x^{-1} gives

$$\Omega_x(2) = \operatorname{tr}(\underline{A}'\underline{A})\Sigma_u = 1 + \alpha^2 = 1.25 \qquad (7.5.6)$$

and

$$\begin{aligned}
\Omega_x(10) &= \sum_{i=0}^{4} \sum_{j=0}^{4} \operatorname{tr}(\underline{A}'^{2(5-j)-1} \underline{A}^{2(5-i)-1})\alpha^j\alpha^i \\
&= \sum_{i=0}^{4} \sum_{j=0}^{4} \operatorname{tr}(\underline{A}'^{2(5-j-1)} \underline{A}'\underline{A}\, \underline{A}^{2(5-i-1)})\alpha^{i+j} \\
&= \sum_{i=0}^{4} \sum_{j=0}^{4} \operatorname{tr}\left[\begin{bmatrix} \alpha^{5-j-1} & 0 \\ 0 & \alpha^{5-j-1} \end{bmatrix} \begin{bmatrix} 1 & 0 \\ 0 & \alpha^2 \end{bmatrix} \begin{bmatrix} \alpha^{5-i-1} & 0 \\ 0 & \alpha^{5-i-1} \end{bmatrix}\right] \alpha^{i+j} \\
&= \sum_{i=0}^{4} \sum_{j=0}^{4} \operatorname{tr}\begin{bmatrix} \alpha^{10-i-j-2} & 0 \\ 0 & \alpha^{10-i-j} \end{bmatrix} \alpha^{i+j} \\
&= 25(\alpha^8 + \alpha^{10}) = 0.122 \qquad (7.5.7)
\end{aligned}$$

Furthermore,

$$\Omega_y(1) = Kp\Sigma_v = 1 \qquad (7.5.8)$$

and

$$\Omega_y(5) = \sum_{i=0}^{4} \sum_{j=0}^{4} \alpha^{4-j} \alpha^{4-i} \alpha^j \alpha^i = 25\alpha^8 = 0.098 . \qquad (7.5.9)$$

Finally, using (3.2.39),

$$G_x(2) = (1 - (1,\ 0)\underline{A}^2\begin{bmatrix}1\\1\end{bmatrix})^2 \not{Z}_{\bar{x}} = (1 - (1,\ 0)\begin{bmatrix}\alpha & 0\\0 & \alpha\end{bmatrix}\begin{bmatrix}1\\1\end{bmatrix})^2 \not{Z}_{\bar{x}}$$

$$= (1 - \alpha)^2 \not{Z}_{\bar{x}} = \not{Z}_u = 1 , \qquad (7.5.10)$$

where

$$\not{Z}_{\bar{x}} = \frac{1}{(1-\alpha)^2} \not{Z}_u .$$

$$G_x(10) = (1 - (1,\ 0)\underline{A}^{10}\begin{bmatrix}1\\1\end{bmatrix})^2 \not{Z}_{\bar{x}} = (1 - (1,\ 0)\begin{bmatrix}\alpha^5 & 0\\0 & \alpha^5\end{bmatrix}\begin{bmatrix}1\\1\end{bmatrix})^2 \not{Z}_{\bar{x}}$$

$$= \frac{(1-\alpha^5)^2}{(1-\alpha)^2} \not{Z}_u = 3.754 , \qquad (7.5.11)$$

$$G_y(1) = \not{Z}_v = 1 , \qquad (7.5.12)$$

and

$$G_y(5) = (1 - \alpha^5)^2 \not{Z}_y = \frac{(1-\alpha^5)^2}{(1-\alpha)^2} \not{Z}_v = 3.754 . \qquad (7.5.13)$$

Now all the pieces are available to compare the MSEs

$$\hat{\not{Z}}(h) = \not{Z}(h) + \frac{1}{T}(m\Omega_y(h) + mG_y(h)) \qquad (7.5.14)$$

and

$$\hat{\not{Z}}^o(h) = \not{Z}^o(h) + \frac{1}{T}(\Omega_x(mh) + G_x(mh)) \qquad (7.5.15)$$

for h = 1 and 5 obtained from the asymptotic theory of Section 7.2. Here T is the sample size of the full process and the sample size of the partial process is T/m. By the foregoing results,

$$\hat{\not{Z}}(1) - \hat{\not{Z}}^o(1) = \frac{1}{T}(m\Omega_y(1) - \Omega_x(m) + mG_y(1) - G_x(m))$$

$$= 1.75/T \qquad (7.5.16)$$

and

$$\hat{\Sigma}(5) - \hat{\Sigma}^{o}(5) = \frac{1}{T}(2\cdot 0.098 - 0.122 + 2\cdot 3.754 - 3.754)$$

$$= 3.828/T \,. \qquad (7.5.17)$$

Obviously the MSE part due to estimating the mean term becomes more important for increasing forecast horizon and for h = 5 the MSE difference is clearly dominated by the difference $mG_y(5) - G_x(10)$.

The MSE differences obtained in the Monte Carlo experiment are given in Table 7.1(a). When the true orders are used (p = 1,2) the results are fully in line with the asymptotic results, that is, the MSE differences are all positive and most are significant at the 5% or 10% level. The same holds if the AR orders are estimated by the three criteria AIC, HQ, and SC. The frequency distributions obtained with these criteria are presented in Table 7.1(b). The maximum orders P = 8 for the full process and P = 4 for the partial process are not restrictive for any of the three sample sizes and with growing length of the simulated series the AR orders are estimated correctly more often by all three criteria. Given the high probability of estimating the AR orders correctly it is not surprising that the results for processes with estimated orders are similar to those for known orders. Similar results were obtained for AR(2) processes $x_t = 1 + \alpha x_{t-2} + u_t$ with $\alpha = 0.2$ and $\alpha = 0.8$.

7.5.2 Bivariate AR Process

Realizations of the bivariate AR(2) process

$$\underline{x}_t = \underline{\nu} + A_2\underline{x}_{t-2} + \underline{u}_t \qquad (7.5.18)$$

were also generated to investigate the effect of increasing the dimension of the considered processes. The following parameters were used:

$$\underline{\nu} = \begin{bmatrix} 1 \\ 1 \end{bmatrix}, \quad A_2 = \begin{bmatrix} 0.5 & -0.66 \\ -0.5 & 0.3 \end{bmatrix}, \quad \text{and } \Sigma_{\underline{u}} = I_2 \,.$$

The matrix A_2 is chosen so that $\underline{x}_t$ is stationary and is otherwise arbitrary. Using m = 2 gives an AR(1) process

$$\underline{y}_t = \underline{x}_{2t} = \underline{\nu} + A_2\underline{y}_{t-1} + \underline{v}_t \quad \text{with} \quad \underline{v}_t = \underline{u}_{2t}$$

Table 7.1. Monte Carlo Results Based on 600 Replications for Univariate Full AR(2) and Partial AR(1) Process

(a) Differences of Forecast MSEs, $\hat{\Sigma}(h) - \hat{\Sigma}^o(h)$ $(\tilde{\Sigma}(h) - \tilde{\Sigma}^o(h))$

sample size T of full process	forecast horizon h		estimation criterion		
		p=1,2	AIC	HQ	SC
60	1	0.04**	0.07**	0.09**	0.07**
	5	0.02	0.03	0.05	0.02
100	1	0.02*	0.04	0.03*	0.03*
	5	0.04**	0.04*	0.05**	0.05**
200	1	0.03**	0.01	0.02*	0.03**
	5	0.02	0.01	0.01	0.01

* significant at 10% level, ** significant at 5% level

(b) Frequency Distributions of Estimated AR Orders in Percent

full process					partial process				
sample size T	AR order	frequency distribution[a] p(AIC)	p(HQ)	p(SC)	sample size T	AR order	frequency distribution[a] p(AIC)	p(HQ)	p(SC)
60	0	2	7	15	30	0	15	19	29
	1	2	2	3		1	62	65	63
	2	63	74	76		2	13	10	7
	3	14	9	4		3	5	3	2
	4	8	5	2		4	6	4	0
	5	4	2	1					
	6	2	1	0					
	7	3	0	0					
	8	2	0	0					
100	0	0	0	2	50	0	3	5	10
	1	0	0	0		1	71	81	84
	2	70	85	94		2	14	9	4
	3	12	9	4		3	7	3	1
	4	7	4	1		4	6	2	0
	5	4	1	0					
	6	4	0	0					
	7	2	0	0					
	8	1	0	0					
200	0	0	0	0	100	0	0	0	1
	1	0	0	0		1	75	87	94
	2	72	91	97		2	14	9	5
	3	12	6	3		3	6	2	0
	4	6	2	0		4	5	1	0
	5	5	0	0					
	6	3	1	0					
	7	2	0	0					
	8	1	0	0					

[a] Some columns do not sum to 100 due to rounding errors.

and again, by Proposition 7.1, the forecasts $\underline{y}_t^o(h)$ and $\underline{y}_t(h)$ based on known processes are identical for h = 1,2,... . The frequency distributions of the orders obtained with AIC, HQ, and SC are given in Table 7.2(a). The maximum AR orders are P = 6 and 4 for $\underline{x}_t$ and $\underline{y}_t$ respectively and they are not restrictive as they are attained very rarely. Again all three criteria choose the correct order more often with increasing sample size and for sample sizes T = 100 and 200 (T = 50 and 100) the consistent criteria HQ and SC choose the correct order with a very high probability.

The results of Sections 7.2 and 7.3 suggest that the predictor $\hat{\underline{y}}_t^o(h)$ ($\tilde{\underline{y}}_t^o(h)$) based on the full process will dominate the predictor $\hat{\underline{y}}_t(h)$ ($\tilde{\underline{y}}_t(h)$) which is based on the imcomplete series with every second observation missing. The MSE differences obtained in the Monte Carlo simulations are given in Table 7.2(b) and are in full agreement with the asymptotic results. Only positive differences are significant at the 10% level and the differences diminish with increasing sample size.

7.5.3 MA(m) Processes

The asymptotic theory of Section 7.3 allows the AR representation of the underlying processes to be of infinite order and requires that the AR orders of the processes used for prediction go to infinity with increasing sample size (see (7.3.3)). Therefore realizations of the univariate MA(2) process

$$x_t = 1 + u_t - 0.5u_{t-2} \ , \quad \Sigma_u = 1, \tag{7.5.19}$$

were generated. Using again m = 2,

$$y_t = x_{2t} = 1 + v_t - 0.5v_{t-1} \quad \text{with} \quad v_t = u_{2t} \ .$$

Since condition (7.1.12) of Proposition 7.1 is satisfied for x_t the predictors $y_t(h)$ and $y_t^o(h)$ are equal for h = 1,2,... , if the processes are assumed known so that the observed MSE differences are due to estimation and specification variability.

The discussion in Sections 7.2 and 7.3 suggests that for estimated processes the MSE $\tilde{\Sigma}^o(h)$ from the full process is again smaller than the MSE $\tilde{\Sigma}(h)$ obtained from the partial process provided the AR orders are chosen according to (7.3.3). The frequency distributions of the AR orders estimated by AIC, HQ, and SC are given in Table 7.3(a). The maximum AR orders are P = 8 and 4 for x_t and y_t respectively. For all three

Table 7.2. Monte Carlo Results Based on 600 Replications for Bivariate Full AR(2) and Partial AR(1) Process

(a) Frequency Distribution of Estimated AR Orders in Percent

full process					partial process				
sample size T	AR order	frequency distribution p(AIC)	p(HQ)	p(SC)	sample size T	AR order	frequency distribution p(AIC)	p(HQ)	p(SC)
60	0	0	0	0	30	0	1	1	3
	1	0	0	0		1	72	85	93
	2	84	96	99		2	14	9	3
	3	8	3	1		3	7	3	1
	4	4	1	0		4	6	1	0
	5	2	0	0					
	6	2	0	0					
100	0	0	0	0	50	0	0	0	0
	1	0	0	0		1	83	94	99
	2	86	98	100		2	10	5	1
	3	8	2	0		3	4	1	0
	4	3	0	0		4	3	0	0
	5	2	0	0					
	6	1	0	0					
200	0	0	0	0	100	0	0	0	0
	1	0	0	0		1	87	98	100
	2	89	99	100		2	9	2	0
	3	7	1	0		3	2	0	0
	4	3	0	0		4	2	0	0
	5	1	0	0					
	6	0	0	0					

(b) Differences of Forecast MSEs, $\hat{\Sigma}(h) - \hat{\Sigma}^o(h)$ $(\tilde{\Sigma}(h) - \tilde{\Sigma}^o(h))$

sample size T of full process	fore-cast horizon h	p = 1,2 y_1	p = 1,2 y_2	estimation criterion: AIC y_1	AIC y_2	HQ y_1	HQ y_2	SC y_1	SC y_2
60	1	0.06**	0.05*	0.11**	0.10**	0.10**	0.06*	0.11**	0.07**
	5	0.20	0.12	0.26	0.24**	0.26	0.15	0.23	0.14
100	1	0.07**	0.00	0.09**	0.01	0.08**	0.01	0.07**	-0.00
	5	0.06	0.05	0.14	0.08	0.13	0.09	0.06	0.05
200	1	0.00	0.00	0.00	0.00	0.00	0.00	0.00	0.00
	5	0.01	-0.01	-0.02	-0.00	0.01	-0.01	0.01	-0.01

* significant at 10% level, ** significant at 5% level

Table 7.3. Monte Carlo Results Based on 600 Replications for Full MA(2) and Partial MA(1) Process

(a) Frequency Distributions of Estimated AR Orders in Percent

full process					partial process				
sample size T	AR order	frequency distribution			sample size T	AR order	frequency distribution		
		p(AIC)	p(HQ)	p(SC)			p(AIC)	p(HQ)	p(SC)
60	0	4	9	24	30	0	9	14	25
	1	0	0	0		1	39	43	50
	2	39	58	64		2	29	27	20
	3	4	3	1		3	11	8	4
	4	27	19	10		4	12	8	2
	5	6	4	1					
	6	10	5	1					
	7	5	1	0					
	8	6	1	0					
100	0	0	2	6	50	0	2	5	11
	1	0	0	0		1	34	44	55
	2	29	55	75		2	36	35	28
	3	2	1	1		3	15	10	4
	4	39	32	16		4	13	6	2
	5	6	2	1					
	6	15	7	1					
	7	3	1	0					
	8	7	1	0					
200	0	0	0	0	100	0	0	0	1
	1	0	0	0		1	17	28	48
	2	9	31	61		2	42	47	41
	3	0	0	0		3	26	19	9
	4	45	52	37		4	16	7	2
	5	5	2	0					
	6	23	12	3					
	7	6	1	0					
	8	13	3	0					

(b) Differences of Forecast MSEs, $\tilde{\Sigma}(h) - \tilde{\Sigma}^o(h)$

sample size T of full process	forecast horizon h	estimation criterion		
		AIC	HQ	SC
60	1	0.05	0.10**	0.08**
	5	0.00	0.01	0.01
100	1	0.04*	0.02	0.03
	5	0.00	-0.01	-0.00
200	1	0.00	0.02	0.02
	5	0.02*	0.00	0.01

* significant at 10% level, ** significant at 5% level

criteria the averages of the order estimates increase with growing sample size in accordance with condition (7.3.3).

The MSE differences $\tilde{\Sigma}(h) - \tilde{\Sigma}^{o}(h)$ are shown in Table 7.3(b). They are positive except in two cases and, in accordance with the asymptotic theory, only positive differences are significant. Thus, the asymptotic theory is a good indicator for what actually occurred under the conditions of the simulation experiment.

Since this and the previous examples are borderline cases in that m assumes its minimum value of 2, realizations of the univariate MA(3) process

$$x_t = 1 + u_t - 0.5u_{t-3}, \ \Sigma_u = 1 , \qquad (7.5.20)$$

were also generated and every third observation (m = 3) was used to obtain the process $y_{\mathfrak{t}}$, that is,

$$y_{\mathfrak{t}} = x_{3\mathfrak{t}} = 1 + v_{\mathfrak{t}} - 0.5v_{\mathfrak{t}-1}, \ v_{\mathfrak{t}} = u_{3\mathfrak{t}},$$

so that again $\Sigma^{o}(h) = \Sigma(h)$ by Proposition 7.1. The maximum AR orders used for estimating the orders of x_t and $\underset{\sim}{y}_{\mathfrak{t}}$ were P = 9 and 4 respectively. For this process the differences $\tilde{\Sigma}(h) - \tilde{\Sigma}^{o}(h)$ were all positive in accordance with the asymptotic theory.

Moreover, realizations of a bivariate MA(2) process similar to (7.5.19) were generated and the $\underline{y}_{\mathfrak{t}}$ process was obtained by deleting every second observation. Also in this case the MSE differences were mostly positive and only positive differences were significant at the 10% level. Hence, the small sample results were in line with the asymptotic theory of Section 7.3.

7.5.4 Univariate MA(1) Process

So far only processes have been considered where it is preferable to use the full process for estimation and specification. In Section 7.3 it is argued that for an MA(q) process x_t with $q < m$, using the partial process for prediction may result in smaller MSEs if only pure AR processes are fitted. Therefore, the MA(1) process

$$x_t = 1 + u_t + 0.5u_{t-1} , \quad \text{with} \quad \Sigma_u = 1 , \qquad (7.5.21)$$

is also considered. If every second observation is missing (m = 2), a partial white noise process

$$y_t = 1 + v_t \text{ , where } v_t = u_{2t} + 0.5u_{2t-1} \text{ ,} \tag{7.5.22}$$

is obtained.

Assuming that AR processes of finite order p are fitted to x_t the approximate MSE of $\tilde{y}_t^o(h)$ is,

$$\tilde{\Sigma}^o(h) = (1 + \frac{p}{T})\Sigma^o(h) + \frac{1}{T}G_x(mh) \tag{7.5.23}$$

according to the discussion in Section 7.3. On the other hand, if y_t is detected to be white noise, the approximate MSE of $\tilde{y}_t(h)$ is

$$\tilde{\Sigma}(h) = \Sigma(h) + \frac{1}{T}G_y(h) = \Sigma(h) + \frac{1}{T}mG_y(h), \tag{7.5.24}$$

where $T = T/m$ has been used. Since condition (7.1.12) of Proposition 7.1 is satisfied, $\Sigma(h) = \Sigma^o(h)$ for h = 1,2,... . Hence,

$$\tilde{\Sigma}(h) - \tilde{\Sigma}^o(h) = -\frac{p}{T}\Sigma(h) + \frac{1}{T}(mG_y(h) - G_x(mh)). \tag{7.5.25}$$

For instance, for h = 1,

$$\Sigma(1) = \Sigma_y = \Sigma_v = 1.25,$$

and

$$G_y(1) = \Sigma_y = \Sigma_v = 1.25.$$

To evaluate $G_x(2)$, note that for an AR process

$$x_t = \mu + \sum_{i=1}^{\infty} \alpha_i (x_{t-i} - \mu) + u_t \tag{7.5.26}$$

the optimal 2-step predictor is

$$\begin{aligned} x_t(2) &= \mu + \alpha_1(x_t(1) - \mu) + \alpha_2(x_t - \mu) + \dots \\ &= \mu + \alpha_1[\sum_{i=1}^{\infty} \alpha_i(x_{t+1-i} - \mu) - \mu] + \alpha_2(x_t - \mu) + \dots \end{aligned}$$

so that

$$\begin{aligned} \frac{\partial x_t(2)}{\partial \mu} &= 1 + \alpha_1(-\sum_{i=1}^{\infty} \alpha_i - 1) - \alpha_2 - \alpha_3 - \dots \\ &= 1 + \alpha_1(\alpha(1) - 2) + \alpha(1) + \alpha_1 - 1 \\ &= (1 + \alpha_1)\alpha(1) - \alpha_1 \text{ ,} \end{aligned} \tag{7.5.27}$$

where

$$\alpha(z) = 1 - \sum_{i=1}^{\infty} \alpha_i z^i .$$

Thus, for the present case, where $\alpha_i = (-0.5)^i$,

$$\frac{\partial x_t(2)}{\partial \mu} = \frac{1-0.5}{1+0.5} + 0.5 = \frac{5}{6} .$$

Furthermore,

$$\Sigma_{\bar{x}} = (1 + 0.5)^2 \Sigma_u = (\tfrac{3}{2})^2$$

and consequently,

$$G_x(2) = (\frac{\partial x_t(2)}{\partial \mu})^2 \Sigma_{\bar{x}} = 1.5625 . \qquad (7.5.28)$$

Hence, using (7.5.25),

$$\tilde{\Sigma}(1) - \tilde{\Sigma}^o(1) = -1.25\frac{p}{T} + \frac{1}{T}(2.5 - 1.5625)$$

$$= (-1.25p + 0.9375)/T \qquad (7.5.29)$$

which is negative if $p \geq 1$. Of course, the difference between the two MSEs is small if p is small.

In Table 7.4(a) the frequency distributions of the AR orders obtained by AIC, HQ, and SC are given. The maximum AR orders are P = 8 and 4 for x_t and $\mathcal{y}_\mathcal{t}$, respectively. The three criteria tend to increase the estimated AR order for x_t on average with growing sample size which is in line with (7.3.3a) so that (7.5.23) may be a reasonable approximation to the MSEs of the forecasts based on the full process. On the other hand, for $\mathcal{y}_\mathcal{t}$ an AR(0) is chosen more frequently when $\mathcal{T} = T/m$ increases. This is precisely the situation described in the foregoing so that the 1-step MSEs of the partial process are expected to be smaller than the MSEs from the full process. In other words, $\tilde{\Sigma}(1) - \tilde{\Sigma}^o(1)$ is expected to be negative. The differences obtained in the Monte Carlo experiment are reported in Table 7.4(b) where negative values are found in eight out of nine cases and only negative differences are significant for the 1-step MSEs.

For increasing forecast horizon h, $G_x(mh)$ can be shown to approach $\Sigma_{\bar{x}} = 2.25$ (replace the matrix $\underline{A}$ in (3.2.38) by an infinite order matrix). Thus, the difference in (7.5.25) remains negative for h = 5.

Table 7.4. Monte Carlo Results Based on 600 Replications for Full MA(1) and Partial MA(0) Process

(a) Frequency Distributions of Estimated AR Orders in Percent

full process					partial process				
sample size T	AR order	frequency distribution p(AIC)	p(HQ)	p(SC)	sample size T	AR order	frequency distribution p(AIC)	p(HQ)	p(SC)
60	0	1	3	8	30	0	73	82	93
	1	28	39	56		1	10	8	5
	2	43	43	32		2	8	5	1
	3	11	8	3		3	4	3	1
	4	6	4	1		4	6	3	1
	5	4	1	0					
	6	4	2	0					
	7	2	1	0					
	8	1	0	0					
100	0	0	0	1	50	0	75	85	93
	1	15	29	49		1	12	8	5
	2	48	55	47		2	7	4	2
	3	16	10	3		3	3	2	1
	4	11	5	1		4	4	1	0
	5	3	1	0					
	6	3	1	0					
	7	3	0	0					
	8	2	0	0					
200	0	0	0	0	100	0	75	89	96
	1	4	11	27		1	12	6	3
	2	42	61	63		2	6	3	2
	3	26	20	8		3	4	1	0
	4	14	8	2		4	3	1	0
	5	6	1	0					
	6	3	0	0					
	7	3	0	0					
	8	3	0	0					

(b) Differences of Forecast MSEs, $\tilde{\Sigma}(h) - \tilde{\Sigma}^o(h)$

sample size T of full process	forecast horizon h	estimation criterion AIC	HQ	SC
60	1	-0.02	0.01	-0.05*
	5	0.01	0.00	0.01
100	1	-0.03	-0.02	-0.02
	5	-0.00	-0.01	-0.00
200	1	-0.01	-0.03*	-0.03**
	5	0.01	0.01*	0.01**

* significant at 10% level, ** significant at 5% level

This is not clearly reflected in the 5-step MSEs from the Monte Carlo experiment. Most of the differences in Table 7.4(b) are positive for h = 5. The reason may be that the mean term dominates the long term forecasts when only low order AR processes are fitted and the mean is estimated more accurately from the full process than from the partial process ($m\Sigma_{\bar{y}} > \Sigma_{\bar{x}}$). Note that $y_t^o(5)$ is actually a 10-step forecast of the x_t process. Especially the fact that the 5-step MSE differences are significantly positive for the parsimonious criteria HQ and SC (see Table 7.4(a)) supports this explanation.

In summary, this example shows that in small samples it is possible that superior short-term forecasts are obtained when a series with systematically missing observations is used rather than the full series. In practice, however, such a situation may not be very likely to occur because if the partial process y_t is recognized to be white noise the process mean is known to be the optimal predictor and may be computed from the full series rather than fitting some AR process.

7.5.5 Summary of Small Sample Results

In summary, it seems that the asymptotic theories of Sections 7.2 and 7.3 are good indicators for the small sample efficiencies of the two predictors $\underline{y}_t(h)$ and $\underline{y}_t^o(h)$. The Monte Carlo results show that in small samples the predictor $\tilde{\underline{y}}_t(h)$ based on series with systematically missing observations can in fact be superior to the predictor $\tilde{\underline{y}}_t^o(h)$ which is based on the full series although this is perhaps not a very likely occurence since in practice the underlying processes for which it occurs may not be very common. In general $\underline{y}_t^o(h)$ is superior to $\underline{y}_t(h)$ if the data generation processes are known and the same applies for most estimated processes other than the special cases considered. In the next section two empirical examples will be discussed, where the data generation processes are possibly approximately of the types considered in the simulation study.

7.6 EMPIRICAL EXAMPLES

In this section two sets of economic data are analyzed to illustrate the behavior of the two predictors under investigation in practice. The first series consists of quarterly, seasonally adjusted U.S. Personal Consumption Expenditures, and the second series is the quarterly U.S. Gross Private Domestic Investment used earlier for illustrative purposes.

7.6.1 Consumption Expenditures

The quarterly, seasonally adjusted U.S. Personal Consumption Expenditures (z_t) for the period 1947.I to 1972.IV used in this example are given in the Appendix of the book. For the period 1947.I - 1968.IV the model

$$(1-L)z_t = \underset{(0.58)}{2.69} + \underset{(0.11)}{0.33}\,(1-L)z_{t-2} + u_t \;, \quad \tilde{\Sigma}_u = 14.74 \;, \tag{7.6.1}$$

was identified and estimated using the Box-Jenkins approach. As usual, the numbers in parentheses are estimated standard errors. Since most of this chapter deals with stationary processes, define $x_t = (1-L)z_t$, that is, x_t consists of the first differences of the quarterly consumption data. Assuming that x_t is indeed generated by the process

$$x_t = 2.69 + 0.33x_{t-2} + u_t \;, \tag{7.6.2}$$

and using a partial process $y_t = x_{2t}$ that consists of the second and fourth quarter values, a situation similar to the one discussed in Section 7.5.1 is obtained. Given the simulation results one would expect that x_t provides slightly better forecasts for y_t than a model for y_t that is only based on every other value of the x_t series. Note that if it were known that x_t is actually generated by (7.6.2) the theoretical forecast MSEs $\Sigma(h)$ and $\Sigma^{o}(h)$ would be identical for h = 1,2,... by Proposition 7.1.

Using the three criteria AIC, SC, and HQ for fitting AR processes and a maximum AR order of P = 14 the following models for x_t were obtained:

$$\text{AIC, HQ: } x_t = \underset{(0.69)}{2.44} + \underset{(0.10)}{0.07}\,x_{t-1} + \underset{(0.11)}{0.32}\,x_{t-2} + u_t \;, \quad \tilde{\Sigma}_u = 14.83 \;, \tag{7.6.3}$$

$$\text{SC: } x_t = \underset{(0.43)}{3.92} + u_t \;, \quad \tilde{\Sigma}_u = 16.05 \;. \tag{7.6.4}$$

With a maximum AR order of P = 8, the following models were obtained for y_t:

$$\text{AIC, HQ: } y_t = \underset{(1.43)}{2.63} + \underset{(0.16)}{0.27}\, y_{t-1} - \underset{(0.17)}{0.25}\, y_{t-2} + \underset{(0.17)}{0.16}\, y_{t-3}$$

$$- \underset{(0.17)}{0.23}\, y_{t-4} + \underset{(0.17)}{0.36}\, y_{t-5} + v_t \,, \quad \tilde{\Sigma}_v = 16.29 \,, \tag{7.6.5}$$

$$\text{SC: } y_t = \underset{(0.60)}{3.71} + v_t \,, \quad \tilde{\Sigma}_v = 15.87 \,. \tag{7.6.6}$$

Since the generation process of y_t would be an AR(1) if (7.6.2) were in fact the true generation process of x_t, an AR(1) model was also estimated for y_t:

$$y_t = \underset{(0.84)}{3.05} + \underset{(0.15)}{0.17}\, y_{t-1} + v_t \,, \quad \tilde{\Sigma}_v = 16.13 \,. \tag{7.6.7}$$

Using all six models (7.6.2) - (7.6.7) forecasts were computed for y_t for the postsample years 1969 - 1972 and the corresponding MSEs are shown in Table 7.5(a). Note that the MSEs for forecast horizon h = 1 are based on eight squared errors of 1-step forecasts for the postsample period. Similarly, the 2-step MSEs are based on seven 2-step forecasts and so on. Comparing only the forecasts from the Box-Jenkins model for x_t with those from the AR(1) model for y_t the results are fully in line with the theoretical and Monte Carlo findings of the previous sections. The forecasts $\tilde{y}^o_t(h)$ based on all quarterly data x_t dominate the forecasts $\tilde{y}_t(h)$ based on the series y_t with systematically missing observations for h = 1,2,3,4. The same holds for h = 1,2 for the AR models based on AIC and HQ. Surprisingly, the heavily parameterized AIC-HQ-model (7.6.5) for y_t does slightly better than its x_t counterpart (7.6.3) for forecast horizons h = 3 and 4. This result can perhaps be explained by the small number of forecasts on which these MSEs are based. The models for both x_t and y_t chosen by the SC criterion are white noise processes. Since more observations are used for estimating the intercept term in (7.6.4) it was to be expected that this model supplies forecasts that are slightly superior to the $\tilde{y}_t(h)$ based on (7.6.6). The MSEs for the SC models in Table 7.5(a) confirm this expectation.

If the original data z_t are considered and every second observation is deleted the resulting partial process, say $z_t = z_{2t}$, is nonstationary. For the first differences of z_t all three criteria have chosen an AR(1) model when a maximum order of P = 8 was allowed:

$$(1-L)z_t = \underset{(1.41)}{5.42} + \underset{(0.15)}{0.34}\,(1-L)z_{t-1} + w_t \,, \quad \tilde{\Sigma}_w = 29.25 \,. \tag{7.6.8}$$

Table 7.5. MSEs of Forecasts for Second and Fourth Quarters of Seasonally Adjusted Quarterly U.S. Personal Consumption Expenditures

(a) First Differences

forecast horizon h	forecasts based on full quarterly series			forecasts based on partial series of second and fourth quarter data		
	AIC, HQ	SC	Box-Jenkins	AIC, HQ	SC	AR(1)
1	35	46	36	40	47	41
2	50	52	51	53	54	53
3	60	61	61	59	62	62
4	72	73	72	69	74	75

(b) Original Series

forecast horizon h	forecasts based on full quarterly series			forecasts based on partial series of second and fourth quarter data
	AIC, HQ	SC	Box-Jenkins	AIC, HQ, SC
1	89	112	90	89
2	277	315	278	272
3	491	518	483	472
4	879	760	847	832

Again the estimates are obtained from the data for 1947 - 1968. This model and the processes in (7.6.1), (7.6.3), and (7.6.4) were used to compute forecasts for the nonstationary z_t series for 1969 - 1972. From the discussion at the end of Section 7.4 one would expect that a predictor based on the full series is superior to one based on the partial series. The MSEs of the z_t forecasts are given in Table 7.5(b). It turns out that the forecasts from the partial process (7.6.8) are optimal for h = 1,2, and 3. For h = 4, the random walk model (7.6.4) for the full series forecasts best. The somewhat unexpected outcome may be due to the small number of forecasts on which the MSEs are based. Also, it is of course possible that the Personal Consumption Expenditures violate any of the assumptions underlying the analysis of this chapter. For instance, there may be structural changes in the estimation or forecasting period.

7.6.2 Investment

The investment data considered in earlier chapters are used as a further example. The Box-Jenkins model obtained in Chapter 5 for the Gross Private Domestic Investment (z_t) is

$$(1-L)z_t = \underset{(0.25)}{1.06} + u_t - \underset{(0.09)}{0.59}\, u_{t-4} \;, \quad \tilde{\Sigma}_u = 28.9 \;, \qquad (7.6.9)$$

(see (5.6.30)). Defining $x_t = (1-L)z_t$, that is, x_t represents the first differences of the original investment data, and denoting the series of fourth quarter values by y_t (= x_{4t}) the MSEs $\Sigma(h)$ and $\Sigma^o(h)$ of the y_t forecasts are identical for known processes. The process x_t is similar to the processes discussed in Section 7.5.3 and the results of that section suggest that $\tilde{\Sigma}(h) > \tilde{\Sigma}^o(h)$ when pure AR processes are fitted to x_t and y_t. Using again the data for the period 1947 - 1968 and a maximum AR order of P = 14, AIC and HQ have chosen the AR(4) in (5.6.4) for x_t while SC has chosen the white noise (AR(0)) model in (5.6.5). The models obtained for y_t when allowing a maximum AR order of P = 4 are:

$$\text{AIC, HQ:}\quad y_t = \underset{(1.32)}{2.71} - \underset{(0.26)}{0.85}\, y_{t-1} - \underset{(0.32)}{0.54}\, y_{t-2} - \underset{(0.25)}{0.24}\, y_{t-3} + v_t \;, \quad \tilde{\Sigma}_v = 26.42 \;, \qquad (7.6.10)$$

$$\text{SC:}\quad y_t = \underset{(1.16)}{1.60} - \underset{(0.18)}{0.51}\, y_{t-1} + v_t \;, \quad \tilde{\Sigma}_v = 26.91 \qquad (7.6.11)$$

The resulting forecast MSEs for y_t based on the postsample data for 1969 - 1972 are given in Table 7.6(a). Note that the MSEs for forecast horizons 1 and 2 are in this case based only on 4 and 3 postsample predictions, respectively. In all cases the forecasts $\tilde{y}_t^o(h)$ based on quarterly data are superior to the corresponding $\tilde{y}_t(h)$ based on annual data. This result is fully in line with the theoretical and Monte Carlo findings of the previous sections.

For completeness AR models for the series z_t of fourth quarter values of the original, nonstationary series z_t were also fitted. All three criteria AIC, HQ, and SC have chosen the random walk model

$$(1-L)z_t = \underset{(3.33)}{4.05} + w_t \;, \quad \tilde{\Sigma}_w = 233 \;. \tag{7.6.12}$$

The MSEs for the forecasts of the nonstationary series z_t obtained from the full z_t series and the partial process (7.6.12) are given in Table 7.6(b). For h = 1 the AR(4) model chosen by AIC and HQ for the first differences of the full quarterly series is inferior to the other forecasts. Comparing only the SC model for the z_t series and the partial process, the forecasts based on the full series and the partial series are almost identical. This is in line with results of the next chapter.

7.7 CONCLUDING REMARKS

In this chapter two different predictors for time series with systematically missing observations or temporally aggregated stock variables have been compared. Overall the results confirm what might have been expected using common sense. If more information is used, better forecasts result. In other words, even if, e.g., only forecasts of the fourth quarters of forthcoming years are of interest, it will generally be better to base these forecasts on available data for all quarters of previous years rather than use a forecasting model for past fourth quarter values only. This conclusion is reached by using asymptotic theory and small sample simulation results.

There are, however, exceptions to this general rule. For instance, if the series of systematically missing observations (aggregated stock variables) is white noise and the full series is a low order MA process, it may be preferable to use only the former rather than an AR model fitted to the latter. Two empirical examples are used to illustrate the theoretical conclusions.

In practice a model based on a partial series with systematically

Table 7.6. MSEs of Fourth Quarter Forecasts of Seasonally Adjusted Quarterly U.S. Gross Private Domestic Investment

(a) First Differences

forecast horizon h	forecasts based on full quarterly series		forecasts based on partial series of fourth quarter data	
	AIC, HQ	SC	AIC, HQ	SC
1	65	51	74	71
2	31	23	45	37

(b) Original Series

forecast horizon h	forecasts based on full quarterly series		forecasts based on partial series of fourth quarter data
	AIC, HQ	SC	AIC, HQ, SC
1	287	229	231
2	492	554	559

missing observations may of course provide forecasts superior to those from the full series if model misspecifications are present. One form of misspecification that may be of particular importance in the present context was noted by Cleveland and Tiao (1979). These authors point out that for some time series a different model may be needed for different seasons (e.g., quarters or months). Thus, using the AR model fitting procedures or standard Box-Jenkins methodology and constructing one model for all seasons may result in a model that provides forecasts inferior to those based on data for a particular season. In the next chapter temporally aggregated flow variables will be discussed in some detail.

7.A APPENDIX: PROOF OF RELATION (7.2.18)

In the following the notation of Section 7.2 is used. In (7.2.18) it is claimed that

$$\mathrm{tr}(\underline{A}'^{m-1}\Gamma^{-1}\underline{A}^{m-1}\Gamma) < mK . \tag{7.A.1}$$

Using (7.2.15) it suffices to show that

$$\mathrm{tr}(A_m'^{i}\Sigma_{\underline{x}}^{-1}A_m^{i}\Sigma_{\underline{x}}) < K \quad \text{for} \quad i = 1,2,\ldots . \tag{7.A.2}$$

For i = 1 this inequality follows because

$$\begin{aligned}\mathrm{tr}(A_m'\Sigma_{\underline{x}}^{-1}A_m\Sigma_{\underline{x}}) &= \mathrm{tr}(\Sigma_{\underline{x}}^{-1}A_m\Sigma_{\underline{x}}A_m') \\ &= \mathrm{tr}[\Sigma_{\underline{x}}^{-1}A_m(\sum_{n=0}^{\infty}A_m^n\Sigma_{\underline{u}}A_m^{n'})A_m'] \\ &= \mathrm{tr}[\Sigma_{\underline{x}}^{-1}(\sum_{n=1}^{\infty}A_m^n\Sigma_{\underline{u}}A_m^{n'} + \Sigma_{\underline{u}} - \Sigma_{\underline{u}})] \\ &= \mathrm{tr}(I_K) - \mathrm{tr}(\Sigma_{\underline{x}}^{-1}\Sigma_{\underline{u}}) \\ &= K - \mathrm{tr}(\Sigma_{\underline{u}}^{1/2}\Sigma_{\underline{x}}^{-1}\Sigma_{\underline{u}}^{1/2}) < K\end{aligned}$$

since $\Sigma_{\underline{u}}^{1/2}\Sigma_{\underline{x}}^{-1}\Sigma_{\underline{u}}^{1/2}$ is positive definite and thus has a trace greater than zero.

Now the proof proceeds by induction. Suppose (7.A.2) holds for $i = j - 1$.

$$\mathrm{tr}(A_m'^{j}\Sigma_{\underline{x}}^{-1} A_m^{j}\Sigma_{\underline{x}}) = \mathrm{tr}(\Sigma_{\underline{x}}^{-1}A_m^{j} \Sigma_{\underline{x}}A_m^{j'})$$

$$= \mathrm{tr}[\Sigma_{\underline{x}}^{-1}A_m^{j}(\sum_{n=0}^{\infty} A_m^{n}\Sigma_{\underline{u}}A_m^{n'})A_m^{j'}]$$

$$= \mathrm{tr}[\Sigma_{\underline{x}}^{-1}A_m^{j-1}(\Sigma_{\underline{x}} - \Sigma_{\underline{u}})A_m'^{j-1}]$$

$$= \mathrm{tr}(\Sigma_{\underline{x}}^{-1}A_m^{j-1}\Sigma_{\underline{x}}A_m'^{j-1}) - \mathrm{tr}(\Sigma_{\underline{x}}^{-1}A_m^{j-1}\Sigma_{\underline{u}}A_m'^{j-1}) .$$

The first of these two terms is less than K by induction assumption and the last term

$$\mathrm{tr}(\Sigma_{\underline{x}}^{-1}A_m^{j-1}\Sigma_{\underline{u}}A_m'^{j-1}) = \mathrm{tr}(\Sigma_{\underline{u}}^{1/2}A_m'^{j-1}\Sigma_{\underline{x}}^{-1}A_m^{j-1}\Sigma_{\underline{u}}^{1/2}) > 0.$$

Thereby (7.A.2) is proved. Q.E.D.

CHAPTER 8. TEMPORAL AGGREGATION OF FLOW VARIABLES

Adding the values of a variable associated with consecutive time periods is the type of temporal aggregation considered in this chapter. Examples of flow variables where this form of aggregation is common are income, consumption expenditures, sales, imports, etc.. For instance, the annual income is the sum of monthly or quarterly incomes. In this chapter forecasts of the aggregate will be investigated.

There are numerous situations where predictions of temporally aggregated flow variables are of interest. Some such situations are mentioned in Chapter 6. Other examples are annual revenues that are required for planning an annual budget and the monthly number of applications that have to be handled within a month. Of course, the monthly figure is the sum of the daily applications and hence a temporal aggregate. Forecasts of the monthly numbers may be of interest in order to determine the size of the staff required to handle the applications within the maximum time that is tolerated by the applicants. Another case where the results of this chapter are of interest is mentioned in Section 7.4. If temporal aggregation of stock variables is treated and the generation process of the disaggregate series is stationary in the first differences then the stationary part of the aggregate is just the sum of consecutive first differences of the disaggregate series.

In Chapter 6 it was shown that forecasts from temporally disaggregated data are more efficient in terms of mean squared error than forecasts based on aggregated time series if the data generating processes are known vector ARMA processes. For example, if monthly income values are available then, based on the results of Chapter 6, using a monthly forecasting model is preferable to forecasting with an annual model even if interest centers on predictions for annual income. This result is a consequence of using a larger information set if forecasts are based on the disaggregate rather than the temporally aggregated time series. Given the results for contemporaneous aggregation and for temporal aggregation of stock variables one question of interest is whether the predictor based on the disaggregate series will remain optimal if the data generation process is unknown and has to be estimated.

In Section 8.1 the data generation processes are again assumed to be known. Although the results for this case were already given in more general form in Chapter 6, for illustrative purposes, it seems useful to consider the special case of temporal aggregation of flow variables in detail here. For this special case necessary and sufficient conditions for equality of the predictors based on the disaggregate and the aggregated variables are given that are more easily applicable than those of Chapter 6. In Section 8.2 the case of estimated coefficients is discussed and in Section 8.3 the consequences of fitting AR processes whose orders increase with the sample size are investigated. In those two sections the asymptotic theories of Chapter 3, Sections 3.2 and 3.3, are utilized. Some remarks on the nonstationary case are made in Section 8.4 and small sample results are discussed in Section 8.5. The consumption and investment data used in the previous chapter will again serve as examples in Section 8.6 and some concluding comments on forecasting temporally aggregated flow variables are contained in Section 8.7.

Similar, though more specialized work on temporal aggregation of flow variables has been reported by a number of authors in recent articles. For instance, Abraham (1982), Ahsanullah & Wei (1984a, b), Amemiya & Wu (1972), Brewer (1973), Tiao (1972), Wei (1978a), Weiss (1984) and others consider temporal aggregation of univariate series, whereas special multivariate models are treated by Engle & Liu (1972), Moriguchi (1970), Teräsvirta (1981), Tiao & Wei (1976), Wei (1978b), Wei & Mehta (1980), and Zellner & Montmarquette (1971) among others. In the latter articles the estimation of distributed lag models from temporally aggregated data is considered. In contrast, in this chapter multivariate series generated by general vector ARMA processes are treated and estimation is only of interest with regard to the forecasting problem (see also Lütkepohl (1986c)).

8.1 FORECASTING WITH KNOWN PROCESSES

It is assumed again that the disaggregate, basic process $\underline{x}_t = (x_{1t}, \dots, x_{Kt})'$ is a K-dimensional stationary stochastic process with MA representation

$$\underline{x}_t = \underline{\mu}_x + \sum_{i=0}^{\infty} \Phi_i \underline{u}_{t-i} = \underline{\mu}_x + \Phi(L)\underline{u}_t \quad , \quad \Phi_0 = I_K \, , \tag{8.1.1}$$

where $\underline{\mu}_x = E(\underline{x}_t)$ is the process mean, $\underline{u}_t = (u_{1t}, \dots, u_{Kt})'$ is K-dimensional white noise with nonsingular covariance matrix $\Sigma_{\underline{u}}$ and

$$\det(\Phi(z)) \neq 0 \quad \text{for} \quad |z| < 1. \tag{8.1.2}$$

In this section $\underline{x}_t$ is not required to have an AR representation. One may think of $\underline{x}_t$ as a vector ARMA process.

The process obtained by temporally aggregating $\underline{x}_t$ over m periods is denoted by $\underline{y}_t$, that is,

$$\underline{y}_t = \underline{x}_{mt} + \underline{x}_{mt-1} + \dots + \underline{x}_{mt-m+1}. \tag{8.1.3}$$

This process has also an MA representation by the results in Chapter 6, say

$$\underline{y}_t = \underline{\mu}_y + \sum_{i=0}^{\infty} N_i \underline{v}_{t-i} = \underline{\mu}_y + N(L)\underline{v}_t \;, \quad N_0 = I_K \;, \tag{8.1.4}$$

where L is the lag operator, shifting the macro time index backwards by one period, $\underline{\mu}_y = E(\underline{y}_t) = m\underline{\mu}_x$,

$$\det(N(z)) \neq 0 \quad \text{for} \quad |z| < 1, \tag{8.1.5}$$

and $\underline{v}_t$ is K-dimensional white noise with covariance matrix $\Sigma_{\underline{v}}$. From Chapter 6, Section 6.5, it is known that $\underline{y}_t$ has an ARMA representation if $\underline{x}_t$ is from the ARMA class.

The optimal h-step predictor of the $\underline{x}_t$ process based on $\{\underline{u}_s | s \leq t\}$ is

$$\underline{x}_t(h) = \underline{\mu}_x + \sum_{i=0}^{\infty} \Phi_{h+i}\underline{u}_{t-i} \tag{8.1.6}$$

and the corresponding MSE matrix is

$$\Sigma_{\underline{x}}(h) = \sum_{i=0}^{h-1} \Phi_i \Sigma_{\underline{u}} \Phi_i' \;. \tag{8.1.7}$$

Accordingly, the optimal h-step predictor of the aggregate based on $\{\underline{v}_s | s \leq t\}$ is

$$\underline{y}_t(h) = \underline{\mu}_y + \sum_{i=0}^{\infty} N_{h+i}\underline{v}_{t-i} \tag{8.1.8}$$

with corresponding MSE matrix

$$\Sigma(h) = \sum_{i=0}^{h-1} N_i \Sigma_{\underline{v}} N_i' \;. \tag{8.1.9}$$

If the disaggregate process is available, $\underline{y}_t(h)$ is in general not the optimal predictor of the aggregate. Rather the optimal predictor based on $\{\underline{u}_s | s \le mt\}$ is

$$\underline{y}_t^o(h) = \underline{x}_{mt}(mh) + \underline{x}_{mt}(mh-1) + \ldots + \underline{x}_{mt}(mh-m+1) \qquad (8.1.10)$$

(see Chapter 6). Denoting the MSE matrix of the 1-step to r-step predictor of the $\underline{x}_t$ process as usual by $\underline{\Sigma}_{\underline{x}}(r)$, i.e.,

$$\underline{\Sigma}_{\underline{x}}(r) = E\begin{bmatrix} \underline{x}_{t+1} - \underline{x}_t(1) \\ \vdots \\ \underline{x}_{t+r} - \underline{x}_t(r) \end{bmatrix}\begin{bmatrix} \underline{x}_{t+1} - \underline{x}_t(1) \\ \vdots \\ \underline{x}_{t+r} - \underline{x}_t(r) \end{bmatrix}',$$

the MSE matrix of $\underline{y}_t^o(h)$ can be written as

$$\Sigma^o(h) = F_h \underline{\Sigma}_{\underline{x}}(mh) F_h' , \qquad (8.1.11)$$

where

$$F_h = (\underbrace{0 \quad \ldots \quad 0}_{(K \times (h-1)mK)} \underbrace{I_K \quad \ldots \quad I_K}_{(K \times mK)}) \qquad (8.1.12)$$

is a (K x hmK) matrix.

The predictor $\underline{y}_t^o(h)$ being superior to $\underline{y}_t(h)$ means that

$$\Sigma^o(h) \le \Sigma(h). \qquad (8.1.13)$$

In other words, $\Sigma(h) - \Sigma^o(h)$ is positive semidefinite. For univariate ARMA(1,1) processes exact values for the relative efficiencies of the two predictors are given by Ahsanullah & Wei (1984b).

In Chapter 6 it is shown that for special disaggregate processes $\underline{x}_t$ the two predictors are identical. In the following proposition another necessary and sufficient condition for equality of the predictors is given. The condition is easy to check and is therefore useful in practice (see Lütkepohl (1986c)).

<u>PROPOSITION 8.1</u>

Let $\underline{x}_t$, $\underline{y}_t$, $\underline{y}_t(h)$, and $\underline{y}_t^o(h)$ be as defined in (8.1.1), (8.1.3), (8.1.8), and (8.1.10) respectively. Then

$$\underline{y}_t(h) = \underline{y}_t^o(h) \quad \text{for} \quad h = 1,2,\ldots \qquad (8.1.14)$$

if and only if

$$(1 + z + \dots + z^{m-1})(\sum_{i=0}^{\infty} \Phi_i z^i)$$

$$= \left[\sum_{j=0}^{\infty} (\Phi_{jm} + \dots + \Phi_{jm-m+1}) z^{jm}\right]\left[\sum_{i=0}^{m-1} (\Phi_0 + \Phi_1 + \dots + \Phi_i) z^i\right] , \quad (8.1.15)$$

where $\Phi_j = 0$ for $j < 0$.

Proof.
Note that equality of the two predictors for h = 1 implies equality for h > 1. Thus, it suffices to show that

$$\underline{y}_t(1) = \underline{y}_t^o(1) = \underline{x}_{mt}(1) + \dots + \underline{x}_{mt}(m) \quad (8.1.16)$$

or, in other words,

$$\underline{v}_{t+1} = \underline{y}_{t+1} - \underline{y}_t(1) = \underline{y}_{t+1} - \underline{y}_t^o(1)$$

$$= \left[\sum_{i=0}^{m-1} (I_K + \Phi_1 + \dots + \Phi_i) L^i\right] \underline{u}_{m(t+1)} \quad (8.1.17)$$

is equivalent to condition (8.1.15).

If (8.1.15) holds and, without loss of generality, the mean terms are assumed to be zero,

$$\underline{y}_t = \sum_{j=0}^{\infty} N_j \underline{v}_{t-j} = (1 + L + \dots + L^{m-1}) \underline{x}_{mt}$$

$$= (1 + L + \dots + L^{m-1})(\sum_{i=0}^{\infty} \Phi_i L^i) \underline{u}_{mt}$$

$$= \left[\sum_{j=0}^{\infty} (\Phi_{jm} + \Phi_{jm-1} + \dots + \Phi_{jm-m+1}) L^{jm}\right]\left[\sum_{i=0}^{m-1} (I_K + \Phi_1 + \dots + \Phi_i) L^i\right] \underline{u}_{mt}$$

$$= \sum_{j=0}^{\infty} (\Phi_{jm} + \dots + \Phi_{jm-m+1}) \underline{v}_{t-j} .$$

Thus,

$$\underline{v}_t = \left[\sum_{i=0}^{m-1} (I_K + \Phi_1 + \dots + \Phi_i) L^i\right] \underline{u}_{mt}$$

and equality of the two predictors follows from (8.1.17).

In turn, if (8.1.17) holds,

$$\underline{y}_t = \sum_{j=0}^{\infty} N_j \underline{v}_{t-j}$$

$$= \sum_{j=0}^{\infty} N_j \left[\sum_{i=0}^{m-1} (I_K + \Phi_1 + \ldots + \Phi_i) \underline{u}_{m(t-j)-i} \right], \tag{8.1.18}$$

where again a zero mean term is assumed without loss of generality. Hence, the coefficient matrix of $\underline{u}_{m(t-j)}$ is N_j. On the other hand,

$$\underline{y}_t = \sum_{k=0}^{m-1} \underline{x}_{mt-k} = \sum_{k=0}^{m-1} \sum_{i=0}^{\infty} \Phi_i \underline{u}_{mt-k-i} . \tag{8.1.19}$$

Since $\underline{u}_{mt-k-i} = \underline{u}_{m(t-j)}$ if i = jm - k, the coefficient matrix of $\underline{u}_{m(t-j)}$ in (8.1.19) is

$$\sum_{k=0}^{m-1} \Phi_{jm-k} . \tag{8.1.20}$$

Equality of (8.1.18) and (8.1.19) implies that this matrix is equal to N_j. Substituting N_j in (8.1.18) by (8.1.20) shows that (8.1.15) holds.

Q.E.D.

The condition (8.1.15) in Proposition 8.1 means that if the MA operator of $\underline{x}_t$ is multiplied by $(1 + z + \ldots + z^{m-1})$ it has a multiplicative structure. This result has interesting consequences. First, if $\underline{x}_t$ is a purely seasonal process with seasonal period m, that is, if $\Phi_i = 0$ unless i is an integer multiple of m, then condition (8.1.15) is obviously satisfied. In other words, if

$$\underline{x}_t = \underline{\mu}_x + \sum_{i=0}^{\infty} \Phi_{im} \underline{u}_{t-im} , \tag{8.1.21}$$

then $\underline{y}_t(h) = \underline{y}_t^o(h)$ for h = 1,2,... . Second, in contrast to a result for stock variables in Section 7.1, for a finite order MA(q) process $\underline{x}_t$ with $0 < q < m$ the two predictors are usually not identical for forecast horizon h = 1 if flow variables are considered. For this case, (8.1.15) means that

$$(1+z+\ldots+z^{m-1})(I_K + \Phi_1 z+\ldots+\Phi_q z^q)$$

$$= \left[I_K+(\Phi_1+\ldots+\Phi_q)z^m\right]\left[I_K+(I_K+\Phi_1)z+\ldots+(I_K+\Phi_1+\ldots+\Phi_q)z^{m-1}\right]$$

which is usually not satisfied because the left-hand side is a polynomial of degree q+m-1 while the right-hand side is of degree 2m-1.

Another result of interest that is mentioned in Chapter 6 is that

$$\Sigma(h) - \Sigma^{o}(h) \rightarrow 0 \quad \text{for} \quad h \rightarrow \infty, \tag{8.1.22}$$

that is, the two pedictors become identical if the forecast horizon goes to infinity.

These results hold under the restrictive assumption that the considered processes are known. Forecasting with estimated processes will be investigated in the following sections.

8.2 FORECASTS BASED ON PROCESSES WITH ESTIMATED COEFFICIENTS

It is now assumed that the basic, disaggregate process $\underline{x}_t$ satisfies the conditions of Section 3.2. In particular, $\underline{x}_t$ is a K-dimensional, Gaussian, stationary and invertible ARMA process with known, finite orders p and q. The parameters including the mean terms are assumed to be estimated by ML using time series of length T. It is shown in Section 3.2 that an approximate MSE matrix for the vector of 1-step to r-step predictors is

$$\hat{\underline{\Sigma}}_{\underline{x}}(r) = \underline{\Sigma}_{\underline{x}}(r) + \frac{1}{T}(\underline{\Omega}_{\underline{x}}(r) + \underline{G}_{\underline{x}}(r)) , \tag{8.2.1}$$

where $\underline{\Sigma}_{\underline{x}}(r)$ is the MSE matrix for known processes, $\underline{\Omega}_{\underline{x}}(r)$ is the MSE contribution from estimating the ARMA parameters (see (3.2.8)), and $\underline{G}_{\underline{x}}(r)$ comes from estimating the mean terms (see (3.2.19)). Using (8.2.1) the predictor $\hat{y}^{o}_t(h)$ with estimated coefficients has asymptotic MSE matrix

$$\hat{\Sigma}^{o}(h) = F_h\hat{\underline{\Sigma}}_{\underline{x}}(mh)F_h' = \Sigma^{o}(h) + \frac{1}{T}(F_h\underline{\Omega}_{\underline{x}}(mh)F_h' + F_h\underline{G}_{\underline{x}}(mh)F_h') , \tag{8.2.2}$$

where F_h is defined in (8.1.12).

Since $\underline{x}_t$ is a Gaussian, stationary and invertible vector ARMA process the same holds for y_t (see Section 6.5) and, applying the results of Section 3.2 once more, the asymptotic MSE matrix

$$\hat{\Sigma}(h) = \Sigma(h) + \frac{m}{T}(\Omega_{y}(h) + G_{y}(h)) \tag{8.2.3}$$

is obtained for the predictor $\hat{y}_t(h)$ with estimated coefficients. Here the sample size used for estimating the coefficients of $\underline{y}_t(h)$ is assumed to be $T = T/m$ and $\Omega_{\underline{y}}(h)$ is due to estimating the ARMA parameters while $G_{\underline{y}}(h)$ represents the uncertainty from estimating the mean terms.

Obviously, the systematic terms $\Sigma^o(h)$ and $\Sigma(h)$ in (8.2.2) and (8.2.3) dominate the asymptotic MSEs for large T. Thus, if the difference $\Sigma(h) - \Sigma^o(h)$ is positive definite ($\Sigma(h) > \Sigma^o(h)$) so that $\underline{y}_t^o(h)$ strictly dominates $\underline{y}_t(h)$ for known processes, the same will hold for estimated processes when the sample size used for estimation is large.

Furthermore, if the forecast horizon h goes to infinity both predictors approach the mean of the $\underline{y}_t$ process and thus, $F_h\Omega_{\underline{x}}(mh)F_h'$ and $\Omega_{\underline{y}}(h)$ tend to zero, while $G_{\underline{y}}(h)$ and $F_hG_{\underline{x}}(mh)F_h'$ converge to $\Sigma_{\overline{\underline{y}}}$ and $m^2\Sigma_{\overline{\underline{x}}}$ respectively. Here $\Sigma_{\overline{\underline{y}}}$ denotes the covariance matrix of the asymptotic distribution of $\sqrt{T}(\overline{\underline{y}} - \underline{\mu}_y)$, where

$$\overline{\underline{y}} = \frac{1}{T}\sum_{t=1}^{T} \underline{y}_t \qquad (8.2.4)$$

is the vector of sample means. Also, $\Sigma_{\overline{\underline{x}}}$ is the covariance matrix of the asymptotic distribution of $\sqrt{T}\,(\overline{\underline{x}} - \underline{\mu}_x)$ with

$$\overline{\underline{x}} = \frac{1}{T}\sum_{t=1}^{T} \underline{x}_t \; . \qquad (8.2.5)$$

Note that for $h\to\infty$, $\hat{\underline{y}}_t^o(h) \to m\overline{\underline{x}}$ and therefore the MSE part due to estimation uncertainty approaches $m^2\Sigma_{\overline{\underline{x}}}/T$. Since

$$\overline{\underline{y}} = \frac{1}{T}m\sum_{t=1}^{T} \underline{x}_t = m\overline{\underline{x}} \; , \qquad (8.2.6)$$

it follows that

$$\sqrt{T}\;(\overline{\underline{y}} - \underline{\mu}_y) = \sqrt{T/m}\;(m\overline{\underline{x}} - m\underline{\mu}_x) = \sqrt{m}\,\sqrt{T}\;(\overline{\underline{x}} - \underline{\mu}_x) \; ,$$

so that

$$m\Sigma_{\overline{\underline{y}}} = m^2\Sigma_{\overline{\underline{x}}} \qquad (8.2.7)$$

and hence,

$$\hat{\Sigma}(h) - \hat{\Sigma}^o(h) \to 0 \quad \text{for} \quad h \to \infty. \qquad (8.2.8)$$

In other words, the two predictors become identical for long range forecasting even if estimated coefficients are used.

It may be worth pointing out that (8.2.6) explains why the two predictors for the nonstationary investment data compared in Section 7.6.2 are almost identical for the random walk models (see the SC results in Table 7.6(b)). It was mentioned earlier that temporal aggregation of stock variables that are stationary in first differences comes down to analyzing temporally aggregated flow variables in the stationary parts. Of course, if a nonzero mean white noise is considered the mean terms are the only parameters to be estimated. Based on (8.2.6) one may expect that the two predictors are exactly identical. However, in Section 7.6.2, $\mathcal{T}$ is not exactly equal to T/m.

For the presently considered case of temporal aggregation of flow variables the impact of the estimation variability on the short term forecast MSEs can be studied most easily for processes where $\mathcal{Z}^o(1) = \mathcal{Z}(1)$. One such process will be treated in some detail in the following.

For the AR(m) process

$$\underline{x}_t = \underline{\nu}_x + A_m \underline{x}_{t-m} + \underline{u}_t \tag{8.2.9}$$

with corresponding aggregate $\underline{y}_{\mathcal{t}} = \underline{x}_{m\mathcal{t}} + \dots + \underline{x}_{m\mathcal{t}-m+1}$ the condition (8.1.15) of Proposition 8.1 is satisfied so that $\mathcal{Z}(h) = \mathcal{Z}^o(h)$ for $h = 1,2,\dots$. The aggregate is an AR(1) process,

$$\underline{y}_{\mathcal{t}} = \underline{\nu}_y + A_m \underline{y}_{\mathcal{t}-1} + \underline{v}_{\mathcal{t}} , \tag{8.2.10}$$

where $\underline{v}_{\mathcal{t}} = \underline{u}_{m\mathcal{t}} + \dots + \underline{u}_{m\mathcal{t}-m+1}$ so that

$$\mathcal{Z}_{\underline{v}} = m\mathcal{Z}_{\underline{u}}. \tag{8.2.11}$$

In comparing the MSE parts due to parameter estimation the following notation will be used:

$$\Gamma = E\left[\begin{bmatrix} \underline{x}_t \\ \underline{x}_{t-1} \\ \vdots \\ \underline{x}_{t-m+1} \end{bmatrix} (\underline{x}_t', \dots, \underline{x}_{t-m+1}')\right] = I_m \otimes \mathcal{Z}_{\underline{x}} , \tag{8.2.12}$$

where $\mathcal{Z}_{\underline{x}}$ is the covariance matrix of $\underline{x}_t$.

$$\underline{A} = \begin{bmatrix} 0 & 0 & \dots & 0 & A_m \\ I_K & 0 & \dots & 0 & 0 \\ 0 & I_K & & \cdot & \cdot \\ \vdots & \vdots & \ddots & \vdots & \vdots \\ 0 & 0 & \dots & I_K & 0 \end{bmatrix} (mK \times mK). \tag{8.2.13}$$

Note that

$$\underline{A}^i = \underset{(mK \times mK)}{\begin{bmatrix} 0 & 0 & \dots & 0 & A_m & 0 & \dots & 0 & 0 \\ 0 & 0 & \dots & 0 & 0 & A_m & \dots & 0 & 0 \\ \vdots & \vdots & \ddots & \vdots & \vdots & \vdots & \ddots & \vdots & \vdots \\ 0 & 0 & \dots & 0 & 0 & 0 & \dots & A_m & 0 \\ 0 & 0 & \dots & 0 & 0 & 0 & \dots & 0 & A_m \\ I_K & 0 & \dots & 0 & 0 & 0 & \dots & 0 & 0 \\ 0 & I_K & \dots & 0 & 0 & 0 & \dots & 0 & 0 \\ \vdots & \vdots & \ddots & \vdots & \vdots & \vdots & \ddots & \vdots & \vdots \\ 0 & 0 & \dots & I_K & 0 & 0 & \dots & 0 & 0 \end{bmatrix}} = \begin{bmatrix} 0 & I_i \otimes A_m \\ I_{m-i} \otimes I_K & 0 \end{bmatrix}, \tag{8.2.14}$$

$$i = 1,2,\dots m$$

and

$$\underline{A}^{mj} = \begin{bmatrix} A_m^j & & 0 \\ & \ddots & \\ 0 & & A_m^j \end{bmatrix} = \begin{bmatrix} I_i \otimes A_m^j & 0 \\ 0 & I_{m-i} \otimes A_m^j \end{bmatrix}, \quad j = 1,2,\dots \tag{8.2.15}$$

so that

$$\underline{A}^{mj+i} = \underline{A}^{mj}\underline{A}^i = \begin{bmatrix} 0 & I_i \otimes A_m^{j+1} \\ I_{m-i} \otimes A_m^j & 0 \end{bmatrix} \tag{8.2.16}$$

for $i = 1,\dots,m$ and $j = 1,2,\dots$.

Using this notation, (8.2.16) and (3.2.39) gives

$$F_h \underline{G}_{\underline{X}}(mh) F_h' =$$

$$= (I_K \ \dots \ I_K) \left[\begin{bmatrix} I_K \\ I_K \\ \vdots \\ I_K \end{bmatrix} - \begin{bmatrix} (I_K \ 0 \ \dots \ 0)\underline{A}^{m(h-1)+1} \\ (I_K \ 0 \ \dots \ 0)\underline{A}^{m(h-1)+2} \\ \vdots \\ (I_K \ 0 \ \dots \ 0)\underline{A}^{mh} \end{bmatrix} \begin{bmatrix} I_K \\ I_K \\ \vdots \\ I_K \end{bmatrix} \right] \Sigma_{\underline{X}} \begin{bmatrix} \dots \\ \dots \\ \vdots \\ \dots \end{bmatrix}' \begin{bmatrix} I_K \\ I_K \\ \vdots \\ I_K \end{bmatrix}$$

$$= (I_K \ \dots \ I_K) \begin{bmatrix} I_K - A_m^h \\ \vdots \\ I_K - A_m^h \end{bmatrix} \Sigma_{\underline{\bar{x}}} \begin{bmatrix} I_K - A_m^h \\ \vdots \\ I_K - A_m^h \end{bmatrix}' \begin{bmatrix} I_K \\ \vdots \\ I_K \end{bmatrix}$$

$$= m^2 (I_K - A_m^h) \Sigma_{\underline{\bar{x}}} (I_K - A_m^h)' \quad . \tag{8.2.17}$$

Furthermore, using (3.2.39) and (8.2.7),

$$G_{\underline{y}}(h) = (I_K - A_m^h) \Sigma_{\underline{\bar{y}}} (I_K - A_m^h)' = m(I_K - A_m^h) \Sigma_{\underline{\bar{x}}} (I_K - A_m^h)' . \tag{8.2.18}$$

Consequently,

$$\frac{1}{T} G_{\underline{y}}(h) = \frac{m}{T} G_{\underline{y}}(h) = \frac{1}{T} F_h G_{\underline{x}}(mh) F_h' \quad . \tag{8.2.19}$$

In other words, the relative efficiency of the two predictors is not affected by the level of aggregation of the data used for estimating the mean terms.

Assuming that $\underline{x}_t$ is estimated as an unrestricted AR(m),

$$\underline{x}_t = \underline{\nu}_x + A_1 \underline{x}_{t-1} + \dots + A_m \underline{x}_{t-m} + \underline{u}_t \ , \tag{8.2.20}$$

it follows from (3.2.31) that

$$\Omega_{\underline{x}}(m) = \left[\sum_{j=0}^{l-1} \sum_{i=0}^{k-1} \operatorname{tr}\{(\underline{A}')^{l-1-j} \Gamma^{-1} \underline{A}^{k-1-i} \Gamma\} \ \Phi_j \Sigma_{\underline{u}} \Phi_i' \right]_{l,k = 1,\dots,m}$$

$$= \begin{bmatrix} \operatorname{tr}\{(\underline{A}')^0 \Gamma^{-1} \underline{A}^0 \Gamma\} \Sigma_{\underline{u}} & \dots & \operatorname{tr}\{(\underline{A}')^0 \Gamma^{-1} \underline{A}^{m-1} \Gamma\} \Sigma_{\underline{u}} \\ \vdots & \ddots & \vdots \\ \operatorname{tr}\{(\underline{A}')^{m-1} \Gamma^{-1} \underline{A}^0 \Gamma\} \Sigma_{\underline{u}} & \dots & \operatorname{tr}\{(\underline{A}')^{m-1} \Gamma^{-1} \underline{A}^{m-1} \Gamma\} \Sigma_{\underline{u}} \end{bmatrix} , \tag{8.2.21}$$

where it has been used that the MA representation of $\underline{x}_t$ is

$$\underline{x}_t = \underline{\mu}_x + \sum_{i=0}^{\infty} \Phi_i \underline{u}_{t-i} = \underline{\mu}_x + \sum_{i=0}^{\infty} A_m^i \underline{u}_{t-mi} \tag{8.2.22}$$

so that Φ_i is zero unless i is an integer multiple of m. In the Appendix of this chapter (Section 8.A) it is shown that

$$\operatorname{tr}\{(\underline{A}')^j \Gamma^{-1} \underline{A}^i \Gamma\} = 0 \quad \text{for } i \neq j \text{ and } 0 \leq i,j < m , \tag{8.2.23}$$

so that $\Omega_{\underline{x}}(m)$ is block diagonal. Furthermore, using (8.2.12) and (8.2.14),

$$(\underline{A}')^i \Gamma^{-1} \underline{A}^i \Gamma = \begin{bmatrix} I_K & & & & 0 \\ & \ddots & & & \\ & & I_K & & \\ & & & A_m' \Sigma_{\underline{x}}^{-1} A_m \Sigma_{\underline{x}} & \\ & & & & \ddots \\ 0 & & & & A_m' \Sigma_{\underline{x}}^{-1} A_m \Sigma_{\underline{x}} \end{bmatrix}$$

$$= \begin{bmatrix} I_{(m-i)K} & 0 \\ 0 & I_i \otimes A_m' \Sigma_{\underline{x}}^{-1} A_m \Sigma_{\underline{x}} \end{bmatrix} , \quad i = 0,1,\dots,m \quad (8.2.24)$$

From the Appendix of Chapter 7 (Section 7.A) it is known that

$$\mathrm{tr}\{A_m' \Sigma_{\underline{x}}^{-1} A_m \Sigma_{\underline{x}}\} < K \quad (8.2.25)$$

so that

$$\mathrm{tr}\{(\underline{A}')^i \Gamma^{-1} \underline{A}^i \Gamma\} < (m - i)K + iK = mK . \quad (8.2.26)$$

These results imply

$$F_1 \Omega_{\underline{x}}(m) F_1' = \sum_{i=0}^{m-1} \mathrm{tr}\{(\underline{A}')^i \Gamma^{-1} \underline{A}^i \Gamma\} \Sigma_{\underline{u}} < m^2 K \Sigma_{\underline{u}} , \quad (8.2.27)$$

where F_1 is as defined in (8.1.12) with $h = 1$. On the other hand,

$$\Omega_{\underline{y}}(1) = K \Sigma_{\underline{v}} = Km \Sigma_{\underline{u}} \quad (8.2.28)$$

(see (3.2.34)). Consequently,

$$F_1 \Omega_{\underline{x}}(m) F_1' < m \Omega_{\underline{y}}(1) . \quad (8.2.29)$$

In other words, although the two predictors $\underline{y}_t(1)$ and $\underline{y}_t^o(1)$ are identical for known processes, $\hat{\underline{y}}_t^o(1)$ dominates $\hat{\underline{y}}_t(1)$ if estimated parameters are used. Thus, even if $\underline{x}_t$ is such that no gains in forecast efficiency are obtained for known processes, using the disaggregate data for estimating the process parameters is still desirable. Note that this result obtains although $\underline{x}_t$ is estimated in unrestricted form, that is, $A_1,\ldots,A_{m-1}$ are estimated in addition to A_m. If the coefficient matrices $A_1,\ldots,A_{m-1}$ were set to zero it follows from the properties of ML estimation that A_m can be estimated more efficiently asymptotically from the $\underline{x}_t$ data than from the aggregate $\underline{y}_t$ data (see also Wei (1978a) and Ahsanullah & Wei (1984a)).

Of course, the situation considered in the foregoing is a very special one and it is of interest whether or not it can be generalized. First, if $\underline{x}_t$ is an AR(mp) process of the form

$$\underline{x}_t = \underline{\nu}_x + \sum_{i=1}^{p} A_{mi}\underline{x}_{t-mi} + \underline{u}_t$$

a similar result as above can be derived. Second, for forecast horizons $h > 1$ it becomes increasingly more difficult to compare the two asymptotic forecast MSE matrices. I have found no evidence that there are processes satisfying (8.1.15) for which

$$F_h(\Omega_{\underline{x}}(mh) + G_{\underline{x}}(mh))F_h' > m(\Omega_{\underline{y}}(h) + G_{\underline{y}}(h)),$$

although I am unable to give a general proof of this result. Thus, it seems that temporal aggregation of flow variables generally results in efficiency losses in forecasts if ARMA coefficients are estimated. This result differs from the conclusions for contemporaneous aggregation and temporal aggregation of stock variables in Chapters 5 and 7. Of course, no efficiency will be lost in the present case if $\underline{x}_t$ is a white noise process (see (8.2.7)).

So far it has been assumed that the ARMA orders of $\underline{x}_t$ and $\underline{y}_t$ are known. The previous results also apply if the orders are estimated consistently. In the next section the asymptotic theory of Section 3.3 is used to compare the two predictors for estimated processes.

8.3 FORECASTING WITH AUTOREGRESSIVE PROCESSES OF UNKNOWN ORDER

In this section the situation described in Chapter 3, Section 3.3 , is assumed. That is, the basic, disaggregate process $\underline{x}_t$ (and thus the temporal aggregate $\underline{y}_t$) is assumed to have an AR representation of possibly infinite order and finite order AR processes are fitted to $\underline{x}_t$ and $\underline{y}_t$ for prediction. The AR order is a function $p(T)$ of the sample size T and goes to infinity with T, although much more slowly. More precisely,

$$p(T) \to \infty \text{ and } \frac{p(T)^3}{T} \to 0 \quad \text{for} \quad T \to \infty . \qquad (8.3.1)$$

In addition, the other assumptions of Section 3.3 are assumed to hold for $\underline{x}_t$ and $\underline{y}_t$. The process means are assumed to be zero and are not estimated since estimation of the mean has been considered in the previous section.

Under these conditions, an approximate MSE matrix for the 1-step to r-step forecasts of $\underline{x}_t$ is

$$\tilde{\Sigma}_{\underline{x}}(r) = (1 + \frac{Kp(T)}{T})\Sigma_{\underline{x}}(r) \qquad (8.3.2)$$

(see (3.3.9)). Thus, the approximate MSE matrix of $\tilde{y}_t^o(h)$, based on the estimated process $\underline{x}_t$, is

$$\tilde{\Sigma}^o(h) = (1 + \frac{Kp(T)}{T}) F_h \Sigma_{\underline{x}}(mh) F_h'$$

$$= (1 + \frac{Kp(T)}{T}) \Sigma^o(h) , \qquad (8.3.3)$$

where F_h is as defined in (8.1.12). On the other hand, using the estimated aggregate $\underline{y}_t$ for prediction, the following approximate MSE matrix is obtained:

$$\tilde{\Sigma}(h) = (1 + \frac{Kp(\mathcal{T})}{\mathcal{T}}) \Sigma(h) , \qquad (8.3.4)$$

where $\mathcal{T}$ is the length of the temporally aggregated series used for estimating $\underline{y}_t$.

Consequently, as in the case of known orders and estimated coefficients, if $\Sigma^o(h) < \Sigma(h)$, the same holds for $\tilde{\Sigma}^o(h)$ and $\tilde{\Sigma}(h)$, provided T is large enough. Here condition (8.3.1) is used. It implies that $p(T)/T \to 0$ and hence $p(\mathcal{T})/\mathcal{T} \to 0$ if $T \to \infty$. If $\underline{x}_t$ satisfies condition (8.1.15) of Proposition 8.1 and thus $\Sigma^o(h) = \Sigma(h)$ for h = 1,2,..., the difference between the MSEs of forecasts from the aggregated estimated process and aggregated forecasts from the disaggregate estimated process becomes

$$\tilde{\Sigma}(h) - \tilde{\Sigma}^o(h) = (\frac{p(\mathcal{T})}{\mathcal{T}} - \frac{p(T)}{T}) K \Sigma(h) \qquad (8.3.5)$$

which is likely to be positive definite if p is chosen by the same rule for both the aggregated and the disaggregate series. Take, for instance, $p(T) = T^{1/(3+\delta)}$, where δ is some positive number so that (8.3.1) is satisfied, and use $\mathcal{T} = T/m$. Then (8.3.5) is easily seen to be positive definite (see also Section 7.3, (7.3.4)).

In summary, what has been shown here is that even under the most favorable conditions for the temporally aggregated process of flow variables, if the forecast MSEs for known processes are identical (i.e., $\Sigma(h) = \Sigma^o(h)$), the disaggregate process is preferable when the orders and coefficients are estimated, that is, in this case $\tilde{\Sigma}(h) - \tilde{\Sigma}^o(h)$ is likely to be positive definite. This result, however, relies on asymptotic theory and the choice of $p(\cdot)$. If $p(\cdot)$ were a linear function of its argument and $\mathcal{T} = T/m$, then $mp(\mathcal{T}) - p(T) = 0$ and hence $\tilde{\Sigma}(h) = \tilde{\Sigma}^o(h)$. However, condition (8.3.1) rules out this choice of $p(\cdot)$ since it violates $p(T)^3/T \to 0$ for $T \to \infty$. On the other hand, (8.3.1) is an asymptotic requirement and hence, in small samples, the difference $mp(\mathcal{T}) - p(T)$ may be negative. Consequently the above conclusion, that temporal aggregation is even more likely to result in a loss of forecast precision if estimated rather than known processes are used, depends on the choice of $p(\cdot)$.

For the case of aggregated stock variables an example was given in Section 7.3 for which, in practice, $mp(\mathcal{T}) - p(T)$ is likely to be negative. In that section an MA(q) was considered which is white noise if every m-th observation is used as aggregate. In the present case in which consecutive $\underline{x}_t$ values are added such an example will not work. Recall that it follows from Proposition 8.1 that for a finite order MA(q) process $\underline{x}_t$ with $0 < q < m$, the predictor $\underline{y}^o_t(1)$ dominates $\underline{y}_t(1)$ even if the true data generation processes are known.

In practice a choice of the AR order must be made on the basis of a particular fixed sample and the small sample properties of the resulting forecasts are of interest. A small sample investigation will be discussed in Section 8.5.

8.4 TEMPORALLY AGGREGATED NONSTATIONARY PROCESSES

For temporally aggregated nonstationary processes that represent flow variables similar comments can be made as for stock variables (see Section 7.4). More precisely, the predictor based on the disaggregate process will be at least as good as the one based on the aggregated process, and the predictors will not become identical for growing forecast horizon. That is,

$$\Sigma^o(h) \le \Sigma(h) \;, \quad h = 1,2,\ldots \;, \tag{8.4.1}$$

if the nonstationarity can be removed by differencing. For instance, if $\underline{x}_t$ is stationary after differencing once, i.e.,

$$\underline{x}_t^s = \underline{x}_t - \underline{x}_{t-1} \tag{8.4.2}$$

is stationary and $\underline{y}_\tau = \underline{x}_{2\tau} + \underline{x}_{2\tau-1}$ (i.e., m = 2), then

$$\underline{y}_\tau^s = \underline{y}_\tau - \underline{y}_{\tau-1} = \underline{x}_{2\tau} + \underline{x}_{2\tau-1} - \underline{x}_{2\tau-2} - \underline{x}_{2\tau-3}$$

$$= \underline{x}_{2\tau}^s + 2\underline{x}_{2\tau-1}^s + \underline{x}_{2\tau-2}^s \tag{8.4.3}$$

is stationary (see Section 6.4.1). Since

$$\underline{x}_t(r) = \underline{x}_t + \sum_{i=1}^{r} \underline{x}_t^s(i) \tag{8.4.4}$$

is the optimal r-step predictor of the disaggregate process,

$$\underline{y}_\tau^o(1) = \underline{x}_{2\tau}(1) + \underline{x}_{2\tau}(2)$$

$$= 2\underline{x}_{2\tau} + 2\underline{x}_{2\tau}^s(1) + \underline{x}_{2\tau}^s(2)$$

$$= \underline{y}_\tau + \underline{x}_{2\tau}^s + 2\underline{x}_{2\tau}^s(1) + \underline{x}_{2\tau}^s(2) \tag{8.4.5}$$

is the optimal 1-step predictor of the aggregate based on the disaggregate process. On the other hand, the optimal 1-step predictor based on the aggregate is

$$\underline{y}_\tau(1) = \underline{y}_\tau + \underline{y}_\tau^s(1) \; . \tag{8.4.6}$$

Given the relationship in (8.4.3) it is clear that $\underline{y}_\tau^o(1)$ dominates $\underline{y}_\tau(1)$. Moreover, the example shows that Proposition 8.1 is not valid for nonstationary processes. More precisely, if condition (8.1.15) holds for the MA representation of $\underline{x}_t^s$, this does not imply that the predictors $\underline{y}_\tau^o(h)$ and $\underline{y}_\tau(h)$ are identical. In fact, the contrary is true. If $\underline{x}_t^s$ and $\underline{x}_t$ are as in (8.4.2) and (8.1.15) holds for the MA representation of $\underline{x}_t^s$, then $\underline{y}_\tau(1) \neq \underline{y}_\tau^o(1)$ and the latter strictly dominates the former.

For estimated nonstationary processes the comments at the end of Section 7.4 also apply for the present case of temporal aggregation of flow variables. If the stationary parts of the disaggregate process and the aggregate satisfy the conditions of Sections 8.2 or 8.3 and if the required order of differencing is known, asymptotic MSE matrices are easy to obtain from the results of the previous sections (see also Section 3.4).

8.5 SMALL SAMPLE COMPARISON

A Monte Carlo investigation was carried out to study the small sample properties of the two predictors. The design of the simulation experiment is the same as in the previous chapter. For the details the reader is referred to Sections 5.5.1 and 7.5. Most simulated processes considered in detail in the following satisfy condition (8.1.15) of Proposition 8.1 so that the forecast MSEs are identical for known processes. For these processes the observed MSE differences will exclusively result from estimation and specification variability. Of course, it is this part of the MSEs that is of interest here. Therefore, processes satisfying (8.1.15) are particularly suited here.

8.5.1 A Univariate AR Process

The first process investigated in the simulation study is the univariate AR(2)

$$x_t = 1 + 0.5x_{t-2} + u_t \quad , \quad \Sigma_u = 1 \ . \tag{8.5.1}$$

Using an aggregation period of $m = 2$ the temporally aggregated process $y_t = x_{2t} + x_{2t-1}$ is the AR(1)

$$y_t = 2 + 0.5y_{t-1} + v_t \quad , \quad \Sigma_v = 2 \ , \tag{8.5.2}$$

where $v_t = u_{2t} + u_{2t-1}$. The process x_t is similar to (8.2.9) and satisfies (8.1.15) so that $\Sigma(h) = \Sigma^o(h)$ for known processes.

The maximum AR orders considered in the simulation study in estimating the processes are P = 8 and 4 for the disaggregate AR(2) and the aggregate AR(1) respectively. In Table 8.1(a) the frequency distributions of the estimated AR orders are given. The upper bounds for the AR orders are not attained very often by any of the criteria and thus these bounds are not restrictive. As was to be expected on the basis of the asymptotic results mentioned in Section 2.5.1, SC estimates the AR order correctly with a very high probability when the sample size is large, whereas AIC tends to overestimate the order even if T = 200 (for the disaggregate series) or T = 100 (for the aggregated series).

The differences of the forecast MSEs obtained from the aggregate and the disaggregate series ($\tilde{\Sigma}(h) - \tilde{\Sigma}^o(h)$) are reported in Table 8.1(b). In the first column of the table the differences between the MSEs obtained by using the true AR orders are given. For almost all sample

Table 8.1. Monte Carlo Results Based on 600 Replications for Univariate Disaggregate AR(2) and Aggregated AR(1) Process

(a) Frequency Distributions of Estimated AR Orders in Percent

disaggregate process					aggregated process				
sample size T	AR order	frequency distribution p(AIC)	p(HQ)	p(SC)	sample size T	AR order	frequency distribution p(AIC)	p(HQ)	p(SC)
60	0	2	7	15	30	0	14	19	28
	1	2	2	3		1	55	59	61
	2	63	74	76		2	14	11	8
	3	14	9	4		3	9	6	3
	4	8	5	2		4	8	5	1
	5	4	2	1					
	6	2	1	0					
	7	3	0	0					
	8	2	0	0					
100	0	0	0	2	50	0	3	5	9
	1	0	0	0		1	68	77	82
	2	70	85	94		2	14	11	7
	3	12	9	4		3	8	5	1
	4	7	4	1		4	7	3	1
	5	4	1	0					
	6	4	0	0					
	7	2	0	0					
	8	1	0	0					
200	0	0	0	0	100	0	0	0	0
	1	0	0	0		1	75	88	96
	2	72	91	97		2	12	7	3
	3	12	6	3		3	8	3	1
	4	6	2	0		4	5	1	0
	5	5	0	0					
	6	3	1	0					
	7	2	0	0					
	8	1	0	0					

(b) Differences of Forecast MSEs ($\hat{\Sigma}(h) - \hat{\Sigma}^o(h)$ and $\tilde{\Sigma}(h) - \tilde{\Sigma}^o(h)$)

sample size T of disaggregate process	forecast horizon h	p = 1,2	estimation criterion AIC	HQ	SC
60	1	0.06*	0.19**	0.24**	0.10*
	5	0.01	0.02	0.05	0.01
100	1	0.01	0.05	0.06*	0.05*
	5	-0.01	0.04	0.01	0.03*
200	1	0.01	0.03	0.04*	0.04*
	5	0.00	-0.01	0.00	-0.00

* significant at 5% level, ** significant at 1% level

sizes and forecast horizons the MSEs from the disaggregate data are smaller than those from the aggregate data, i.e., $\hat{\mathcal{Z}}(h) - \hat{\mathcal{Z}}^{o}(h)$ and $\tilde{\mathcal{Z}}(h) - \tilde{\mathcal{Z}}^{o}(h)$ are positive in accordance with the asymptotic results of Sections 8.2 and 8.3. Furthermore, using again the test statistic given in Section 3.5, only positive differences are significant at the usual levels. Comparing the MSE differences obtained with known and estimated AR orders, in most cases the former are smaller than the latter. That is, based on this Monte Carlo experiment, it seems that in small samples, when the AR order is unknown, it is even more important to use the disaggregate rather than the aggregated data. Overall the small sample conclusions are in full agreement with the asymptotic results of the previous sections. Note, however, that the conditions of the simulation experiment are not quite in line with those underlying the asymptotic theory of Section 8.3 since the AR orders do not tend to infinity with increasing sample size (see Table 8.1(a)). Also, in Section 8.3 the processes are allowed to have an infinite AR representation. Therefore realizations of finite order MA processes were also generated.

8.5.2 A Univariate MA(2) Process

The next process used in the Monte Carlo study is the univariate MA(2)

$$x_t = 1 + u_t - 0.5u_{t-2} \quad , \quad \mathcal{Z}_u = 1 \ , \tag{8.5.3}$$

and again the period of temporal aggregation is $m = 2$. Thus, the aggregated process $y_t = x_{2t} + x_{2t-1}$ is the MA(1)

$$y_t = 2 + v_t - 0.5v_{t-1} \quad , \quad \mathcal{Z}_v = 2 \ . \tag{8.5.4}$$

From Proposition 8.1 it follows that the forecast MSEs for known processes are identical for $h = 1,2,\ldots$.

Again 600 realizations of the disaggregate process (8.5.3) were generated. The estimated AR orders for three different sample sizes are given in Table 8.2(a). The maximum AR orders for the disaggregate and the aggregated processes are $P = 8$ and 4 respectively and again these upper bounds do not appear to be very restrictive as they are not attained very often. However, now the AR orders chosen by the three criteria increase on average with the sample size in accordance with (8.3.1).

Table 8.2. Monte Carlo Results Based on 600 Replications for Univariate Disaggregate MA(2) and Aggregated MA(1) Process

(a) Frequency Distributions of Estimated AR Orders in Percent

disaggregate process					aggregated process				
sample size T	AR order	frequency distribution p(AIC)	p(HQ)	p(SC)	sample size T	AR order	frequency distribution p(AIC)	p(HQ)	p(SC)
60	0	3	9	24	30	0	9	13	23
	1	0	0	0		1	38	44	49
	2	43	57	62		2	31	28	22
	3	4	3	2		3	11	9	4
	4	26	23	11		4	12	7	2
	5	5	2	1					
	6	10	4	1					
	7	5	1	0					
	8	5	2	0					
100	0	0	2	8	50	0	2	6	12
	1	0	0	0		1	32	43	53
	2	33	55	73		2	38	36	28
	3	2	2	1		3	16	11	5
	4	35	29	16		4	12	5	1
	5	6	2	1					
	6	14	6	2					
	7	5	2	0					
	8	6	2	0					
200	0	0	0	0	100	0	0	0	1
	1	0	0	0		1	16	31	51
	2	9	30	63		2	45	45	38
	3	1	1	0		3	25	18	9
	4	44	50	34		4	15	7	1
	5	7	3	1					
	6	22	11	2					
	7	5	2	0					
	8	12	3	0					

(b) Differences of Forecast MSEs ($\tilde{Z}(h) - \tilde{Z}^o(h)$)

sample size T of disaggregate process	forecast horizon h	estimation criterion AIC	HQ	SC
60	1	-0.10*	-0.06	-0.08
	5	0.02	0.01	0.04
100	1	0.02	0.03	0.05
	5	-0.00	0.01	-0.00
200	1	0.02	0.01	-0.03
	5	-0.00	-0.00	0.01

* significant at 5% level

The differences between the forecast MSEs from aggregate and disaggregate data are given in Table 8.2(b) and are mostly positive in accordance with the asymptotic theory of Section 8.3. For T = 60 (T = 30) and forecast horizon h = 1, the aggregate models chosen by AIC provide significantly better forecasts than the corresponding disaggregate models. In some other cases $\tilde{\Sigma}(h) - \tilde{\Sigma}^o(h)$ are also negative. These differences, however, are not significant at the 5% level. Hence, especially for moderate and large sample sizes the results for the process (8.5.3) are in accordance with the asymptotic theory.

8.5.3 A Univariate MA(3) Process

To investigate the consequences of increasing the aggregation period m, 600 realizations of the univariate MA(3) process

$$x_t = 1 + u_t - 0.5u_{t-3} \quad , \quad \Sigma_u = 1 \; , \qquad (8.5.5)$$

were generated. Aggregating over m = 3 periods results in the aggregate $y_t = x_{3t} + x_{3t-1} + x_{3t-2}$ which is again an MA(1),

$$y_t = 3 + v_t - 0.5v_{t-1} \quad , \quad \Sigma_v = 3 \; , \qquad (8.5.6)$$

where $v_t = u_{3t} + u_{3t-1} + u_{3t-2}$. Again $\Sigma(h) = \Sigma^o(h)$ holds by Proposition 8.1 if the processes are assumed known.

The maximum AR orders were in this case P = 9 and 4 for the disaggregate and aggregate data, respectively. The frequency distributions of the AR order estimates are given in Table 8.3(a) for the sample sizes T = 90, 150, and 300 (T = 30, 50, 100) for the disaggregate (aggregate) process. As was to be expected, the upper bound (P = 9) is selected more often by AIC for the disaggregate data than in the previous example which is based on an MA(2). For all three criteria the estimated AR orders increase on average, however, with increasing sample size in accordance with condition (8.3.1) of Section 8.3.

In Table 8.3(b) the differences of the forecast MSEs $(\tilde{\Sigma}(h) - \tilde{\Sigma}^o(h))$ are presented. The aggregated forecasts based on disaggregate data $(\tilde{y}_t^o(h))$ are mostly better than the corresponding forecasts from aggregate data. Only for sample size T = 90 and forecast horizon h = 1 the SC and HQ forecasts and for T = 150 the SC 1-step forecasts of the aggregated process out-perform the forecasts based on disaggregate data. These MSE differences are not significant at the 5% level, though. Thus,

Table 8.3. Monte Carlo Results Based on 600 Replications for Univariate Disaggregate MA(3) and Aggregated MA(1) Process

(a) Frequency Distributions of Estimated AR Orders in Percent

disaggregate process					aggregated process				
sample size T	AR order	frequency distribution p(AIC)	frequency distribution p(HQ)	frequency distribution p(SC)	sample size T	AR order	frequency distribution p(AIC)	frequency distribution p(HQ)	frequency distribution p(SC)
90	0	1	5	24	30	0	8	14	25
	1	0	0	1		1	39	43	47
	2	0	0	0		2	30	27	20
	3	39	60	62		3	13	10	6
	4	7	6	4		4	11	7	2
	5	4	2	0					
	6	29	20	8					
	7	7	3	0					
	8	3	1	0					
	9	12	3	0					
150	0	0	0	5	50	0	2	5	11
	1	0	0	0		1	32	44	56
	2	0	0	0		2	37	34	27
	3	22	53	81		3	17	12	5
	4	3	5	3		4	11	5	1
	5	2	1	0					
	6	43	33	11					
	7	9	4	0					
	8	4	1	0					
	9	17	4	0					
300	0	0	0	0	100	0	0	0	1
	1	0	0	0		1	16	30	48
	2	0	0	0		2	46	48	42
	3	4	28	65		3	24	17	8
	4	1	2	1		4	15	6	2
	5	0	0	0					
	6	52	58	34					
	7	7	2	0					
	8	3	1	0					
	9	33	10	0					

(b) Differences of Forecast MSEs ($\tilde{\ell}(h) - \tilde{\ell}^o(h)$)

sample size T of disaggregate process	forecast horizon h	estimation criterion AIC	estimation criterion HQ	estimation criterion SC
90	1	0.03	-0.05	-0.17
	5	0.11*	0.09*	0.08*
150	1	0.07	0.05	-0.03
	5	0.06	0.02	0.02
300	1	0.10*	0.07	0.03
	5	0.00	0.00	0.02

* significant at 5% level

overall the results are again in accordance with the asymptotic theory of Section 8.3.

8.5.4 A Bivariate MA Process

To analyze whether similar results hold when a higher dimensional process is considered, 600 realizations of the bivariate MA(2) process

$$\underline{x}_t = \begin{bmatrix} x_{1t} \\ x_{2t} \end{bmatrix} = \begin{bmatrix} 1 \\ 1 \end{bmatrix} + \begin{bmatrix} u_{1t} \\ u_{2t} \end{bmatrix} + \begin{bmatrix} -0.5 & 0.66 \\ 0.5 & 0.3 \end{bmatrix} \begin{bmatrix} u_{1,t-2} \\ u_{2,t-2} \end{bmatrix}, \quad \Sigma_{\underline{u}} = I_2 , \quad (8.5.7)$$

were generated. Upon aggregation over m = 2 periods the process

$$\underline{y}_t = \begin{bmatrix} y_{1t} \\ y_{2t} \end{bmatrix} = \begin{bmatrix} 2 \\ 2 \end{bmatrix} + \underline{v}_t + \begin{bmatrix} -0.5 & 0.66 \\ 0.5 & 0.3 \end{bmatrix} \underline{v}_{t-1} , \quad \Sigma_{\underline{v}} = 2I_2 , \quad (8.5.8)$$

results. Here

$$\underline{v}_t = \begin{bmatrix} v_{1t} \\ v_{2t} \end{bmatrix} = \begin{bmatrix} u_{1,2t} + u_{1,2t-1} \\ u_{2,2t} + u_{2,2t-1} \end{bmatrix} .$$

The process $\underline{x}_t$ is chosen so that an AR representation exists and the forecast MSEs obtained from the aggregate and the disaggregate process are identical by Proposition 8.1 if the processes are assumed known, that is, $\Sigma(h) = \Sigma^o(h)$ for h = 1,2,... . Otherwise the choice of the process is arbitrary.

The AR order estimation results for sample sizes T = 60, 100, 200 (T = 30, 50, 100) are given in Table 8.4(a) and the differences between the estimated MSEs are shown in Table 8.4(b). The maximum AR orders for the disaggregate and the aggregate data are 6 and 4, respectively. These upper bounds have been used to keep the computation costs in reasonable limits although it turns out that the bounds are somewhat restrictive especially for the AIC criterion and sample size T = 200. Nevertheless, for all three criteria the estimated orders tend to increase with increasing sample size which is in line with condition (8.3.1). Again the differences between the MSEs of $\tilde{\underline{y}}_t(h)$ and $\tilde{\underline{y}}_t^o(h)$ are positive or not significantly different at the 5% level as predicted by the asymptotic theory of Section 8.3.

Table 8.4. Monte Carlo Results Based on 600 Replications for Bivariate Disaggregate MA(2) and Aggregated MA(1) Process

(a) Frequency Distributions of Estimated AR Orders in Percent

disaggregate process					aggregated process				
sample size T	AR order	frequency distribution p(AIC)	p(HQ)	p(SC)	sample size T	AR order	frequency distribution p(AIC)	p(HQ)	p(SC)
60	0	0	5	37	30	0	2	7	23
	1	0	0	1		1	24	40	53
	2	23	59	59		2	37	34	20
	3	2	2	0		3	18	11	3
	4	45	30	3		4	19	9	2
	5	6	1	0					
	6	24	4	0					
100	0	0	0	6	50	0	0	0	5
	1	0	0	0		1	12	35	60
	2	6	47	83		2	39	43	32
	3	0	1	0		3	27	15	3
	4	46	45	12		4	22	6	0
	5	5	2	0					
	6	42	6	0					
200	0	0	0	0	100	0	0	0	0
	1	0	0	0		1	0	8	38
	2	0	5	55		2	25	53	55
	3	0	0	0		3	36	26	7
	4	23	65	45		4	40	14	1
	5	1	0	0					
	6	76	30	0					

(b) Differences of Forecast MSEs ($\tilde{\Sigma}(h) - \tilde{\Sigma}^o(h)$)

sample size T of disaggregate process	forecast horizon h	estimation criterion AIC y_{1t}	AIC y_{2t}	HQ y_{1t}	HQ y_{2t}	SC y_{1t}	SC y_{2t}
60	1	0.16	0.17	0.07	0.08	-0.22	-0.08
	5	0.14	0.17**	0.06	0.13*	0.04	0.03
100	1	0.09	0.11	0.09	-0.00	0.04	-0.02
	5	0.05	0.01	0.06	-0.02	0.00	-0.02
200	1	-0.00	-0.03	0.02	-0.02	-0.00	-0.05
	5	0.02	-0.04	0.02	0.01	0.01	-0.00

* significant at 5% level, ** significant at 1% level

8.5.5 A System With a Stock and a Flow Variable

Just for illustrative purposes it may be interesting to consider the process (8.5.7) with a different type of temporal aggregation. It follows immediately from Proposition 7.1 that treating the variables as stock variables and aggregating by deleting every other observation for each variable results in a process for which the forecasts based on the full and the partial process are identical. Thus, in this respect there is no difference between treating the variables as stock or flow variables. On the other hand, it was mentioned in Section 6.3 that the situation is different if one variable is treated as a flow variable and the other as a stock variable. Therefore the process

$$\underline{y}_t = \begin{bmatrix} y_{1t} \\ y_{2t} \end{bmatrix} = \begin{bmatrix} x_{1,2t} + x_{1,2t-1} \\ x_{2,2t} \end{bmatrix} \tag{8.5.9}$$

was also considered. The MSE differences obtained for this process are presented in Table 8.5. Obviously, the differences for the 1-step forecasts are all quite substantial. They are much greater than in the previous example (see Table 8.4(b)) and they do not go to zero for growing sample size T. This clearly shows that the MSE differences are not only due to estimation variability.

The picture is a bit different for the 5-step forecasts. Their MSE differences are much smaller and tend to zero for growing T. The reason is that for an MA(1) the optimal h-step forecast is the process mean for h > 1. It is easy to see that for the present type of aggregation $\underline{y}_t$ is also an MA(1) process (see Section 6.5, Proposition 6.1) so that $\underline{y}_t(h) = \underline{y}_t^{o}(h)$ for h > 1. Hence, the 5-step MSE differences are again due to estimation and specification variability only. This is nicely reflected in the generated MSEs in Table 8.5.

Overall the Monte Carlo study shows that the asymptotic theories of Sections 8.2 and 8.3 are good indicators of the small sample performance of the two predictors under investigation. This holds at least for most processes used in this simulation study. In the next section two examples based on real life data are considered.

Table 8.5. Monte Carlo Results Based on 600 Replications for a System Involving a Flow and a Stock Variable

Differences of Forecast MSEs $(\tilde{\Sigma}(h) - \tilde{\Sigma}^{o}(h))$

sample size T of disaggregate process	forecast horizon h	estimation criterion AIC		HQ		SC	
		y_{1t}	y_{2t}	y_{1t}	y_{2t}	y_{1t}	y_{2t}
60	1	0.97**	0.31**	0.91**	0.21**	0.46**	0.11*
	5	0.05	0.09**	0.02	0.09**	0.04	0.06**
100	1	0.65**	0.21**	0.69**	0.17**	0.51**	0.14**
	5	0.01	0.03	-0.00	0.01	-0.01	0.02
200	1	0.48**	0.21**	0.52**	0.21**	0.44**	0.17**
	5	-0.03	0.01	-0.02	0.01	-0.03	0.00

* significant at 5% level, ** significant at 1% level .

8.6 EXAMPLES

In this section the seasonally adjusted, quarterly U.S. Personal Consumption Expenditures and Gross Private Domestic Investment series given in the Appendix of this study are used again as examples to illustrate the results of the previous sections. The same data were analyzed in Section 7.6. Again the period 1947 to 1969 is used for estimation and the 1969 to 1972 data are used for assessing the relative forecast performance of the predictors based on disaggregate and temporally aggregated series.

8.6.1 Consumption

Denoting the first differences of the quarterly Personal Consumption Expenditures by x_t the corresponding Box-Jenkins model for the data generation process was found to be the AR(2)

$$x_t = 2.69 + 0.33x_{t-2} + u_t \tag{8.6.1}$$

(see Section 7.6, (7.6.2)). This process is similar to (8.5.1) and, providing (8.6.1) is the true generation process of the x_t data, aggregation to semiannual data does not result in a loss in forecast efficiency if the forecasts are based on known processes. Therefore the semiannual process $\mathcal{y}_t = x_{2t} + x_{2t-1}$ will be considered. Note that the series x_t begins with the second quarter of 1947 whereas $\mathcal{y}_t$ begins with the second half year of 1947. Furthermore, the process $\mathcal{y}_t$ represents a temporal aggregate of the first differences of Personal Consumption Expenditures and not of the original data. In other words, $\mathcal{y}_t$ effectively represents first differences of the second and fourth quarter values of the original consumption series.

AR models were fitted in the usual way to both x_t and $\mathcal{y}_t$ using the three criteria AIC, HQ, and SC and maximum orders of $P = 14$ and 8 for the quarterly and semiannual data, respectively. The models for the x_t series are given in Chapter 7, (7.6.3) (AIC, HQ) and (7.6.4) (SC), and all criteria have chosen the same model for $\mathcal{y}_t$:

$$\text{AIC, HQ, SC:}\quad \mathcal{y}_t = \underset{(1.41)}{5.42} + \underset{(0.15)}{0.34}\, \mathcal{y}_{t-1} + v_t\,, \quad \tilde{\Sigma}_v = 29.25, \tag{8.6.2}$$

where the numbers in parentheses are, as usual, estimated standard errors and $\tilde{\Sigma}_v$ is the estimate of the white noise variance with degrees of freedom correction.

The models for x_t and y_t were used to compute semiannual h-step forecasts $\tilde{y}^o_t(h)$ and $\tilde{y}_t(h)$ for the postsample period 1969 - 1972. Thus, there are eight 1-step forecasts based on the disaggregate series, $\tilde{y}^o_t(1),\ldots,\tilde{y}^o_{t+7}(1)$, and eight 1-step forecasts based on the aggregated semiannual series $\tilde{y}_t(1),\ldots,\tilde{y}_{t+7}(1)$. Similarly, there are seven 2-step forecasts, six 3-step forecasts and so on. These forecasts were used to compute the h-step MSEs given in Table 8.6(a). For the AIC and HQ criterion the MSEs from quarterly and semiannual forecasts are very similar. This is roughly in accordance with the asymptotic theory and the simulation results of the previous sections although one would have expected the MSEs from quarterly data to be slightly better than those from semiannual data. The SC criterion has chosen the white noise model (7.6.4) for the quarterly data and the AR(1) model (8.6.2) for the semiannual data. The latter predicts markedly better than the former for forecast horizons h = 1 and 2. One possible explanation for this deviation from the simulation results may be that the conditions underlying the present example are not the same as those of the Monte Carlo experiment. In this example the MSEs are based on a single, limited realization of the underlying data generation process while the simulation results are based on a large number of independent realizations. Furthermore, the number of forecasts on which the MSEs in Table 8.6 are based is relatively small. Of course, a predictor being superior to a competitor under the MSE criterion does not imply that every single forecast provided by the former is better than a competing forecast.

Based on the results of Section 8.4 one would expect that the forecasts based on quarterly data are clearly superior if the levels rather than the first differences are considered. Denoting the original data by z_t the semiannual process is $z_t = z_{2t} + z_{2t-1}$. AR models were also fitted to the first differences of the z_t (semiannual original consumption) process. The following models were obtained when a maximum order of P = 8 was considered:

$$\text{AIC:}\quad (1 - \underset{(0.17)}{0.60}L + \underset{(0.21)}{0.43}L^2 - \underset{(0.22)}{0.25}L^3 + \underset{(0.21)}{0.04}L^4 - \underset{(0.18)}{0.32}L^5)(1-L)z_t$$

$$= \underset{(3.80)}{5.98} + w_t \;,\quad \tilde{\Sigma}_w = 82.30\;, \tag{8.6.3}$$

$$\text{HQ:}\quad (1 - \underset{(0.16)}{0.65}L + \underset{(0.16)}{0.27}L^2)(1-L)z_t = \underset{(2.89)}{10.07} + w_t \;,\quad \tilde{\Sigma}_w = 86.57, \tag{8.6.4}$$

$$\text{SC:}\quad (1 - \underset{(0.14)}{0.54}L)(1-L)z_t = \underset{(2.57)}{7.79} + w_t \;,\quad \tilde{\Sigma}_w = 88.51\;, \tag{8.6.5}$$

Table 8.6. MSEs of Forecasts for Semiannual Consumption Data

(a) First Differences

forecast horizon h	forecasts based on quarterly data		forecasts based on semiannual data
	AIC, HQ	SC	AIC, HQ, SC
1	89	112	89
2	116	128	115
3	145	149	143
4	176	178	173

(b) Original Series

forecast horizon h	forecasts based on quarterly data		forecasts based on semiannual data		
	AIC, HQ	SC	AIC	HQ	SC
1	189	227	204	192	174
2	730	835	798	757	689
3	1393	1482	978	1093	1205
4	2694	2288	1418	2038	2235

where L denotes the lag operator for the macro time index t.

The MSEs obtained for the original semiannual consumption data are given in Table 8.6(b). Despite the theoretical results the forecasts based on semiannual data are better than those from the quarterly models. For h = 1 and 2 the forecasts from the SC model (8.6.5) are optimal and for h = 3 and 4 the AIC forecasts from (8.6.3) are best. The reasons for this result may be the same as for the first differences mentioned previously.

8.6.2 Investment

The second set of example data consists of the quarterly, seasonally adjusted U.S. Gross Private Domestic Investment (z_t). Denoting the first differences again by x_t the Box-Jenkins model given in Section 7.6.2 is

$$x_t = 1.06 + u_t - 0.59u_{t-4} \cdot \tag{8.6.6}$$

Using m = 4, that is,

$$y_t = x_{4t} + x_{4t-1} + x_{4t-2} + x_{4t-3}$$

is an annual series, this example is similar to (8.5.3) and (8.5.5). Note that the series of annual data starts in 1948 whereas the first value of the x_t series is associated with the second quarter of 1947. Assuming that (8.6.6) is in fact the true data generation process, the forecast MSEs obtained from known disaggregate and aggregated processes are identical, i.e., $\Sigma(h) = \Sigma^o(h)$, by Proposition 8.1.

Using P = 14 and 4 as maximum AR orders for the quarterly and annual data, respectively, the AR models obtained for x_t are given in Chapter 5, (5.6.4) (for AIC and HQ) and (5.6.5) (for SC) and for y_t the white noise model

$$y_t = \underset{(3.33)}{4.05} + v_t \quad , \quad \tilde{\Sigma}_v = 233 \tag{8.6.7}$$

is chosen by all three criteria AIC, HQ, and SC. The corresponding forecast MSEs obtained for the postsample years 1969 to 1972 are given in Table 8.7(a). Note that the 1-step and 2-step MSEs are only based on 4 and 3 annual forecasts, respectively. The best forecasts are obtained with the white noise (AR(0)) model (5.6.5) chosen by SC for the quar-

Table 8.7. MSEs of Forecasts for Annual Investment Data

(a) First Differences

forecast horizon h	forecasts based on quarterly data			forecasts based on annual data
	AIC, HQ (AR(4))	SC (AR(0))	subset AR	AIC, HQ, SC (AR(0))
1	287	229	291	231
2	297	294	339	297

(b) Original Series

forecast horizon h	forecasts based on quarterly data		forecasts based on annual data
	AIC, HQ	SC	AIC, HQ, SC
1	2223	1895	2737
2	4579	5551	4798

terly x_t data.

In order to investigate whether the inferior performance of the AR(4) (5.6.4) model chosen by AIC and HQ may be blamed to the nonparsimonious parameterization of the model, a more parsimonious version, for which the parameters at lags 1, 2, and 3 are set to zero was also used for prediction (see (5.6.14)). Recall that in (5.6.4) the coefficients at lags 1, 2, and 3 are, in absolute value, considerably less than twice their respective standard errors. The MSEs of the subset AR model (5.6.14) are also given in Table 8.7(a). These MSEs are even worse than those of the full AR(4) model. Thus, the forecast performance of the quarterly model is not improved by setting insignificant coefficients to zero. A discussion of reasons for the poor performance of a model based on disaggregate data was given in Section 8.6.1 and will not be repeated here.

Also for this example the levels rather than first differences were aggregated and forecasts were computed for the annual levels. The model obtained for the series z_t of annual levels of investment is a random walk for all three criteria,

$$(1 - L) z_t = \underset{(10.30)}{17.03} + w_t \quad , \quad \tilde{\Sigma}_w = 2229 \ , \qquad (8.6.8)$$

where a maximum AR order of P = 4 was used for the first differences of z_t. The resulting MSEs of the annual forecasts for the original series are presented in Table 8.7(b). From the discussion in Section 8.4 one would expect that the forecasts based on quarterly data outperform those based on annual data and this is what happens for this example. The only exception is the 2-step forecast MSE of the quarterly random walk which exceeds the 2-step forecast MSE of the annual model (8.6.8).

More examples of forecast comparisons for temporally aggregated real life time series are given by Wei (1978a) and Abraham (1982). In the latter article it is also found that forecasts from the disaggregate series are not necessarily superior to forecasts based on the aggregate.

8.7 SUMMARY AND CONCLUSIONS

In this chapter the relative performance of predictors based on temporally aggregated and disaggregated processes has been investigated for the case of flow variables where consecutive values are added to obtain the aggregate. In Chapter 6 it was shown that if the data generation processes are known, then, under common assumptions, the forecast MSEs of the aggregated process are greater than or equal to the MSEs obtained from the disaggregate process. Using asymptotic theory and small sample simulations it has been investigated in this chapter whether the result for known processes carries over to the situation where the process orders and parameters have to be estimated from the available data as is usually the case in practice. Overall the results suggest that also if the process orders and/or coefficients are unknown, using the disaggregate data is preferable. Thus, the fact that in practice temporally aggregated data sometimes do provide better forecasts than the disaggregate data (see e.g., Section 8.6 and Abraham (1982)) cannot be explained by the asymptotic theory discussed in this chapter. Possible reasons may be (1) that the sample size is too small for the asymptotic theory to be approximately valid or (2) that the assumptions such as structural stability over time, underlying the asymptotic theory are violated or (3) that a specific estimate obtained on the basis of a single realization of the data generation process is not a good approximation to the actual forecast MSE of the underlying process.

8.A APPENDIX: PROOF OF RELATION (8.2.23)

In the following proof the notation of Section 8.2 is used. It is stated in (8.2.23) that

$$\mathrm{tr}\{(\underline{A}')^{j}\Gamma^{-1}\underline{A}^{i}\Gamma\} = 0 \quad \text{for} \quad i \neq j \text{ and } 0 \leq i, j < m . \qquad (8.A.1)$$

Note that

$$\Gamma = I_m \otimes \Sigma_{\underline{x}} = \begin{bmatrix} I_{m-i} \otimes \Sigma_{\underline{x}} & 0 \\ 0 & I_i \otimes \Sigma_{\underline{x}} \end{bmatrix} , \quad i = 0,1,\dots,m ,$$

and

$$\underline{A}^{i} = \begin{bmatrix} 0 & I_i \otimes A_m \\ I_{m-i} \otimes I_K & 0 \end{bmatrix}$$

(see (8.2.14)). Hence,

$$\underline{A}^i\Gamma = \begin{bmatrix} 0 & I_i \otimes A_m \Sigma_{\underline{x}} \\ I_{m-i} \otimes \Sigma_{\underline{x}} & 0 \end{bmatrix} .$$

Similarly,

$$(\underline{A}')^j\Gamma^{-1} = \begin{bmatrix} 0 & I_{m-j} \otimes I_K \\ I_j \otimes A_m' & 0 \end{bmatrix} \begin{bmatrix} I_j \otimes \Sigma_{\underline{x}}^{-1} & 0 \\ 0 & I_{m-j} \otimes \Sigma_{\underline{x}}^{-1} \end{bmatrix}$$

$$= \begin{bmatrix} 0 & I_{m-j} \otimes \Sigma_{\underline{x}}^{-1} \\ I_j \otimes A_m' \Sigma_{\underline{x}}^{-1} & 0 \end{bmatrix} .$$

Thus, $(\underline{A}')^j\Gamma^{-1}\underline{A}^i\Gamma$ has zero diagonal for $i \neq j$ and (8.A.1) follows.

Q.E.D.

CHAPTER 9. JOINT TEMPORAL AND CONTEMPORANEOUS AGGREGATION

After having considered the consequences of forecasting with estimated processes for contemporaneous aggregation in Chapter 5 and for temporal aggregation in Chapters 7 and 8 the two types of aggregation will be treated jointly in this chapter. In practice the two types of aggregation are often both present. For instance, the annual tax revenues of a country that consists of a number of states, is the sum of the monthly revenues in each state. Thus, the total figure is obtained by aggregating over time (temporally) and over regions (contemporaneously). In this chapter the particular type of temporal and contemporaneous aggregation is considered where all the disaggregate figures are simply added as in the foregoing example. This simplification is justified because it suffices to illustrate the pertinent problems. On the other hand, it helps to simplify some of the arguments.

Since the general case of temporal and contemporaneous aggregation has been treated in Chapter 6 for known processes, the main focus of this chapter will be on forecasting with estimated processes. The six predictors introduced in Chapter 6 will be considered. Forecasts for the aggregate are assumed to be desired. For instance, in the previous example, forecasts of the annual total tax revenues from all the states are assumed to be of interest.

The organization of this chapter is as follows. In Section 9.1 a summary of the processes and predictors of interest is given and in Sections 9.2 and 9.3 the predictors are compared for estimated processes. The asymptotic results of Chapter 3 are used in that comparison. Some small sample results obtained with a Monte Carlo experiment are discussed in Section 9.4 and U.S. investment data are again used as an example in Section 9.5. A summary of the findings of this chapter and some concluding remarks are given in Section 9.6. Some of the results of this chapter are summarized in Lütkepohl (1986d) where only four of the predictors are compared.

9.1 SUMMARY OF PROCESSES AND PREDICTORS

In this section some notation from Chapter 6 is reviewed and the processes and predictors of interest are specified for the special form of aggregation considered in this chapter. The basic disaggregate process is again denoted by $\underline{x}_t = (x_{1t},\ldots,x_{Kt})'$. It is assumed to be a K-dimensional, nondeterministic, stationary stochastic process with MA and AR representation as in many previous sections. Adding the components of $\underline{x}_t$ gives the contemporaneously aggregated process

$$z_t = x_{1t} + \ldots + x_{Kt} \tag{9.1.1}$$

and temporal aggregation of $\underline{x}_t$ over m periods gives

$$\underline{\bar{z}}_{\ell} = (\bar{z}_{1\ell},\ldots,\bar{z}_{K\ell})' = \underline{x}_{m\ell} + \underline{x}_{m\ell-1} + \ldots + \underline{x}_{m\ell-m+1} \; . \tag{9.1.2}$$

Furthermore contemporaneous and temporal aggregation of $\underline{x}_t$ results in the univariate process

$$\begin{aligned} y_{\ell} &= z_{m\ell} + \ldots + z_{m\ell-m+1} \\ &= \bar{z}_{1\ell} + \ldots + \bar{z}_{K\ell} \\ &= \sum_{k=1}^{K} \sum_{i=0}^{m-1} x_{k,m\ell-i} \; . \end{aligned} \tag{9.1.3}$$

It is assumed that y_{ℓ} represents the variable of which forecasts are desired. Thus, a special type of temporal and contemporaneous aggregation is considered. Since the aforementioned processes are used continuously throughout this chapter they are summarized in Table 9.1.

The six predictors of interest in the following have been discussed in detail in Chapter 6. They are summarized in Table 6.2. For the particular form of aggregation considered now, they are reviewed in Table 9.2. Since forecasts of an univariate variable are analyzed here, the MSEs are denoted by lower case letters. Some basic relations between the MSEs will be reviewed next.

The predictor $y_{\ell}^{o}(h)$, based on the completely disaggregated process, uses the largest information base and is therefore optimal among all six predictors. In other words,

$$\sigma_o^2(h) \le \sigma^2(h),\ \sigma_*^2(h),\ \bar{\sigma}_o^2(h),\ \sigma_u^2(h),\ \bar{\sigma}_u^2(h) . \tag{9.1.4}$$

Table 9.1. Processes Used for Prediction

$\underline{x}_t = (x_{1t},\ldots,x_{Kt})'$	(disaggregate process)
$z_t = x_{1t} + \ldots + x_{Kt}$	(contemporaneously aggregated process)
$\underline{\bar{z}}_{\mathit{t}} = (\bar{z}_{1\mathit{t}},\ldots,\bar{z}_{K\mathit{t}})' =$	
$= \underline{x}_{m\mathit{t}} + \underline{x}_{m\mathit{t}-1} + \ldots + \underline{x}_{m\mathit{t}-m+1}$	(temporally aggregated process)
$y_{\mathit{t}} = z_{m\mathit{t}} + z_{m\mathit{t}-1} + \ldots + z_{m\mathit{t}-m+1}$	
$= \bar{z}_{1\mathit{t}} + \ldots + \bar{z}_{K\mathit{t}}$	
$= \sum_{k=1}^{K} \sum_{i=0}^{m-1} x_{k,m\mathit{t}-i}$	(temporally and contemporaneously aggregated process)

Table 9.2. Predictors and MSEs for Aggregated Process

Predictor	Description	MSE
$y_t^o(h) = \sum_{k=1}^{K} \sum_{i=0}^{m-1} x_{k,mt}(mh-i)$	Prediction of the disaggregate process and aggregation of the predictions	$\sigma_o^2(h)$
$y_t(h)$	Direct prediction of the aggregated process	$\sigma^2(h)$
$y_t^*(h) = \sum_{i=0}^{m-1} z_{mt}(mh-i)$	Prediction of the contemporaneously aggregated process and temporal aggregation of the predictions	$\sigma_*^2(h)$
$\bar{y}_t^o(h) = \sum_{k=1}^{K} \bar{z}_{kt}(h)$	Prediction of the temporally aggregated process and contemporaneous aggregation of the predictions	$\bar{\sigma}_o^2(h)$
$y_t^u(h) = \sum_{k=1}^{K} \sum_{i=0}^{m-1} x_{k,mt}^u(mh-i)$	Prediction of the univariate components of the disaggregate process and aggregation of the univariate predictions	$\sigma_u^2(h)$
$\bar{y}_t^u(h) = \sum_{k=1}^{K} \bar{z}_{kt}^u(h)$	Prediction of the univariate components of the temporally aggregated process and contemporaneous aggregation of the univariate predictions	$\bar{\sigma}_u^2(h)$

Furthermore, the predictor $y_t(h)$ based on the fully aggregated process is less efficient than $y_t^*(h)$ which is based on the contemporaneously aggregated process and $\bar{y}_t^o(h)$ which is based on the temporally aggregated process, that is,

$$\sigma^2(h) \geq \sigma_o^2(h), \sigma_*^2(h), \bar{\sigma}_o^2(h). \tag{9.1.5}$$

Moreover, the predictor $\bar{y}_t^u(h)$, based on the univariate components of the temporally aggregated process, is dominated by $\bar{y}_t^o(h)$ which is based on the multivariate temporally aggregated process and by the predictor $y_t^u(h)$ based on univariate predictions of the components of $\underline{x}_t$, that is,

$$\bar{\sigma}_u^2(h) \geq \sigma_o^2(h), \bar{\sigma}_o^2(h), \sigma_u^2(h). \tag{9.1.6}$$

On the other hand, a general ranking of $y_t(h)$, $y_t^u(h)$, and $\bar{y}_t^u(h)$ cannot be given, that is, it depends on the correlation structure of the disaggregate process $\underline{x}_t$ and the period of aggregation m which one of the three predictors is optimal. Also, whether using the contemporaneously aggregated process for prediction results in smaller MSEs than using the temporally aggregated process depends on $\underline{x}_t$ and m. Finally, all six predictors converge to the mean of y_t when the forecast horizon h goes to infinity,

$$\sigma_o^2(h), \sigma^2(h), \sigma_*^2(h), \bar{\sigma}_o^2(h), \sigma_u^2(h), \bar{\sigma}_u^2(h) \underset{h\to\infty}{\longrightarrow} \sigma_y^2, \tag{9.1.7}$$

where σ_y^2 denotes the variance of y_t.

If the basic, disaggregate process $\underline{x}_t$ is nonstationary and stationarity can be achieved by differencing, the relations (9.1.4), (9.1.5), and (9.1.6) still hold. On the other hand (9.1.7) does not carry over to the nonstationary case, that is, the different predictors will not become identical for long-range forecasting. In the following, mostly stationary processes will be considered.

All the results of this section are given in Chapter 6 and rely, of course, on the assumption that the involved processes are known. In the following sections the contribution of the estimation uncertainty to the MSEs will be considered assuming that estimated processes are used for prediction.

9.2 PREDICTION BASED ON PROCESSES WITH ESTIMATED COEFFICIENTS

9.2.1 General Results

It is assumed now that the disaggregate process $\underline{x}_t$ is a stationary and invertible, K-dimensional, Gaussian vector ARMA process. This implies that the aggregated processes listed in Table 9.1 are also stationary and invertible Gaussian ARMA processes (see Section 6.5). The coefficients of these processes are assumed to be unknown and their ARMA orders are known. The coefficients are assumed to be estimated by a ML (maximum likelihood) procedure or a method that is asymptotically equivalent to ML using a realization of a process that is independent of the process used for prediction, but has the same stochastic structure. The sample size used for estimation is assumed to be T for temporally disaggregated processes and T/m for temporally aggregated processes. For the moment it is also assumed that $\underline{x}_t$ and hence all the aggregated processes have zero mean and mean terms are not estimated. Comments on estimating mean terms will be made later on.

Using these assumptions, asymptotic MSEs for the six predictors follow from the results in Section 3.2. For instance, the asymptotic MSE matrix of a vector of forecasts $[\hat{\underline{x}}_{m\ell}(mh-m+1)', \hat{\underline{x}}_{m\ell}(mh-m+2)',\dots, \hat{\underline{x}}_{m\ell}(mh)']'$ is

$$\hat{\underline{\Sigma}}_{\underline{x}}(mh) = \underline{\Sigma}_{\underline{x}}(mh) + \frac{1}{T}\underline{\Omega}_{\underline{x}}(mh) , \qquad (9.2.1)$$

where $\underline{\Sigma}_{\underline{x}}(mh)$ is as defined in (3.1.15) and $\underline{\Omega}_{\underline{x}}(mh)$ is as defined in (3.2.8). As in previous chapters, a caret denotes quantities involving or related to estimated coefficients. For instance, $\hat{\underline{x}}_t(h)$ denotes the forecast $\underline{x}_t(h)$ with actual coefficients replaced by ML estimators. From the asymptotic MSE matrix in (9.2.1) an asymptotic MSE of the predictor $\hat{y}^o_\ell(h)$, based on the disaggregate process with estimated coefficients, can be obtained:

$$\begin{aligned}\hat{\sigma}^2_o(h) &= F_{mhK,mK}\hat{\underline{\Sigma}}_{\underline{x}}(mh)F'_{mhK,mK} \\ &= \sigma^2_o(h) + \frac{1}{T}F_{mhK,mK}\underline{\Omega}_{\underline{x}}(mh)F'_{mhK,mK} .\end{aligned} \qquad (9.2.2)$$

Here and in the following $F_{i,j}$ denotes the $(1 \times i)$ row vector

$$F_{i,j} = (\underbrace{0,\dots,0}_{i-j} , \underbrace{1,\dots,1}_{j}) . \qquad (9.2.3)$$

Asymptotic MSEs of the other predictors can be obtained in a similar way. For instance, the asymptotic MSE of the predictor $\hat{y}_t(h)$, based on temporally and contemporaneously aggregated data, is

$$\hat{\sigma}^2(h) = \sigma^2(h) + \frac{m}{T}\Omega_y(h), \qquad (9.2.4)$$

where $\sigma^2(h)$ is the MSE of $y_t(h)$, T/m is the length of the aggregated time series used for estimation, and $\Omega_y(h)$ is the variance of the asymptotic distribution of $\sqrt{T/m}[\hat{y}_t(h) - y_t(h)]$ (see (3.2.2) and (3.2.3)). Note that the parameters of the process y_t are assumed to be estimated using only the temporally and contemporaneously aggregated data. An analogous assumption is made for the other processes. All six resulting asymptotic MSEs are summarized in Table 9.3 where the notation corresponds to the notation in Chapter 3. For instance, $\underline{\Omega}_{x_k}(mh)$ is the covariance matrix of the asymptotic distribution of

$$\sqrt{T}\begin{bmatrix} \hat{x}_{kt}(1) & - & x_{kt}(1) \\ & \vdots & \\ \hat{x}_{kt}(mh) & - & x_{kt}(mh) \end{bmatrix}$$

(see (3.2.7)).

In all cases the asymptotic MSE is the sum of the MSE for a known process and a term reflecting the estimation uncertainty. Given the assumption that independent processes are used for estimation and forecasting, the additivity of the two terms is in all cases easy to derive. For example,

$$y_{t+h} - \hat{y}_t(h) = [y_{t+h} - y_t(h)] + [y_t(h) - \hat{y}_t(h)].$$

The first term on the right-hand side involves only innovations associated with periods after period t whereas the second term involves only variables up to period t. Thus the two terms are independent and the variance of their sum is the sum of their variances. The same argument, in general, does not work for the predictors based on univariate component series because the univariate white noise series generating the component processes will generally not constitute a multivariate white noise process. Therefore the two terms on the right-hand side of

Table 9.3. Summary of Asymptotic MSEs of Predictors With Estimated Coefficients

Predictor	Asymptotic MSE	Remarks
$\hat{y}^{o}_{t}(h)$	$\hat{\sigma}^2_o(h) = \sigma^2_o(h) + \frac{1}{T} F_{mhK,mK} \Omega_{\underline{x}}(mh) F'_{mhK,mK}$	see (3.2.9)
$\hat{y}_{t}(h)$	$\hat{\sigma}^2(h) = \sigma^2(h) + \frac{m}{T} \Omega_{y}(h)$	see (3.2.4)
$\hat{y}^{*}_{t}(h)$	$\hat{\sigma}^2_*(h) = \sigma^2_*(h) + \frac{1}{T} F_{mh,m} \Omega_{\underline{z}}(mh) F'_{mh,m}$	see (3.2.9)
$\hat{\bar{y}}^{o}_{t}(h)$	$\hat{\bar{\sigma}}^2_o(h) = \bar{\sigma}^2_o(h) + \frac{m}{T} F_{K,K} \Omega_{\bar{\underline{z}}}(h) F'_{K,K}$	see (3.2.4)
$\hat{y}^{u}_{t}(h)$	$\hat{\sigma}^2_u(h) = \sigma^2_u(h) + \frac{1}{T} F_{mh,m} \left[\sum_{k=1}^{K} \Omega_{\underline{x}_k}(mh) \right] F'_{mh,m}$	see (3.2.9) if components of $\underline{x}_t$ are independent
$\hat{\bar{y}}^{u}_{t}(h)$	$\hat{\bar{\sigma}}^2_u(h) = \bar{\sigma}^2_u(h) + \frac{m}{T} \sum_{k=1}^{K} \Omega_{\bar{z}_k}(h)$	see (3.2.4)

$$\begin{bmatrix} \underline{x}_{mt+mh-m+1} - \hat{\underline{x}}^{u}_{mt}(mh-m+1) \\ \vdots \\ \underline{x}_{mt+mh} - \hat{\underline{x}}^{u}_{mt}(mh) \end{bmatrix}$$

$$= \begin{bmatrix} \underline{x}_{mt+mh-m+1} - \underline{x}^{u}_{mt}(mh-m+1) \\ \vdots \\ \underline{x}_{mt+mh} - \underline{x}^{u}_{mt}(mh) \end{bmatrix} + \begin{bmatrix} \underline{x}^{u}_{mt}(mh-m+1) - \hat{\underline{x}}^{u}_{mt}(mh-m+1) \\ \vdots \\ \underline{x}^{u}_{mt}(mh) - \hat{\underline{x}}^{u}_{mt}(mh) \end{bmatrix}$$

will in general not be independent. Independence is guaranteed, however, if the component series are independent (see also the corresponding discussion in Section 5.2.2). Therefore the independence assumption is made in Table 9.3. A weaker assumption could be made but is not used here for simplicity.

For all six MSEs listed in Table 9.3 the terms due to estimation variability approach zero as T increases. Thus, for large enough samples,

$$\hat{\sigma}^2_o(h) < \hat{\sigma}^2(h),\ \hat{\sigma}^2_*(h),\ \hat{\bar{\sigma}}^2_o(h),\ \hat{\sigma}^2_u(h),\ \hat{\bar{\sigma}}^2_u(h)\ , \tag{9.2.5}$$

provided the strict inequality holds in (9.1.4) for the MSEs of the known processes. In other words, if there is sufficient sample information, the predictor based on completely disaggregated data is best even if estimated coefficients are used. This result holds if $y^o_t(h)$, with known coefficients, strictly dominates the other predictors.

Similarly, if a strict inequality holds in (9.1.5) ,

$$\hat{\sigma}^2(h) > \hat{\sigma}^2_o(h),\ \hat{\sigma}^2_*(h),\ \hat{\bar{\sigma}}^2_o(h) \tag{9.2.6}$$

provided T is large enough. That is, if the predictor based on the fully aggregated process is inferior to $y^o_t(h)$, $y^*_t(h)$, and $\bar{y}^o_t(h)$, then the same will hold for processes with estimated coefficients, given the available sample information is sufficiently rich. A similar comment applies for the relation (9.1.6).

If the forecast horizon h tends to infinity all six predictors approach the known mean of the aggregate y_t so that no estimated parameters will be involved. Therefore all asymptotic MSEs converge to the variance of y_t. If the means of the different processes were unknown and were estimated by the sample means, then it is easy to see that even in this case the predictors all become identical for $h \to \infty$. All predictors then converge to the sample mean of y_t.

The case in which the MSEs are identical for known processes is of particular interest. In this situation the relative predictor performance depends solely on that part of the MSEs which is due to the estimation variability. The question arises whether the MSE orderings in (9.1.4), (9.1.5), and (9.1.6) are maintained in this case. It has been shown in Chapter 5 that if there is only contemporaneous aggregation, a predictor based on the aggregated process may be superior to a predictor that results from aggregating forecasts of the disaggregate process. On the other hand, in Chapter 8 temporal aggregation of the present type was shown to be subversive of forecast precision, that is, even if the MSEs for the known processes are identical, the predictor based on a temporally aggregated process will in general be strictly inferior to the aggregated forecasts from the disaggregate process when estimated coefficients are used. Thus, a question of particular interest in the present context is, which forces dominate when both temporal and contemporaneous aggregation are present. This question will be considered in the following subsection using a particular process as an example.

9.2.2 An Example

In the following the example AR(m) process

$$\underline{x}_t = A_m \underline{x}_{t-m} + \underline{u}_t \tag{9.2.7}$$

with $A_m = \alpha I_K$, $0 < |\alpha| < 1$, will be considered in detail. It follows from Chapter 6, Section 6.3, that for this disaggregate process the predictors are identical if known processes are used for forecasting, i.e.,

$$\sigma_o^2(h) = \sigma^2(h) = \sigma_*^2(h) = \bar{\sigma}_o^2(h) = \sigma_u^2(h) = \bar{\sigma}_u^2(h) \ . \tag{9.2.8}$$

Thus, MSE differences will be due to using estimated coefficients.

Suppose the investigator knows the order of the process but does not know the various parameter restrictions. In that situation, in order to obtain a forecast $\hat{y}_{\mathcal{t}}^o(h)$, an unconstrained AR(m)

$$\underline{x}_t = A_1 \underline{x}_{t-1} + \dots + A_m \underline{x}_{t-m} + \underline{u}_t \tag{9.2.9}$$

is estimated. Then the matrix $\Omega_{\underline{x}}(m)$ has the form

$$\underline{\Omega}_{\underline{x}}(m) = \left[\sum_{j=0}^{l-1} \sum_{i=0}^{k-1} \operatorname{tr}\{\underline{A}'^{\,l-1-j}\Gamma^{-1}\underline{A}^{k-1-i}\Gamma\}\Phi_j \not{Z}_{\underline{u}} \Phi_i' \right]_{l,k = 1,\dots,m} \tag{9.2.10}$$

where

$$\underline{A} = \begin{bmatrix} 0 & 0 & \dots & 0 & A_m \\ I_K & 0 & \dots & 0 & 0 \\ 0 & I_K & & 0 & 0 \\ \vdots & \vdots & \ddots & \vdots & \vdots \\ 0 & 0 & \dots & I_K & 0 \end{bmatrix}, \quad (mK \times mK)$$

$$\Gamma = E\left[\begin{bmatrix} \underline{x}_t \\ \underline{x}_{t-1} \\ \vdots \\ \underline{x}_{t-m+1} \end{bmatrix} \left[\underline{x}_t', \underline{x}_{t-1}', \dots, \underline{x}_{t-m+1}' \right] \right], \quad (mK \times mK)$$

the Φ_i are the coefficient matrices of the MA representation of $\underline{x}_t$ and $\not{Z}_{\underline{u}}$ is the covariance matrix of $\underline{u}_t$ as before (see (3.2.31)).

The special form of $\underline{x}_t$ in (9.2.7) implies an MA representation

$$\underline{x}_t = \sum_{i=0}^{\infty} \Phi_{im}\underline{u}_{t-im}, \tag{9.2.11}$$

where

$$\Phi_{im} = A_m^i = \alpha^i I_K . \tag{9.2.12}$$

Thus,

$$\underline{\Omega}_{\underline{x}}(m) = \begin{bmatrix} \operatorname{tr}\{\underline{A}'^{0}\Gamma^{-1}\underline{A}^{0}\Gamma\}\not{Z}_{\underline{u}} & \dots & \operatorname{tr}\{\underline{A}'^{0}\Gamma^{-1}\underline{A}^{m-1}\Gamma\}\not{Z}_{\underline{u}} \\ \vdots & \ddots & \vdots \\ \operatorname{tr}\{\underline{A}'^{m-1}\Gamma^{-1}\underline{A}^{0}\Gamma\}\not{Z}_{\underline{u}} & \dots & \operatorname{tr}\{\underline{A}'^{m-1}\Gamma^{-1}\underline{A}^{m-1}\Gamma\}\not{Z}_{\underline{u}} \end{bmatrix}.$$

Furthermore,

$$\Gamma = \begin{bmatrix} \not{Z}_{\underline{x}} & 0 & \dots & 0 \\ 0 & \not{Z}_{\underline{x}} & & 0 \\ \vdots & & \ddots & \vdots \\ 0 & 0 & \dots & \not{Z}_{\underline{x}} \end{bmatrix} = \frac{1}{1-\alpha^2}(I_m \otimes \not{Z}_{\underline{u}})$$

since $\underline{\Sigma}_{\underline{x}} = E(\underline{x}_t\underline{x}_t') = \frac{1}{1-\alpha^2}\underline{\Sigma}_{\underline{u}}$. Moreover,

$$\underline{A}^i = \begin{bmatrix} 0 & I_i \otimes A_m \\ I_{m-i} \otimes I_K & 0 \end{bmatrix} \quad (mK \times mK)$$

and thus,

$$tr(\underline{A}'^j\Gamma^{-1}\underline{A}^i\Gamma) = 0 \quad \text{for} \quad i \neq j \text{ and } i,j \leq m,$$

and

$$\underline{A}'^i\underline{A}^i = \begin{bmatrix} I_{m-i} \otimes I_K & 0 \\ 0 & I_i \otimes A_m'A_m \end{bmatrix} \quad \text{for } i \leq m,$$

(see Chapter 8, (8.2.14) and 8.A). Hence,

$$tr(\underline{A}'^i\Gamma^{-1}\underline{A}^i\Gamma) = tr(\underline{A}'^i\underline{A}^i) = (m-i)K + iK\alpha^2, \qquad i = 0,1,\dots,m, \quad (9.2.13)$$

because $A_m'A_m = \alpha^2 I_K$. It follows that

$$\underline{\Omega}_{\underline{x}}(m) = \begin{bmatrix} mK & 0 & \dots & 0 \\ 0 & (m-1)K + K\alpha^2 & & 0 \\ \vdots & \vdots & \ddots & \vdots \\ 0 & 0 & \dots & K + (m-1)K\alpha^2 \end{bmatrix} \otimes \underline{\Sigma}_{\underline{u}}. \quad (9.2.14)$$

This matrix permits to evaluate

$$\hat{\sigma}_o^2(1) = \sigma^2(1) + \frac{1}{T}F_{mK,mK}\underline{\Omega}_{\underline{x}}(m)F'_{mK,mK} . \quad (9.2.15)$$

To evaluate the other MSEs in Table 9.3 the aggregate processes implied by (9.2.7) are needed. These are listed in Table 9.4. By a similar reasoning as above, the variances and covariances of the asymptotic distributions of the predictors can be derived. The results are given in Table 9.5. Using these quantities and assuming $\underline{\Sigma}_{\underline{u}} = I_K$ it is easy to derive explicit expressions for the asymptotic MSEs of Table 9.3. These expressions are presented in Table 9.6. For example, $\hat{\sigma}_o^2(1)$ is obtained by noting that

Table 9.4. Processes Implied by $\underline{x}_t = \alpha \underline{x}_{t-m} + \underline{u}_t$

$\underline{x}_t = \alpha \underline{x}_{t-m} + \underline{u}_t \; , \; \Sigma_{\underline{u}} = E(\underline{u}_t \underline{u}_t')$	(basic, disaggregate process)
$z_t = \alpha z_{t-m} + v_t \; , \; \sigma_v^2 = F_{K,K} \Sigma_{\underline{u}} F_{K,K}'$	(contemporaneously aggregated process)
$\overline{\underline{z}}_{\mathcal{t}} = \alpha \overline{\underline{z}}_{\mathcal{t}-1} + \overline{\underline{w}}_{\mathcal{t}} \; , \; \Sigma_{\overline{\underline{w}}} = m \Sigma_{\underline{u}}$	(temporally aggregated process)
$y_{\mathcal{t}} = \alpha y_{\mathcal{t}-1} + \upsilon_{\mathcal{t}} \; , \; \sigma_\upsilon^2 = m F_{K,K} \Sigma_{\underline{u}} F_{K,K}'$	(temporally and contemporaneously aggregated process)
$x_{kt} = \alpha x_{k,t-m} + u_{kt} \; , \; \sigma_k^2 = E(u_{kt}^2)$	(k-th component of $\underline{x}_t$)
$\overline{z}_{k\mathcal{t}} = \alpha \overline{z}_{k,\mathcal{t}-1} + \overline{w}_{k\mathcal{t}} \; , \; \sigma_{\overline{w}_k}^2 = m \sigma_k^2$	(k-th component of $\overline{\underline{z}}_{\mathcal{t}}$)

Table 9.5. Asymptotic Covariance Matrices Related to Predictors With Estimated Coefficients

$$\Omega_{\underline{X}}(m) = \begin{bmatrix} mK & & & \\ & (m-1)K + K\alpha^2 & & 0 \\ & & \ddots & \\ 0 & & & K + (m-1)K\alpha^2 \end{bmatrix} \otimes \Sigma_{\underline{u}}$$

$$\Omega_{y}(1) = \sigma_{\upsilon}^2 = mF_{K,K}\Sigma_{\underline{u}}F'_{K,K}$$

$$\Omega_{\underline{Z}}(m) = (F_{K,K}\Sigma_{\underline{u}}F'_{K,K}) \begin{bmatrix} m & & & \\ & (m-1) + \alpha^2 & & 0 \\ & & \ddots & \\ 0 & & & 1 + (m-1)\alpha^2 \end{bmatrix}$$

$$\Omega_{\bar{\underline{Z}}}(1) = K\Sigma_{\bar{\underline{w}}} = mK\Sigma_{\underline{u}}$$

$$\Omega_{\underline{X}_k}(m) = \sigma_k^2 \begin{bmatrix} m & & & \\ & (m-1) + \alpha^2 & & 0 \\ & & \ddots & \\ 0 & & & 1 + (m-1)\alpha^2 \end{bmatrix}$$

$$\Omega_{\bar{z}_k}(1) = m\sigma_k^2$$

Table 9.6. Asymptotic MSEs of Predictors With Estimated Coefficients: Disaggregate Process $\underline{x}_t = \alpha\underline{x}_{t-m} + \underline{u}_t$, $\Sigma_{\underline{u}} = I_K$

$$\hat{\sigma}_o^2(1) = \sigma^2(1) + \frac{1}{T}F_{mK,mK}\Omega_{\underline{x}}(1)F'_{mK,mK}$$

$$= \sigma^2(1) + \frac{K}{T}\sum_{i=0}^{m-1}((m-i)K + iK\alpha^2)$$

$$= \sigma^2(1) + \frac{K^2}{T}(m^2 - (1-\alpha^2)\frac{m-1}{2}m)$$

$$\hat{\sigma}^2(1) = \sigma^2(1) + \frac{m}{T}\Omega_y(1) = \sigma^2(1) + \frac{m^2K}{T}$$

$$\hat{\sigma}_*^2(1) = \sigma^2(1) + \frac{1}{T}F_{m,m}\Omega_{\underline{z}}(m)F'_{m,m} = \sigma^2(1) + \frac{K}{T}\sum_{i=0}^{m-1}(m-i+i\alpha^2)$$

$$= \sigma^2(1) + \frac{K}{T}(m^2 - (1-\alpha^2)\frac{m-1}{2}m)$$

$$\hat{\bar{\sigma}}_o^2(1) = \sigma^2(1) + \frac{m}{T}F_{K,K}\Omega_{\bar{\underline{z}}}(1)F'_{K,K} = \sigma^2(1) + \frac{m^2K^2}{T}$$

$$\hat{\sigma}_u^2(1) = \sigma^2(1) + \frac{1}{T}F_{m,m}\left[\sum_{k=1}^{K}\Omega_{\underline{x}_k}(m)\right]F'_{m,m}$$

$$= \sigma^2(1) + \frac{K}{T}\sum_{i=0}^{m-1}(m-i+i\alpha^2) = \sigma^2(1) + \frac{K}{T}(m^2 - (1-\alpha^2)\frac{m-1}{2}m)$$

$$\hat{\bar{\sigma}}_u^2(1) = \sigma^2(1) + \frac{m}{T}\sum_{k=1}^{K}\Omega_{\bar{z}_k}(1) = \sigma^2(1) + \frac{m^2K}{T}$$

$$F_{mK,mK}\Omega_{\underline{x}}(m)F'_{mK,mK} = K\sum_{i=0}^{m-1}((m-i)K + iK\alpha^2)$$

$$= K^2(m^2-(1-\alpha^2)\sum_{i=1}^{m-1} i)$$

$$= K^2(m^2-(1-\alpha^2)\frac{m-1}{2}m) \quad . \tag{9.2.16}$$

Using the quantities in Table 9.6 it is easy to compare the asymptotic MSEs of all six 1-step predictors. Note that $\alpha \neq 0$ and $m > 1$ implies

$$m^2 - (1-\alpha^2)\frac{m-1}{2}m < m^2 \tag{9.2.17}$$

because $|\alpha| < 1$ to ensure stationarity. Hence, the relation

$$\hat{\sigma}_*^2(1) = \hat{\sigma}_u^2(1) < \hat{\sigma}_o^2(1),\ \hat{\sigma}^2(1),\ \hat{\bar{\sigma}}_o^2(1),\ \hat{\bar{\sigma}}_u^2(1) \tag{9.2.18}$$

follows. In other words, forecasting the contemporaneously aggregated process and temporally aggregating the forecasts is now optimal. Asymptotically equivalent forecasts result by predicting the univariate components of the disaggregate process individually and aggregating the obtained forecasts temporally and contemporaneously. All other 1-step forecasts are strictly inferior to these two predictors. Also, it follows from Table 9.6 that computing multivariate forecasts of the temporally aggregated process and aggregating them contemporaneously is strictly inferior to all other forecasts. That is,

$$\hat{\bar{\sigma}}_o^2(1) > \hat{\sigma}_o^2(1),\ \hat{\sigma}^2(1),\ \hat{\sigma}_*^2(1),\ \hat{\sigma}_u^2(1),\ \hat{\bar{\sigma}}_u^2(1). \tag{9.2.19}$$

These results illustrate what is already known from Chapters 5 and 8: Using a contemporaneously aggregated process may lead to forecast improvements while temporal aggregation tends to reduce the forecast efficiency.

It can also be seen from Table 9.6 which forces dominate if there is contemporaneous as well as temporal aggregation. A comparison of $\hat{\sigma}_o^2(1)$ (MSE of forecast based on completely disaggregated process) and $\hat{\sigma}^2(1)$ (MSE of forecast based on fully aggregated process) reveals that their relative efficiency depends on the number K of components of the disaggregate process $\underline{x}_t$ and the number m of periods over which the process is temporally aggregated. If K = m,

$$\hat{\sigma}^2(1) - \hat{\sigma}_o^2(1) = \frac{m^3}{T}\{1 - m + (1-\alpha^2)\frac{m-1}{2}\}$$

$$= \frac{m^3}{T}(1 - m)(1 - \frac{1-\alpha^2}{2}) < 0 \quad \text{for } m \geq 2, \qquad (9.2.20)$$

since $|\alpha| < 1$. Thus, the losses due to temporal aggregation are offset by the efficiency gains due to contemporaneous aggregation and hence, the predictor based on the completely aggregated process asymptotically outperforms the predictor based on the fully disaggregate process.

If the mean of the process $\underline{x}_t$ in (9.2.7) is not assumed known but is estimated, it is easy to see that this adds the same quantity to each of the asymptotic MSEs in Table 9.3 (see also Sections 5.2 and 8.2). Therefore the discussion of an estimated mean term is not very interesting in the context of this example.

9.2.3 Conclusions for Processes With Estimated Coefficients

In summary, the investigation of this section shows that, if the six predictors are based on processes with estimated coefficients rather than known processes, their relative efficiencies may change. Specifically, the "optimal" predictor $y_t^o(h)$, based on the disaggregate process, may not be optimal anymore if the process parameters are estimated. It turns out that efficiency losses may result from using contemporaneously disaggregated rather than aggregated processes, whereas temporal aggregation generally tends to reduce the forecast precision. However, efficiency gains due to contemporaneous aggregation can offset the losses resulting from temporal aggregation.

Note that the efficiency gains from contemporaneous aggregation are essentially a consequence of estimating too many parameters in the unconstrained disaggregate model (see Section 5.2). Ignoring the white noise covariance matrix $\Sigma_{\underline{u}}$, the process in (9.2.7) contains only the single parameter α. If this constraint had been taken into account in the estimation, the predictor $\hat{y}_t^o(h)$, based on the completely disaggregated process, would retain its optimality property. In practice, however, the relevant restrictions are often unknown so that estimating an unconstrained process is not an unreasonable assumption.

Of course, the example process (9.2.7) with $\Sigma_u = I_K$, for which the relative efficiencies of the six predictors have been analyzed, is of a very special kind. The individual component series x_{kt} of $\underline{x}_t$ all have the same AR structure and are independent. It must not be forgotten that, in general, the predictor $\hat{y}_t^o(h)$, based on the fully disaggregate process, is optimal even if estimated coefficients are used. Only under rather special circumstances it may lose its optimality property. Assuming that these asymptotic considerations are valid in small samples, the question is whether or not, for a particular data set, these special circumstances are given. For instance, returning to the introductory example, the monthly tax revenues of the different states are generated by a process of the type (9.2.7) if the revenues in different states are independent and have the same univariate structure and moreover the revenues in different months are generated by structurally identical but independent processes. In this case it may be advantageous to use either contemporaneously aggregated data for prediction or forecast the monthly revenues of the different states individually with univariate time series models and then aggregate the forecasts temporally and contemporaneously. Of course, the first predictor is most attractive whenever all component series are independent and have an identical stochastic structure while the second predictor is to be preferred whenever the AR structure of the components may differ (see Chapter 5). For these predictors to be optimal it is not required that revenues in different months of the year are independent.

In this section the ARMA orders are assumed known. The results remain valid if the orders are estimated consistently. In the next section the asymptotic theory of Section 3.3 will be used to compare the forecast MSEs if estimated processes with unknown orders are used for prediction. A Monte Carlo investigation of the small sample validity of the asymptotic results of this and the next section will be reported in Section 9.4.

9.3 PREDICTION BASED ON ESTIMATED PROCESSES WITH UNKNOWN ORDERS

9.3.1 General Comments

In order to apply the asymptotic results of Section 3.3, it is assumed that the disaggregate K-dimensional system $\underline{x}_t$ is a stationary Gaussian process and has an AR representation of possibly infinite order. Its mean is known to be zero and is not estimated. It follows that the other processes in Table 9.1 are also stationary and Gaussian and have AR representations. Moreover, the other conditions of Section 3.3 are assumed to hold. In particular, finite order AR processes are fitted to the data by multivariate least squares. The orders p(T) of the fitted processes depend on the sample size T used for estimation in such a way that

$$p(T) \to \infty \text{ and } \frac{p(T)^3}{T} \to 0 \quad \text{if } T \to \infty. \tag{9.3.1}$$

In other words, the orders go to infinity with the sample size, at a much slower rate, though. A lower bound for the speed by which p(T) goes to infinity depends on the data generation process and is given in (2.4.47). Estimation and forecasting is assumed to be based on independent processes with identical stochastic structures. Forecasts and MSEs obtained in this way will be furnished with a tilde (~) in the following. The sample size used for estimating temporally disaggregated processes is denoted by T and for temporally aggregated processes T/m data is assumed to be available for estimation.

The asymptotic MSEs of the six predictors under the aforementioned conditions are given in Table 9.7. For example, the asymptotic MSE of $\tilde{y}^o_t(h)$, which is based on the disaggregate data, is

$$\tilde{\sigma}^2_o(h) = (1 + \frac{Kp(T)}{T})\sigma^2_o(h) \ . \tag{9.3.2}$$

This expression follows directly from the asymptotic MSE matrix of the 1-step to r-step predictors given in Section 3.3.1, Proposition 3.2,

$$\tilde{\underline{\Sigma}}_{\underline{X}}(r) = (1 + \frac{Kp(T)}{T})\underline{\Sigma}_{\underline{X}}(r) \ ,$$

where $\underline{\Sigma}_{\underline{X}}(r)$ is the MSE matrix when a known process is used for prediction. Thus, $\tilde{\sigma}^2_o(h) = F_{mhK,mK}\tilde{\underline{\Sigma}}_{\underline{X}}(mh)F'_{mhk,mK}$ is of the form given in (9.3.2). Here $F_{mhK,mK}$ is as defined in (9.2.3).

For the last two MSEs in Table 9.7, $\tilde{\sigma}^2_u(h)$ and $\tilde{\bar{\sigma}}^2_u(h)$, the additional assumption is made that the component series are independent and the same order p(T) or p(T/m) is chosen for each component. The independence assumption has been discussed in more detail in Section 9.2.1. Similar arguments apply here. All MSEs consist of the MSE for a known process and a term due to estimation and specification error that vanishes with growing sample size by (9.3.1). The additive form of these two terms is obtained by noting that, for example, the forecast error associated with $\tilde{y}_t(h)$ is

$$y_{t+h} - \tilde{y}_t(h) = [y_{t+h} - y_t(h)] + [y_t(h) - \tilde{y}_t(h)] \ . \tag{9.3.3}$$

Independence of the two terms in brackets implies that the variance of $y_{t+h} - \tilde{y}_t(h)$ is the sum of the variances of the terms in brackets. Similar arguments apply for the other predictors. Only for $\tilde{y}^u_t(h)$ and

Table 9.7. Asymptotic MSEs of Predictors Based on Processes With Unknown Orders and Estimated Coefficients

Predictor	Asymptotic MSE
$\tilde{y}_t^o(h)$ (based on disaggregate data)	$\tilde{\sigma}_o^2(h) = (1 + \frac{Kp(T)}{T})\sigma_o^2(h)$
$\tilde{y}_t(h)$ (based on temporally and contemporaneously aggregated data)	$\tilde{\sigma}^2(h) = (1 + \frac{p(T/m)}{T/m})\sigma^2(h)$
$\tilde{y}_t^*(h)$ (based on contemporaneously aggregated data)	$\tilde{\sigma}_*^2(h) = (1 + \frac{p(T)}{T})\sigma_*^2(h)$
$\tilde{\bar{y}}_t^o(h)$ (based on temporally aggregated data)	$\tilde{\bar{\sigma}}_o^2(h) = (1 + \frac{Kp(T/m)}{T/m})\bar{\sigma}_o^2(h)$
$\tilde{y}_t^u(h)$ (based on disaggregate univariate series)	$\tilde{\sigma}_u^2(h) = (1 + \frac{p(T)}{T})\sigma_u^2(h)$ a)
$\tilde{\bar{y}}_t^u(h)$ (based on temporally aggregated univariate series)	$\tilde{\bar{\sigma}}_u^2(h) = (1 + \frac{p(T/m)}{T/m})\bar{\sigma}_u^2(h)$ a)

a) provided the same order p(T) [p(T/m)] is chosen for each component series and the components of $\underline{x}_t$ ($\underline{\bar{z}}_t$) are independent

$\tilde{y}^u_t(h)$, in general, breaking down the forecasting errors as in (9.3.3) will not result in two independent terms. Independence of the two terms can be obtained, however, by assuming that the individual components of $\underline{x}_t$ and $\bar{\underline{z}}_t$ are independent (see Section 9.2.1).

The assumption that all orders $p(T)$ $[p(T/m)]$ are identical is merely a convenience. Allowing a different order for each component would make the notation more cumbersome. For example, denoting the order of the AR process fitted to the k-th component of $\bar{\underline{z}}_t$ by $p_k(\cdot)$ the asymptotic MSE of $\tilde{y}^u_t(h)$ is

$$\tilde{\sigma}^2_u(h) = F_{K,K}\begin{bmatrix} (1 + \frac{p_1(T/m)}{T/m})\bar{\sigma}^2_1(h) & & 0 \\ & \ddots & \\ 0 & & (1 + \frac{p_K(T/m)}{T/m})\bar{\sigma}^2_K(h) \end{bmatrix} F'_{K,K} ,$$

where $\bar{\sigma}^2_k(h)$ is the h-step forecasting MSE of the k-th component of $\bar{\underline{z}}_t$ if the corresponding univariate process is known. Note that all the $p_k(\cdot)$ have to satisfy the conditions (9.3.1). Therefore, for the following discussion little is gained by allowing the $p_k(\cdot)$ to be different for different k.

9.3.2 Comparison of MSEs

Condition (9.3.1) guarantees that all six MSEs approach their counterparts for known processes fast as T goes to infinity. Thus, if for instance the disaggregate process $\underline{x}_t$ is such that the predictor $y^o_t(h)$ dominates the five other predictors, then the same will hold for $\tilde{y}^o_t(h)$ if the sample size (length of time series) is large enough. On the other hand, if $\underline{x}_t$ is such that some predictors are identical when based on the known processes, then $\tilde{y}^o_t(h)$ may be dominated by other predictors. For instance, if the components of $\underline{x}_t$ are independent so that $\sigma^2_o(h) = \sigma^2_*(h)$,

$$\tilde{\sigma}^2_*(h) - \tilde{\sigma}^2_o(h) = (1 - K)\frac{p(T)}{T}\sigma^2_o(h) , \qquad (9.3.4)$$

which is negative for $K > 1$. Thus, in this case, using the contemporaneously aggregated process for prediction is better in an asymptotic MSE sense than basing the forecast on the fully disaggregate process $\underline{x}_t$. This result was also obtained in Section 5.3.

A comparison of $\tilde{y}^o_t(h)$ and the corresponding predictor $\tilde{y}_t(h)$, based on the temporally and contemporaneously aggregated process, shows that

$$\tilde{\sigma}^2(h) - \tilde{\sigma}_o^2(h) = \frac{\sigma^2(h)}{T}[mp(\frac{T}{m}) - Kp(T)] , \qquad (9.3.5)$$

provided the two predictors are identical for known processes ($\sigma^2(h) = \sigma_o^2(h)$). Whether the quantity in (9.3.5) is positive or negative depends on the length of the period of temporal aggregation m, the number of component series K and the function $p(\cdot)$. Assuming, in conjunction with condition (9.3.1), that

$$p(T) = T^{1/(3+\delta)} , \qquad (9.3.6)$$

where δ is some positive number, gives

$$[m(\frac{T}{m})^{1/(3+\delta)} - KT^{1/(3+\delta)}] = \left[\frac{m}{m^{1/(3+\delta)}} - K\right]T^{1/(3+\delta)}$$

$$= (m^{(2+\delta)/(3+\delta)} - K)T^{1/(3+\delta)} \qquad (9.3.7)$$

which is always negative if $K \geq m > 1$. Depending on δ it will also often be negative if K is substantially less than m. Suppose, for instance, that a monthly process is temporally aggregated to obtain an annual process so that m = 12 and assume that δ is very close to zero. Then the expression in (9.3.7) is negative for $K \geq 6$. Hence, using the fully aggregated process for forecasting may be superior to aggregating the forecasts of the fully disaggregated process provided the length of the period of temporal aggregation m is not large compared to the number of component series K that are aggregated contemporaneously.

This result suggests that also when the process orders are assumed unknown, temporal aggregation reduces the forecast efficiency while contemporaneous aggregation may result in forecast improvements. This conclusion is in agreement with the results in Chapters 5 and 8. One implication is that when all six predictors are identical for known processes, the predictor $\tilde{y}_t^*(h)$ which is based on contemporaneously aggregated data is optimal. Assuming that the univariate components of $\underline{x}_t$ are independent, $p(\cdot)$ is such that

$$p(T) < mp(T/m) , \qquad (9.3.8)$$

and all predictors are identical for known processes, it is easy to see that

$$\tilde{\sigma}_*^2(h) = \tilde{\sigma}_u^2(h) < \tilde{\sigma}_o^2(h),\ \tilde{\sigma}^2(h),\ \tilde{\bar{\sigma}}_o^2(h),\ \tilde{\bar{\sigma}}_u^2(h) \ . \tag{9.3.9}$$

Furthermore, under these conditions the predictor $\tilde{\bar{y}}_t(h)$ based on the temporally aggregated multivariate process is least efficient, that is,

$$\tilde{\bar{\sigma}}_o^2(h) > \tilde{\sigma}_o^2(h),\ \tilde{\sigma}^2(h),\ \tilde{\sigma}_*^2(h),\ \tilde{\sigma}_u^2(h),\ \tilde{\bar{\sigma}}_u^2(h) \ . \tag{9.3.10}$$

Using the expressions in Table 9.7 makes it easy to perform other comparisons. Note that all results are in agreement with the results for processes with known orders and estimated coefficients derived in Section 9.2. Here, however, they crucially depend on the assumption for the AR orders $p(\cdot)$.

9.3.3 Summary and Discussion of Results for Processes With Unknown Orders

The foregoing results show that the overall ranking of the predictors may change if the underlying processes are not known and must be specified and estimated on the basis of the available data. Note, however, that equality of some or all predictors holds only for special disaggregate processes $\underline{x}_t$ and it is not obvious that such processes are likely to be met in practice. For instance, all predictors are identical for forecast horizons $h = 1,2,...$ if the individual component series all have the same MA structure, are intertemporally uncorrelated with each other and there is no correlation between observations s periods apart if s is not an integer multiple of m. Although these are only sufficient and not necessary conditions for the equality of the predictors based on known processes, they indicate the special nature of processes $\underline{x}_t$ for which equality of all predictors holds for all h.

Of course, for $\tilde{y}_t^o(h)$ to lose its optimality property it is not necessary that all predictors are identical. If, for instance, the individual components of $\underline{x}_t$ are independent but may have different correlation structures, then $y_t^o(h) = y_t^u(h)$ and thus, the predictor $\tilde{y}_t^u(h)$, based on univariate models for the component series of $\underline{x}_t$, will be superior to $\tilde{y}_t^o(h)$ for any h. Nevertheless, these are fairly special conditions and, for real life data, the predictor $\tilde{y}_t^o(h)$ may still be optimal in most cases.

On the other hand, all the results of this section are based on asymptotic theory and it is possible that in small samples the optimality of $\tilde{y}_t^o(h)$ is lost even if equality of the predictors does not hold exactly for known processes. In particular, the requirements for the process orders are very much asymptotic conditions as explained in previous chapters. In this context it may be worth noting again that for any stationary, nondeterministic process all the predictors become approximately identical as the forecast horizon h goes to infinity. Thus, for long range forecasting $\tilde{y}_t^o(h)$ may not be optimal in small samples. In the next section some simulation results are discussed to investigate whether or not the asymptotic theory is a good indicator for the small sample performance of the six predictors.

9.4 MONTE CARLO COMPARISON OF PREDICTORS

Realizations of a bivariate (K = 2), finite order AR process of the type (9.2.7) considered in Section 9.2 and of a bivariate MA process were generated to compare the small sample efficiencies of the six predictors under investigation. The length of the period of temporal aggregation for both processes is m = 2. For both bivariate processes the white noise processes consist of independent pseudo normal random numbers with zero mean and variance 1, generated by a NAG library subroutine. Thus, the covariance matrix of the white noise processes is the identity matrix. MSEs of 1-step and 5-step ahead forecasts of the temporal and contemporaneous aggregate y_t will be reported for three different sample sizes T = 60, 100, and 200 for temporally disaggregated series and the corresponding lengths of the temporally aggregated series are T/2. In addition to the sample values, lagged values are taken from the presample period where required for (multivariate) LS estimation. For each of the two processes 600 realizations were generated and for each realization 50 values were discarded at the beginning of the series to reduce the impact of starting-up values. All processes have been estimated without zero restrictions for the parameters. In accordance with the asymptotic theory of Section 9.3 only pure, finite order AR processes were fitted to the data. The three criteria AIC, HQ, and SC were used to choose the orders p of the processes fitted to the aggregated and disaggregated series. The statistic $\hat{\rho}$ given in Section 3.5 is used to assess the significance of differences between the forecast MSEs. Thus the design of the Monte Carlo experiment is essentially the same as in Chapters 5, 7, and 8. The simulation results for the two processes will now be discussed in detail.

9.4.1 Simulation Results for AR Process

The first process used in the simulation study is the bivariate AR(2)

$$\underline{x}_t = \underline{\nu} + A\underline{x}_{t-2} + \underline{u}_t , \qquad (9.4.1)$$

where $\underline{x}_t = (x_{1t},x_{2t})'$, $\underline{u}_t = (u_{1t},u_{2t})'$, $\underline{\nu} = (1,1)'$, $A = 0.5I_2$, and $\Sigma_{\underline{u}} = I_2$. This type of process has been discussed in detail in Section 9.2 (see (9.2.7)). The implied aggregate and component processes for $m = 2$ are

$$z_t = 2 + 0.5z_{t-2} + v_t , \quad \sigma_v^2 = 2 , \qquad (9.4.2)$$

$$\underline{\bar{z}}_{\mathcal{t}} = \begin{bmatrix} 2 \\ 2 \end{bmatrix} + 0.5\underline{\bar{z}}_{\mathcal{t}-1} + \underline{\bar{w}}_{\mathcal{t}} , \quad \Sigma_{\underline{\bar{w}}} = 2I_2 , \qquad (9.4.3)$$

$$y_{\mathcal{t}} = 4 + 0.5y_{\mathcal{t}-1} + \nu_{\mathcal{t}} , \quad \sigma_\nu^2 = 4 , \qquad (9.4.4)$$

$$x_{kt} = 1 + 0.5x_{k,t-2} + u_{kt} , \quad \sigma_{u_k}^2 = 1 , \quad k = 1,2 , \qquad (9.4.5)$$

$$\bar{z}_{k\mathcal{t}} = 2 + 0.5\bar{z}_{k,\mathcal{t}-1} + \bar{w}_{k\mathcal{t}} , \quad \sigma_{\bar{w}_k}^2 = 2 , \quad k = 1,2 , \qquad (9.4.6)$$

(see Table 9.4). Thus, all the processes are of finite order AR type. The MSEs of all resulting predictors are identical for known processes, i.e. (9.2.8) holds. Using such a process is useful because MSE differences will only result from estimating the processes and the MSE parts due to estimation are of primary interest here.

If the predictors are obtained using estimated coefficients while assuming that the process orders are known, the following relationships among the asymptotic MSEs were found in Section 9.2:

$$\hat{\sigma}_*^2(1) = \hat{\sigma}_u^2(1) < \hat{\sigma}_o^2(1), \ \hat{\sigma}^2(1), \ \hat{\bar{\sigma}}_o^2(1), \ \hat{\bar{\sigma}}_u^2(1) , \qquad (9.4.7)$$

that is, the predictors based on contemporaneously aggregated data or the univariate components of the disaggregate process are best (see (9.2.18)). Also,

$$\hat{\bar{\sigma}}_o^2(1) > \hat{\sigma}_o^2(1), \ \hat{\sigma}^2(1), \ \hat{\sigma}_*^2(1), \ \hat{\sigma}_u^2(1), \ \hat{\bar{\sigma}}_u^2(1) , \qquad (9.4.8)$$

that is, the predictor based on the temporally aggregated multivariate process is inferior to all other predictors. Note, however, that the assumptions underlying the asymptotic theory in Section 9.2 are not strictly satisfied in the Monte Carlo experiment. While it was assumed in Section 9.2 that independent processes are used for estimation and forecasting, the same series is used for both purposes in the simulations because this is a more realistic approach from a practical point of view.

In Table 9.8 the MSEs obtained in the simulation experiment are given for different sample sizes and forecast horizons h = 1 and 5. By and large the simulation results are in agreement with the asymptotic results. In Table 9.9 the differences between the empirical MSEs are displayed in qualitative form for the case where the true AR orders are used. The asymptotic inequalities (9.4.7) and (9.4.8) are indeed in most cases satisfied. Out of the 78 cases listed in Table 9.9, in three cases only the MSE differences are significant at the 5% level when (9.4.7) or (9.4.8) is not satisfied.

In the upper part of Table 9.8 (true order), for sample sizes T = 200 (T/m = 100 for temporally aggregated series) all MSEs are very close together. This again is in agreement with the asymptotic theory since for large samples the difference between the MSEs should diminish due to increased estimation precision. Note that for all three sample sizes the 5-step MSEs are very close together. Thus, for long term forecasting there is no clear winner. This again is in line with the asymptotic considerations because the 5-step forecasts are approximately the sample means given that only low order AR processes have been fitted.

In Section 9.2 it was shown that the gains due to contemporaneous aggregation off-set the losses incurred by temporal aggregation if m = K as in the present case. Thus the asymptotic MSE $\hat{\sigma}^2(1)$ is lower than $\hat{\sigma}_o^2(1)$ for the present process. In Table 9.8 it can be seen that this holds also for the small samples considered in the Monte Carlo study.

It is perhaps worth noting that a comparison of the sizes of the MSEs for different sample sizes is not useful given a number of replications of R = 600. Although this number may seem quite high, the standard errors of the MSEs are still substantial. For example, if the MSEs had been computed from known instead of estimated processes, their standard errors for $y_t(h)$ would be

$$\sigma^2(h)\sqrt{2/R} \; . \qquad (9.4.9)$$

This number is, for instance, $4\sqrt{2/600} = 0.231$ for $y_t(1)$ (see Chapter 5, Section 5.5.2). Since the MSEs are computed using estimated coefficients their standard errors are likely to be even greater. The correlation of MSEs for different sample sizes, on the other hand, will be relatively

Table 9.8. Forecast MSEs for Temporally and Contemporaneously Aggregated Bivariate AR(2)

order	sample size T of disaggregate process	forecast horizon h	forecast MSEs					
			$\sigma_o^2(h)$	$\sigma^2(h)$	$\sigma_*^2(h)$	$\bar{\sigma}_o^2(h)$	$\sigma_u^2(h)$	$\bar{\sigma}_u^2(h)$
true order, p = 1 or 2	60	1	4.80	4.60	4.58	4.90	4.64	4.67
		5	6.31	6.27	6.28	6.37	6.36	6.39
	100	1	4.13	4.06	4.03	4.22	4.04	4.10
		5	5.83	5.82	5.83	5.81	5.83	5.83
	200	1	3.84	3.77	3.78	3.80	3.73	3.71
		5	5.20	5.23	5.22	5.19	5.19	5.18
p(AIC)	60	1	4.92	5.01	4.72	5.31	4.69	4.95
		5	6.36	6.43	6.32	6.56	6.40	6.51
	100	1	4.20	4.22	4.10	4.37	4.10	4.20
		5	5.83	5.85	5.83	5.78	5.87	5.92
	200	1	3.86	3.78	3.87	3.84	3.78	3.77
		5	5.20	5.24	5.26	5.19	5.20	5.27
p(HQ)	60	1	4.90	4.96	4.64	5.30	4.72	4.83
		5	6.33	6.44	6.31	6.49	6.41	6.45
	100	1	4.15	4.16	4.06	4.29	4.10	4.16
		5	5.83	5.82	5.84	5.79	5.82	5.89
	200	1	3.84	3.77	3.80	3.81	3.75	3.75
		5	5.20	5.23	5.22	5.19	5.19	5.23
p(SC)	60	1	5.25	4.95	4.73	5.17	4.74	4.86
		5	6.31	6.37	6.29	6.38	6.35	6.39
	100	1	4.25	4.17	4.10	4.34	4.09	4.16
		5	5.83	5.83	5.84	5.81	5.83	5.84
	200	1	3.84	3.76	3.78	3.81	3.75	3.76
		5	5.20	5.22	5.22	5.19	5.19	5.18

Table 9.9. Relations Between MSEs When the AR Orders are Known - Underlying Disaggregate Process: Bivariate AR(2)

	T	h	$\hat{\sigma}_o^2(h)$	$\hat{\sigma}^2(h)$	$\hat{\bar{\sigma}}_o^2(h)$	$\hat{\bar{\sigma}}_u^2(h)$
$\hat{\sigma}_*^2(h)$	60	1	$<^a$	$<$	$<^a$	$<$
		5	$<$	$>$	$<^a$	$<^a$
	100	1	$<^a$	$<$	$<^a$	$<$
		5	$<$	$>$	$>$	$<$
	200	1	$<^a$	$>$	$<$	$>$
		5	$>^a$	$>$	$>$	$>^a$
$\hat{\sigma}_u^2(h)$	60	1	$<^a$	$>$	$<^a$	$<$
		5	$<$	$>$	$<$	$<$
	100	1	$<$	$<$	$<^a$	$<^a$
		5	$<$	$>$	$>$	$<$
	200	1	$<^a$	$<$	$<$	$>$
		5	$<$	$<^a$	$<$	$>$

	T	h	$\hat{\sigma}_o^2(h)$	$\hat{\sigma}^2(h)$	$\hat{\sigma}_*^2(h)$	$\hat{\sigma}_u^2(h)$	$\hat{\bar{\sigma}}_u^2(h)$
$\hat{\bar{\sigma}}_o^2(h)$	60	1	$>$	$>^a$	$>^a$	$>^a$	$>^a$
		5	$>^a$	$>^a$	$>^a$	$>$	$<$
	100	1	$>^a$	$>^a$	$>^a$	$>^a$	$>^a$
		5	$<$	$<$	$<$	$<$	$<$
	200	1	$<$	$>$	$>$	$>$	$>^a$
		5	$<$	$<^a$	$<$	$>$	$>$

a) significant at 5% level.

low. Therefore, the standard errors in (9.4.9) give an indication of their sampling variability. This does not mean, however, that 600 replications is too small a number to draw any conclusions from the Monte Carlo experiment. In fact, as indicated by the statistic $\hat{\rho}$ from Section 3.5, a comparison of MSEs for the same sample size and forecast horizon is meaningful as these MSEs are based on the same data and therefore are highly correlated.

For the present example the process orders were also estimated by the criteria AIC, HQ, and SC. The maximum order for nontemporally aggregated series was $P = 6$ and for temporally aggregated series $P = 4$ was used. The resulting frequency distributions for the orders are given in Table 9.10. The maximum orders were not very restrictive since they were not attained very often. The consistent criteria HQ and SC have picked the correct order quite often for $T = 100$ and 200 ($T/m = 50$, 100 for temporally aggregated data). All three criteria have a tendency to underestimate the true order more frequently when less sample information is available. The AR orders chosen do not necessarily increase on average with increasing sample size, however, as required by the asymptotic theory in Section 9.3 (see (9.3.1)). Furthermore in the comparison of MSEs in Section 9.3 it was assumed that the same order $p(T)$ $[p(T/m)]$ is chosen for all nontemporally [temporally] aggregated processes. This condition is clearly violated. For instance, the average orders for $\underline{x}_t$ and z_t chosen by SC are 1.21 and 1.73, respectively, for $T = 60$. Similar comments apply for other criteria, sample sizes, and processes.

Also, the condition $p(T) < m\, p(T/m)$ which was used in comparing the MSEs in Section 9.3 (see (9.3.8)) is not satisfied on the average in the simulation study. For example, for $T/m = 30$, SC chooses an average order of 0.83 for y_t and, for $T = 60$, it chooses an average order of 1.73 for z_t. The latter is obviously more than twice as much as the former value. Similar results hold for other criteria and processes.

Thus, the asymptotic assumptions imposed for the process orders in Section 9.3 to derive asymptotic results are not satisfied in the present Monte Carlo study in small samples. From a practical point of view it seems nevertheless more logical to use some specification criterion for determining the order rather than specifying an arbitrary number or sequence of numbers that satisfies asymptotic conditions. In practice usually only one set of data is available for which a process order must be chosen.

The MSEs resulting from the processes with estimated orders are also given in Table 9.8. For the consistent criteria HQ and SC, one

Table 9.10. Frequency Distribution of Estimated AR Orders in Percent - Underlying Disaggregate Process: Bivariate AR(2)*

sample size T	AR order	$\underline{x}_t = (x_{1t}, x_{2t})'$			z_t			x_{1t}			x_{2t}		
		p(AIC)	p(HQ)	p(SC)	p(AIC)	p(HQ)	p(SC)	p(AIC)	p(HQ)	p(SC)	p(AIC)	p(HQ)	p(SC)
60	0	2	9	39	4	8	17	3	7	13	2	7	15
	1	0	1	1	1	2	3	1	1	1	1	2	2
	2	76	86	60	70	77	75	74	82	82	67	78	77
	3	11	2	0	12	7	4	9	6	3	13	7	5
	4	5	2	0	7	4	2	5	3	1	7	4	1
	5	3	1	0	4	2	0	5	2	0	6	2	0
	6	3	0	0	3	1	0	4	1	0	4	1	0
100	0	0	1	7	0	0	2	0	1	2	0	0	3
	1	0	0	0	0	0	0	0	0	1	0	0	0
	2	87	97	93	75	89	94	77	88	95	72	87	93
	3	8	2	0	10	7	3	10	6	2	13	9	4
	4	3	1	0	7	3	0	6	3	1	6	3	1
	5	2	0	0	4	1	0	4	2	0	4	1	0
	6	1	0	0	4	1	0	3	1	0	5	0	0
200	0	0	0	0	0	0	0	0	0	0	0	0	0
	1	0	0	0	0	0	0	0	0	0	0	0	0
	2	89	99	100	72	91	97	77	95	98	77	92	98
	3	7	1	0	13	7	3	9	4	2	11	6	2
	4	3	0	0	6	1	0	7	2	0	6	1	0
	5	1	0	0	5	0	0	4	0	0	4	1	0
	6	1	0	0	5	0	0	2	1	0	2	0	0

*) Some columns do not sum to 100 due to rounding errors.

Table 9.10. (continued)*

sample size T/m	AR order	y_t p(AIC)	y_t p(HQ)	y_t p(SC)	$\bar{z}_t = (\bar{z}_{1t}, \bar{z}_{2t})'$ p(AIC)	$\bar{z}_t$ p(HQ)	$\bar{z}_t$ p(SC)	$\bar{z}_{1t}$ p(AIC)	$\bar{z}_{1t}$ p(HQ)	$\bar{z}_{1t}$ p(SC)	$\bar{z}_{2t}$ p(AIC)	$\bar{z}_{2t}$ p(HQ)	$\bar{z}_{2t}$ p(SC)
30	0	14	18	29	12	21	42	13	17	28	13	19	26
	1	62	65	62	66	69	56	63	66	64	61	64	65
	2	13	11	7	12	7	2	11	9	6	14	11	7
	3	7	4	1	5	2	0	7	5	2	8	4	2
	4	5	3	1	6	1	0	6	4	1	5	2	1
50	0	3	5	9	1	4	12	2	4	8	3	4	9
	1	72	80	83	81	91	88	72	81	87	72	80	85
	2	14	11	6	12	5	1	13	9	4	14	10	5
	3	6	3	1	3	1	0	8	4	1	6	4	1
	4	5	2	1	2	0	0	5	2	1	6	2	0
100	0	0	0	0	0	0	0	0	0	0	0	0	2
	1	78	89	94	86	98	100	78	90	98	76	88	96
	2	11	7	4	10	2	0	11	7	2	13	9	4
	3	8	2	1	3	0	0	7	2	1	6	2	0
	4	3	1	0	1	0	0	4	1	0	5	1	0

*) Some columns do not sum to 100 due to rounding errors.

would expect, for large samples, to find similar results as in the case where the true order is assumed known. This expectation is in fact confirmed by the results in Table 9.8. Moreover, for T = 60 and 100(T/m = 30 and 50) $\tilde{y}^*_t(1)$ and $\tilde{y}^u_t(1)$ are best for all three criteria and $\tilde{\tilde{y}}^o_t(1)$ is the worst predictor using AIC or HQ. These results are fully in line with the asymptotic results of Sections 9.2 and 9.3. Using the SC criterion $\tilde{\sigma}^2_o(1)$ is the largest MSE for T = 60. One reason for the predictor $\tilde{y}^o_t(1)$, based on the disaggregate multivariate process, to be inferior to the other predictors may be that SC often underestimates the true AR order for this sample size. In Table 9.10 it can be seen that p(SC) = 0 in 39% of all cases for the disaggregate process $\underline{x}_t$. Note, however, that, using the statistic $\hat{\rho}$, the difference between $\tilde{\sigma}^2_o(1)$ and $\tilde{\tilde{\sigma}}^2_o(1)$ is not significant at the 5% level.

For longer term forecasting (h = 5) or large sample size (T = 200, T/m = 100), all MSEs are very close together and most of the differences are not significant at the 5% level. For large samples this is in accordance with the asymptotic theory whereas for h = 5 a similar argument applies as in the case of known process orders. That is, since mostly low-order processes are involved the forecasts are approximately the sample means in most cases. This explains the similarity of the forecasts.

Overall the asymptotic theory seems to be a good guide to the small sample performance of the different predictors for the AR process considered in this subsection. This conclusion holds despite the discrepancies between the asymptotic assumptions and the conditions governing the Monte Carlo experiment. In the next subsection the simulation results for an MA process will be discussed.

9.4.2 Simulation Results for MA Process

The second process used for simulation purposes is the bivariate MA(2)

$$\begin{bmatrix} x_{1t} \\ x_{2t} \end{bmatrix} = \begin{bmatrix} 1 \\ 1 \end{bmatrix} + \begin{bmatrix} u_{1t} \\ u_{2t} \end{bmatrix} + \begin{bmatrix} 0.5 & 0 \\ 0 & 0.5 \end{bmatrix} \begin{bmatrix} u_{1,t-2} \\ u_{2,t-2} \end{bmatrix}, \quad \Sigma_{\underline{u}} = I_2, \qquad (9.4.10)$$

which has an infinite AR representation, a situation fully in line with the asymptotic theory of Section 9.3. Temporal aggregation over two periods (m = 2) yields the bivariate MA(1)

$$\begin{bmatrix} \bar{z}_{1t} \\ \bar{z}_{2t} \end{bmatrix} = \begin{bmatrix} 2 \\ 2 \end{bmatrix} + \begin{bmatrix} \bar{w}_{1t} \\ \bar{w}_{2t} \end{bmatrix} + \begin{bmatrix} 0.5 & 0 \\ 0 & 0.5 \end{bmatrix} \begin{bmatrix} \bar{w}_{1,t-1} \\ \bar{w}_{2,t-1} \end{bmatrix}, \quad \Sigma_{\bar{\underline{w}}} = 2I_2 , \qquad (9.4.11)$$

where $\bar{z}_{kt} = x_{k,2t} + x_{k,2t-1}$ and $\bar{w}_{kt} = u_{k,2t} + u_{k,2t-1}$. Furthermore, contemporaneous aggregation of the two components of (9.4.10) results in the univariate MA(2)

$$z_t = x_{1t} + x_{2t} = 2 + v_t + 0.5v_{t-2}, \quad \sigma_v^2 = 2 , \qquad (9.4.12)$$

where $v_t = u_{1t} + u_{2t}$. Joint temporal and contemporaneous aggregation gives the MA(1) process

$$y_t = 4 + \nu_t + 0.5\nu_{t-1}, \quad \sigma_\nu^2 = 4 , \qquad (9.4.13)$$

where $y_t = x_{1,2t} + x_{1,2t-1} + x_{2,2t} + x_{2,2t-1}$ and $\nu_t = u_{1,2t} + u_{1,2t-1} + u_{2,2t} + u_{2,2t-1}$. The univariate component series of $\underline{x}_t$ are MA(2) processes,

$$x_{kt} = 1 + u_{kt} + 0.5u_{k,t-2} , \qquad (9.4.14)$$

and the component series of $\bar{\underline{z}}_t$ are MA(1) processes,

$$\bar{z}_{kt} = 2 + \bar{w}_{kt} + 0.5\bar{w}_{k,t-1} , \quad \text{for} \quad k = 1,2. \qquad (9.4.15)$$

For these processes the MSEs of the six predictors are all identical when the processes are assumed to be known (see Section 6.3). On the other hand, using the asymptotic theory of Section 9.3 the following relations are obtained for the MSEs based on estimated processes:

$$\tilde{\sigma}_*^2(h) = \tilde{\sigma}_u^2(h) < \tilde{\sigma}_o^2(h),\ \tilde{\sigma}^2(h),\ \tilde{\bar{\sigma}}_o^2(h),\ \tilde{\bar{\sigma}}_u^2(h) \qquad (9.4.16)$$

(see (9.3.9)) and

$$\tilde{\bar{\sigma}}_o^2(h) > \tilde{\sigma}_o^2(h),\ \tilde{\sigma}^2(h),\ \tilde{\sigma}_*^2(h),\ \tilde{\sigma}_u^2(h),\ \tilde{\bar{\sigma}}_u^2(h) \qquad (9.4.17)$$

(see (9.3.10)), provided the orders are chosen in the way discussed in Section 9.3.

In the simulation experiment the orders are again selected by the three criteria AIC, HQ, and SC. The frequency distributions of the order estimates are displayed in Table 9.11. The maximum order for series that are not temporally aggregated is again P = 6 for all three sample sizes T = 60, 100, and 200, whereas for temporally aggregated series the maximum AR order is P = 4. Again these choices of the maximum orders are not very restrictive since none of the three selection criteria has chosen the maximum order very often (in most cases for much less than 20% of the replications). All criteria increase the average order chosen with increasing sample size which is in agreement with conditions (9.3.1). Like for the AR process, the following (asymptotic) conditions for $p(\cdot)$ are required for the inequalities (9.4.16) and (9.4.17) to hold: (i) The orders $p(T)$ [$p(T/m)$] for all processes based on nontemporally [temporally] aggregated data are the same and (ii) $p(T) < mp(T/m)$ or, in other words, the orders of the processes based on nontemporally aggregated data are less than twice the orders for the corresponding aggregated processes. Again, for the finite samples these conditions are clearly not satisfied. For instance, the orders chosen on average for the nontemporally aggregated series $\underline{x}_t$ and z_t are quite different. For T = 60, p(AIC), p(HQ), and p(SC) are on average 2.89, 1.64, and 0.52, respectively, for $\underline{x}_t$. The corresponding figures for z_t are 3.60, 2.56, and 1.73. Thus, (i) is violated. Similar results hold for $\mathfrak{y}_t$ and $\bar{\mathfrak{z}}_t$. Also, the inequality $p(T) < mp(T/m)$ is not in all cases satisfied on average.

The MSEs obtained in the Monte Carlo experiment are given in Table 9.12. For the AIC criterion they are in good agreement with what one would expect on the basis of the asymptotic theory of Section 9.3. More precisely, the inequalities (9.4.16) and (9.4.17) are either satisfied or the difference between the MSEs is not significant at the 5% level. In Table 9.13 the differences between the MSEs obtained with AIC are indicated. The upper part of Table 9.13 refers to the inequalities in (9.4.16). Note that $\tilde{\sigma}_u^2(h)$ (forecasts based on disaggregate univariate components) and $\tilde{\sigma}_*^2(h)$ (forecasts based on contemporaneously aggregated process) are in most cases not significantly different, the only exception being when T = 60 and h = 5. This again is in agreement with asymptotic theory. Table 9.13 shows that the inequalities (9.4.16) are more often significant for small sample sizes. This is also in line with the asymptotic theory which suggests that the differences disappear when the sample size becomes large.

The lower part of Table 9.13 refers to the inequalities (9.4.17). Again the differences between $\bar{\tilde{\sigma}}_o^2(h)$ (forecasts based on the temporally aggregated multivariate process) and all other MSEs are either significant and have the expected sign or they are insignificant. For T = 100

Table 9.11. Frequency Distribution of Estimated AR Orders in Percent - Underlying Disaggregate Process: Bivariate MA(2)*

sample size T	AR order	$\underline{x}_t = (x_{1t}, x_{2t})'$			z_t			x_{1t}			x_{2t}		
		p(AIC)	p(HQ)	p(SC)	p(AIC)	p(HQ)	p(SC)	p(AIC)	p(HQ)	p(SC)	p(AIC)	p(HQ)	p(SC)
60	0	5	29	73	5	11	29	4	11	29	5	11	31
	1	1	3	5	1	3	6	1	2	3	2	3	5
	2	50	54	22	38	47	48	37	47	48	35	49	48
	3	7	4	1	7	7	4	7	7	4	7	7	4
	4	27	9	0	32	25	12	34	26	15	36	24	11
	5	7	1	0	10	4	1	10	5	1	10	6	1
	6	4	0	0	8	3	1	8	2	0	6	1	0
100	0	0	6	39	1	1	7	0	2	9	0	2	10
	1	0	0	1	0	0	0	0	0	0	0	0	1
	2	40	78	59	25	46	65	24	44	64	27	47	67
	3	4	3	1	4	6	3	4	4	4	4	4	2
	4	44	13	1	47	39	23	49	40	21	47	38	18
	5	8	0	0	13	5	1	12	5	1	11	6	2
	6	5	0	0	10	3	1	12	5	1	11	4	0
200	0	0	0	1	0	0	0	0	0	0	0	0	0
	1	0	0	0	0	0	0	0	0	0	0	0	0
	2	13	63	97	9	25	54	9	25	56	8	27	56
	3	1	1	0	1	2	2	1	1	1	1	1	2
	4	65	35	3	54	59	41	55	61	40	56	59	38
	5	8	0	0	11	6	2	12	5	1	12	6	2
	6	14	1	0	25	9	2	24	9	2	24	7	2

*) Some columns do not sum to 100 due to rounding errors.

Table 9.11. (continued)*

sample size T/m	AR order	y_t p(AIC)	y_t p(HQ)	y_t p(SC)	$\bar{z}_t = (\bar{z}_{1t}, \bar{z}_{2t})'$ p(AIC)	$\bar{z}_t$ p(HQ)	$\bar{z}_t$ p(SC)	$\bar{z}_{1t}$ p(AIC)	$\bar{z}_{1t}$ p(HQ)	$\bar{z}_{1t}$ p(SC)	$\bar{z}_{2t}$ p(AIC)	$\bar{z}_{2t}$ p(HQ)	$\bar{z}_{2t}$ p(SC)
30	0	15	22	34	17	30	62	12	20	35	16	21	35
	1	31	34	34	37	39	30	31	35	39	32	36	40
	2	32	29	24	30	24	7	35	32	22	32	30	21
	3	11	8	5	8	4	1	10	7	3	11	8	3
	4	12	7	3	9	3	0	12	6	1	10	5	1
50	0	2	5	14	3	12	36	2	6	14	3	6	16
	1	31	40	50	39	57	55	28	41	51	34	42	52
	2	44	42	31	42	28	9	45	40	32	40	39	28
	3	10	7	3	8	2	0	11	7	2	10	7	3
	4	13	6	2	8	2	0	14	7	1	13	6	1
100	0	0	0	1	0	0	3	0	0	1	0	1	2
	1	15	27	43	20	48	81	14	24	44	19	31	48
	2	50	55	50	58	48	16	50	56	47	48	50	46
	3	18	12	5	15	4	0	18	14	6	18	11	4
	4	17	6	1	8	0	0	18	6	2	15	8	2

*) Some columns do not sum to 100 due to rounding errors.

Table 9.12. Forecasting MSEs for Temporally and Contemporaneously Aggregated Bivariate MA(2)

order	sample size T of disaggregate process	forecast horizon h	forecast MSEs $\sigma_o^2(h)$	$\sigma^2(h)$	$\sigma_*^2(h)$	$\bar{\sigma}_o^2(h)$	$\sigma_u^2(h)$	$\bar{\sigma}_u^2(h)$
p(AIC)	60	1	4.90	4.79	4.63	5.28	4.46	4.68
		5	5.46	5.60	5.34	5.54	5.11	5.32
	100	1	4.08	4.02	3.98	4.26	3.84	3.84
		5	4.94	4.98	4.97	5.03	4.95	5.06
	200	1	4.64	4.53	4.51	4.80	4.45	4.52
		5	5.32	5.33	5.33	5.30	5.31	5.35
p(HQ)	60	1	4.99	4.82	4.72	5.24	4.51	4.76
		5	5.04	5.53	5.36	5.51	5.08	5.22
	100	1	4.13	4.00	4.07	4.15	3.91	3.82
		5	4.92	4.98	4.96	4.97	4.97	4.97
	200	1	4.66	4.60	4.55	4.78	4.48	4.53
		5	5.32	5.35	5.33	5.34	5.32	5.31
p(SC)	60	1	5.06	5.03	4.95	4.97	4.70	4.87
		5	5.04	5.46	5.33	5.18	5.02	5.17
	100	1	4.49	4.15	4.20	4.38	4.03	4.00
		5	4.93	4.98	4.97	4.96	4.95	4.95
	200	1	4.58	4.64	4.60	4.70	4.46	4.59
		5	5.32	5.37	5.33	5.32	5.30	5.31

Table 9.13. Relations Between MSEs when AR Orders are Determined by AIC - Underlying Disaggregate Process: Bivariate MA(2)

	T	h	$\tilde{\sigma}_o^2(h)$	$\tilde{\sigma}^2(h)$	$\tilde{\tilde{\sigma}}_o^2(h)$	$\tilde{\tilde{\sigma}}_u^2(h)$
$\tilde{\sigma}_*^2(h)$	60	1	$<^a$	$<$	$<^a$	$<$
		5	$<^a$	$<^a$	$<^a$	$>$
	100	1	$<$	$<$	$<^a$	$>$
		5	$>$	$<$	$<$	$<$
	200	1	$<^a$	$<$	$<^a$	$<$
		5	$>$	$=$	$>$	$<$
$\tilde{\sigma}_u^2(h)$	60	1	$<^a$	$<^a$	$<^a$	$<^a$
		5	$<^a$	$<^a$	$<^a$	$<^a$
	100	1	$<^a$	$<$	$<^a$	$=$
		5	$>$	$<$	$<$	$<^a$
	200	1	$<^a$	$<$	$<^a$	$<$
		5	$<$	$<$	$>$	$<$

	T	h	$\tilde{\sigma}_o^2(h)$	$\tilde{\sigma}^2(h)$	$\tilde{\sigma}_*^2(h)$	$\tilde{\sigma}_u^2(h)$	$\tilde{\tilde{\sigma}}_u^2(h)$
$\bar{\tilde{\sigma}}_o^2(h)$	60	1	$>^a$	$>^a$	$>^a$	$>^a$	$>^a$
		5	$>$	$<$	$>^a$	$>^a$	$>^a$
	100	1	$>$	$>^a$	$>^a$	$>^a$	$>^a$
		5	$>$	$>$	$>$	$>$	$<$
	200	1	$>^a$	$>^a$	$>^a$	$>^a$	$>^a$
		5	$<$	$<$	$<$	$<$	$<$

a) significant at 5% level.

and 200 and h = 5 all differences are insignificant. In summary, Table 9.13 shows that, using AIC for determining the AR order, the small sample results are quite nicely in line with what one would expect on the basis of the asymptotic theory of Section 9.3 despite the deviations from the conditions underlying the large sample theory. As a further confirmation of this conclusion note that the predictor $\tilde{y}_t^o(1)$, based on the fully disaggregated data, is inferior to the predictor $\tilde{y}_t(1)$, based on fully aggregated data, that is, $\tilde{\sigma}_o^2(1) > \tilde{\sigma}^2(1)$, for all three sample sizes. The differences are not significant though.

For the HQ criterion the inequalities (9.4.16) and (9.4.17) are also in most cases satisfied when significant differences are present (see Table 9.14). The only exceptions are that $\tilde{\sigma}_*^2(5)$ is significantly greater than $\tilde{\sigma}_o^2(5)$ for T = 60 and $\tilde{\sigma}_*^2(1)$ is significantly greater than $\tilde{\tilde{\sigma}}_u^2(1)$ for T = 100. For longer term forecasting (h = 5) and T = 100 or 200 (T/m = 50 or 100 for temporally aggregated processes) the differences are again insignificant. Thus, like for AIC, using the HQ criterion, the small sample results are overall in accordance with the asymptotic theory.

The situation is somewhat different for the SC criterion. Table 9.15 is based on the results obtained by SC and also relates to the inequalities (9.4.16) and (9.4.17). Here the direction of the inequality signs between the MSEs is not always in agreement with the large sample inequalities. This result can be interpreted as an indication that the asymptotic theory cannot be used to predict the forecast efficiencies of the different predictors if a parsimonious model building procedure is used. Note that using SC does not necessarily result in inferior forecasts although most 1-step MSEs obtained with this criterion exceed the corresponding AIC MSEs.

9.4.3 Discussion of Small Sample Results

The foregoing small sample results show that the asymptotic theory of Sections 3 and 4 is a good indicator of the small sample performance of the different predictors provided that the orders are assumed to be known or AIC or HQ are used to determine the AR orders. If the underlying disaggregate process is an AR process of the type (9.4.1), then SC also performs in accordance with asymptotic theory.

Of course, these results are only based on two different processes and generalizations should be made cautiously. It is, however, worth noting that the predictor $y_t^u(h)$, based on the univariate components of the disaggregate process has performed extremely well in the small sam-

Table 9.14. Relations Between MSEs when AR Orders are Determined by HQ - Underlying Disaggregate Process: Bivariate MA(2)

	T	h	$\tilde{\sigma}_o^2(h)$	$\tilde{\sigma}^2(h)$	$\tilde{\bar{\sigma}}_o^2(h)$	$\tilde{\bar{\sigma}}_u^2(h)$
	60	1	<[a]	<	<[a]	<
		5	>[a]	<[a]	<[a]	>
$\tilde{\sigma}_*^2(h)$	100	1	<	>	<	>[a]
		5	>	<	<	<
	200	1	<	<	<[a]	>
		5	>	<	<	>
	60	1	<[a]	<[a]	<[a]	<[a]
		5	>	<[a]	<[a]	<[a]
$\tilde{\sigma}_u^2(h)$	100	1	<[a]	<	<[a]	>
		5	>	<	=	=
	200	1	<[a]	<	<[a]	<
		5	=	<	<	>

	T	h	$\tilde{\sigma}_o^2(h)$	$\tilde{\sigma}^2(h)$	$\tilde{\sigma}_*^2(h)$	$\tilde{\sigma}_u^2(h)$	$\tilde{\bar{\sigma}}_u^2(h)$
	60	1	>	>[a]	>[a]	>[a]	>[a]
		5	>[a]	<	>[a]	>[a]	>[a]
$\tilde{\bar{\sigma}}_o^2(h)$	100	1	>	>	>	>[a]	>[a]
		5	>	<	>	=	=
	200	1	>	>[a]	>[a]	>[a]	>[a]
		5	>	<	>	>	>

a) significant at 5% level.

Table 9.15. Relations Between MSEs when AR Orders are Determined by SC - Underlying Disaggregate Process: Bivariate MA(2)

	T	h	$\tilde{\sigma}_o^2(h)$	$\tilde{\sigma}^2(h)$	$\bar{\tilde{\sigma}}_o^2(h)$	$\bar{\tilde{\sigma}}_u^2(h)$
	60	1	<	<	<	>
		5	>[a]	<[a]	>[a]	>[a]
$\tilde{\sigma}_*^2(h)$	100	1	<[a]	>	<	>
		5	>[a]	<	>	>
	200	1	>	<	<	>
		5	>	<	>	>
	60	1	<[a]	<[a]	<	<
		5	<	<[a]	<[a]	<[a]
$\tilde{\sigma}_u^2(h)$	100	1	<[a]	<	<[a]	>
		5	>	<	<	=
	200	1	<	<[a]	<[a]	<[a]
		5	<	<[a]	<	<

	T	h	$\tilde{\sigma}_o^2(h)$	$\tilde{\sigma}^2(h)$	$\tilde{\sigma}_*^2(h)$	$\tilde{\sigma}_u^2(h)$	$\bar{\tilde{\sigma}}_u^2(h)$
	60	1	<	<	>	>	>
		5	>[a]	<[a]	<[a]	>[a]	>
$\bar{\tilde{\sigma}}_o^2(h)$	100	1	<	>	>	>[a]	>[a]
		5	>	<	<	>	>
	200	1	>[a]	>	>	>[a]	>
		5	=	<[a]	<	>	>

a) significant at 5% level.

ple experiment. The Monte Carlo study does allow the conclusion that there are conditions under which the predictor based on the multivariate disaggregate process is inferior to other predictors. Using univariate forecasting models may be an attractive alternative if the individual components are uncorrelated.

This result sheds doubt on the usefulness of full AR models as forecasting tools. Their ease of application makes them an attractive choice in practice. However, subset AR methods may be preferable since they can be implemented with very little extra costs and asymptotic theory suggests that imposing parameter restrictions results in more efficient estimates and thus forecasts, provided the restrictions are correct.

9.5 FORECASTS OF U.S. GROSS PRIVATE DOMESTIC INVESTMENT

To illustrate the theoretical results the quarterly, seasonally adjusted U.S. investment data given in the Appendix of the book will be used again. As in previous chapters the years 1947 - 1968 will be used for model specification and estimation and the forecast comparison will be based on the data for 1969 - 1972. Results obtained by aggregating the (supposedly) stationary first differenced series will be discussed first and then the forecast MSEs for the original data will be compared.

9.5.1 First Differences of Investment Data

The bivariate system consisting of the variables

x_{1t} - first differences of quarterly Fixed Investment

and

x_{2t} - first differences of quarterly Change in Business Inventories

will be considered and it is assumed that forecasts of annual changes in Gross Private Domestic Investment y_t are desired. The first available values for x_{1t} and x_{2t} are associated with the second quarter of 1947. The contemporaneously aggregated series is $z_t = x_{1t} + x_{2t}$ and represents changes in quarterly Gross Private Domestic Investment. This series also originates in the second quarter of 1947.

Using m = 4 the temporally aggregated series are

$\bar{z}_{1t}$ - annual changes in Fixed Investment,

$\bar{z}_{2t}$ - annual changes in Change in Business Inventories,

and

$$y_t = \bar{z}_{1t} + \bar{z}_{2t} \text{ - annual changes in total investment.}$$

All three series originate in 1948 since a first quarter value of 1947 is not available. Thus, we have T = 87 quarterly observations and $\mathcal{T}$ = 21 annual values.

It seems plausible to suspect that the two disaggregate component series x_{1t} and x_{2t} are intertemporally correlated and do not have identical correlation structures. Therefore, given the results of the previous sections one would expect that the predictor $y_t^o(h)$, based on the disaggregate process $\underline{x}_t = (x_{1t}, x_{2t})'$, is optimal. Also, $y_t(h)$, which is based on the temporally and contemporaneously aggregated data, is expected to be inferior to the predictor based on temporally aggregated data, $\bar{y}_t^o(h)$, and the predictor based on contemporaneously aggregated data, $y_t^*(h)$.

Pure AR models were fitted to all series in accordance with the theory in Section 9.3. The maximum AR orders that were considered are P = 14 and 4 for quarterly and annual series, respectively. All three criteria, AIC, HQ, and SC were used for determining the AR order and the resulting models are given in Tables 9.16 and 9.17 for quarterly and annual data, respectively. Although the quarterly and some of the annual models are given in previous chapters, they are summarized here for completeness. In the tables the numbers in parentheses underneath the estimates are estimated standard errors and the variance-covariance estimates are corrected for degrees of freedom, that is, for instance, the elements of $\tilde{\Sigma}_u$ are sums of squares and cross-products divided by degrees of freedom. In the search procedure for determining the AR order the first P (14 for quarterly data and 4 for annual data) values were used as presample values. After having determined the order, say $\tilde{p}$, the models have been reestimated using only the first $\tilde{p}$ observations as presample values as explained in Chapter 2.

The models in Tables 9.16 and 9.17 were used to compute four 1-step forecasts for the annual changes in Gross Private Domestic Investment for the postsample years 1969 - 1972. The resulting average squared forecasting errors are given in Table 9.18. The smallest MSE is indeed $\tilde{\sigma}_o^2(1)$ for all three criteria. On the other hand, for AIC and HQ, $\tilde{\sigma}^2(1)$, based on fully aggregated annual total investment data, does not exceed $\tilde{\bar{\sigma}}_o^2(1)$ and $\tilde{\sigma}_*^2(1)$, which are based on temporally and contemporaneously aggregated data, respectively. In fact, $\tilde{\bar{\sigma}}_o^2(1)$ and $\tilde{\sigma}^2(1)$ are identical for all three criteria. This, of course, is a consequence of choosing

Table 9.16. AR Models for First Differences of Quarterly Investment Data

x_{1t} - first differences of quarterly Fixed Investment

x_{2t} - first differences of quarterly Change in Business Inventories

Models for bivariate quarterly series $\underline{x}_t = (x_{1t}, x_{2t})'$

AIC:

$$\underline{x}_t = \begin{bmatrix} 0.78 \\ (0.29) \\ \\ -0.55 \\ (0.57) \end{bmatrix} + \begin{bmatrix} 0.49 & 0.17 \\ (0.12) & (0.06) \\ & \\ 0.42 & -0.27 \\ (0.23) & (0.11) \end{bmatrix} \underline{x}_{t-1} + \begin{bmatrix} -0.17 & -0.07 \\ (0.13) & (0.06) \\ & \\ 0.05 & -0.10 \\ (0.25 & (0.12) \end{bmatrix} \underline{x}_{t-2}$$

$$+ \begin{bmatrix} 0.05 & -0.05 \\ (0.13) & (0.06) \\ & \\ 0.15 & -0.01 \\ (0.25) & (0.12) \end{bmatrix} \underline{x}_{t-3} + \begin{bmatrix} -0.18 & -0.07 \\ (0.11) & (0.06) \\ & \\ 0.13 & -0.45 \\ (0.21) & (0.12) \end{bmatrix} \underline{x}_{t-4} + \underline{u}_t, \tilde{\underline{\Sigma}}_u = \begin{bmatrix} 5.06 & 2.15 \\ 2.15 & 19.3 \end{bmatrix}$$

SC, HQ:

$$\underline{x}_t = \begin{bmatrix} 0.62 \\ (0.27) \\ \\ -0.32 \\ (0.53) \end{bmatrix} + \begin{bmatrix} 0.40 & 0.17 \\ (0.09) & (0.05) \\ & \\ 0.48 & -0.30 \\ (0.19) & (0.11) \end{bmatrix} \underline{x}_{t-1} + \underline{u}_t, \ \tilde{\underline{\Sigma}}_u = \begin{bmatrix} 5.64 & 2.58 \\ 2.58 & 21.8 \end{bmatrix}$$

Models for quarterly total investment $z_t = x_{1t} + x_{2t}$

AIC, HQ:

$$z_t = \underset{(0.64)}{1.17} + \underset{(0.10)}{0.13}z_{t-1} + \underset{(0.10)}{0.11}z_{t-2} + \underset{(0.10)}{0.02}z_{t-3} - \underset{(0.10)}{0.42}z_{t-4} + v_t ,$$

$$\tilde{\sigma}_v^2 = 31.5$$

SC:

$$z_t = \underset{(0.66)}{1.07} + v_t, \ \tilde{\sigma}_v^2 = 37.3$$

Models for quarterly Fixed Investment x_{1t}

AIC:

$$x_{1t} = \underset{(0.30)}{0.83} + \underset{(0.11)}{0.49}x_{1,t-1} - \underset{(0.12)}{0.14}x_{1,t-2} + \underset{(0.12)}{0.02}x_{1,t-3}$$

$$- \underset{(0.11)}{0.25}x_{1,t-4} + w_{1t}, \ \tilde{\sigma}_{w_1}^2 = 5.81$$

SC, HQ:

$$x_{1t} = \underset{(0.29)}{0.58} + \underset{(0.10)}{0.46}x_{1,t-1} + w_{1t}, \ \tilde{\sigma}_{w_1}^2 = 6.26$$

Model for quarterly Change in Business Inventories x_{2t}

AIC, SC, HQ:

$$x_{2t} = \underset{(0.49)}{0.11} - \underset{(0.10)}{0.19}x_{2,t-1} + \underset{(0.10)}{0.07}x_{2,t-2} + \underset{(0.10)}{0.06}x_{2,t-3}$$

$$- \underset{(0.10)}{0.43}x_{2,t-4} + w_{2t}, \ \tilde{\sigma}_{w_2}^2 = 19.7$$

Table 9.17. AR Models for Annual Figures of First Differences of Quarterly Investment Data

$\bar{z}_{1t}$ - annual changes of Fixed Investment

$\bar{z}_{2t}$ - annual changes of Change in Business Inventories

Model for bivariate annual series $\underline{\bar{z}}_t = (\bar{z}_{1t}, \bar{z}_{2t})'$

AIC, HQ, SC:

$$\underline{\bar{z}}_t = \begin{bmatrix} \underset{(1.51)}{3.82} \\ \underset{(2.29)}{0.23} \end{bmatrix} + \underline{\bar{w}}_t, \quad \tilde{\underline{\Sigma}}_{\bar{w}} = \begin{bmatrix} 48.1 & 37.9 \\ 37.9 & 109.7 \end{bmatrix}$$

Model for annual total investment $y_t = \bar{z}_{1t} + \bar{z}_{2t}$

AIC, HQ, SC: $y_t = \underset{(3.33)}{4.05} + v_t, \quad \tilde{\sigma}_v^2 = 233$

Model for annual Fixed Investment $\bar{z}_{1t}$

AIC, HQ, SC: $\bar{z}_{1t} = \underset{(1.51)}{3.82} + w_{1t}, \quad \tilde{\sigma}_{w_1}^2 = 48.1$

Models for annual Change in Business Inventories $\bar{z}_{2t}$

AIC, HQ:

$$\bar{z}_{2t} = \underset{(1.56)}{0.59} - \underset{(0.19)}{0.67}\bar{z}_{2,t-1} - \underset{(0.22)}{0.55}\bar{z}_{2,t-2} - \underset{(0.18)}{0.39}\bar{z}_{2,t-3} + w_{2t}, \quad \tilde{\sigma}_{w_2}^2 = 40.8$$

SC:

$$\bar{z}_{2t} = \underset{(2.29)}{0.23} + w_{2t}, \quad \tilde{\sigma}_{w_2}^2 = 109,7$$

Table 9.18. MSEs of Predictors for First Differences of Gross Private Domestic Investment

	$\tilde{\sigma}_o^2(1)$	$\tilde{\sigma}^2(1)$	$\tilde{\sigma}_*^2(1)$	$\bar{\tilde{\sigma}}_o^2(1)$	$\tilde{\sigma}_u^2(1)$	$\bar{\tilde{\sigma}}_u^2(1)$
AIC	192	231	287	231	266	244
HQ	186	231	287	231	212	244
SC	186	231	229	231	212	231

a white noise (AR(0))model for both the bivariate temporally aggregated series $\bar{z}_t$ and the fully aggregated series y_t (see Table 9.17). The predictor $\tilde{y}_t^u(1)$, based on univariate forecasting models, results in quite impressive MSEs. It is second best for SC and HQ. This predictor is expected to perform particularly well if the component series are uncorrelated. As was to be expected on the basis of the asymptotic theory, $\tilde{\sigma}_u^2(1)$ is smaller than $\tilde{\tilde{\sigma}}_u^2(1)$, which is based on the temporally aggregated univariate component series. This, however, does not hold when the AIC criterion is applied.

Overall these results are in line with the theoretical findings of the previous sections. The slight deviations can have various reasons: (1) Due to the small number of forecasts on which they are based, there is a good chance that the observed MSEs are far away from the actual MSEs of the underlying processes. (2) The MSEs in Table 9.18 are based on a single limited realization of the underlying data generation process, while the simulation results are based on a large number of independent realizations of the considered processes. (3) The data generation process may not satisfy the basic assumptions on which the theoretical results of the previous sections rely.

9.5.2 Aggregation of Original Investment Data

The original (nonstationary) data were used to compute forecasts for annual Gross Private Domestic Investment. The disaggregate component series are now

x_{1t} - quarterly Fixed Investment

and

x_{2t} - Change in Business Inventories.

Contemporaneous aggregation gives the quarterly total investment $z_t = x_{1t} + x_{2t}$ and, using $m = 4$, temporal aggregation gives the annual series $\bar{z}_{kt} = x_{k,4t} + x_{k,4t-1} + x_{k,4t-2} + x_{k,4t-3}$, $k = 1,2$. The fully aggregated series $y_t = \bar{z}_{1t} + \bar{z}_{2t}$ is total annual investment. Note that now the quarterly series begin with the first quarter of 1947 and the annual series also originate in 1947. Thus, for estimation and model specification $T = 88$ quarterly data and $T/m = 22$ annual data are available.

Based on the discussion in Section 9.1 and previous chapters one would expect the forecasts based on the fully disaggregated quarterly process $\underline{x}_t = (x_{1t}, x_{2t})'$ to be best again and the forecasts based on fully aggregated annual data y_t to result in greater MSEs than $\tilde{\bar{y}}^o_t(h)$, $\tilde{y}^*_t(h)$ which are based on temporally and contemporaneously aggregated data, respectively.

Assuming that stationarity can be achieved by taking first differences of all series the same models result for the quarterly data that were obtained in the previous subsection (replace $\underline{x}_t$, x_{kt}, and z_t in Table 9.16 by first differences $(1-L)\underline{x}_t$, $(1-L)x_{kt}$, and $(1-L)z_t$, respectively). On the other hand, the models for the annual data may be different from those in Table 9.17 since now the first differences of the temporally aggregated data rather than the aggregated differenced data are modeled. The resulting estimated processes are presented in Table 9.19, where again a maximum order of P = 4 was used in the search procedures. With the exception of $\bar{z}_{2t}$ (Change in Business Inventories) white noise models are chosen for the first differences of all series. Note, however, that the models nevertheless differ from the annual models in Table 9.17 (see also the discussion in Section 8.4)

The 1-step forecast MSEs computed on the basis of these models are given in Table 9.20. They agree quite well with the expected results. For all three criteria (AIC, HQ, SC) the forecasts based on the disaggregate, bivariate, quarterly series are optimal, that is, $\tilde{\sigma}^2_o(1)$ is smaller than any of the other MSEs. Furthermore, the predictors based on quarterly data are better than those based on temporally aggregated annual data, that is, $\tilde{\sigma}^2_o(1)$, $\tilde{\sigma}^2_*(1)$, and $\tilde{\sigma}^2_u(1)$ are lower than $\tilde{\sigma}^2(1)$, $\tilde{\bar{\sigma}}^2_o(1)$, and $\tilde{\bar{\sigma}}^2_u(1)$. Moreover, the forecasts $\tilde{y}_t(1)$, based on fully aggregated (annual total investment) data, have the largest MSE, i.e., $\tilde{\sigma}^2(1)$ exceeds all other MSEs. Note, that the differences between $\tilde{\sigma}^2(1)$ and $\tilde{\bar{\sigma}}^2_o(1)$ are due to rounding errors. All these results hold regardless of the criterion used.

9.6 SUMMARY AND CONCLUSIONS

In Chapter 6 and in this chapter the relative efficiencies of six predictors for a variable that results from temporally and contemporaneously aggregating a set of disaggregate variables have been compared. The mean squared error has been used as a measure of forecast performance. The six predictors are obtained by

(1) temporally and contemporaneously aggregating forecasts from a multivariate model for the disaggregate data;
(2) forecasting the temporally and contemporaneously aggregated variable directly;

Table 9.19. AR Models for Annual Investment Data

$\bar{z}_{1t}$ - annual Fixed Investment

$\bar{z}_{2t}$ - annual Change in Business Inventories

Model for bivariate annual series $\bar{\underline{z}}_t = (\bar{z}_{1t}, \bar{z}_{2t})'$

AIC, HQ, SC:
$$(1-L)\bar{\underline{z}}_t = \begin{bmatrix} \underset{(5.60)}{15.34} \\ \underset{(5.46)}{1.71} \end{bmatrix} + \bar{\underline{w}}_t, \quad \tilde{\Sigma}_{\bar{w}} = \begin{bmatrix} 659 & 473 \\ 473 & 627 \end{bmatrix}$$

Model for annual total investment $y_t = \bar{z}_{1t} + \bar{z}_{2t}$

AIC, HQ, SC: $(1-L)y_t = \underset{(10.30)}{17.03} + v_t, \quad \tilde{\sigma}_v^2 = 2229$

Model for annual Fixed Investment $\bar{z}_{1t}$

AIC, HQ, SC: $(1-L)\bar{z}_{1t} = \underset{(5.60)}{15.34} + w_{1t}, \quad \tilde{\sigma}_{w_1}^2 = 659$

Model for annual Change in Business Inventories $\bar{z}_{2t}$

AIC, HQ, SC:
$$(1-L)\bar{z}_{2t} = \underset{(4.27)}{2.71} - \underset{(0.20)}{0.29}\,(1-L)\bar{z}_{2,t-1} - \underset{(0.19)}{0.57}\,(1-L)\bar{z}_{2,t-2} - \underset{(0.19)}{0.25}\,(1-L)\bar{z}_{2,t-3} + w_{2t}, \quad \tilde{\sigma}_{w_2}^2 = 297$$

Table 9.20. MSEs of Predictors for Gross Private Domestic Investment

	$\tilde{\sigma}_o^2(1)$	$\tilde{\sigma}^2(1)$	$\tilde{\sigma}_*^2(1)$	$\bar{\tilde{\sigma}}_o^2(1)$	$\tilde{\sigma}_u^2(1)$	$\bar{\tilde{\sigma}}_u^2(1)$
AIC	1354	2737	2223	2726	1906	2652
HQ	1360	2737	2223	2726	1558	2652
SC	1360	2737	1895	2726	1558	2652

(3) forecasting the contemporaneously aggregated series and temporally aggregating the forecasts;
(4) forecasting the temporally aggregated system of variables and contemporaneously aggregating the forecasts;
(5) using univariate forecasting methods for the individual components of the disaggregate system and temporally and contemporaneously aggregating the forecasts; and
(6) computing univariate forecasts for the component series of the temporally aggregated process and contemporaneously aggregating the forecasts.

The first predictor has the smallest MSE if the underlying data generation mechanisms are known nondeterministic, stationary, stochastic processes. For long-term forecasting, as the forecasting horizon goes to infinity, the MSEs of all predictors converge to the variance of the aggregated process and hence the predictors become equivalent provided the basic disaggregate process is stationary and nondeterministic. The results for known processes were obtained in Chapter 6.

In practice the data generation processes are usually unknown and have to be estimated from the given time series. Therefore, in this chapter the performance of the different predictors has been investigated under the assumptions that (i) the disaggregate data are generated by a stationary vector ARMA process with known orders and unknown coefficients and (ii) the data are generated by a process of unknown orders and coefficients. The asymptotic results of Chapter 3 have been used in this analysis. Asymptotically, as the sample size increases, in either case the contribution of the estimation variability to the forecast MSEs vanishes under the assumptions made in Sections 9.2 and 9.3. Thus, if one predictor is strictly superior to another predictor for known processes, then the same will hold in large samples for the predictors based on estimated processes.

In order to focus on the MSE parts due to estimation the case in which the predictors are identical for known processes has been treated in detail. This situation occurs, for instance, when all component series have the same covariance structure and are uncorrelated, and there is no correlation between variables that are noninteger multiples of the period of temporal aggregation apart. In that situation, the first predictor, based on the multivariate disaggregate process, may lose its optimality property. Since using contemporaneously aggregated processes may increase the forecast efficiency while temporal aggregation is destructive to forecast efficiency, the third predictor, based on the contemporaneously aggregated process, and the fifth predictor, based on the individual components of the disaggregate process, become optimal. The predictor based on the temporally aggregated multivariate process, on the other hand, is least attractive. These asymptotic results have been checked in a Monte Carlo study which indicates that in small samples the choice of the process orders may be a critical factor for the asymptotic results to remain valid.

Of course, processes for which all predictors are identical have a very special correlation structure. However, the first predictor may lose its optimality property already under less restrictive assumptions. For example, if all component series are uncorrelated, the predictor based on the disaggregate univariate components will be optimal if the process coefficients and orders are unknown and have to be estimated.

Returning to the introductory example and assuming that the monthly tax revenues from the different states are generated by processes of the type considered in this study, the foregoing results imply that forecasts of the annual total tax revenues should preferably be based on the monthly data for each of the states. If it is known that the revenues in different states are uncorrelated or nearly uncorrelated, univariate forecasting methods should be used to forecast the monthly revenues for each of the states. These forecasts should then be temporally and contemporaneously aggregated in order to obtain the desired forecast for the total annual revenues from all states. Similarly, if the revenues of the different states are known to be uncorrelated and have the same stochastic structure, then the predictor based on the total monthly figures or again the predictor based on univariate models for the monthly revenues from each of the states should be adapted. If the sample size is large, the first predictor which is based on a multivariate model for the monthly revenue figures of the different states is always recommended provided, of course, that the general assumptions underlying this study are satisfied.

In this chapter U.S. investment data have been used to illustrate the theoretical findings. The forecast MSEs for this data are overall in accordance with what one would expect on the basis of the theoretical and Monte Carlo results.

In conclusion, the first predictor, based on a multivariate model for the disaggregate system, will often be optimal in practice if the data generation processes satisfy the assumptions of this chapter. In some cases the use of other predictors is to be favored, however. For example, if the component series are uncorrelated, forecasts based on univariate models for the individual components will be preferable. Note, however, that the results of this chapter rely to some extent on the particular way of model construction and estimation. Possible constraints on the parameters are not taken into account since they will often not be known in practice. If statistical methods were used, for instance, to determine zero constraints that could be placed on some of the AR coefficients, the results may change in favor of the first predictor. Zero constraints could be placed on the parameters by using subset AR methods for model building.

The findings of this chapter can easily be extended in two ways. First, instead of using simply sums of variables as aggregates, weighted sums could be considered. Second, the aggregate y_t could be allowed to be a multivariate process with components that are temporal and contemporaneous aggregates. These generalizations are easy to handle in the framework developed in Chapter 6. They do, however, involve a slightly more elaborate notation and have therefore not been considered in this chapter. Moreover, nonstationary processes can be analyzed in a similar way if stationarity can be obtained by differencing (see Chapters 5, 6, and 8).

CHAPTER 10. EPILOGUE

10.1 SUMMARY AND CONCLUSIONS

In this study a number of predictors for temporal and/or contemporaneous aggregates have been compared using the MSE as measure of forecast precision. In particular, the impact of the level of aggregation of the data used for prediction has been investigated. The following results have been obtained in this study.

If the data generation process is known, disaggregation as much as possible results in optimal forecasts. This conclusion is hardly surprising because the information base for the forecasts is extended by disaggregation. The critical assumption for this result to hold is, however, that the true data generation process has to be used for prediction. In practice, for real life data, this condition is virtually always violated. Therefore the consequences of using estimated processes for prediction have been considered. For this case the solution to the aggregation problem is a bit more difficult because the contribution of the estimation variability to the forecast MSEs depends also on the aggregation level of the data used for estimation. For contemporaneous aggregation it has been shown that the MSE part due to estimation variability may be greater if the disaggregate data are used for estimating the disaggregate process rather than estimating the aggregated process from aggregate data. In other words, if high dimensional systems are aggregated contemporaneously, using the high dimensional system to obtain a multivariate forecast of the components and then aggregating the forecasts gives a predictor for the aggregate that may be inferior to direct prediction of the aggregate. In this study only consistent estimation has been considered so that for large samples the contribution of the estimation variability decreases and becomes negligible relative to the systematic part of the forecast MSEs. Thus, for relatively short series only, a forecast from a disaggregate process will be significantly inferior to a direct forecast of the aggregate. Moreover, this situation can occur only if the systematic differences of the MSEs (differences between the MSEs obtained for known processes) do not off-set the differences due to estimation. However, it has been shown by way of simulations that the situation where a direct forecast of the aggregate dominates a forecast from a multivariate model can indeed arise for sample sizes usually available in practice.

On the other hand, if it is possible to limit the estimation variability in a multivariate system by imposing parameter constraints then using the disaggregate system will be worthwhile. This result could be summarized by noting that a heavily parameterized system should be used cautiously for prediction if there is insufficient data to get precise estimates of its coefficients. Stated in this way the result should not be surprising.

As a compromise between predicting the components of the disaggregate system with multivariate methods and forecasting the aggregate directly, a predictor based on univariate models for the component series has been considered. The predictor is obtained by contemporaneously aggregating the univariate forecasts of the individual components of the disaggregate system. The resulting predictor is optimal if the components of the disaggregate system are uncorrelated. It may always be a good choice if the data generation processes are unknown so that estimated processes have to be used and the correlation among the components is not strong. The predictor has the disadvantage of being inferior to predicting the aggregate directly for some processes, even if the data generation processes are known. In other words, the systematic part of the MSE of the direct predictor may be smaller than the systematic part of the MSE of the predictor based on univariate forecasts. Therefore the latter predictor should be used cautiously if strong intertemporal relationships are suspected to be present among the components.

For long range forecasting all three predictors mentioned in the foregoing become identical for known stationary, nondeterministic processes. The optimal long term forecasts for such processes converge to the process means. The situation is different for nonstationary processes for which one predictor may significantly dominate the others for all forecast horizons for known and estimated processes alike.

For temporal aggregation it depends on the type of the variables whether forecasting the aggregate directly may become optimal. For stock variables, where the aggregate can be regarded as a series of systematically missing observations, the situation is similar to contemporaneous aggregation. That is, forecasts based on a series with systematically missing observations may have smaller MSEs than predictors based on the full (disaggregate) series. It seems, however, that this will only happen in rather special situations and the suggestion is to use the full series if that is available and safisfies the general conditions underlying this study (for instance, if the series can be described at least approximately by an ARMA model).

Forecasting a temporally aggregated flow variable which is the sum of consecutive disaggregate values the results of this study suggest that it is always preferable to use disaggregate data if available. Compared to the case of known processes the relative forecast efficiency will in general increase if disaggregate data is used for estimating the processes.

From these results it follows that, if a variable is a contemporaneous and temporal aggregate, in general it will be a good idea to use disaggregate data for predictions of the aggregate. This does not mean, however, that it is necessarily a good idea to construct a high dimensional forecasting model, forecast the disaggregate components and then aggregate the forecasts to obtain the desired prediction. This strategy can be recommended only if the estimation variability can be limited in the multivariate system. In other words, practical strategies for multiple time series modelling are called for that use the available sample information in a way that is optimal for forecasting. If the disaggregate components are not strongly interrelated, it may be a good strategy to predict them individually with univariate methods and then aggregate the obtained forecasts.

10.2 SOME REMAINING PROBLEMS

In practice the forecaster often has no choice between data of different levels of aggregation. For instance, quarterly forecasts may be desired when only quarterly data is available. In that case it may not be very helpful to know that better forecasts could be obtained by getting disaggregate (e.g., monthly) data. Nevertheless in some situations it may not be too difficult to obtain disaggregate data and the forecaster should at least be aware that there is an option to use them beneficially. One problem in this context is to assess the size of the gains in forecast precision that can be expected from using disaggregate data. Getting an estimate of the gain would permit to evaluate whether the expense for getting the disaggregate data is worthwhile.

Assuming that disaggregate data is available the results of this study may still not be useful for a forecaster who has to predict an aggregate. It must be emphasized that the previous analysis rests on some basic assumptions and most results will not hold without them. One basic assumption relates to the class of processes considered. The assumption that the data is generated by nondeterministic stochastic processes that are stationary or can be made stationary by differencing means that many types of nonstationarities are excluded. For example, a change in a tax law may change the structure of some economic time series in a particular period. Such nonstationarities can usually not be taken care of by differencing.

In this study the MSE has been used as the measure of forecast precision. As mentioned in the introduction to Chapter 3 this measure is not always of interest. If other loss functions are to be minimized further investigations may be necessary to determine whether the results remain valid for the loss functions of interest.

Nonlinear aggregation is another interesting topic of considerable practical relevance that has not been considered in the foregoing. For instance, real GNP is the ratio of nominal GNP and a price index. In the context of this example, one remaining question of interest is whether forecast improvements of real GNP can be obtained by using nominal GNP and price level data.

Although the previous discussion shows that some problems related to forecasting aggregated time series remain unsolved, it is hoped that this study will provide a useful base for further investigations.

APPENDIX. DATA USED FOR EXAMPLES

The data used in the example sections of this study are presented here to enable the reader to replicate the results. All the data are taken from The National Income and Product Accounts of the United States, 1929 - 1974, published by the U.S. Department of Commerce, Bureau of Economic Analysis. The quarterly, seasonally adjusted series of Fixed Investment, Change in Business Inventories, Gross Private Domestic Investment, and Personal Consumption Expenditures for the years 1947 to 1972 are given. The figures are the quarterly totals at annual rates in billions of 1972 dollars. The investment series are plotted in Figures 2.1, 2.2, and 5.1.

t	Quarter	Fixed Investment	Change in Business Inventories	Gross Private Domestic Investment	Personal Consumption Expenditures
1	1947.I	69.6	0.1	69.7	302.7
2	II	67.6	-0.9	66.6	307.3
3	III	69.5	-2.9	66.7	307.6
4	IV	74.7	2.7	77.5	307.2
5	1948.I	77.1	4.1	81.2	309.3
6	II	77.4	5.6	83.0	312.5
7	III	76.6	6.9	83.5	313.1
8	IV	76.1	5.3	81.4	316.1
9	1949.I	71.8	-0.3	71.5	316.5
10	II	68.9	-7.1	61.8	320.5
11	III	68.5	-2.5	66.0	320.0
12	IV	70.6	-7.7	63.0	323.1
13	1950.I	75.4	4.4	79.8	328.3
14	II	82.3	7.7	90.0	334.3
15	III	88.2	8.0	96.2	348.9
16	IV	86.9	22.1	109.0	340.8
17	1951.I	83.4	13.4	96.8	346.5
18	II	80.3	19.9	100.3	338.5
19	III	79.4	14.6	94.0	341.4
20	IV	78.6	7.0	85.5	342.8
21	1952.I	79.3	7.3	86.6	343.5
22	II	80.3	-2.7	77.6	349.5
23	III	75.3	5.4	80.8	351.0
24	IV	80.6	7.2	87.8	359.6

t	Quarter	Fixed Investment	Change in Business Inventories	Gross Private Domestic Investment	Personal Consumption Expenditures
25	1953.I	83.9	3.9	87.9	363.7
26	II	84.2	5.1	89.3	365.3
27	III	84.4	1.9	86.2	364.4
28	IV	83.8	-5.0	78.8	363.5
29	1954.I	82.8	-3.4	79.4	364.4
30	II	84.1	-4.1	80.0	367.1
31	III	87.0	-2.7	84.2	372.7
32	IV	88.5	1.5	90.0	379.5
33	1955.I	92.1	5.9	98.0	386.2
34	II	96.1	8.0	104.1	393.2
35	III	98.3	7.8	106.1	397.4
36	IV	98.8	9.2	108.0	403.6
37	1956.I	96.6	7.5	104.2	404.1
38	II	97.4	5.5	102.9	404.8
39	III	97.6	4.9	102.5	406.0
40	IV	96.6	5.4	102.0	410.2
41	1957.I	96.2	2.5	98.7	412.6
42	II	95.3	2.9	98.2	413.2
43	III	96.4	3.7	100.1	416.1
44	IV	94.9	-3.0	91.9	416.9
45	1958.I	90.0	-6.8	83.2	411.9
46	II	87.2	-6.2	81.1	415.7
47	III	88.0	0.3	88.4	421.8
48	IV	93.0	5.3	98.3	426.5
49	1959.I	98.3	5.0	103.3	435.1
50	II	101.6	13.0	114.6	440.8
51	III	102.6	-0.4	102.3	444.4
52	IV	101.4	8.2	109.6	445.6
53	1960.I	104.9	13.5	118.5	449.2
54	II	101.8	4.9	106.7	455.1
55	III	98.8	3.0	101.8	453.6
56	IV	98.6	-3.9	94.7	454.1
57	1961.I	97.7	-3.8	93.9	454.8
58	II	99.2	1.9	101.2	460.8
59	III	101.3	6.6	107.9	462.2
60	IV	104.6	6.7	111.3	471.1
61	1962.I	106.1	10.6	116.7	475.3
62	II	109.9	9.2	119.1	480.7
63	III	111.1	8.0	119.1	484.4
64	IV	110.1	4.7	114.8	490.8
65	1963.I	110.7	7.6	118.3	493.9
66	II	116.0	7.0	122.9	498.3
67	III	118.5	9.3	127.8	504.8
68	IV	122.0	7.1	129.2	508.4
69	1964.I	124.0	6.1	130.1	517.4
70	II	124.0	8.0	131.9	526.4
71	III	124.9	7.3	132.2	535.0
72	IV	126.4	7.9	134.3	536.0

t	Quarter	Fixed Investment	Change in Business Inventories	Gross Private Domestic Investment	Personal Consumption Expenditures
73	1965.I	133.4	13.4	146.7	546.7
74	II	137.9	10.6	148.5	551.4
75	III	140.1	12.4	152.5	559.8
76	IV	143.8	8.8	152.6	574.5
77	1966.I	147.5	13.5	161.0	581.7
78	II	146.2	17.8	164.0	582.8
79	III	145.0	15.1	160.1	589.0
80	IV	139.7	20.5	160.2	590.8
81	1967.I	136.4	14.6	150.9	595.1
82	II	139.6	7.5	147.1	602.9
83	III	141.1	12.2	153.3	605.8
84	IV	145.5	13.8	159.4	608.8
85	1968.I	148.9	6.3	155.1	620.8
86	II	148.9	11.8	160.6	628.0
87	III	150.7	9.2	159.9	640.8
88	IV	155.0	7.6	162.6	644.0
89	1969.I	159.1	9.8	168.9	649.9
90	II	158.4	12.2	170.6	653.0
91	III	158.1	13.4	171.6	656.8
92	IV	154.3	6.8	161.1	661.9
93	1970.I	151.8	2.9	154.7	665.4
94	II	150.0	4.8	154.8	668.7
95	III	150.4	6.3	156.7	673.6
96	IV	149.5	3.3	152.7	668.0
97	1971.I	154.3	7.9	162.2	682.3
98	II	158.4	10.0	168.4	689.5
99	III	162.1	5.0	167.0	693.6
100	IV	166.0	3.7	169.7	702.3
101	1972.I	174.3	4.8	179.1	713.7
102	II	176.1	10.1	186.2	728.1
103	III	178.2	12.1	190.2	737.5
104	IV	186.7	10.8	197.6	752.8

BIBLIOGRAPHY

ABRAHAM, B. (1982), "Temporal Aggregation and Time Series," International Statistical Review, 50, 285-291.

AHSANULLAH, M. & W.W.S. WEI (1984a),"The Effects of Time Aggregation on the AR(1) Process," Computational Statistics Quarterly, 1, 343-352.

AHSANULLAH, M. & W.W.S. WEI (1984b), "Effects of Temporal Aggregation on Forecasts in an ARMA(1,1) Process," American Statistical Association, Proceedings of the Business and Economic Statistics Section, 297-302.

AKAIKE, H. (1969), "Fitting Autoregressive Models for Prediction," Annals of the Institute of Statistical Mathematics, 21, 243-247.

AKAIKE, H. (1971), "Autoregressive Model Fitting for Control," Annals of the Institute of Statistical Mathematics, 23, 163-180.

AKAIKE, H. (1973), "Information Theory and an Extension of the Maximum Likelihood Principle," in B.N. PETROV & F. CSÁKI (eds.), 2nd International Symposium on Information Theory, Budapest: Acadêmiai Kiadô, 267-281.

AKAIKE, H. (1974), "A New Look at the Statistical Model Identification," IEEE Transactions on Automatic Control, AC - 19, 716-723.

AMEMIYA, T. & R.Y. WU (1972), "The Effect of Aggregation on Prediction in the Autoregressive Model," Journal of the American Statistical Association, 67, 628-632.

ANDERSON, O.D. (1975a), "Moving Average Processes," Statistician, 24, 283-297.

ANDERSON, O.D. (1975b), "On a Lemma Associated with Box, Jenkins and Granger," Journal of Econometrics, 3, 151-156.

ANDERSON, O.D. (1978), "Concerning one of T.W. Anderson's Theorems - A Correction to 'Forecasting Aggregates of Independent ARIMA Processes' by Rose," Metron, 36, 99-103.

ANDERSON, T.W. (1971), The Statistical Analysis of Time Series, New York: John Wiley.

ANDERSON, T.W. (1980), "Maximum Likelihood Estimation for Vector Autoregressive Moving Average Models," in D.R. BRILLINGER & G.C. TIAO (eds.), Directions in Time Series, Institute of Mathematical Statistics, 49-59.

ANSLEY, C.F., W.A. SPIVEY & W.J. WROBLESKI (1977), "On the Structure of Moving Average Processes," Journal of Econometrics, 6, 121-134.

BAILLIE, R.T. (1979), "Asymptotic Prediction Mean Squared Error for Vector Autoregressive Models," Biometrika, 66, 675-678.

BAILLIE, R.T. (1980), "Predictions from ARMAX Models," Journal of Econometrics, 12, 365-374.

BAILLIE, R.T. (1981), "Prediction from the Dynamic Simultaneous Equation Model with Vector Autoregressive Errors," Econometrica, 49, 1331-1337.

BARONE, P. & R. ROY (1983), "On a Stability Test for Estimated Multivariate Autoregressive-Moving Average Models," American Statistical Association, Proceedings of the Business and Economic Statistics Section, 650-653.

BERGSTROM, A.R. (1984), "Continuous Time Stochastic Models and Issues of Aggregation over Time," in Z. GRILICHES & M.D. INTRILIGATOR (eds.), Handbook of Econometrics, Vol. II, Amsterdam: North-Holland, 1145-1212.

BHANSALI, R.J. (1978), "Linear Prediction by Autoregressive Model Fitting in the Time Domain," Annals of Statistics, 6, 224-231.

BHANSALI, R.J. (1981), "Effects of Not Knowing the Order of an Autoregressive Process on the Mean Squared Error of Prediction - 1," Journal of the American Statistical Association, 76, 588-597.

BOX, G.E.P. & G.M. JENKINS (1976), Time Series Analysis: Forecasting and Control, San Francisco: Holden-Day.

BREWER, K.R.W. (1973), "Some Consequences of Temporal Aggregation and Systematic Sampling for ARMA and ARMAX Models," Journal of Econometrics, 1, 133-154.

CHAN, W.Y.T. & K.F. WALLIS (1978), "Multiple Time Series Modeling: Another Look at the Mink-Muskrat Interaction," Applied Statistics, 27, 168-175.

CHOW, G.C. & A.-L. LIN (1971), "Best Linear Unbiased Interpolation, Distribution and Extrapolation of Time Series by Related Series," Review of Economics and Statistics, 53, 372-375.

CLEVELAND, W.P. & G.C. TIAO (1979), "Modeling Seasonal Time Series," Economie Appliquée, 32, 107-129.

CLINE, D.B. & P.J. BROCKWELL (1985), "Linear Prediction of ARMA Processes with Infinite Variance," Stochastic Processes and Their Applications, 19, 281-296.

DEISTLER, M., W.T.M. DUNSMUIR & E.J. HANNAN (1978), "Vector Linear Time Series Models: Corrections and Extensions," Advances in Applied Probability, 10, 360-372.

DEISTLER M. & E.J. HANNAN (1981), "Some Properties of the Parameterization of ARMA Systems with Unknown Order," Journal of Multivariate Analysis, 11, 474-484.

DICKEY, D.A., W.R. BELL & R.B. MILLER (1986), "Unit Roots in Time Series Models: Tests and Implications," American Statistician, 40, 12-26.

DICKEY, D.A. & W.A. FULLER (1979), "Distribution of the Estimators for Autoregressive Time Series with Unit Root," Journal of the American Statistical Association, 74, 427-431.

DUNN, D.M., W.H. WILLIAMS & T.L. DeCHAINE (1976), "Aggregate Versus Subaggregate Models in Local Area Forecasting," Journal of the American Statistical Association, 71, 68-71.

DUNSMUIR, W.T.M. & E.J. HANNAN (1976), "Vector Linear Time Series Models," Advances in Applied Probability, 8, 339-364.

ENGLE, R.F., D.F. HENDRY & J.F. RICHARD (1983), "Exogeneity," Econometrica, 51, 277-304.

ENGLE, R.F. & T.-C. LIU (1972), "Effects of Aggregation over Time on Dynamic Characteristics of an Econometric Model," in B.G. HICKMAN (ed.), Econometric Models of Cyclical Behaviors, Vol. 2, New York: Columbia University Press, 673-737.

FERNÁNDEZ, R.B. (1981), "A Methodological Note on the Estimation of Time Series," Review of Economics and Statistics, 63, 471-476.

FULLER, W.A. (1976), Introduction to Statistical Time Series, New York: John Wiley.

FULLER, W.A. & D.P. HASZA (1980), "Predictors for the First-Order Autoregressive Process," Journal of Econometrics, 13, 139-157.

FULLER, W.A. & D.P. HASZA (1981), "Properties of Predictors for Autoregressive Time Series," Journal of the American Statistical Association, 76, 155-161.

FULLER, W.A., D.P. HASZA & J.J. GOEBEL (1981), "Estimation of Parameters of Stochastic Difference Equations," Annals of Statistics, 9, 531-543.

GEWEKE, J. (1978), "Temporal Aggregation in the Multiple Regression Model," Econometrica, 46, 643-661.

GEWEKE, J. (1982), "Causality, Exogeneity and Inference," in W. HILDENBRAND (ed.), Advances in Econometrics, New York: Cambridge University Press, 209-235.

GEWEKE, J., R. MEESE & W. DENT (1983), "Comparing Alternative Tests of Causality in Temporal Systems: Analytic Results and Experimental Evidence," Journal of Econometrics, 21, 161-194.

GINSBURGH, V.A. (1973), "A Further Note on the Derivation of Quarterly Figures Consistent With Annual Data," Applied Statistics, 22, 368-374.

GOOIJER, J.G. de, B. ABRAHAM, A. GOULD, & L. ROBINSON (1985), "Methods for Determining the Order of an Autoregressive - Moving Average Process: A Survey," International Statistical Review, 53, 301-329.

GRANGER, C.W.J. (1969a), "Prediction with a Generalized Cost of Error Function," Operations Research Quarterly, 20, 199-207.

GRANGER, C.W.J. (1969b), "Investigating Causal Relations by Econometric Models and Cross-Spectral Methods," Econometrica, 37, 424-438.

GRANGER, C.W.J. (1984), "Implications of Aggregation with Common Factors," paper presented at the European Meeting of the Econometric Society, Madrid.

GRANGER, C.W.J. & M.J. MORRIS (1976), "Time Series Modelling and Interpretation," Journal of the Royal Statistical Society A, 139, 246-257.

GRANGER, C.W.J. & P. NEWBOLD (1977), Forecasting Economic Time Series, New York: Academic Press.

HANNAN, E.J. (1969), "The Identification of Vector Mixed Autoregressive Moving Average Systems," Biometrika, 56, 223-225.

HANNAN, E.J. (1970), Multiple Time Series, New York: John Wiley.

HANNAN, E.J. (1976), "The Identification and Parameterization of ARMAX and State Space Forms," Econometrica, 44, 713-723.

HANNAN, E.J. (1979), "The Statistical Theory of Linear Systems," in P.R. Krishnaiah (ed.), Developments in Statistics, New York: Academic Press, 83-121.

HANNAN, E.J., W.T.M. DUNSMUIR & M. DEISTLER (1980), "Estimation of Vector ARMAX Models," Journal of Multivariate Analysis, 10, 275-295.

HANNAN, E.J. & B.G. QUINN (1979), "The Determination of the Order of an Autoregression," Journal of the Royal Statistical Society B, 41, 190-195.

HARVEY, A.C. & R.G. PIERSE (1984), "Estimating Missing Observations in Economic Time Series," Journal of the American Statistical Association, 79, 125-131.

HASZA, D.P. & W.A. Fuller (1979), "Estimation for Autoregressive Processes with Unit Roots," Annals of Statistics, 7, 1106-1120.

HASZA, D.P. & W.A. FULLER (1982), "Testing for Nonstationary Parameter Specifications in Seasonal Time Series Models," Annals of Statistics, 10, 1209-1216.

HSIAO, C. (1979), "Autoregressive Modeling of Canadian Money and Income Data," Journal of the American Statistical Association, 74, 553-560.

HILLMER, S.C. & G.C. TIAO (1979), "Likelihood Function of Stationary Multiple Autoregressive Moving Average Models," Journal of the American Statistical Association,74, 652-660.

JONES, R.H. (1962), "Spectral Analysis With Regularly Missed Observations," Annals of Mathematical Statistics, 32, 455-461.

JONES, R.H. (1980), "Maximum Likelihood Fitting of ARMA Models to Time Series With Missing Observations," Technometrics, 22, 389-395.

JUDGE, G.G., R.C. HILL, W.E. GRIFFITHS, H. LÜTKEPOHL & T.-C. LEE (1982), Introduction to the Theory and Practice of Econometrics, New York: John Wiley.

JUDGE, G.G., W.E. GRIFFITHS, R.C. HILL, H. LÜTKEPOHL & T.-C. LEE (1985), The Theory and Practice of Econometrics, Second Edition, New York: John Wiley.

KANG, H. (1986), "Univariate ARIMA Forecasts of Defined Variables," Journal of Business & Economic Statistics, 4, 81-86.

KIRCHGÄSSNER, G. (1981), Einige neuere statistische Verfahren zur Erfassung kausaler Beziehungen zwischen Zeitreihen, Göttingen: Vandenhoeck & Ruprecht.

KOHN, R. (1982), "When is an Aggregate of a Time Series Efficiently Forecast by its Past?" Journal of Econometrics, 18, 337-349.

KUNITOMO, N. & T. YAMAMOTO (1985), "Properties of Predictors in Misspecified Autoregressive Time Series Models," Journal of the American Statistical Association, 80, 941-950.

LANG, S. (1969), Real Analysis, Reading, Massachusetts: Addison-Wesley.

LEWIS, R. & G. REINSEL (1982), "Prediction of Multivariate Time Series by Autoregressive Model Fitting," American Statistical Association, Proceedings of the Business and Economic Statistics Section, 149-154.

LITTERMAN, R.B. (1983), "A Random Walk, Markov Model for the Distribution of Time Series," Journal of Business & Economic Statistics, 1, 169-173.

LÜTKEPOHL, H. (1982a), "Differencing Multiple Time Series: Another Look at Canadian Money and Income Data," Journal of Time Series Analysis, 3, 235-243.

LÜTKEPOHL, H. (1982b), "Non-Causality Due to Omitted Variables," Journal of Econometrics, 19, 367-378.

LÜTKEPOHL, H. (1984a), "Linear Transformations of Vector ARMA Processes," Journal of Econometrics, 26, 283-293.

LÜTKEPOHL, H. (1984b), "Forecasting Contemporaneously Aggregated Vector ARMA Processes," Journal of Business & Economic Statistics, 2, 201-214.

LÜTKEPOHL, H. (1984c), "Linear Aggregation of Vector Autoregressive Moving Average Processes," Economics Letters, 14, 345-350.

LÜTKEPOHL, H. (1985a), "Comparison of Criteria for Estimating the Order of a Vector Autoregressive Process," Journal of Time Series Analysis, 6, 35-52.

LÜTKEPOHL, H. (1985b), "The Joint Asymptotic Distribution of Multistep Prediction Errors of Estimated Vector Autoregressions," Economics Letters, 17, 103-106.

LÜTKEPOHL, H. (1985c), "Comparison of Three Predictors for Contemporaneously Aggregated Time Series," Methods of Operations Research, 50, 317-333.

LÜTKEPOHL, H. (1986a), Prognose aggregierter Zeitreihen, Göttingen: Vandenhoeck & Ruprecht.

LÜTKEPOHL, H. (1986b), "Forecasting Vector ARMA Processes With Systematically Missing Observations," Journal of Business & Economic Statistics, 4, 375-390.

LÜTKEPOHL, H. (1986c), "Forecasting Temporally Aggregated Vector ARMA Processes," Journal of Forecasting, 5, forthcoming.

LÜTKEPOHL, H. (1986d), "Comparison of Predictors for Temporally and Contemporaneously Aggregated Time Series," International Journal of Forecasting, 2, forthcoming.

LÜTKEPOHL, H. & S. DORNBUSCH (1983), "A Computer Program for Fitting Subset Vector Autoregressions," Beiträge des Fachbereichs Wirtschaftswissenschaften der Universität Osnabrück Nr. 8303.

MORIGUCHI, C. (1970), "Aggregation over Time in Macroeconomic Relations," International Economic Review, 11, 427-440.

NEUDECKER, H. (1969), "Some Theorems on Matrix Differentiation with Special Reference to Kronecker Matrix Products," Journal of the American Statistical Association, 65, 953-963.

NEWBOLD, P. (1982), "Causality Testing in Economics," in O.D. ANDERSON (ed.), Time Series Analysis: Theory and Practice I, Amsterdam: North-Holland, 701-716.

NIEMI, H. (1984), "Theoretical Properties of Linear Predictors for ARIMA Models," Scandinavian Journal of Statistics, 11, 113-122.

NIJMAN, T.E. (1985), Missing Observations in Dynamic Macroeconomic Modeling, Amsterdam: Free University Press.

NIJMAN, T.E. & F.C. PALM (1986), "The Construction and Use of Approximations for Missing Quarterly Observations: A Model-Based Approach," Journal of Business & Economic Statistics, 4, 47-58.

PALM, F.C. & T.E. NIJMAN (1984), "Missing Observations in the Dynamic Regression Model," Econometrica, 52, 1415-1435.

PANKRATZ, A. (1983), Forecasting with Univariate Box-Jenkins Models: Concepts and Cases, New York: John Wiley.

PARZEN, E. (1963), "On Spectral Analysis With Missing Observations and Amplitude Modulation," Sankhyá, Ser. A, 25, 383-392.

PAULSEN, J. (1984), "Order Determination of Multivariate Autoregressive Time Series With Unit Roots," Journal of Time Series Analysis, 5, 115-127.

PAULSEN, J. & D. TJØSTHEIM (1985), "On the Estimation of Residual Variance and Order in Autoregressive Time Series," Journal of the Royal Statistical Society B, 47, 216-228.

PENM, J.H.W. & R.D. TERRELL (1982), "On the Recursive Fitting of Subset Autoregressions," Journal of Time Series Analysis, 3, 43-59.

PENM, J.H.W. & R.D. TERRELL (1984), "Multivariate Subset Autoregressive Modelling With Zero Constraints for Detecting 'Overall Causality'," Journal of Econometrics, 24, 311-330.

PRIESTLEY, M.B. (1981), Spectral Analysis and Time Series, Vol. I and II, London: Academic Press.

QUENOUILLE, M.H. (1958), "Discrete Autoregressive Schemes with Varying Time-Intervals," Metrika, 1, 21-27.

QUINN, B.G. (1980), "Order Determination for a Multivariate Autoregression," Journal of the Royal Statistical Society B, 42, 182-185.

RAO, M.M. (1978), "Asymptotic Distribution of an Estimator of the Boundary Parameter of an Unstable Process," Annals of Statistics, 6, 185-190.

REINSEL, G. (1980), "Asymptotic Properties of Prediction Errors for the Multivariate Autoregressive Model Using Estimated Parameters," Journal of the Royal Statistical Society B, 42, 328-333.

REINSEL, G. (1983), "Some Results on Multivariate Autoregressive Index Models," Biometrika, 70, 145-156.

RISSANEN, J. (1978), "Modeling by Shortest Data Description," Automatica, 14, 465-471.

ROSE, D.E. (1977), "Forecasting Aggregates of Independent ARIMA Processes," Journal of Econometrics, 5, 323-345.

SAID, S.E. & D.A. DICKEY (1984), "Testing for Unit Roots in Autoregressive - Moving Average Models of Unknown Order," Biometrika, 71, 599-607.

SAID, S.E. & D.A. DICKEY (1985), "Hypothesis Testing in ARIMA(p,1,q) Models," Journal of the American Statistical Association, 80, 369-374.

SARGENT, T.J. & C.A. SIMS (1977), "Business Cycle Modeling Without Pretending to Have Too Much A Priori Economic Theory," in New Methods in Business Cycle Research: Proceedings from a Conference, Federal Reserve Bank of Minneapolis, Minnesota, 45-109.

SCHMIDT, P. (1974), "The Asymptotic Distribution of Forecasts in the Dynamic Simulation of an Econometric Model," Econometrica, 42, 303-309.

SCHÖNFELD, P. (1980), "Fehlspezifikation dynamischer Modelle durch temporale Aggregation," in Empirische Wirtschaftsforschung, Festschrift für R. Krengel, Berlin: Duncker & Humblot, 253-266.

SCHWARZ, G. (1978), "Estimating the Dimension of a Model," Annals of Statistics, 6, 461-464.

SERFLING, R.J. (1980), Approximation Theorems of Mathematical Statistics, New York: John Wiley.

SHIBATA, R. (1976), "Selection of the Order of an Autoregressive Model by Akaike's Information Criterion," Biometrika, 63, 117-126.

SHIBATA, R. (1980), "Asymptotically Efficient Selection of the Order of the Model for Estimating Parameters of a Linear Process," Annals of Statistics, 8, 147-164.

SIMS, C.A. (1971), "Discrete Approximations to Continuous Time Distributed Lags in Econometrics," Econometrica, 39, 545-563.

SPITZER, J.J. & R.T. BAILLIE (1983), "Small-Sample Properties of Predictions From the Regression Model With Autoregressive Errors," Journal of the American Statistical Association, 78, 258-263.

STRAM, D.O. & W.W.S. WEI (1986), "Temporal Aggregation in the ARIMA Process," Journal of Time Series Analysis, 7, 279-292.

TERÄSVIRTA, T. (1977), "The Invertibility of Sums of Discrete MA and ARMA Processes," Scandinavian Journal of Statistics, 4, 165-170.

TERÄSVIRTA, T. (1981), "Temporal Aggregation in Finite Distributed Lag Models," paper presented at the European Meeting of the Econometric Society, Amsterdam.

TIAO, G.C. (1972), "Asymptotic Behaviour of Temporal Aggregates of Time Series," Biometrika, 59, 525-531.

TIAO, G.C. & G.E.P. BOX (1981), "Modeling Multiple Time Series With Applications," Journal of the American Statistical Association, 76, 802-816.

TIAO, G.C. & I. GUTTMAN (1980), "Forecasting Contemporal Aggregates of Multiple Time Series," Journal of Econometrics, 12, 219-230.

TIAO, G.C. & W.S. WEI (1976), "Effect of Temporal Aggregation on the Dynamic Relationship of Two Time Series Variables," Biometrika, 63, 513-523.

TJØSTHEIM, D. (1981), "Granger-Causality in Multiple Time Series," Journal of Econometrics, 17, 157-176.

TJØSTHEIM, D. & J. PAULSEN (1983), "Bias of Some Commonly-Used Time Series Estimates," Biometrika, 70, 389-399.

TSAY, R.S. (1984), "Order Selection in Nonstationary Autoregressive Models," Annals of Statistics, 12, 1425-1433.

WALLIS, K.F. (1977), "Multiple Time Series Analysis and the Final Form of Econometric Models," Econometrica, 45, 1481-1497.

WEI, W.W.S. (1978a), "Some Consequences of Temporal Aggregation in Seasonal Time Series Models," in A. ZELLNER (ed.), Seasonal Analysis of Economic Time Series, U.S. Department of Commerce, Bureau of the Census, 433-444.

WEI, W.W.S. (1978b), "The Effect of Temporal Aggregation on Parameter Estimation in Distributed Lag Model," Journal of Econometrics, 8, 237-246.

WEI, W.W.S. (1981), "Effect of Systematic Sampling on ARIMA Models," Communications in Statistics - Theory and Methods, A10, 2389-2398.

WEI, W.W.S. & B. ABRAHAM (1981), "Forecasting Contemporal Time Series Aggregates," Communications in Statistics - Theory and Methods, A10, 1335-1344.

WEI, W.W.S. & J. MEHTA (1980), "Temporal Aggregation and Information Loss in a Distributed Lag Model," in O.D. ANDERSON, Analysing Time Series, Amsterdam: North-Holland, 391-400.

WEISS, A.A. (1984), "Systematic Sampling and Temporal Aggregation in Time Series Models," Journal of Econometrics, 26, 271-281.

WERNER, H.-J. (1982), "On the Temporal Aggregation in Discrete Dynamical Systems," in R.F. DRENICK & F. KOZIN (eds), System Modeling and Optimization, New York: Springer, 819-825.

YAMAMOTO, T. (1976), "Asymptotic Mean Square Prediction Error for an Autoregressive Model with Estimated Coefficients," Applied Statistics, 25, 123-127.

YAMAMOTO, T. (1980), "On the Treatment of Autocorrelated Errors in the Multiperiod Prediction of Dynamic Simultaneous Equation Models," International Economic Review, 21, 735-748.

YAMAMOTO, T. (1981), "Prediction of Multivariate Autoregressive - Moving Average Models," Biometrika, 68, 485-492.

YAMAMOTO, T. (1982), "Shrunken Predictors for Autoregressive Models," Technical Report No. 352, Institute for Mathematical Studies in the Social Science, Stanford University.

ZELLNER, A. (1966), "On the Analysis of First Order Autoregressive Models with Incomplete Data," International Economic Review, 7, 72-76.

ZELLNER, A. & C. MONTMARQUETTE (1971), "A Study of Some Aspects of Temporal Aggregation Problems in Econometric Analyses," Review of Economics and Statistics, 53, 335-342.

ZELLNER, A. & F. PALM (1974), "Time Series Analysis and Simultaneous Equation Econometric Models," Journal of Econometrics, 2, 17-54.

Vol. 184: R. E. Burkard and U. Derigs, Assignment and Matching Problems: Solution Methods with FORTRAN-Programs. VIII, 148 pages. 1980.

Vol. 185: C. C. von Weizsäcker, Barriers to Entry. VI, 220 pages. 1980.

Vol. 186: Ch.-L. Hwang and K. Yoon, Multiple Attribute Decision Making – Methods and Applications. A State-of-the-Art-Survey. XI, 259 pages. 1981.

Vol. 187: W. Hock, K. Schittkowski, Test Examples for Nonlinear Programming Codes. V. 178 pages. 1981.

Vol. 188: D. Bös, Economic Theory of Public Enterprise. VII, 142 pages. 1981.

Vol. 189: A. P. Lüthi, Messung wirtschaftlicher Ungleichheit. IX, 287 pages. 1981.

Vol. 190: J. N. Morse, Organizations: Multiple Agents with Multiple Criteria. Proceedings, 1980. VI, 509 pages. 1981.

Vol. 191: H. R. Sneessens, Theory and Estimation of Macroeconomic Rationing Models. VII, 138 pages. 1981.

Vol. 192: H. J. Bierens: Robust Methods and Asymptotic Theory in Nonlinear Econometrics. IX, 198 pages. 1981.

Vol. 193: J. K. Sengupta, Optimal Decisions under Uncertainty. VII, 156 pages. 1981.

Vol. 194: R. W. Shephard, Cost and Production Functions. XI, 104 pages. 1981.

Vol. 195: H. W. Ursprung, Die elementare Katastrophentheorie. Eine Darstellung aus der Sicht der Ökonomie. VII, 332 pages. 1982.

Vol. 196: M. Nermuth, Information Structures in Economics. VIII, 236 pages. 1982.

Vol. 197: Integer Programming and Related Areas. A Classified Bibliography. 1978 – 1981. Edited by R. von Randow. XIV, 338 pages. 1982.

Vol. 198: P. Zweifel, Ein ökonomisches Modell des Arztverhaltens. XIX, 392 Seiten. 1982.

Vol. 199: Evaluating Mathematical Programming Techniques. Proceedings, 1981. Edited by J.M. Mulvey. XI, 379 pages. 1982.

Vol. 200: The Resource Sector in an Open Economy. Edited by H. Siebert. IX, 161 pages. 1984.

Vol. 201: P. M. C. de Boer, Price Effects in Input-Output-Relations: A Theoretical and Empirical Study for the Netherlands 1949–1967. X, 140 pages. 1982.

Vol. 202: U. Witt, J. Perske, SMS – A Program Package for Simulation and Gaming of Stochastic Market Processes and Learning Behavior. VII, 266 pages. 1982.

Vol. 203: Compilation of Input-Output Tables. Proceedings, 1981. Edited by J. V. Skolka. VII, 307 pages. 1982.

Vol. 204: K. C. Mosler, Entscheidungsregeln bei Risiko: Multivariate stochastische Dominanz. VII, 172 Seiten. 1982.

Vol. 205: R. Ramanathan, Introduction to the Theory of Economic Growth. IX, 347 pages. 1982.

Vol. 206: M. H. Karwan, V. Lotfi, J. Telgen, and S. Zionts, Redundancy in Mathematical Programming. VII, 286 pages. 1983.

Vol. 207: Y. Fujimori, Modern Analysis of Value Theory. X, 165 pages. 1982.

Vol. 208: Econometric Decision Models. Proceedings, 1981. Edited by J. Gruber. VI, 364 pages. 1983.

Vol. 209: Essays and Surveys on Multiple Criteria Decision Making. Proceedings, 1982. Edited by P. Hansen. VII, 441 pages. 1983.

Vol. 210: Technology, Organization and Economic Structure. Edited by R. Sato and M. J. Beckmann. VIII, 195 pages. 1983.

Vol. 211: P. van den Heuvel, The Stability of a Macroeconomic System with Quantity Constraints. VII, 169 pages. 1983.

Vol. 212: R. Sato and T. Nôno, Invariance Principles and the Structure of Technology. V, 94 pages. 1983.

Vol. 213: Aspiration Levels in Bargaining and Economic Decision Making. Proceedings, 1982. Edited by R. Tietz. VIII, 406 pages. 1983.

Vol. 214: M. Faber, H. Niemes und G. Stephan, Entropie, Umweltschutz und Rohstoffverbrauch. IX, 181 Seiten. 1983.

Vol. 215: Semi-Infinite Programming and Applications. Proceedings, 1981. Edited by A. V. Fiacco and K. O. Kortanek. XI, 322 pages. 1983.

Vol. 216: H. H. Müller, Fiscal Policies in a General Equilibrium Model with Persistent Unemployment. VI, 92 pages. 1983.

Vol. 217: Ch. Grootaert, The Relation Between Final Demand and Income Distribution. XIV, 105 pages. 1983.

Vol. 218: P. van Loon, A Dynamic Theory of the Firm: Production, Finance and Investment. VII, 191 pages. 1983.

Vol. 219: E. van Damme, Refinements of the Nash Equilibrium Concept. VI, 151 pages. 1983.

Vol. 220: M. Aoki, Notes on Economic Time Series Analysis: System Theoretic Perspectives. IX, 249 pages. 1983.

Vol. 221: S. Nakamura, An Inter-Industry Translog Model of Prices and Technical Change for the West German Economy. XIV, 290 pages. 1984.

Vol. 222: P. Meier, Energy Systems Analysis for Developing Countries. VI, 344 pages. 1984.

Vol. 223: W. Trockel, Market Demand. VIII, 205 pages. 1984.

Vol. 224: M. Kiy, Ein disaggregiertes Prognosesystem für die Bundesrepublik Deutschland. XVIII, 276 Seiten. 1984.

Vol. 225: T. R. von Ungern-Sternberg, Zur Analyse von Märkten mit unvollständiger Nachfragerinformation. IX, 125 Seiten. 1984

Vol. 226: Selected Topics in Operations Research and Mathematical Economics. Proceedings, 1983. Edited by G. Hammer and D. Pallaschke. IX, 478 pages. 1984.

Vol. 227: Risk and Capital. Proceedings, 1983. Edited by G. Bamberg and K. Spremann. VII, 306 pages. 1984.

Vol. 228: Nonlinear Models of Fluctuating Growth. Proceedings, 1983. Edited by R. M. Goodwin, M. Krüger and A. Vercelli. XVII, 277 pages. 1984.

Vol. 229: Interactive Decision Analysis. Proceedings, 1983. Edited by M. Grauer and A. P. Wierzbicki. VIII, 269 pages. 1984.

Vol. 230: Macro-Economic Planning with Conflicting Goals. Proceedings, 1982. Edited by M. Despontin, P. Nijkamp and J. Spronk. VI, 297 pages. 1984.

Vol. 231: G. F. Newell, The M/M/∞ Service System with Ranked Servers in Heavy Traffic. XI, 126 pages. 1984.

Vol. 232: L. Bauwens, Bayesian Full Information Analysis of Simultaneous Equation Models Using Integration by Monte Carlo. VI, 114 pages. 1984.

Vol. 233: G. Wagenhals, The World Copper Market. XI, 190 pages. 1984.

Vol. 234: B. C. Eaves, A Course in Triangulations for Solving Equations with Deformations. III, 302 pages. 1984.

Vol. 235: Stochastic Models in Reliability Theory. Proceedings, 1984. Edited by S. Osaki and Y. Hatoyama. VII, 212 pages. 1984.

Vol. 236: G. Gandolfo, P. C. Padoan, A Disequilibrium Model of Real and Financial Accumulation in an Open Economy. VI, 172 pages. 1984.

Vol. 237: Misspecification Analysis. Proceedings, 1983. Edited by T. K. Dijkstra. V, 129 pages. 1984.

Vol. 238: W. Domschke, A. Drexl, Location and Layout Planning. IV, 134 pages. 1985.

Vol. 239: Microeconomic Models of Housing Markets. Edited by K. Stahl. VII, 197 pages. 1985.

Vol. 240: Contributions to Operations Research. Proceedings, 1984. Edited by K. Neumann and D. Pallaschke. V, 190 pages. 1985.

Vol. 241: U. Wittmann, Das Konzept rationaler Preiserwartungen. XI, 310 Seiten. 1985.

Vol. 242: Decision Making with Multiple Objectives. Proceedings, 1984. Edited by Y. Y. Haimes and V. Chankong. XI, 571 pages. 1985.

Vol. 243: Integer Programming and Related Areas. A Classified Bibliography 1981–1984. Edited by R. von Randow. XX, 386 pages. 1985.

Vol. 244: Advances in Equilibrium Theory. Proceedings, 1984. Edited by C. D. Aliprantis, O. Burkinshaw and N. J. Rothman. II, 235 pages. 1985.

Vol. 245: J. E. M. Wilhelm, Arbitrage Theory. VII, 114 pages. 1985.

Vol. 246: P. W. Otter, Dynamic Feature Space Modelling, Filtering and Self-Tuning Control of Stochastic Systems. XIV, 177 pages. 1985.

Vol. 247: Optimization and Discrete Choice in Urban Systems. Proceedings, 1983. Edited by B. G. Hutchinson, P. Nijkamp and M. Batty. VI, 371 pages. 1985.

Vol. 248: Plural Rationality and Interactive Decision Processes. Proceedings, 1984. Edited by M. Grauer, M. Thompson and A. P. Wierzbicki. VI, 354 pages. 1985.

Vol. 249: Spatial Price Equilibrium: Advances in Theory, Computation and Application. Proceedings, 1984. Edited by P. T. Harker. VII, 277 pages. 1985.

Vol. 250: M. Roubens, Ph. Vincke, Preference Modelling. VIII, 94 pages. 1985.

Vol. 251: Input-Output Modeling. Proceedings, 1984. Edited by A. Smyshlyaev. VI, 261 pages. 1985.

Vol. 252: A. Birolini, On the Use of Stochastic Processes in Modeling Reliability Problems. VI, 105 pages. 1985.

Vol. 253: C. Withagen, Economic Theory and International Trade in Natural Exhaustible Resources. VI, 172 pages. 1985.

Vol. 254: S. Müller, Arbitrage Pricing of Contingent Claims. VIII, 151 pages. 1985.

Vol. 255: Nondifferentiable Optimization: Motivations and Applications. Proceedings, 1984. Edited by V. F. Demyanov and D. Pallaschke. VI, 350 pages. 1985.

Vol. 256: Convexity and Duality in Optimization. Proceedings, 1984. Edited by J. Ponstein. V, 142 pages. 1985.

Vol. 257: Dynamics of Macrosystems. Proceedings, 1984. Edited by J.-P. Aubin, D. Saari and K. Sigmund. VI, 280 pages. 1985.

Vol. 258: H. Funke, Eine allgemeine Theorie der Polypol- und Oligopolpreisbildung. III, 237 pages. 1985.

Vol. 259: Infinite Programming. Proceedings, 1984. Edited by E. J. Anderson and A. B. Philpott. XIV, 244 pages. 1985.

Vol. 260: H.-J. Kruse, Degeneracy Graphs and the Neighbourhood Problem. VIII, 128 pages. 1986.

Vol. 261: Th. R. Gulledge, Jr., N. K. Womer, The Economics of Made-to-Order Production. VI, 134 pages. 1986.

Vol. 262: H. U. Buhl, A Neo-Classical Theory of Distribution and Wealth. V, 146 pages. 1986.

Vol. 263: M. Schäfer, Resource Extraction and Market Structure. XI, 154 pages. 1986.

Vol. 264: Models of Economic Dynamics. Proceedings, 1983. Edited by H. F. Sonnenschein. VII, 212 pages. 1986.

Vol. 265: Dynamic Games and Applications in Economics. Edited by T. Başar. IX, 288 pages. 1986.

Vol. 266: Multi-Stage Production Planning and Inventory Control. Edited by S. Axsäter, Ch. Schneeweiss and E. Silver. V, 264 pages. 1986.

Vol. 267: R. Bemelmans, The Capacity Aspect of Inventories. IX, 165 pages. 1986.

Vol. 268: V. Firchau, Information Evaluation in Capital Markets. VII, 103 pages. 1986.

Vol. 269: A. Borglin, H. Keiding, Optimality in Infinite Horizon Economies. VI, 180 pages. 1986.

Vol. 270: Technological Change, Employment and Spatial Dynamics. Proceedings 1985. Edited by P. Nijkamp. VII, 466 pages. 1986.

Vol. 271: C. Hildreth, The Cowles Commission in Chicago, 1939–1955. V, 176 pages. 1986.

Vol. 272: G. Clemenz, Credit Markets with Asymmetric Information. VIII, 212 pages. 1986.

Vol. 273: Large-Scale Modelling and Interactive Decision Analysis. Proceedings, 1985. Edited by G. Fandel, M. Grauer, A. Kurzhanski and A. P. Wierzbicki. VII, 363 pages. 1986.

Vol. 274: W. K. Klein Haneveld, Duality in Stochastic Linear and Dynamic Programming. VII, 295 pages. 1986.

Vol. 275: Competition, Instability, and Nonlinear Cycles. Proceedings, 1985. Edited by W. Semmler. XII, 340 pages. 1986.

Vol. 276: M. R. Baye, D. A. Black, Consumer Behavior, Cost of Living Measures, and the Income Tax. VII, 119 pages. 1986.

Vol. 277: Studies in Austrian Capital Theory, Investment and Time. Edited by M. Faber. VI, 317 pages. 1986.

Vol. 278: W. E. Diewert, The Measurement of the Economic Benefits of Infrastructure Services. V, 202 pages. 1986.

Vol. 279: H.-J. Büttler, G. Frei and B. Schips, Estimation of Disequilibrium Models. VI, 114 pages. 1986.

Vol. 280: H. T. Lau, Combinatorial Heuristic Algorithms with FORTRAN. VII, 126 pages. 1986.

Vol. 281: Ch.-L. Hwang, M.-J. Lin, Group Decision Making under Multiple Criteria. XI, 400 pages. 1987.

Vol. 282: K. Schittkowski, More Test Examples for Nonlinear Programming Codes. V, 261 pages. 1987.

Vol. 283: G. Gabisch, H.-W. Lorenz, Business Cycle Theory. VII, 229 pages. 1987.

Vol. 284: H. Lütkepohl, Forecasting Aggregated Vector ARMA Processes. X, 323 pages. 1987.

GPSR Compliance

The European Union's (EU) General Product Safety Regulation (GPSR) is a set of rules that requires consumer products to be safe and our obligations to ensure this.

If you have any concerns about our products, you can contact us on ProductSafety@springernature.com

In case Publisher is established outside the EU, the EU authorized representative is:

Springer Nature Customer Service Center GmbH
Europaplatz 3
69115 Heidelberg, Germany

Batch number: 10845480

Printed by Printforce, the Netherlands